SECURITY COOPERATION IN AFRICA

SECURITY

COOPERATION

IN AFRICA

A Reappraisal

Benedikt Franke

FIRST**FORUM**PRESS

A DIVISION OF LYNNE RIENNER PUBLISHERS, INC. • BOULDER & LONDON

Published in the United States of America in 2009 by
FirstForumPress
A division of Lynne Rienner Publishers, Inc.
1800 30th Street, Boulder, Colorado 80301
www.firstforumpress.com

and in the United Kingdom by
FirstForumPress
A division of Lynne Rienner Publishers, Inc.
3 Henrietta Street, Covent Garden, London WC2E 8LU

Library of Congress Cataloging-in-Publication Data
A Cataloging-in-Publication record for this book
is available from the Library of Congress.
ISBN: 978-1-935049-09-8

British Cataloguing in Publication Data
A Cataloguing in Publication record for this book
is available from the British Library.

This book was produced from digital files prepared by the author
using the FirstForumComposer.

Printed and bound in the United States of America

 The paper used in this publication meets the requirements
of the American National Standard for Permanence of
Paper for Printed Library Materials Z39.48-1992.

5 4 3 2 1

Contents

Tables and Figures

Tables

Figures

Acknowledgments

An African (*Twi*) proverb holds that "ingratitude is sooner or later fatal to its author". Hence, turning to the acknowledgments is not only one of the most enjoyable moments of writing a book but might also be one of its most rational.

Over the last years, I have accumulated a wide variety of debts, and enumerating them inevitably brings back the feeling of gratitude that has become such a valued companion of my research. In fact, I have been fortunate to encounter this feeling so often that it will be difficult to single out but a few of its creators.

I must begin by expressing my heartfelt gratitude to Philip Towle from the Centre of International Studies in Cambridge for his advice and gentle guidance. Without him, this book would not have been written. I also owe enormous debts to Eliot Cohen, Alan Kuperman, Bill Zartman and Thomas Mahnken who nurtured both my interest in Africa's indigenous security efforts and my aspiration to analyze them in the form of a book.

Many other people gave generously of their valuable time to comment on previous versions of this manuscript. They spared me from many errors and their suggestions for revisions have greatly improved the final outcome. Special thanks must go to James Mayall and David Francis for providing particularly constructive comments during our meeting in Cambridge, Paul Williams for the elaborate candidness of his critiques and Sophia Gollwitzer for her unfailing support and unstinting advice. The comments provided by the anonymous reviewers of FirstForumPress also proved highly useful.

Most of this book could not have been written without the help of the plethora of people (more than 150) who consented to be interviewed for it. They are not all quoted directly in it, but they all helped to inform its argument. I am particularly indebted to the African Defense Attachés to the UN, the late Major-General Ishaya Hassan, Johan Potgieter and the staffs of the AU's Peace Support Operations Division in Addis Ababa and the EASBRIG Planning Element in Nairobi, Richard Gowan from New York University's Center on International Cooperation, Abdel-Kader Haireche from the UN Department of Peacekeeping Operations Liaison Team to the African Union, Simone Kopfmüller from the GTZ and the German Defense Attachés in Africa, especially Colonels Josef Gerner, Jens Biesterfeldt and Werner Rauber.

A number of people and institutions have made my research visits to Africa truly wonderful experiences. I am particularly grateful to the Mwalimu Nyerere Foundation in Dar es Salaam, and especially its president Salim Ahmed Salim and its executive director Gallus Abedi, for the kind hospitality and cooperation they provided to me during my prolonged stay in Tanzania, and the European Council Delegation to Ethiopia for its generous support during my time in Addis Ababa. I also had the great fortune to meet Colonel Reinhard Linz, the EU's Military Liaison Officer to the AU, who with stupendous kindness offered me more assistance than I could ever have hoped for. I would also like to express my gratitude to the former director of the AU's Peace Support Operations Department, Bereng Mtimkulu, who, over several months, granted me such unrestricted access to his work and staff that I had soon, in his words, "become part of the furniture" at the African Union Headquarters.

I am also indebted to Cambridge's Centre of International Studies, the German Council on Foreign Relations, the *Institut de Hautes Études Internationales et du Développement* in Geneva and the Academic Council on the United Nations System for giving me the opportunity to present my research in a collegial atmosphere, and to the Kurt Hahn Trust and the African Studies Centre for generously funding several re-search visits. I am also particularly grateful to Richard Caplan and Oxford's Department of Politics and International Relations for their support during my post-doctoral fellowship in the city of dreaming spires. Finally, I would like to thank Lynne Rienner, Claire Vlcek and the fantastic team at FirstForumPress for their patience and invaluable counsel in the preparation of the final manuscript.

My greatest debt, however, is to my parents for their advice and loving support. The most consistent motivation to complete this book was the desire to dedicate it to them in gratitude.

Benedikt Franke

1
Introduction

This book deals with the increasing extent and quality of inter-African cooperation in the area of peace and security. In particular, it deals with the efforts of the African Union (AU), an inter-governmental organization to which all but one of Africa's 54 states belong, to establish what it calls the African Peace and Security Architecture. Among other components, this institutional architecture is eventually supposed to comprise a military standby force of approximately 15,000 to 20,000 troops which can be used to stop genocides and other crimes against humanity and an elaborate early warning mechanism which is to process information from around the continent and thus allow for a timely assessment of and responses to security threats. While news coverage of the ongoing atrocities in the Congo, Sudan and Somalia and the electoral scandals in Kenya and Zimbabwe continues to cast a penumbra of doubt over the ability of the continent to realize this ambitious project, the member states of the AU have already achieved some remarkable successes on the way. For example, they have created a multi-layered and poly-centric governance structure to manage their security relations that evolves around a Peace and Security Council akin to the Security Council of the United Nations. They have also agreed on a Common African Defense and Security Policy, incorporated a plethora of existing regional security and conflict management mechanisms into one coherent (continental) approach and conducted a number of independent peace operations in places such as Burundi, Darfur, the Comoros and Somalia.

All of this makes a notable change from the past. For reasons ranging from the dynamics of the Cold War, the continent's unfinished liberation and the limitations of its own founding charter, the AU's institutional predecessor, the Organization of African Unity (OAU) had never been able to encourage similar levels of inter-state cooperation. On the contrary, the OAU's almost 40-year existence was marked by its inability to provide an institutional basis for inter-African security cooperation. As the Cold War came to an end, this inability led Africa's states to turn to regional organizations like the Economic Community of West African States (ECOWAS) to fill the institutional void and eventually caused them to replace the OAU with a more promising African Union modeled after the European archetype. Given the fate of its predecessor, the swiftness with which the AU has revitalized the quest for what Ali Mazrui once called a "Pax Africana that is protected and maintained by Africa herself" calls for a reappraisal of inter-African security cooperation.[1]

With this in mind, the purpose of this book is twofold. Its empirical objective is to offer a detailed description of the historical evolution and contemporary pattern of inter-state security cooperation on the continent. In particular, it seeks to shed light on (1) the multitude of initiatives that preceded the creation of the AU's security architecture, (2) the path to and details of that creation, (3) the structure, role and current state of the AU's new institutions and mechanisms, and (4) the remaining challenges to effective inter-African security cooperation. In the process, it explores a number of elementary questions. For example, to what extent does contemporary security cooperation on the African continent differ from previous initiatives, and what accounts for these differences? What can continent-wide projects like the African Standby Force or the Continental Early Warning System tell us about the state and direction of contemporary security cooperation in Africa? Is there a qualitative difference between the security cooperation observed at the regional level and that taking place at the continental level? What is the role of international support in all of this?

At the same time, the book also has two theoretical objectives, namely, (1) to offer a constructivist interpretation of the dynamics of security cooperation in contemporary Africa and (2) to mine the continent's emerging security architecture for new insights on international cooperation in general. Relying on African realities such as collective identities and shared values to explain the increasing extent and quality of security cooperation on the continent, it seeks to draw attention to the need to complement rationalist-systemic theories of inter-state cooperation with a detailed understanding of social processes. To this purpose, it focuses on the role of ideational factors such as shared historical experiences and common aspirations, but also of ideologies like Pan-Africanism, concepts like the African Renaissance and processes like norm diffusion in the induction and evolution of inter-state cooperation on the continent.

Underlying these objectives is the aspiration to answer two fundamental research questions, namely, why have Africa's states chosen to intensify their cooperation in the field of peace and security over the last decade, and what does this cooperation look like today. However straightforward these questions may seem, both their theoretical complexity and the ongoing evolution of inter-state security cooperation in Africa prevent equally straightforward answers. In this respect, the findings discussed in chapters ten, eleven and twelve should be taken not so much as definitive pronouncements, but rather as indicators and stimuli for future research agendas. At the very least, they should generate further debate and discussion on inter-African security cooperation, and thus help to address the notable imbalance in the academic literature on cooperation that originally motivated this study.

Argument

The book is built on two core arguments, namely, (1) that the current developments on the African continent enable a detailed understanding of the motivations for, and evolutionary patterns of, complex inter-state security cooperation, and (2) that a constructivist approach offers a useful theoretical lens through which to examine these motivations and evolutionary patterns as well as their institutional manifestations. Given the ongoing marginalization of Africa in International Relations (IR) theory as well as the continuing dominance of rationalist-systemic theories of international cooperation, both arguments call for some initial justification.

It is certainly true that Africa is no longer as absent from theorizing about world politics as Kevin Dunn once lamented.[2] Instead, there has been a notable increase in the literature on the role of Africa in world politics and related issue areas such as security and development.[3] However, given that more than one out of seven people and one out of four nations in the world are African, the amount of IR scholarship that analyzes the continent for theory-building purposes is still insignificant.[4] This omission is a long-standing problem. Bernard Magubane, for example, reminds us that much of the historical literature that has influenced Western thought displays an uncritical ignorance of Africa. For example, Hegel in the *Introduction to the Philosophy of History* states:

> At this point we leave Africa, not to mention it again. For it is no historical part of the world, it has no movement or development to exhibit. Historical movement in it – that is in its northern part – belongs to the Asiatic or European world. What we properly understand by Africa is the unhistorical, underdeveloped spirit still involved in the conditions of mere nature, and which had to be presented here as on the childhood of the world's history.[5]

Over the centuries, such stereotypical and largely Eurocentric presentation of Africa has glossed over the essence and theoretical relevance of the continent's political realities. As a direct result, a notable inattention to African politics has become deeply ingrained in the dominant approaches within IR theory.[6] Both realism and neo-liberal institutionalism, for example, fail to accord the continent a place in their systemic analyses – despite their positivist epistemological pretension to provide *general* theories of international relations. In line with the realist catchphrase recorded by Thucydides in his Melian Dialogue that "the strong do what they can and the weak suffer what they must",[7] for these theories Africa appears to exist only to the extent that it is acted upon.

While realism and liberalism are under attack from many quarters and on many grounds, this apparent imbalance between the pretension of universality and the exclusion of Africa remains virtually unexamined. The book argues that Africa's recent move from *ad hoc* security initiatives to permanently institutionalized cooperation offers a unique chance to address this unfortunate gap in theorizing inter-state relations. Coupled with the increasing willingness of the continent's states to conduct all-African peace operations, it not only provides a rich and heavily under-explored area for theoretical investigation, but also underlines Africa's claim for a place in contemporary theory-building and testing.

I also contend that, contrary to the deterministic preconceptions of most other IR theories, the open and process-orientated approach of constructivism can account for the intensification of inter-African security cooperation and, even more importantly, offers an attractive theoretical framework for its analysis.[8] Developed in part to overcome the inability of rationalist approaches to explain collective action, including the resolution of security dilemmas, constructivism goes much further than the dominant theories of security cooperation in portraying international relations as social constructs susceptible to limitless reformulation over time rather than as a static concept fixed to definable and unchanging conditions. While the realist – neo-liberal institutionalist debate has been primarily concerned with studying the barriers to cooperation, constructivists such as Alexander Wendt, Emmanuel Adler and Michael Barnett concentrate on how, under certain conditions, transnational forces and state interactions can generate the trust, reciprocity, shared knowledge and common identities necessary to transform global politics and overcome Hobbesian anarchy.[9] Constructivism thereby draws on the explanatory power of inter-subjective factors such as ideas, beliefs and norms and social processes such as identity and interest formation rather than deep structure to explain international relations. It is exactly because it "sees IR differently" that constructivism is so well suited to studying security cooperation in theoretically-marginalized regions like Africa.[10]

Naturally, this should not be taken to mean that the material forces of rationalist theories have lost their importance to the study of international cooperation, nor that we are witnessing the decline of the Westphalian nation state in Africa. Nonetheless, the African experience shows that the attention to the concern for power and sovereignty that undoubtedly continues to permeate international relations must be complemented by an understanding of the occasions in which these concerns are balanced against competing objectives or even muted altogether. Without such an understanding it is simply impossible to comprehend the recent proliferation of cooperative ventures on the African continent, particularly in the field of peace and security. Constructivism should thus be seen as a complementary theory which does not attempt to refute rationalist explanations of international cooperation as much as it seeks to expand them. Its great conceptual advantage over other theories is that its ideas can sit comfortably with the prevalence of "realist" behavior in some parts of the continent, while at the same time allowing for the role of inter-subjective factors such as the integrative and unifying force of Pan-Africanism, or the desire for continental emancipation.

Methodology

The dual purpose of this book necessitates a clearly defined methodology. Analogous to the works of Waltz, Keohane and also Wendt, I adopt a state-centric approach to international relations in my discussion of cooperation. The rationales for choosing such an approach have already been outlined by these authors in great detail and with great skill, so here it suffices to restate two important reassurances.[11] First, the choice of the state as analytical unit does in no way entail a conceptual disregard for the pivotal role of non-state actors in the promotion of international cooperation. Several studies have drawn attention to the important links between states and non-state actors in this respect, and though fully investigating them would exceed the scope of this book, they need to be kept in mind, and are referred to at junctures where they have an important bearing on the policies of states.[12] Second, despite its systemic perspective, this study does recognize the crucial role of domestic politics. This role is particularly important in Africa, where, as Jeffrey Herbst has pointed out, leaders have to be highly attentive to domestic concerns when making decisions about international engagements in order to protect their national power bases.[13] The occasional consideration of such unit-level factors, however, should not distract from the main level of analysis of the book, namely, the systemic interaction between states.

While I thus choose the same level of analysis employed by Waltz and Wendt, I go one step further, subdividing this level into two interdependent but separate layers of systemic investigation, namely, a regional layer of inter-state cooperation and a continental layer of inter-state cooperation. Africa's emerging peace and security architecture is unique in the extent to which the continental level relies on regional organizations as pillars and implementation organs of its policies. A separate analysis of the two layers not only takes account of this important characteristic of contemporary security cooperation in Africa, but may also yield important insights into the possibility of different motivations for, and evolutions of, cooperation at the two layers. One criticism of previous attempts at theorizing inter-state security cooperation, including that of Wendt, virtually omnipresent throughout this book, is that their unconditional reliance on a monolithic level of systemic analysis glosses over conceptually rich patterns of inter-state relations. The African experience shows that it is important to differentiate between regional and continental cooperation, not least because of the different numbers of actors involved and the different rationales at play, and that doing so makes a difference to thinking about international cooperation.

While the definition of the continental layer is relatively straightforward, namely, all 53 member states of the AU, writers have offered several definitions of "the regional level".[14] These differ widely, both in their depth and significance. This book adopts a functional perspective on regionalism, defining its organizational aspect as *a notion encompassing entities, which may, but do not necessarily, belong to a geographically determinable area, having either common or disparate attributes and values, but which seek the accomplishment of common goals.*[15] The distinctive force of this proposed definition is its emphasis on abstract values over mere physical proximity, and the possibility that states claiming to belong to a region may have divergent values. This definition reflects the reality in Africa where members of a single regional organization vaunt extremely diverse political systems varying from absolute monarchy and democracy to militocracy. It is on the basis of political and economic aspirations amongst states moving towards closer cooperation rather than mere geographical proximity or communality of values that an effective system of regional collective security emerged after the Cold War.

Apart from its unusual geographic focus and sub-divided level of analysis, this work must be distinguished from previous discussions of inter-state security cooperation also by the substance of its engagement with sociological concepts and the extent to which it relies on historical retrospectives (nearly a quarter of its volume is dedicated to the evolution of security cooperation). Both features spring directly from the choice of the African continent as empirical test-case, for even a cursory glance at its institutional landscape reveals the crucial role of shared historical experiences and collective identities in the evolution of inter-state security relations. Without a detailed understanding of these historical experiences or occasional recourse to conceptual tools like symbolic interactionism and structuration theory in order to gauge their effects, an analysis of Africa's emerging patterns of security cooperation is bound to miss important parts of the puzzle.[16]

The choice of case studies also requires some explanation. In order to assess the extent and quality of contemporary inter-state security cooperation, I look at two central pillars of Africa's emerging peace and security architecture in particularly great detail, namely, the African Standby Force (ASF) and the Continental Early Warning System (CEWS). Both are highly prestigious projects which are supported by Africa's states and the international community alike. While this significantly reduces their chances of failure, this is not why they were chosen here as examples of inter-African security cooperation. Rather they were selected for three very practical reasons. First, they relate to the most sensitive areas of security cooperation, namely, information sharing and military integration, and thus allow for what Stephan van Evera has called a "strong test" of the seriousness of cooperation.[17] Second, their two very different *raisons d'être*, namely, the anticipation and prevention of conflict (for the CEWS) and the management of conflict (for the ASF) cover the full spectrum of contemporary inter-African security cooperation. Third, their heavily regionalized but centrally coordinated character makes for an interesting test of the divisibility of the systemic into separate levels of analysis, and thus for the methodological approach adopted in this book.

Given the substantial debates in the field, it is also necessary to define the two central concepts of the book, namely, *cooperation* and *security*, in order to avoid confusion and equivocation. Beginning with *cooperation*, Robert Keohane's definition of the term as "mutual adjustment of policies by two or more states" comes closer than others to the meaning that most analysts seem to have in mind when they use it, and thus will be the one used here.[18] This definition successfully distinguishes accords reached as a result of cooperation from those reached on the basis of coercion, when the adjustment of policies is not mutual, and from the "coincidence of preferences" or harmony of interests, where all states follow their own national interests and the result is accord without conflict.

The exact meaning of *security* has long been hotly debated and there is no consensus in sight.[19] On the contrary, over the years, this seemingly straightforward term has come to encompass everything from survival and the absence of a military threat to the freedom from fear and want,[20] gradually turning into what Walter Gallie once called an "essentially contested concept".[21] Ken Booth, for example, has equated the concept with the "emancipation from the social, physical, economic, political and other constraints that stop people from carrying out what they would freely choose to do",[22] while Paul Williams paraphrases Alexander Wendt to argue that "security is what people make it".[23] The usage of the term *security* is thus inevitably fraught with conceptual difficulties. This is particularly true in the African context, for no other part of the world has had so little control over its own security agenda. Reflecting the extent of their involvement in the continent's affairs, external actors such as former colonial powers, but also the United Nations and the European Union, have essentially shaped the discussion about the meaning of "African security" in their own image. As a result, a notable dichotomy has developed between African and non-African conceptions of "African security".[24] While for many African leaders regime survival undoubtedly continues to play the central role, non-African decision-makers generally focus on the increasingly popular and easier-to-sell notions of "new threats" and "human security" which they have superimposed on the African debate.[25] In order to account for both conceptions of security, I follow the emerging Critical Security Studies literature in defining the term in the broadest sense possible as "the alleviation of threats to cherished values".[26]

Organization of the Book

The book is organized into twelve chapters. Following this introduction, the second chapter lays the theoretical groundwork for the ensuing discussion by drawing attention to the limits of rational-systemic theories of international relations and introducing social constructivism as a more appropriate framework for theorizing inter-state security cooperation in Africa. In particular, it highlights the importance of constructivist concepts like collective identities, norm diffusion, social learning and community-building for understanding the increasing extent and quality of inter-African cooperation.

In order to provide vital context, the next three chapters analyze the attempts at establishing some sort of continental security cooperation which preceded the creation of the AU and which had a profound impact on the way in which its security architecture has evolved. Emphasizing the rationales offered for attempting to centralize the responsibility for peace and security as well as the many obstacles to such centralization, chapters three, four and five track the quest for continental security cooperation through the past century. Chapter three thereby covers the feeble attempts of Africa's freedom fighters to join forces, the repeated failure to establish an African High Command in the early years of decolonization, the inability of the OAU's Defense Commission to agree on a common defense structure and the OAU's ineffective peacekeeping operation in Chad. Chapter four details the subsequent devolution of security cooperation to the regional level as well as the supporting efforts of Western actors. On the basis of this retrospective journey, chapter five discusses the reasons for the revival of continental security cooperation at the turn of the 21st century and elaborates on the structural, conceptual and philosophical differences from the continent's previous cooperative ventures.

Chapter six covers the remarkable surge in AU-led peace operations that accompanied the development of institutionalized security structures on the continent. It elaborates on the nature, structure and significance of the AU Mission in Burundi (AMIB), the AU missions in Sudan (AMIS I, II and IIE), the AU operations on the Comoros (AMISEC, MAES and Operation Democracy) and the African Mission in Somalia (AMISOM).

Chapter seven shifts the focus back to the institutional level and details the AU's emerging peace and security architecture and its organizational components including the Peace and Security Council, the Panel of the Wise, the Military Staff Committee and the Special (Peace) Fund. It also provides an analysis of the AU's Peace & Security Directorate as well as its various divisions and discusses the consensus-building role of the Common African Defense and Security Policy.

In order to assess the quality and extent of contemporary inter-state security cooperation in Africa, the next two chapters examine the two remaining pillars of the AU's security architecture, namely the African Standby Force and the Continental Early Warning System. While both chapters go into great detail to demonstrate the complexity of these undertakings, they do not seek to provide an exhaustive description of the ASF and CEWS. Rather they focus on those aspects that help to highlight the state of contemporary inter-African security cooperation.

Chapter eight discusses the attempt of Africa's states to establish a continental quick reaction force in order to improve their ability to respond to violent conflict and humanitarian catastrophes. It first elaborates on the concept, structure and operationalization of the ASF before it turns to the AU's five regional partner organizations and their efforts to establish component standby brigades. As they are the most advanced regional brigades, the chapter focuses on the East African Standby Brigade, the ECOWAS Standby Force and the brigade of the Southern African Development Community.

Chapter nine begins by presenting the concept of the Continental Early Warning System and its current state of implementation. As in the previous chapter, this general introduction is followed by a review of the progress made by the continent's regional and sub-regional organizations in developing their respective component early warning systems. Given their advanced stage of development and model character, the chapter pays special attention to the mechanisms set up by the Intergovernmental Authority on Development and the Economic Community of West African States.

Chapters ten and eleven summarize the findings of the book. Chapter ten distils the empirical observations into a number of key characteristics of contemporary inter-state security cooperation in Africa. These characteristics include the Africanization of security, the diffusion of liberal norms, the institutionalization of cooperation, the emergence of (security) communities, the consolidation of institutional partnerships and the dependence on international support.

Chapter eleven elaborates on some of the main challenges to effective inter-African security cooperation. Emphasizing those challenges that have not yet received as much attention as the obvious scarcity of financial and military resources, it covers the problems arising from asymmetrical regionalization, the proliferation of intergovernmental organizations, overlapping institutional memberships, the nature and quality of international support measures, the ulterior motives of some African states and the lack of institutional capacity at all levels of cooperation.

The final chapter discusses the implications of these observations for theorizing security cooperation, both in Africa and beyond. It draws attention to the importance of constructivist concepts like collective identities, norm diffusion, social learning and community-building in the evolution of inter-African cooperation, the crucial role played by institutions in fostering this cooperation and the need to be open to different logics of regionalization. I conclude by arguing that none of this book's findings signify that the material forces of rational choice theory have lost their importance to the study of international cooperation. Instead, the African experience merely shows that the attention to the concern for power and sovereignty that permeates international relations must be complemented by an understanding of the occasions where these concerns are balanced against competing objectives or even muted altogether.

Notes

[1]   See Ali Mazrui, *Towards a Pax Africana: A Study in Ideology and Ambition* (Chicago: Chicago University Press, 1967), 216.

[2]   Kevin Dunn, "Africa and International Relations Theory," in *Africa's Challenge to International Relations Theory*, ed. Kevin Dunn and Timothy Shaw (Basingstoke: Palgrave, 2001), 2.

[3]   See, for instance, Christopher Clapham, *Africa and the International System: The Politics of State Survival* (Cambridge: Cambridge University Press, 1996), John Harbeson and Donald Rothchild, eds., *Africa in World Politics: Reforming Political Order* (Boulder: Westview Press, 2008), Ian Taylor and Paul Williams, eds., *Africa in International Politics: External Involvement on the Continent* (London: Routledge, 2003). For peace and security see, for example, Shannon Field, ed., *Peace in Africa: Towards a Collaborative Security Regime* (Johannesburg: Institute for Global Dialogue, 2004), David Francis, ed., *Peace & Conflict in Africa* (London: Zed Books, 2008).

[4]   For notable exceptions see the works of Paul Williams, Jürgen Haacke and Mohammed Ayoob.

[5]   Georg Wilhelm Friedrich Hegel quoted in Bernard Magubane, "The African Renaissance in Historical Perspective," in *African Renaissance*, ed. M Makgoba (Cape Town: Mafube & Tafelberg, 1999), 25.

[6]   See Kevin Dunn and Timothy Shaw, eds., *Africa's Challenge to International Relations Theory* (Basingstoke: Palgrave, 2001).

[7]   See Robert Strassler, ed., *The Landmark Thucydides: A Comprehensive Guide to the Peloponnesian War* (New York: Touchstone, 1998), 242.

[8]   For a similar, yet more radical argument see Amitav Acharya, "Beyond Anarchy: Third World Instability and International Order after the Cold War," in *International Relations Theory and the Third World*, ed. Stephanie Neuman (New York: St. Martin's Press, 1998), Kal Holsti, "International Relations Theory and Domestic War in the Third World: The Limits of Relevance," in *International Relations Theory and the Third World*, ed. Stephanie Neuman (New York: St. Martin's Press, 1998).

[9]   See, for example, Emanuel Adler, "Seizing the Middle Ground: Constructivism in International Relations," *European Journal of International Relations* 3, no. 3 (1997), Emanuel Adler and Michael Barnett, *Security Communities* (Cambridge: Cambridge University Press, 1998), Alexander

Wendt, "Anarchy Is What States Make of It: The Social Construction of Power Politics," *International Organization* 46, no. 2 (1992).
   [10]   A. Tickner, "Seeing IR Differently: Notes from the Third World," *Millennium: Journal of International Studies* 32, no. 2 (2003).
   [11]   See Alexander Wendt, *Social Theory of International Politics* (Cambridge: Cambridge University Press, 1999), 7-15.
   [12]   See, for example, Thomas Risse-Kappen, "Bringing Transnational Relations Back In: Introduction," in *Bringing Transnational Relations Back In: Non-State Actors, Domestic Structures and International Institutions*, ed. Thomas Risse-Kappen (Cambridge: Cambridge University Press, 1995).
   [13]   Jeffrey Herbst, "Crafting Regional Cooperation in Africa," in *Crafting Cooperation: Regional International Institutions in Comparative Perspective*, ed. Amitav Acharya and Alastair Johnston (Cambridge: Cambridge University Press, 2007), 130.
   [14]   Joseph Nye, for example, defined an international region on the basis of geographical proximity as "a limited number of states linked together by a geographic relationship and by a degree of mutual interdependence". See Joseph Nye, ed., *International Regionalism* (Boston: Little, Brown & Co, 1968), xii. Scholars like Paul Taylor extend such a geographical approach to include the effective distance covered by organizations, that is, the geographical space influenced by particular decisions. See P Taylor, *International Organization in the Modern World* (London: Pinter, 1993). Neo-functionalists like Ernst Haas argue that the deterministic factor in conceptualizing a region is deducible only by reference to the dynamics of integration. See Ernst Haas, *The Uniting of Europe* (Stanford: Stanford University Press, 1968). Teleologists like Bruce Russett measure the existence of a region by gauging the consequences of the practice of it. Bruce Russett, "International Regions and the International System," in *Regional Politics and World Order*, ed. Richard Falk and Saul Mendlovitz (San Francisco: W.H. Freeman, 1973).
   [15]   Adapted from Ademola Abass, *Regional Organizations and the Development of Collective Security - Beyond Chapter VIII of the UN Charter* (Oxford: Hart Publishing, 2004), 25.
   [16]   For a good treatment of symbolic interactionism see Herbert Blumer, *Symbolic Interactionism: Perspective and Method* (Englewood Cliffs: Prentice Hall, 1969). For structuration theory see Anthony Giddens, *The Constitution of Society: Outline of the Theory of Structuration* (Cambridge: Polity Press, 1984).
   [17]   Stephen van Evera, *Guide to Methods for Students of Political Science* (Ithaca: Cornell University Press, 1997), 30-35.
   [18]   Robert Keohane, *After Hegemony: Cooperation and Discord in the World Political Economy* (Princeton: Princeton University Press, 1984), 51-54. Keohane's definition of *cooperation* follows Charles Lindblom's, which uses the notion of policy coordination as an intermediary between cooperation and mutual adjustment of policies. Charles Lindblom, *The Intelligence of Democracy: Decision-Making through Mutual Adjustment* (New York: Free Press, 1965), 287. This definition is now widely accepted.
   [19]   See, for example, David Baldwin, "The Concept of Security," *Review of International Studies* 23, no. 1 (1997): 5-26, Edward Kolodziej, *Security and International Relations* (Cambridge: Cambridge University Press, 2005). For a

good summary of arguments and concepts related to security see Paul Williams, ed., *Security Studies: An Introduction* (London: Routledge, 2008).

[20] An "essentially contested concept" is one for which, by definition, there can be no consensus as to its meaning. See W.B. Gallie, "Essentially Contested Concepts," *Proceedings of the Aristotelian Society* 56 (1956): 167-198.

[21] See David Dewitt, "Common, Comprehensive and Cooperative Security," *The Pacific Review* 7, no. 1 (1994), Robert Mandel, *The Changing Face of National Security: A Conceptual Analysis* (Westport: Greenwood Press, 1994).

[22] Ken Booth, "Security and Emancipation," *Review of International Studies* 17 (1991): 313-326.

[23] Paul Williams, "Thinking About Security in Africa," *International Affairs* 83, no. 6 (2007): 1022.

[24] David Chuter, *Into Africa, Always Something New: Telling Africans what their Security Problems Are*, Conference Presentation, Royal United Services Institute Conference on AFRICOM, 18 February 2008.

[25] This is the result of a study presented by Major Shannon Beebe at the Royal United Services Conference on AFRICOM, 18 February 2008, London. For a detailed discussion of the concepts of human security see Edward Newmann, "Human Security and Constructivism," *International Studies Perspectives* 2, no. 3 (2002), Caroline Thomas and Peter Wilkin, eds., *Globalization, Human Security and the African Experience* (Boulder: Lynne Rienner, 1999). For an elaborate discussion of the concept of security in the African context see Williams, "Thinking About Security in Africa," 1021-1038.

[26] For an excellent discussion of the concept of security see Williams, ed., *Security Studies: An Introduction*, 1-9. For more information about Critical Security Studies see Keith Krause and Michael Williams, eds, *Critical Security Studies: Concepts and Cases* (London: Routledge, 1997).

2
Theorizing Security Cooperation in Africa

Since the end of the Cold War, the gradual intensification of inter-African security cooperation has tempted an increasing number of analysts to explain the underlying dynamics. Over the years, they have offered such a wide variety of perspectives that their enumeration alone could fill an entire volume. For this reason, and not out of a disregard for approaches like post-Marxist world systems theory or feminism, this chapter limits itself to a discussion of the dominant theoretical approaches to inter-state cooperation before it introduces constructivism as alternative theoretical framework. It contends that even though it may be true that parts of the academic community have moved beyond these approaches, rationalist-systemic theories like realism and neo-liberal institutionalism undoubtedly remain the most conceptually advanced, well-debated and, even more importantly, most often applied approaches in contemporary cooperation literature.[1] As such they provide a sound basis and fair target for theoretical discussion and empirical critique.

The chapter begins by arguing that these theories have substantial difficulties in accounting for the extent and quality of inter-state security cooperation currently emerging outside their empirical "comfort zones" in the Western world. As the product of European historical realities, they are inherently biased against the possibility of sustained and meaningful inter-state cooperation in Africa because, their pervasive focus on great powers, their positivist preoccupation with the systemic and materialistic aspects of international relations, as well as their unjustified assertion of universal patterns, causes them to miss essential dynamics in the developing world.

The second part of the chapter introduces social constructivism as a more appropriate theoretical framework. By highlighting the main differences between Alexander Wendt's interpretation of this school of thought and the dominant theories, I seek to demonstrate constructivism's "value added" to the study of inter-state security cooperation. In the process, I elaborate on the inter-subjective foundations of cooperation and introduce the idea of security communities.

The Limitations of Rationalist-Systemic Approaches

Rationalist-systemic theories stress the significance of the broader political structure within which state interaction is embedded. They start from the assumption that anarchy, that is, the absence of sovereign authority that can make and enforce binding agreements on the international level, creates opportunities for states to advance their interests unilaterally and makes it at the same time important and difficult for states to cooperate with one another.[2] The theoretical variants generally differ on the conditions under which cooperation is to be expected, the process by which cooperative action takes place and the overall propensity of states to cooperate. More specifically, realists and neo-liberal institutionalists disagree on the willingness of states to engage in international cooperation given the uncertainties and risks associated with anarchy, the potential of international organizations to mitigate these constraining effects of the anarchic system, the priority of state goals (security vs. political economy) and the importance of relative and absolute gains from cooperation. According to Joseph Grieco, realists thereby view international cooperation as "harder to achieve, more difficult to maintain and more dependent on state power" than do neo-liberal institutionalists.[3]

A number of theorists have applied rationalist-systemic frameworks to the study of post-Cold War African security dynamics. James Goldgeier and Michael McFaul, for example, have characterized Africa as part of a global periphery in which security dynamics continue to be dominated by calculations of material interest and power-balancing.[4] Similarly, Barry Buzan and Ole Waever have argued that Africa's security dynamics are shaped by the relative material capabilities within its various "mutually exclusive" regional security complexes.[5]

While these and other rationalist-systemic theories raise a number of important points with respect to the security dynamics on the continent, they share several methodological and theoretical flaws which limit their relevance to the study of security cooperation in contemporary Africa. On a general level, it is their overstated focus on a certain level of analysis and a predetermination of the conditions which explain state behavior that immediately appear problematic. While realism emphasizes the anarchical character of the international system and the respective ever present possibility of war of all against all to explain selfish state behavior, neo-liberal institutionalism assumes that in every situation states independently of whatever conditions will always seek to maximize their gains, preferably through cooperation, because it is the most rational thing to do. As a result, both schools underestimate levels of analysis other than the international system or the state and posit that the identities and the interests of states are predetermined, fixed and always orientated by a utilitarian rationality.[6] Their resultant focus on rationalism and material structures also leads realism and neo-liberal institutionalism to neglect social processes in general and the "sociological and inter-subjective processes underlying the emergence of cooperation" in particular.[7] Contrary to constructivists like Alexander Wendt who accord inter-subjective processes a crucial role in explaining inter-state cooperation by "constituting identities, interests and threats, by helping actors find common solutions to problems and by defining expectations for behavior",[8] realists and neo-liberal institutionalists emphasize their perspective as lying strictly within the limits of "objective theory-building".[9] Accordingly, both approaches fail, albeit to different degrees, to appreciate the importance of inter-subjective factors, including ideas, norms and beliefs and their role in the emergence and deepening of security cooperation.

On a more Africa-specific level, these general critiques are compounded by both approaches' extreme theoretical marginalization of the developing world in general and the African continent in particular. This marginalization extends beyond practice and is embedded in the approaches themselves.[10] Inevitably reflecting the Western circumstances in which they were formulated as well as their respective political phenomena, realism is the product of European historical realities reaffirmed by the peculiar characteristics of the Cold War just as the advent of neo-liberal institutionalism is inextricably interlinked with that of the European Union. As such, neither has paid much attention to Africa.

It is certainly true that, over the last decade, realist and neo-liberal institutionalist writings have become more heterogeneous and that several scholars have attempted to overcome the apparent inequality of international relations theorizing.[11] English School adherent Mohammed Ayoob, for example, has proposed what he calls "subaltern realism" as analytical tool for grasping the major determinants of developing state behavior, the dominant concerns of developing world elites and the root causes of conflict in the developing world.[12] First put forward in the 1980s, subaltern realism emphasizes the divergence of developing world conditions from those of industrialized core states and thereby aspires to provide a "defense against the theoretical imperialism of the mainstream" and a critical rejoinder to the neo-realism of Kenneth Waltz. Despite their valuable efforts, however, neither subaltern realism nor any of the other *ad hoc* modifications of realism and neo-liberal institutionalism have really been able to penetrate the continuing dominance of their established predecessors.[13] As a result, the apparent fissure between international relations theory and empirical reality in the developing world remains far from bridged.

In the context of this study, five empirical realities prove particularly challenging to rationalist theories of inter-state security cooperation, namely, (1) the nature of the state in Africa, (2) the particular nature of security problems in Africa, (3) the proliferation of regional and continental cooperation schemes, (4) the role of unifying ideologies such as Pan-Africanism and (5) the extent of norm diffusion in Africa.

For both realist and neo-liberal institutionalist theories the state is the central actor in international relations. States are taken to be rational unitary actors motivated by national interests such as the search for power and security. This Hobbesian conception of the state, however, does not necessarily apply to the African state. In fact, one of the few points on which the substantial body of literature on the African state seems to agree is that "it is a very different kind of organization from that which the conventional study of international relations tends to take for granted".[14] Given that they have "so little connection to the established Western concept", Barry Buzan has even argued that African states should be considered an entirely separate class of state, namely *pre-modern* (as opposed to *modern* and *post-modern*).[15] Usually found at the bottom of any conventional ordering of global power, importance and prestige, the African state has been inextricably linked with negative characteristics reaching from "failed", "weak" and "quasi" to "parasitic" and "subordinate".[16] While always at the risk of undue generalization, such portrayals point to an essential epistemological shortcoming of realist and neo-liberal institutionalist approaches which continue to treat the state as the unproblematic starting point of analysis rather than a variable in itself.[17]

By treating the state in this way, traditional IR theory and with it most forms of realism and neo-liberal institutionalism not only privilege the dominant Western discourse, but also mask the complexities of reality.[18] Far from unproblematic, the colonial origin, post-colonial evolution and contemporary nature of the African state are absolutely essential to understand the roots of insecurity in Africa and the resultant attempts at inter-state cooperation.[19] The myopic focus on the state also ignores other actors that are just as important to such an understanding. In line with Christopher Clapham's observation that "the less solid the state, the greater the need to look beyond it for an understanding of how the society that it claims to govern fits into the international system",[20] nations, armed movements, regional strongmen and other non-state actors have to be considered important units of analysis in the African context. Because it simply ignores the influence of such actors and instead assumes that the state is an independent system of power that operates predictably, traditional IR theory has not been able to explain, let alone predict, the behavior of African political actors on the world stage.[21]

Another factor limiting the relevance of realism and neo-liberal institutionalism to the study of contemporary security cooperation in Africa is their overly orthodox notion of security. Both approaches tend to define the concept of security in purely external and systemic terms, that is, security is defined as the immunity (to varying degrees) to external dominance and military threats emanating from outside their borders that states aspire to in the anarchical international system. In the often-cited words of Walter Lippmann, "a state is secure to the extent to which is not in danger of having to sacrifice core values, if it wishes to avoid war, and is able, if challenged, to maintain them by victory in such a war".[22] As so many other concepts central to the two approaches, security is thus unmistakably defined in the state-centric and historically biased terms of the Western academic debate. Not surprisingly, however, the two major characteristics of this traditional definition of security – namely, its external orientation and its strong linkage with systemic theory – are hardly recognizable in Africa. Despite the outward-directed rhetoric of many African leaders, the sense of insecurity that prevails in most African states is that of internal threats to and from the regime in power rather than of external military threats to the sovereign existence of the state *per se*. According to Brian Job, this "insecurity dilemma" is caused by three traits common to most African states.[23] First, there is often no single nation in the state, rather communal groups contending for their own security. Second, the regime often lacks support from significant components of the population, the result being an absence of perceived popular legitimacy to the existence and security interests of the regime. Third, the state generally lacks effective institutional capacities to provide peace and order. These traits are further compounded by the highly personalized nature of African politics and the resultant tendency of regimes to prioritize self-preservation over the security interests of the state.[24] As a result of these characteristics, intra-state conflict has been a far more frequent occurrence in Africa than inter-state war. In fact, using the standard definition of the Correlates of War Project, there have only been three events in Africa's post-colonial history that qualify as inter-state wars, namely, the Ogaden War between Somalia and Ethiopia (1977-78), the war between Uganda and Tanzania (1978) and the border war between

Ethiopia and Eritrea (1998-2000), while there have been hundreds of violent intra-state conflicts.[25] Accordingly, any definition of security in the African context must also take internal and non-systemic components into account.

The proliferation of regional and continental cooperation schemes in Africa presents realism and neo-liberal institutionalism with yet another epistemological problem. Traditionally, their interest in the study of regionalism has been confined predominantly to the highly institutionalized forms of international cooperation among countries in the industrialized world. While the last couple of years have seen a widening of this focus and an increased interest in the developing world, the underlying formalistic approach of both schools of thought has remained virtually unchanged. According to Wil Hout, realist theorizing leads to three expectations concerning regional cooperation in the developing world.[26] First, regional arrangements will be predominantly military security related and necessitate common (external) threat perceptions. Second, the existence of a regional hegemon will facilitate regional cooperation. Third, regionalism will be affected by the relative gains accruing to the different partners in a regional arrangement, which will ultimately deter states from cooperating among themselves. Neo-liberal institutionalists, on the other hand, tend to see regionalist arrangements as regimes through which the allocation of certain public goods can be established. They expect regional arrangements to be negotiated in those situations where states have clearly defined common interests – usually brought about by a high level of interdependence – in creating mechanisms for policy coordination. Adherents to this school of thought also typically argue that the creation of regional arrangements cannot be understood without reference to domestic pressure groups on whose support politicians depend. Given the complex realities of Africa's inter-state relations and the resultant widely varying rationales for regional cooperation reaching from economic development to the joint conduct of peacekeeping operations, however, these traditional theoretical approaches provide only a partial and incomplete guide to understanding contemporary regionalism on the continent. Focused on the comparative interests and powers of states and economic interdependence, neither realist nor neo-liberal institutionalist theories can adequately account for the surge of what Björn Hettne and Fredrik Söderbaum have called the "new regionalisms" in Africa.[27]

The fourth African reality which limits the relevance of rationalist approaches to the study of inter-state security cooperation on the continent is the central role of unifying ideologies such as Pan-Africanism. Discussed in more detail in the next chapter, Pan-

Africanism is a socio-political worldview which seeks to unify and uplift both native Africans and those of the African Diaspora as part of a global African community.[28] It was the ideological centerpiece of Africa's independence movements during decolonization and the basis for many attempts at regional cooperation thereafter. Declared dead somewhat prematurely in the early 1980s,[29] Pan-Africanism has since re-emerged as unifying force in African politics.[30] It now provides the ideological basis for many of the continent's most elaborate inter-state cooperation schemes such as the African Union or the New Partnership for African Development (NEPAD) and there is hardly a political document that does not refer to it at some point.[31] However, neither realism nor neo-liberal institutionalism can account for the fact that "Africa is a political idea as well as a geographical fact".[32] As a result, they fail to appreciate a crucial aspect of inter-state cooperation in Africa, namely, the degree to which regional awareness and a collective identity based on shared historical experiences and cultural ties provide the basis and motivation for such cooperation.

A related difficulty for rationalist theories arises from the fact that Africa's states are increasingly sharing more values than just an ironclad commitment to Pan-Africanism. For instance, the last years have seen the development of what Paul Williams refers to as an "African security culture" built around an emerging consensus on such issues as the responsibility to protect and the rejection of unconstitutional changes of government.[33] According to Williams, security cultures are patterns of thought and argumentation that establish pervasive and durable security preferences by formulating concepts of the role, legitimacy and efficacy of particular approaches to protecting values.[34] Through a process of socialization, they help to establish the core assumptions, beliefs and values of decision-makers about how security challenges can and should be dealt with.[35] Rationalist approaches downplay the importance of shared norms and cultural beliefs to such an extent that they are unable to account for the emergence or intensification of inter-state cooperation on the basis of such a process of norm socialization.

Despite these limitations of both realist and neo-liberal institutionalist approaches in the African context, it has to be pointed out that there are many instances in which one or the other (or even both) schools of thought can provide valuable insights. For example, some of the most important inter-state relationships among African states and between African states and non-African states can be understood in terms of the realist concept of regime security. As Clapham pointed out, "whatever the personal proclivities of African rulers, whatever their dreams or long-term ambitions, a great deal of their immediate behavior is comprehended by the notion that they seem to be most frequently guided in their daily behavior by securing their regimes in power".[36] This corresponds well with non-Western varieties of realism and with Machiavelli's early modern realism.[37] However, while they may apply in instances, for the reasons cited above, realism and neo-liberal institutionalism are only of limited theoretical relevance to the study of security cooperation as undertaken in this book. Because of their pervasive great power bias, their inherent positivist preoccupation with the systemic and materialistic aspects of international relations and their unjustified assertion of universal patterns they fail to capture essential African realities and misinterpret the motives for as well as the evolution of cooperation between African states. As a result, they are unable to account for the substantial differences in origin, design and purpose between security arrangements in Africa and those in the developed world.[38] Thus, for a better understanding of contemporary security cooperation in Africa, it is necessary to open a space for alternative explanatory perspectives and move away from a narrowly-defined and materialist view of rationalist theories such as realism and neo-liberal institutionalism.[39] The book argues that constructivism can offer such an alternative.

Constructivism as an Alternative Analytical Framework

As Maja Zehfuss so rightly pointed out, "the significance of constructivism is established more easily than its identity".[40] Since it was first mentioned by Nicholas Onuf in his book *World of our Making* in 1989,[41] the concept of constructivism has acquired considerable significance in the study of international relations. Within little over a decade it has risen to be one of the top three paradigms in the discipline and increasing numbers of scholars swell its ranks. Despite this rapid ascent to academic prominence, however, it remains difficult to define constructivism in uncontroversial terms.[42] This section does not aspire to provide such a definition, cover each and every concept put forth in the ongoing debate among constructivists and their critics or do justice to the intellectual history of the field. Instead, it merely hopes to distil the central characteristics of this theoretical approach to inter-state cooperation and thus prepare the ground for the ensuing analysis of the AU's security architecture.

Constructivism is not a monolithic theory but rather a label given to a wide variety of approaches to international relations that range from

Alexander Wendt's scientific realism to post-structural constructivism. What all varieties of constructivism share is an inherent skepticism towards the existence of an objective reality. Instead, social meaning is constructed by social interaction which creates a web of norms and rules that govern appropriate action.[43] On this basis, Christian Reus-Smit has identified three common concerns that can serve as a useful starting point.

First, constructivists argue that normative and ideational structures are just as important as material structures. This contrasts starkly with realist as well as neo-liberal institutionalist theories which tend to assume that material structures are the driving force behind world politics. For realists like Kenneth Waltz material conditions "shape and shove" actors' choices and behavior,[44] while neo-liberal institutionalists like Robert Keohane rely on shared norms to facilitate the adjustments of self-interested actors in pursuit of (mutual) material gains. Constructivists, on the other hand, argue that to understand international relations one must adopt a sociological or social/psychological approach and recognize that "the fundamental structures of international politics are *social* rather than strictly material".[45]

Second, constructivists of all stripes agree that ideational structures are important because they shape the identities and therefore interests of actors in world politics.[46] Constructivist scholars like Alexander Wendt reject the rationalist insistence that interests are exogenously given, an idea that underpins both neo-realism and neo-liberalism, and instead share a cognitive, inter-subjective conception of process in which identities and interests are endogenous to interaction.[47] As a result of this recognition that practice influences outcome, they see the social world as *constructed* not given.

The third common concern that binds constructivists is the view that the relationship between agents and structures is mutually constitutive.[48] Contrary to traditional theories which imply that agents and their social constructions are independent and autonomous of each other, constructivism holds that the structures that comprise international society can be altered by the conscious actions of agents. As such, it discards the predetermination of identities, interests or behaviors by the anarchical structure of the system or by individual agent's rational choice.

Wendt's Interpretation of Constructivism

Given the above, it is not surprising that constructivists claim that their approach is a radical break from dominant theorizing in international relations.[49] In fact, it is more than that. It is an explicit reaction to what many scholars see as fundamental shortcomings in prevailing (rationalist) theory about international politics. For constructivists of all stripes, dominant social science assumptions such as static and unchanging identities and interests and the stipulation of a pre-determined trajectory of behavior severely limit social inquiry to means-ends or narrow and self-serving instrumental thinking. As degree and scope of this critique vary substantially across the discipline, this section will focus on the work of Alexander Wendt to briefly outline the main points of contention between constructivism and the traditional theories. Naturally, this is not to mean that other interpretations of constructivism, ranging from its light to heavy versions, are less important, or even false.[50] Given the context of this study, Wendt's pragmatism in seeking to enlarge the scope of explanations of actor behavior, most notably the state, simply seems more appropriate to demonstrate the "value added" of constructivism to the study of inter-state security cooperation than, for example, the radical deconstruction of prevailing behavioral theories preached by heavy constructivists. Following the methodology proposed by Imre Lakatos to test the validity of competing schools of thought,[51] this "value added" will be established by showing that (1) Wendt's constructivism can explain what the traditional theories explain, (2) it can explain facts not addressed by other explanations and (3) it can explain new facts and events that arise within the scope of its explanatory power.

Wendt's interpretation of constructivism has been the subject of exhaustive study ever since his article *Anarchy Is What States Make of It* was published in 1992.[52] The extension of his argument in his book *Social Theory of International Relations* seven years later further consolidated his extraordinary standing in the field.[53] While many scholars disagree with his conclusions Wendt is almost universally credited with advancing the theoretical debate and providing "one of the most sophisticated and hard-hitting constructivist critiques of realism".[54]

Wendt seeks to challenge the core realist premise that anarchy forces states into recurrent security competitions and thus prevents sustained inter-state cooperation. Drawing on Herbert Blumer's symbolic interactionism and Anthony Giddens' structurationist sociology,[55] he argues that social reality develops in interaction and that anarchy does therefore not necessarily lead to spirals of hostility, arms racing and war. Contrary to Waltz and other realists, Wendt holds that the way international relations are conducted "is socially constructed rather than trans-historically given".[56] For this reason, he rejects the realist notion that egoistic state behavior is independent of time, place and culture and that states are thus unable to surmount the security dilemma because it is embedded in the state system.[57] While Wendt accepts that in the initial state of a state-to-state interaction, egoistic self-help behavior is likely to be exhibited,[58] he argues that interaction with other states can lead actors to significant redefinitions of themselves.

Subsumed in his telling phrase "anarchy is what states make of it", Wendt holds that an actor's reality can be transcended by instantiating new social practices and that states are thus not necessarily caught in what Ken Booth has called the "prison of realism",[59] that is, they can act to alter the inter-subjective culture that constitutes the system, solidifying over time the non-egoistic mind-sets needed for sustained cooperation.[60] Hence, if egoistic and militaristic conceptions endure in inter-state relations, it is only because of the interactive practices that reproduce and sustain those conceptions and not because of the structure of the international system *per se*. Consequently, Wendt maintains, the anarchy postulated by Kenneth Waltz is only one of many possible forms of culture and structures of ideas potentially available to states at the macro-level. These forms range from incessant conflict to perpetual peace, from Thomas Hobbes' "war of all against all" through John Locke's social contract to Immanuel Kant's *"ewigem Frieden"*.[61]

These Hobbesian, Lockean and Kantian cultures are further differentiated by the degree to which the actors have internalized the respective norms of the prevailing culture. In the first degree, compliance to the norm is solely a function of coercion. In the second degree, actors conform to the norm not because they see it as legitimate, but merely because they believe it to be in their self-interest. In the third degree, states have finally internalized the behavioral norms as legitimate part of themselves.[62] While acceptance of the prevailing norms at the first two degrees of internalization is purely instrumental and thus consistent with the traditional theories of cooperation, the third degree is consistent with constructivist logic. Hence, each logic of anarchy is characterized by "multiple realizability", that is, the same effect can be reached through different causes.[63] For example, a Kantian culture – characterized by a high degree of cooperation – does not necessarily have to be associated with cultural internalization of the third degree but can also be a product of purely self-interested compliance resulting from the threat of punishment (first degree) or the simple benefits of cooperation (second degree). Similarly, conflictual

Hobbesian systems do not necessarily have to be the product of the material forces of realist theory, but can also arise as social constructions from shared internalized ideas at the third degree. As Dale Copeland put it, "conflict does thus not confirm realism, just as cooperation does not confirm liberalism or constructivism".[64]

While critics may have a point in arguing that Wendt's interpretation of constructivism fails to adequately address problems such as uncertainty and thus some of the central tenets of both realism and neo-liberal institutionalism, its contentions regarding the possibilities for sustained inter-state security cooperation appear firm. Given the centrality of inter-subjective factors in these contentions, the next section will briefly elaborate on the role constructivism accords to norms, ideas, identities and beliefs in the emergence and consolidation of such security cooperation.

The Inter-Subjective Foundations of Cooperation

Traditional cooperation theories, with their emphasis on objective goods such as pre-political national interests and degrees of obligation and mutuality, severely downplay the social and ideational aspects of trans-national security relationships. Constructivism, on the other hand, bases much of its explanatory power on sociological and inter-subjective processes such as collective identity formation, social learning and community building. Its central contention *vis-à-vis* realism and neo-liberal institutionalism is that the dynamic of international politics is neither natural nor given by deep structure, but is rather socially constructed by political actors through their interactions and relationships.[65] As such, constructivism discards the predetermination of identities, interests or behaviors by the anarchical structure of the international system or by actors' rational choice and instead relies on the ideas and beliefs that inform political actors as well as the shared understandings between them as explanatory variables.

Max Weber and Emile Durkheim paved the way for such constructivist thinking over a century ago.[66] Weber implicitly posed the agent-structure problem in insisting that humans are "cultural beings endowed with the capacity and the will to take a deliberate attitude towards the world and to lend it significance".[67] Durkheim, in extending Weber's insights, advanced the notion of a collective conscience, a set of shared ideas and beliefs that informed the thinking and behavior of members of a given society.[68] Building on the contributions of Weber and Durkheim to social thought, scholars like Anthony Giddens began to erect an increasingly sophisticated theoretical edifice. Giddens proposed the concept of structuration as a way of analyzing the relationship between structures and actors.[69] He argued that this relationship involves inter-subjective understanding and meaning and that while structures do constrain actors, actors can also transform structures by thinking about them and acting on them in new ways. This reciprocity provided the basis for Wendt's critique of realism and its emphasis on deep structure. For Wendt, the culture in which states find themselves at any point in time depends on the discursive social practices that reproduce or transform each actor's view of self and other, that is, on the prevailing ideas, norms and identities which generate the actors' material and non-material interests.

Nina Tannenwald defines ideas as "mental constructs held by individuals, sets of distinctive beliefs, principles and attitudes that provide broad orientations for behavior and policy".[70] Contrary to strictly rationalist explanations of international relations where "ideas are unimportant or epiphenomenal either because actors correctly anticipate the results of their actions or because some selective process ensures that only actors who behave as if they were rational succeed",[71] constructivists argue that ideas are the basis of identities and thus interests and ultimately behavior. One way in which ideas shape identities is through norms.

Norms are shared ideas which are defined by Friedrich Kratochwil as "standards of behavior defined in terms of rights and obligations" and by Peter Katzenstein as "collective expectations for proper behavior of actors within a given identity".[72] While all theories of international relations, including neo-liberal institutionalism, recognize the importance of norms, constructivism allows for a much deeper understanding of norms in shaping international relations. Briefly stated, the constructivist definition incorporates both *regulatory* and *constitutive* aspects of norms and their effect on state behavior.[73] Norms not only prescribe and regulate behavior; they also define and constitute identities.

The way in which norms determine identity has been one of the most intensively discussed topics in constructivist thought.[74] A particularly persuasive conceptual pathway has been proposed by Thomas Risse, Stephen Ropp and Kathryn Sikkink. Using the example of human rights, they have developed a five-phased spiral model of norm internalization in which states initially comply with norms merely for tactical reasons but where norms gradually transfer into the habitual behavior of the states and thereby change their identities.[75] As states' identities change, so do their interests for, in the words of Wendt, "what we want depends to a large degree on who we are".[76] Very much in contrast to realist and neo-liberal institutionalist thought where interests are exogenously given, constructivists thus argue that interests are variable and can be determined by reference to "the ideas and norms that are the lens through which states interpret their interests and forge their identities".[77]

This notion of socially constructed state identities and interests runs deep into the heart of constructivist approaches to international cooperation because it theoretically allows for an amelioration of the security dilemma among states. According to constructivists like Wendt, states can eventually overcome the polarizing effects of Hobbesian anarchy and even create trans-national political communities by forming collective identities.[78] Such identities which evolve through sustained social interaction (common experiences), social learning and positive interdependence are seen as the fundamental building blocks of collective action and durable inter-state cooperation. Over time, they can transform egoistic conceptions of self to perceptions of commonality by creating a community of attitudes or, in the words of Emmanuel Adler, a "community of practice".[79] Different types of unit interaction thereby determine the type of collective identity that develops which in turn determines the type of cooperative agreements states create or enter into.

Bruce Cronin discusses four ways in which a trans-national identity can transform the Westphalian self-conception of states assumed by traditional theories into one based on the membership in a conceptual social group.[80] First, trans-national identities provide the members of a social group with a set of norms, boundaries, goals and a social context for interaction. Second, common identities can facilitate cooperation among members of a trans-national group by creating a sense of interdependency with respect to common goals. Third, trans-national identities can help to legitimize a particular form of state or governance structure. Fourth, trans-national identities are often institutionalized within international associations that help to socialize their members according to group norms. These exclusive associations help to highlight and strengthen the identities they embody. To the extent that this is viewed as beneficial for the states involved, the social group grows stronger. Thus, the greater the perceived benefits of group membership, the stronger the identity and the more likely each state will cooperate with the other group members.

Adherents of both realism and neo-liberal institutionalism tend to minimize the importance of identity as an explanatory variable because their theoretical assumptions do not permit any major variation in state behavior. Nor do they see a foundation for cohesive communities among sovereign states. States can have shared interests, but not shared identities. According to Adler and Barnett, "the idea that actors can share values, norms and symbols that provide a social identity and engage in various interactions in myriad spheres that reflect long-term interests, diffuse reciprocity and trust, strikes fear and incredulity in their hearts".[81]

Constructivists, on the other hand, admit that trans-national identities "do not develop easily, that trans-national communities are hard to construct and that the polarizing effects of sovereignty and anarchy are formidable obstacles".[82] Nonetheless, they argue that a theory of community building is integral to a perspective that sees international relations as a process of social learning and identity formation, driven by transactions, interactions and socialization. The idea that states can form an international community is usually attributed to Hedley Bull. According to Bull, a society of states exists "when a group of states, conscious of certain common interests and common values, form a society in the sense that they conceive themselves to be bound by a common set of rules in their relations with one another and share in the working of common institutions".[83] For constructivists, this statement continues to sum up the inter-subjective foundations of international cooperation.

Although the so-called constructivist synthesis in international relations theory is relatively recent, many of its insights discussed above resonate closely with Karl Deutsch's view of international relations as a social and communicative activity. His concept of security communities offers a particularly useful way of understanding how states might reconfigure their perceptions of security by adopting a logic different to that of the security dilemma.

The idea and concept of security communities

A security community is generally defined as a group of states integrated to the point where people have dependable expectations of peaceful change. Initially proposed by Richard van Wagenen in 1952,[84] it was with the seminal 1957 study by Karl Deutsch and his associates that this concept received its first in-depth theoretical and empirical treatment.[85] By that time, however, the systemic theorizing emanating from the *Realpolitik* of the Cold War had already come to dominate the academic discourse to such an extent that few scholars felt attracted to

Deutsch's decidedly sociological concept. Following the end of the Cold War, Emmanuel Adler and Michael Barnett resuscitated the latter hoping to benefit from the best of Deutsch's conceptualization and aiming to correct for its shortcomings by borrowing from four decades of additional theoretical insights.[86]

Deutsch and his associates formulated the concept of security communities "as a contribution to the study of possible ways in which men some day might abolish war".[87] Deeply scarred by the experience of the Second World War (during which Deutsch had to flee from Germany), they sought to explain how and why certain groups have permanently stopped warring and how the conditions underlying this stable peace might be extended over larger and larger areas of the globe. Diverging from the predominantly realist discourse of their time, they focused on the integrative and pacifying effects of shared understandings, trans-national values and transaction flows in order to explain the emergence of so-called security communities within which the formation of a common identity and purpose leads to expectations of peaceful change among the inhabitants. Deutsch and his associates distinguished between amalgamated and pluralistic security communities. While the former relates to the formal merger of two or more previously independent units into a single larger unit with a common government (for example, the United States), units retain their legal independence within the latter (for example, the European Union).[88] Deutsch and his associates identified a list of twelve conditions that were essential for a successful amalgamation of independent states. For the formation of a pluralistic security community, however, they identified only two prerequisites, namely, "the capacity of the participating political units or governments to respond to each other's needs, messages, and actions" and the "compatibility of major values relevant to political decision-making".[89]

Contrary to an alliance, a pluralistic security community is held together by the notion of collective identity and, more specifically, by shared values and meanings rather than merely the perceived need to balance a common threat.[90] According to Deutsch, a trans-national or collective identity develops in the course of sustained interaction between states and through the development of dependable behavior and common norms eventually leads to the emergence of a trans-national community characterized by mutual trust and a sense of affiliation. By arguing that a process of interstate communication and social learning underpins the pacific relations of states in such a community, Deutsch and his associates attempted to steer academic attention from the concept of negative to positive peace and from atomistic models of interstate behavior to the centrality of trans-national social forces.[91] While this proved a lost cause against the backdrop of the Cold War and the omnipresent fear of nuclear war, their study of security communities laid the foundation for the subsequent emergence of a constructivist approach to International Relations.

It took more than 40 years until Emanuel Adler and Michael Barnett resuscitated the concept of security communities. Despite their admiration for Deutsch's scholarly and political vision, they argued that his conceptualization was fraught with theoretical, methodological and conceptual difficulties.[92] In order to overcome these difficulties, they proposed a number of modifications and additions to Deutsch's original schema.

First, they suggested a more thorough definition of the term "security community". This expanded the notion of security from the one-dimensional military security of the Cold War to account for the multiple dimensions of today's inter-community relations and security concerns. While Deutsch's idea of security communities was (quite understandably) influenced by his exposure to the system of collective defense and trans-national cooperation embodied by the North Atlantic Treaty Organization (NATO), Adler and Barnett formulated a definition of the concept that allowed for its application to the international politics of the post-Cold War era (at least in the developed world).

Second, they deepened the concept by distinguishing between two different types of pluralistic security communities, namely loosely-coupled security communities and tightly-coupled security communities. States in a loosely-coupled security community merely expect no bellicose activities from the other members of the community (while maintaining their full sovereignty). States in a tightly coupled-security community, however, have become integrated to the point that they display traits of an almost post-sovereign system of governance, endowed with common supra-national, trans-national and national institutions and some form of a collective security and mutual aid system.[93]

Third, Adler and Barnett elaborated on the evolutionary pattern of security communities. They argued that both loosely and tightly-coupled security communities usually follow a certain growth path in their development and suggested three stylized phases – nascent, ascendant and mature – and a corresponding set of indicators as heuristic devices for its conceptualization. In the initial (nascent) phase, governments contemplate closer cooperation in order to increase their mutual security, reduce transaction costs and encourage further interactions without the explicit purpose of creating a security community.[94]

Ascendant security communities are characterized by a much closer state of integration which has started to transform the environment in which participating states and their citizens are embedded. The emergence of shared expectations and a collective identity as well as the deepening of mutual trust through increasingly institutionalized networks encourage "dependable expectations of peaceful change".[95] The final (mature) stage of development is reached once these expectations are so fully institutionalized in both domestic and supranational settings that war between members of the community has become unimaginable. Instead, states in a mature loosely-coupled security community identify positively with one another and proclaim a similar way of life. States in a mature tightly-coupled security community go even further and express their national identities through the merging of efforts in trans-national organizations such as, for example, an integrated military defense organization.[96]

The fourth helpful addition that Adler and Barnett made to the concept of security communities arises from their discussion of the mutually constitutive relationship between member states and the security community and especially the impact that membership of a security community has on state behavior. This impact, according to Adler and Barnett, is particularly profound in a mature tightly-coupled security community where the identity of a member state (and thus its behavior) is indeed shaped by its membership in that community. While membership does not erode a state's sovereignty (at least not in the case of a pluralistic security community), its socializing effects increase with the maturity of and integration within the community.

Fifth, Adler and Barnett emphasize the central role of international organizations and institutions in this process of socialization. They argue that such organizations and institutions contribute directly and indirectly to the development of security communities through "their capacity to engineer the very conditions – for example, cultural homogeneity, a belief in a common fate and norms of unilateral self-restraint – that assist in the development of mutual trust and shared identities".[97] While both van Wagenen and Deutsch merely touched the subject,[98] Adler, Barnett and some of their co-authors are particularly interested in the trust-building properties of international organizations. They argue that the latter facilitate and encourage trust by establishing norms of behavior, monitoring mechanisms and sanctions to enforce those norms; mediating among conflicting parties; reducing uncertainty by conveying information and producing transparency; expanding material self-interest to be more inclusive and longer term; revealing new areas of mutual interests; and generating the narratives of mutual identification.[99]

With these conceptual clarifications and especially their balanced attention to structures (power and knowledge) and processes (transactions, institutions and social learning) Adler and Barnett have contributed significantly to our understanding of security communities. Other scholars that have also made notable additions or modifications to this concept include Alex Bellamy (on security communities and insider-outsider relationships), Laurie Nathan (on security communities and domestic instability) and Raimo Väyrynen (on comprehensive and interstate security communities).

In his book *Security Communities and their Neighbors*, Alex Bellamy examines the effect the development of security communities has on global politics generally and the relationships between insiders and outsiders in particular.[100] Against the backdrop of an increasing regionalization of security cooperation worldwide he argues that the proliferation of security communities "does not represent the beginning of a Huntingtonian nightmare of a world of civilizational blocs in perpetual conflict with each other".[101] Instead, Bellamy argues, members of a security community eventually project the non-zero sum attitude to security they have grown accustomed to in their relations with each other onto their relations with outsiders (any resultant constitutive effects thereby depend on the type of security community).

Laurie Nathan contends that domestic stability defined as the absence of large-scale violence in a country is a necessary condition of a security community and that the benchmark of dependable expectations of peaceful change should apply not only between states but also within them.[102] While there is certainly a lot of merit to Nathan's argument that whatever the nature of inter-state relations among a group of countries, a citizenry engulfed by internal violence cannot be plausibly be said to inhibit a security community,[103] Raimo Väyrynen has devised a persuasive typology to overcome this problem. He differentiates between comprehensive security communities in which both an inter-state and inter-societal peace prevail and inter-state security communities in which member states are at peace with each other though large-scale violence is still possible within them.[104]

The concept of security communities as discussed by these and other scholars serves well to demonstrate the "value added" of constructivism to the study of inter-state security cooperation as undertaken in this book. First, it raises the possibility that through interactions and socialization, states can manage anarchy and even escape the security dilemma, conditions which realist, neorealist and neo-liberal institutionalist perspectives take as a permanent feature of international relations. Second, the concept offers a theoretical and analytical framework for studying the impact of international (including regional) institutions in promoting peaceful change in international relations. This framework not only challenges the assumptions of realism and neo-realism, but also goes beyond the intellectual parameters established by the realist – neo-liberal institutionalist divide, which have formed a major part of the theoretical debate in international relations in the last decade. Third, the concept highlights the importance of inter-subjective factors such as ideas, norms and beliefs in the emergence and deepening of inter-state cooperation. Fourth, it reintroduces the power of agent-driven change into social analysis.

Despite the brevity of the discussion, the epistemological and heuristic advantages of constructivism over the traditional theories of security cooperation do stand out. Recalling the details of the Lakatosian comparison of competing schools of thought, the previous sections have shown that constructivism can explain what the traditional theories explain (reasons for war and peace), it can explain facts not addressed by realism and neo-liberal institutionalism (the power of ideas) and it can also explain new facts and events that arise within the scope of its explanatory power (collective identities and community building).[105] The following section will demonstrate that constructivism has not only become an attractive alternative to realism and neo-liberal institutionalism in the general sense, but that it also offers a much more appropriate theoretical framework through which to study inter-state security cooperation in the particular context of contemporary Africa.

Constructivism in the African context

Despite the apparent wealth of scholarship on constructivism, many of its central concepts remain severely under-researched. Particularly the narrow focus of the security community literature on the developed world and its institutions has left large geographical and theoretical areas uncovered.[106] In stark contrast to the proliferation of apparent security communities in the Western world (NATO, EU and OSCE),[107] the label is rarely applied to any segment of the developing world with the possible exception of Southeast Asia where Amitav Acharya has triggered an increasingly sophisticated debate on the topic.[108] In Africa, however, a serious discussion about the existence of security communities or the applicability of constructivist theory in general has hardly begun.[109] Even though this is certainly not surprising given the continent's disastrous track record of violent conflicts and humanitarian catastrophes, it also raises the question whether the latter should really disqualify relations among Africa's states as security communities as, for example, Laurie Nathan and Anne Hammerstad have argued.[110] Agreeing with Charles Tilly's warning that such a line of argumentation bears the danger of "smuggling in an implicit comparison with rich western countries" and contending that the presence of wide-spread intrastate conflict should be part of the explanation for the emergence of an African security community rather than a criterion for its disqualification on definitional terms, this section will demonstrate that the concept and its constructivist foundations hold great relevance to the study of inter-state security cooperation in Africa.[111]

As Amitav Acharya has pointed out, when Karl Deutsch and his associates first proposed the idea of security communities, they were seeking to explain the emergence of cooperation among the developed states of the North Atlantic region and not those of the developing world.[112] This has inevitably led to a bias in the theory towards the characteristics of security cooperation in the developed word and the subsequent research has further protracted and consolidated this bias. Especially the frequent evocation of the Kantian notion of democratic peace as philosophy underlying the concept of security communities as well as the emphasis on the necessity of liberal economic interdependence between member states have discouraged research into the possibility of security communities in the developing world.[113] However, even though democratic processes or liberal economics have not necessarily been among the defining characteristics of developing world security dynamics, many other aspects of the security community concept seem well-suited to explain to inter-state cooperation in the developing world. Consequently, a slight redefinition of the concept – away from its liberal roots – as zones of institutionalized security cooperation on the basis of shared values, norms and understandings helps to improve the applicability of the concept to specific areas of the developing world such as Africa.

Such a redefinition has several advantages. First, it allows for common values other than those associated with democratic peace and thus helps to overcome the baseless and unnecessarily restrictive assumption that a liberal democratic and interdependent setting is a necessary precondition for the emergence of security communities. While common values are certainly necessary for community-building, there is no reason why these need to be liberal democratic values. A shared commitment to economic development, regime security and unifying ideologies like Pan-Africanism could compensate for a lack of a high degree of economic interdependence. Moreover, if the former conditions are present, they could pave the way for greater economic and functional cooperation. In other words, interdependence and the development of liberal values could follow, rather than precede, an initial and deliberate attempt at community formation. Such an interpretation also has the advantage of moving the level of analysis away from the masses and towards the elites which typically play a much more pronounced role in the developing world than in the West. It thus allows for an instrumental top-down approach to community-building and helps to de-problematize Africa-specific factors such as the personalistic nature of political leadership, the scarcity of organized interest groups and the cultural cleavage between city and countryside which have previously hampered constructivist analyses of the continent.[114]

Second, the shift in emphasis from war avoidance to institutionalized security cooperation takes account of the particular nature of security problems in Africa. Given the virtual absence of interstate wars in Africa over the past fifty years and the inability of most African militaries to actually wage such a war, the existence of what Ole Waever called "non-war communities" and Arie Kacowicz "zones of peace" is of little relevance to the study of security cooperation in Africa.[115] As the subsequent chapters in this book will show, the continent's states have not come together to face down an external enemy or prevent war between each other as realism or Karl Deutsch's interpretation of security communities would have it respectively, but rather to overcome joint problems arising from the proliferation of violent intra-state conflicts throughout Africa. The proposed redefinition of Adler and Barnett's constructivist typology can account for such *raisons d'être* which differ from the original purposes of a security community.[116] Contrary to the static nature of earlier concepts such as Robert Jervis' "security regimes" or Barry Buzan's "regional security complexes", it also allows for a dynamic and progressive process towards improved overall relations even though, recalling Alexander Wendt's concept of "multiple realizability", it does not necessarily presuppose them.

Third, the constructivist foundation of this redefinition facilitates the combination of the security community concept with the insights of regional integration theory and the multi-dimensionality of Hettne and Söderbaum's new regionalisms. Constructivist ontologies serve well to fuse such distinct theoretical approaches, not only because they provide the main explanatory pillars for both the security community concept and the new regionalism approach,[117] but also because they are able to incorporate insights such as the notion of issue-linkage of more traditional analyses of regional integration like those by Ernst Haas and Philippe Schmitter without falling prey to their materialistic focus.[118] Contrary to rationalist approaches which attempt to explain regional processes and international cooperation purely with the help of strategic interests and relative gains and losses, a constructivist approach to regional cooperation thus allows for "a theoretically rich and promising way of conceptualizing the interaction between material incentives, inter-subjective structures and the identity and interests of the actors".[119]

Given the complexities of the contemporary cooperation efforts in Africa, reaching from regional attempts at joint economic development to the continent-wide establishment of peacekeeping brigades, the theoretical multi-dimensionality of a constructivist approach to inter-African cooperation thus has undeniable advantages over the narrow focus of more conventional theories of international cooperation. Contrary to realism and neo-liberal institutionalism, constructivism can take account of Africa-specific phenomena like the unifying potential of Pan-Africanism, the thirst for continental self-emancipation or the shift from regime security to human security in order to explain the growing interaction of African states. Its emphasis on the importance of ideational forces allows the view that there are many different logics of, and paths to, security cooperation and that the development of security communities in Africa is one of them.

Summary

At first glance neither the concept of security communities nor any of the other concepts of security cooperation currently in the academic discourse such as regional security complexes (Buzan and Weaver),[120] regional security partnerships (Attinà)[121] or zones of peace (Kacowicz)[122] seem applicable to Africa's emerging security architecture.[123] On the contrary, the continuing presence of violent conflict and humanitarian catastrophes in large parts of the continent like the Democratic Republic of the Congo, the Sudan and Somalia has reinforced many people's impression of Africa as a continent characterized by quasi-Hobbesian anarchy rather than elaborate forms of security cooperation. However, the last few years have in fact seen Africa's states making great strides at developing an institutionalized framework for such cooperation.

Rationalist-systemic theories have difficulties to account for this growing interaction between African states. Because of their focus on materialist aspects of cooperation they fail to capture essential African realities such as the importance of Pan-African ideology and the emergence of shared norms. As a result, they misinterpret many of the motivations inducing African states to look into each others' direction and begin to cooperate on increasingly complex matters.

Constructivism on the other hand provides an attractive intellectual point of reference and a viable alternative to the traditional theories because it focuses on the explanatory power of inter-subjective factors such as ideas, beliefs and norms and social processes such as identity and interest formation rather than deep structure to explain international relations. Naturally, this does not mean that the traditional theories and their variants are unimportant or of no use in discussing contemporary African security cooperation. On the contrary, many of their characteristics are clearly visible in what will be described below. For this reason, constructivism should be seen as a complementary theory which does not attempt to refute material and rationalist explanations but rather seeks to expand them. Each of the theories described above has a different understanding of how cooperation works in international affairs and, as Stephen Walt rightly said, "each of these competing perspectives captures important aspects of world politics. Our understanding would be impoverished were our thinking confined to only one of them".[124]

Notes

[1]   For recent noteworthy examples see Mary Farrell, "A Triumph of Realism over Idealism? Cooperation between the European Union and Africa," *Journal of European Integration* 27, no. 3 (2005): 263-283, Anatol Lieven and John Hulsman, *Ethical Realism: A Vision for America's Role in the World* (London: Pantheon Books, 2006), Richard Little, *The Balance of Power in International Relations: Metaphors, Myths and Models* (Cambridge: Cambridge University Press, 2007), Benjamin Miller, *States, Nations and the Great Powers: The Sources of Regional War and Peace* (Cambridge: Cambridge University Press, 2007), Hussein Solomon, *Challenges to Global Security: Geopolitics and Power in an Age of Transition* (London: I.B. Tauris, 2007).

[2]   Anarchy is one of the most contested concepts in international relations theory. See Robert Axelrod and Robert O. Keohane, "Achieving Cooperation under Anarchy: Strategies and Institutions," *World Politics* 38, no. 1 (1985), Helen Milner, "The Assumption of Anarchy in International Relations Theory: A Critique," in *Neorealism and Neoliberalism: The Contemporary Debate*, ed. David Baldwin (New York: Columbia University Press, 1993),

Kenneth Oye, "Explaining Cooperation under Anarchy: Hypotheses and Strategies," *World Politics* 38, no. 1 (1985).

[3] Joseph Grieco, "Understanding the Problem of International Cooperation: The Limits of Neoliberal Institutionalism and the Future of Realist Theory," in *Neorealism and Neoliberalism: The Contemporary Debate*, ed. David Baldwin (New York: Columbia, 1993), 302.

[4] James Goldgeier and Michael McFaul, "A Tale of Two Worlds: Core and Periphery in the Post-Cold War Era," *International Organization* 46, no. 2 (1992): 478.

[5] Barry Buzan and Ole Waever, *Regions and Powers - the Structure of International Security* (Cambridge: Cambridge University Press, 2003).

[6] John Ruggie, *Constructing the World Polity: Essays on International Institutionalization* (New York: Routledge, 1998), 9-10.

[7] See Amitav Acharya, "Collective Identity and Conflict Management in Southeast Asia," in *Security Communities*, ed. Emanuel Adler and Michael Barnett (Cambridge: Cambridge University Press, 1998).

[8] Alexander Wendt, *Social Theory of International Politics* (Cambridge: Cambridge University Press, 1999), 24.

[9] Non-material ideological and psychological factors are not so much rejected by institutionalists as subordinated to the workings of the exterior relations of actor behavior. Like realist theory, institutionalists cross this boundary when it suits their purposes, but the thrust of this school of thought is to stay within the limits of an "objective" perspective in theory-building. Ideas and ideology orient actors in their choices and strategies, but their independent impact on state policies is still viewed as subordinate to the material interests of actors – economic and security – and to changing power relationships. See Judith Goldstein and Robert Keohane, eds., *Ideas and Foreign Policy: Beliefs, Institutions and Political Change* (Ithaca: Cornell University Press, 1993), Robert Keohane, "International Institutions: Two Approaches," *International Studies Quarterly* 32 (1988).

[10] See Kevin Dunn and Timothy Shaw, eds., *Africa's Challenge to International Relations Theory* (Basingstoke: Palgrave, 2001).

[11] See, for example, the edited volume Stephanie Neuman, ed., *International Relations Theory and the Third World* (New York: St. Martin's Press, 1998).

[12] See Mohammed Ayoob, "Inequality and Theorizing in International Relations: The Case for Subaltern Realism," *International Studies Review* 4, no. 3 (2002): 27-48, Mohammed Ayoob, "Subaltern Realism: International Relations Theory Meets the Third World," in *International Relations Theory and the Third World*, ed. Stephanie Neuman (New York: St. Martin's Press, 1998). For a critique of subaltern realism see Michael Barnett, "Radical Chic? Subaltern Realism: A Rejoinder," *International Studies Review* 4, no. 3 (2002): 49-62.

[13] For an interesting discussion see Amitav Acharya and Barry Buzan, "Why Is There No Non-Western International Relations Theory? An Introduction," *International Relations of the Asia-Pacific* 7, no. 3 (2007).

[14] Christopher Clapham, *Africa and the International System: The Politics of State Survival* (Cambridge: Cambridge University Press, 1996), 3-4. The African state has been studied extensively over the last decades. Notable

recent contributions to the literature are Catherine Boon, *Political Topographies of the African State: Territorial Authority and Institutional Choice* (Cambridge: Cambridge University Press, 2003), Ricardo Laremont, ed., *Borders, Nationalism and the African State* (Boulder: Lynne Rienner, 2005), Ahmed Samatar, *The African State: Reconsiderations* (London: Delay, 2002).

[15]   See Barry Buzan, *People, States and Fear*, 2nd ed. (Boulder: Lynne Rienner, 1991).

[16]   For a highly interesting discussion of the academic debate on the African state see Martin Doornbos, "The African State in Academic Debate: Retrospect and Prospect," *Journal of Modern African Studies* 28, no. 2 (1990): 179-198.

[17]   Kevin Dunn, "Madlib #32: The (Blank) African State: Rethinking the Sovereign State in International Relations Theory," in *Africa's Challenge to International Relation's Theory*, ed. Kevin Dunn and Timothy Shaw (Basingstoke: Palgrave, 2001), 46-47.

[18]   Timothy Mitchell, "The Limits of the State: Beyond Statist Approaches and Their Critics," *American Political Science Review* 85, no. 1 (1991).

[19]   Mohammed Ayoob, "State-Making, State-Breaking and State Failure: Explaining the Roots of Third World Insecurity," in *Between Development and Destruction: An Enquiry into the Causes of Conflict in Post-Colonial States*, ed. Luc van de Goor (New York: St. Martin's Press, 1996).

[20]   Clapham, *Africa and the International System: The Politics of State Survival*, 5.

[21]   Assis Malaquias, "Reformulating International Relations Theory: African Insights and Challenges," in *Africa's Challenge to International Relations Theory*, ed. Kevin Dunn and Timothy Shaw (Basingstoke: Palgrave, 2001), 12.

[22]   Walter Lippmann, *US Foreign Policy: Shield of the Republic* (Boston: Little&Brown, 1943), 51.

[23]   Brian Job, "The Insecurity Dilemma," in *The Insecurity Dilemma: National Security of Third World States*, ed. Brian Job (Boulder: Lynne Rienner, 1992), 17-18. See Richard Jackson, "Violent Internal Conflict and the African State: Towards a Framework of Analysis," *Journal of Contemporary African Studies* 20, no. 1 (2002).

[24]   For an elaborate treatment of the phenomenon of personal power policies see Alec Russell, *Big Men, Little People: The Leaders Who Defined Africa* (New York: New York University Press, 1999).

[25]   Douglas Lemke, *Regions of War and Peace* (Cambridge: Cambridge University Press, 2002), 161-194.

[26]   Wil Hout, "Theories of International Relations and the New Regionalism," in *Regionalism across the North-South Divide: State Strategies and Globalization*, ed. Jean Grugel and Wil Hout (London: Routledge, 1999), 16.

[27]   See Andrew Grant and Fredrik Söderbaum, eds., *The New Regionalism in Africa* (Aldershot: Ashgate, 2003), Björn Hettne and Fredrik Söderbaum, "The New Regionalism," *Politeia (Special Issue)* 17, no. 3 (1998).

[28]   For an excellent introduction to the concept of Pan-Africanism and its history see P. Olisanwuche Esedebe, *Pan-Africanism : The Idea and Movement, 1776-1991*, 2nd ed. (Washington, D.C.: Howard University, 1994).

[29]   Samuel Adekoya Oshisanya, *The Ultimate End of Pan-Africanism* (Lagos: S.A. Oshisanya, 1983).

[30]   See Christopher Landsberg, "The Fifth Wave of Pan-Africanism," in *West Africa's Security Challenges: Building Peace in a Troubled Region*, ed. Adekeye Adebajo and Ismail Rashid (Boulder: Lynne Rienner, 2004).

[31]   Mammo Muchie, "Pan-Africanism: An Idea Whose Time Has Come," *Politikon: South African Journal of Political Studies* 27, no. 2 (2000).

[32]   Robert Jackson and Carl Rosberg, "Why Africa's Weak States Persist: The Empirical and the Juridical in Statehood," *World Politics* 35, no. 1 (1982): 17.

[33]   Chapter ten will deal with this topic in more detail. For an excellent discussion of the emerging security culture see Paul Williams, "From Non-Intervention to Non-Indifference: The Origins and Development of the African Union's Security Culture," *African Affairs* 106, no. 423 (2007): 253-279.

[34]   Paul Williams bases his definition on the work of Alastair Johnston, *Cultural Realism: Strategic Culture and Grand Strategy in Chinese History* (Princeton: Princeton University Press, 1995).

[35]   Socialization is defined as the induction of new members into the ways of behavior that are preferred in a society. See Barnes, Carter and Skidmore cited in Thomas Risse, Stephen Ropp, and Kathryn Sikkink, eds., *The Power of Human Rights: International Norms and Domestic Change* (Cambridge: Cambridge University Press, 1999), 11.

[36]   Clapham, *Africa and the International System: The Politics of State Survival*, 5.

[37]   See, for example, John Clark's argument that the notion of regime security derived from realism's central focus on power and interest can serve as theoretical master key to Africa's international relations. John Clark, "Realism, Neo-Realism and Africa's International Relations in the Post-Cold War Era," in *Africa's Challenge to International Relations Theory*, ed. Kevin Dunn and Timothy Shaw (Basingstoke: Palgrave, 2001), 85-102.

[38]   For an interesting discussion on how the nature of threats and inter-state relations determines the kind of security arrangement states enter into, see Celeste Wallander and Robert Keohane, "Risk, Threat and Security Institutions," in *Imperfect Unions: Security Institutions over Time and Space*, ed. Helga Haftendorn, Robert Keohane, and Celeste Wallander (Oxford: Oxford University Press, 1999), 21-47.

[39]   This call has certainly grown louder over the last couple of years. See, for example, the excellent collection of papers in Branwen Jones, ed., *Decolonizing International Relations* (London: Rowman&Littlefield 2006). Particularly noteworthy are Sandra Halperin, "International Relations Theory and the Hegemony of Western Conceptions of Modernity," in *Decolonizing International Relations*, ed. Branwen Jones (London: Rowman&Littlefield, 2006), 43-64, Julian Saurin, "International Relations as the Imperial Illusion; or, the Need to Decolonize IR " in *Decolonizing International Relations*, ed. Branwen Jones (London: Rowman&Littlefield, 2006), 23-42.

40   Maja Zehfuss, *Constructivism in International Relations: The Politics of Reality* (Cambridge: Cambridge University Press, 2002), 2.

41   Nicholas Onuf, *World of Our Making: Rules and Rule in Social Theory and International Relations* (Columbia: University of South Carolina Press, 1989).

42   Even self-declared constructivists seem to have difficulties defining their approach. Emmanuel Adler, for example, situates constructivism between rationalism and critical theory/post-structuralism, while Richard Price and Christian Reus-Smit argue that constructivism is squarely within critical theory. Methodologically, similar problems prevail. Audie Klotz, Jeffrey Checkel and Peter Katzenstein argue that constructivism is compatible with standard research methods while others, including Brian Frederking, argue that constructivism is more consistent with interpretive methods.

43   See Emanuel Adler, "Seizing the Middle Ground: Constructivism in International Relations," *European Journal of International Relations* 3, no. 3 (1997), Ted Hopf, "The Promise of Constructivism in International Relations Theory," *International Security* 23, no. 1 (1998), Richard Price and Christian Reus-Smit, "Dangerous Liaisons? Critical International Theory and Constructivism," *European Journal of International Relations* 4, no. 3 (1998).

44   See Kenneth Waltz, *Theory of International Politics* (New York: Random House, 1979).

45   Alexander Wendt, "Constructing International Politics," *International Security* 20, no. 1 (1995): 71.

46   Christian Reus-Smit, "Constructivism," in *Theories of International Relations*, ed. Scott Burchill (Basingstoke: Palgrave, 2001), 217.

47   See Alexander Wendt, "Anarchy Is What States Make of It: The Social Construction of Power Politics," *International Organization* 46, no. 2 (1992).

48   Reus-Smit, "Constructivism," 219.

49   See Jeffrey Checkel, "The Constructivist Turn in International Relations Theory," *World Politics* 50, no. 2 (1998), Dale Copeland, "The Constructivist Challenge to Structural Realism," in *Constructivism and International Relations*, ed. Stefano Guzzini and Anne Leander (London: Routledge, 2006), Hopf, "The Promise of Constructivism in International Relations Theory.", John Ruggie, "What Makes the World Hang Together? Neo-Utilitarianism and the Social Constructivist Challenge," *International Organization* 52 (1998): 855-885.

50   Light constructivism places special emphasis on domestic politics to explain international relations. See Friedrich Kratochwil, "Constructivism as an Approach to Interdisciplinary Study," in *Constructing International Relations: The Next Generation*, ed. Karin Fierke and Knud Jorgensen (London: M.E. Sharpe, 2001). Heavy constructivism is epistemological to the point that it rejects the notion that knowledge can be divorced from the observer focusing on the psychological make-up of actors to explain international relations. See Vendulka Kubalkova, ed., *Foreign Policy in a Constructed World* (London: M.E. Sharpe, 2001).

51   See Imre Lakatos, "Falsification and the Methodology of Scientific Research Programmes," in *Criticism and the Growth of Knowledge*, ed. Imre Lakatos and Alan Musgrave (Cambridge: Cambridge University Press, 1970),

91-195, Imre Lakatos, *The Methodology of Scientific Research Programmes: Philosophical Papers* (Cambridge: Cambridge University Press, 1978).

[52] See, for example, Stefano Guzzini and Anna Leander, eds., *Constructivism and International Relations: Alexander Wendt and His Critics* (London: Routledge, 2006). For further critiques see Steve Smith, "Wendt's World," *Review of International Studies* 26 (2000): 151-163.

[53] See, for example, Friedrich Kratochwil, "Constructing a New Orthodoxy? Wendt's Social Theory of International Politics and the Constructivist Challenge," *Millennium: Journal of International Studies* 29, no. 1 (2000): 73-101.

[54] Copeland, "The Constructivist Challenge to Structural Realism," 1.

[55] Herbert Blumer, *Symbolic Interactionism: Perspective and Method* (Englewood Cliffs: Prentice Hall, 1969), Anthony Giddens, *The Constitution of Society: Outline of the Theory of Structuration* (Cambridge: Polity Press, 1984).

[56] Zehfuss, *Constructivism in International Relations: The Politics of Reality*, 14.

[57] See, for example, Robert Gilpin who famously argued that "it is doubtful whether or not twentieth-century students of international relations know anything that Thucydides and his fifth-century BC compatriots did not know about the behavior of states". Robert Gilpin, *War and Change in World Politics* (Cambridge: Cambridge University Press, 1982), 227-228.

[58] Wendt, *Social Theory of International Politics*, 322-323.

[59] Ken Booth, *Theory of World Security* (Cambridge: Cambridge University Press, 2007), 31-36.

[60] Copeland, "The Constructivist Challenge to Structural Realism," 2.

[61] Here Wendt has adapted the heuristic division of international politics from Martin Wight and the English School. See Martin Wight, *International Theory: The Three Traditions* (London: Holmes&Meier Publishers, 1992).

[62] See Roy D'Andrade, *The Development of Cognitive Anthropology* (Cambridge: Cambridge University Press, 1995), 227-228, Ian Hurd, "Legitimacy and Authority in International Politics," *International Organization* 53 (1999): 379-408, Melford Spiro, *Culture and Human Nature* (Chicago: Chicago University Press, 1987), 163-164.

[63] On multiple realizability see Benjamin Most and Harvey Starr, "International Relations Theory, Foreign Policy, Substitutability And "Nice" Laws," *World Politics* 36, no. 3 (1984): 383-406.

[64] Copeland, "The Constructivist Challenge to Structural Realism," 7.

[65] See Peter Katzenstein, ed., The Culture of National Security: Norms and Identity in World Politics (New York: Columbia University Press, 1996), Ruggie, Constructing the World Polity: Essays on International Institutionalization, Wendt, "Anarchy Is What States Make of It: The Social Construction of Power Politics.", Alexander Wendt, "Collective Identity Formation and the International State," American Political Science Review 88 (1994).

[66] John Ruggie usefully roots constructivist thinking in the contributions of these early founders of sociology. See Ruggie, *Constructing the World Polity: Essays on International Institutionalization*.

[67] Max Weber, *Gesammelte Aufsätze Zur Wissenschaftslehre*, ed. Johannes Winkelmann, 3rd ed. (Tübingen: J.C.B. Mohr, 1956), 180.

[68]   See Emile Durkheim, *The Division of Labour in Society* (New York: Free Press, 1984), Emile Durkheim, *Ethics and the Sociology of Morals* (Buffalo: Prometheus Books, 1993).

[69]   Giddens, *The Constitution of Society: Outline of the Theory of Structuration*.

[70]   Nina Tannenwald and William Wohlforth, "The Role of Ideas and the End of the Cold War," *Journal of Cold War Studies* 7, no. 2 (2005): 15.

[71]   Goldstein and Keohane, eds., *Ideas and Foreign Policy: Beliefs, Institutions and Political Change*, 4.

[72]   Katzenstein, ed., *The Culture of National Security: Norms and Identity in World Politics*, 5, Friedrich Kratochwil, *Rules, Norms and Decisions: On the Conditions of Practical and Legal Reasoning in International Relations and Domestic Affairs* (Cambridge: Cambridge University Press, 1989), 59.

[73]   There is a large body of literature on this topic. Noteworthy examples are V Shannon, "Norms Are What States Make of Them: The Political Psychology of Norm Violation," *International Studies Quarterly* 44, no. 2 (2000): 355-374, A Wiener, "Contested Compliance: Interventions on the Normative Structure of World Politics," *European Journal of International Relations* 10, no. 2 (2004): 189-234.

[74]   For a highly interesting discussion about norms, identity and the war on terror see Jodie Anstee, "Constructivism, Norms and Identity: A Challenged Relationship?," in *57th Annual Meeting of the Political Studies Association* (University of Bath: 2007).

[75]   Risse, Ropp, and Sikkink, eds., *The Power of Human Rights: International Norms and Domestic Change*.

[76]   Wendt, "Anarchy Is What States Make of It: The Social Construction of Power Politics," 398.

[77]   Kathryn Sikkink, "US Compliance with International Human Rights Law," in *Annual Meeting of the International Studies Association* (Hawaii: 2005), 10.

[78]   See Wendt, "Collective Identity Formation and the International State," 384.

[79]   Emanuel Adler, *Communitarian International Relations: The Epistemic Foundations of International Relations* (New York: Routledge, 2005), 3-28.

[80]   Bruce Cronin, *Community under Anarchy: Transnational Identity and the Evolution of Cooperation* (New York: Columbia University Press, 1999), 34-37.

[81]   Emanuel Adler and Michael Barnett, "Security Communities in Theoretical Perspective," in *Security Communities*, ed. Emanuel Adler and Michael Barnett (Cambridge: Cambridge University Press, 1998), 3.

[82]   Cronin, *Community under Anarchy: Transnational Identity and the Evolution of Cooperation*, 37.

[83]   Hedley Bull, *The Anarchical Society: A Study of Order in World Politics* (London: Macmillan, 1977), 13.

[84]   Richard van Wagenen, *Research in the International Organisation Field: Some Notes on a Possible Focus* (Princeton: Center for Research on World Political Institutions, 1952).

[85] Karl W. Deutsch, *Political Community and the North Atlantic Area - International Organization in the Light of Historical Experience* (Princeton: Princeton University Press, 1957).

[86] Emanuel Adler and Michael Barnett, *Security Communities* (Cambridge: Cambridge University Press, 1998), 29. See also Emanuel Adler and Michael Barnett, "Governing Anarchy: A Research Agenda for the Study of Security Communities," *Ethics and International Affairs* 10 (1996). Even though there were a number of earlier studies on security communities, most of which will be cited in this paper, the work by Adler and Barnett is the most systematic.

[87] Deutsch, *Political Community and the North Atlantic Area - International Organization in the Light of Historical Experience*, 3.

[88] Ibid., 6-7.

[89] Ibid., 66.

[90] Stephen Walt, *The Origins of Alliances* (Ithaca: Cornell University Press, 1987).

[91] "Negative peace" is defined as a situation in which there is no war, but there are preparations and contingency plans for war. "Positive peace", on the other hand, is defined as a situation in which states do not prepare for war nor do they expect other states in their region or zone to do so. This does not necessarily mean that all disputes have been resolved. Issues and disagreements may persist, but no party conceives of force to sort them out. See Andrea Oelsner, "(De-)Securitisation Theory and Regional Peace: Some Theoretical Reflections and a Case Study on the Way to Stable Peace," *EUI Working Paper*, no. 27 (2005): 6-7.

[92] Adler and Barnett, "Security Communities in Theoretical Perspective," 5. For additional critiques of Deutsch's original formulation see also A Lijphart, "Karl W. Deutsch and the New Paradigm in International Relations," in *From Development to Global Community: Essays in Honour of Karl W. Deutsch*, ed. R Merritt and B Russett (London: George Allen and Unwin, 1981).

[93] See Emanuel Adler and Michael Barnett, "A Framework for the Study of Security Communities," in *Security Communities*, ed. Emanuel Adler and Michael Barnett (Cambridge: Cambridge University Press, 1998), 30.

[94] Ibid., 50.

[95] Ibid., 53.

[96] Although a security community does not require military integration, Adler and Barnett argue that "it is quite likely that shared identities will produce a desire for the pooling of military resources". Ibid., 55-57.

[97] Ibid., 43.

[98] See, for example, Richard van Wagenen, "The Concept of Community and the Future of the United Nations," *International Organization* 19, no. 3 (1965): 813.

[99] See Emanuel Adler, "Seeds of Peaceful Change: The OSCE's Security Community-Building Model," in *Security Communities*, ed. Emanuel Adler and Michael Barnett (Cambridge: Cambridge University Press, 1998), Michael Barnett and Emanuel Adler, "Studying Security Communities in Theory, Comparison and History," in *Security Communities*, ed. Emanuel Adler and Michael Barnett (Cambridge: Cambridge University Press, 1998), 418-421, Bruce Russett, "A Neo-Kantian Perspective: Democracy, Interdependence and

International Organisations in Building Security Communities," in *Security Communities*, ed. Emanuel Adler and Michael Barnett (Cambridge: Cambridge University Press, 1998), 377. For a more detailed discussion of the effect of organisations on trust see R Burt and M Knez, "Kinds of Third-Party Effects on Trust," *Rationality and Society* 7, no. 3 (1995): 255-292, Bruce Russett, J Oneal, and D Davis, "The Third Leg of the Kantian Tripod for Peace: Organisations and Militarised Disputes 1950-1985," *International Organization* 52, no. 3 (1998).

[100]   Alex Bellamy, *Security Communities and Their Neighbours: Regional Fortresses or Global Integrators* (New York: Palgrave Macmillan, 2004).

[101]   Ibid., 187.

[102]   See Laurie Nathan, "Domestic Instability and Security Communities," *European Journal of International Relations* 12, no. 2 (2006): 275-299, Laurie Nathan, "Security Communities and the Problem of Domestic Instability," *Crisis States Research Centre Working Paper Series*, no. 55 (2004). For a similar argument with specific reference to Southern Africa see Anne Hammerstad, "Domestic Threats, Regional Solutions? The Challenge of Security Integration in Southern Africa," *Review of International Studies* 31, no. 1 (2005): 69-87.

[103]   According to Nathan, domestic violence precludes the existence of security communities because it renders people and states insecure; it creates the risk of cross-border destabilization; it generates uncertainty and tension among states, inhibiting trust and a sense of collective identity.

[104]   Raimo Väyrynen, "Stable Peace through Security Communities? Steps Towards Theory-Building," in *Stable Peace among Nations*, ed. Arie Kacowicz, Ole Elgstrom, and Magnus Jerneck (Lanham: Rowman and Littlefield, 2000), 163.

[105]   See Lakatos, "Falsification and the Methodology of Scientific Research Programmes," 91-195, Lakatos, *The Methodology of Scientific Research Programmes: Philosophical Papers*.

[106]   There are a number of notable exceptions such as, for example, the works on the Association of South East Asian Nations (ASEAN) by Amitav Acharya. However, given the lack of similar studies on Africa, most of the Russian periphery, Central Asia or Central America it seems fair to say that the developing world has not received its share of academic attention and scrutiny.

[107]   See Adler, "Seeds of Peaceful Change: The OSCE's Security Community-Building Model.", Vincent Pouliot, "The Alive and Well Transatlantic Security Community: A Theoretical Reply to Michael Cox," *European Journal of International Relations* 12, no. 1 (2006), Andrej Tusicisny, "Globalization, Value Change and Security Community Building in Europe," in *Third European Consortium for Political Research* (Budapest: 2005), Michael Williams and Iver Neumann, "From Alliance to Security Community: NATO, Russia and the Power of Identity," *Millennium: Journal of International Studies* 29, no. 2 (2000).

[108]   See, for example, Amitav Acharya, "The Association of Southeast Asian Nations: Security Community or Defense Community?," *Pacific Affairs* 64, no. 2 (1991), Amitav Acharya, *Constructing a Security Community in Southeast Asia: ASEAN and the Problem of Regional Order* (London: Routledge, 2001), Alan Collins, "Forming a Security Community: Lessons from

ASEAN," *International Relations of the Asia-Pacific* 7, no. 2 (2007), John Garofano, "Power, Institutions, and the ASEAN Regional Forum: A Security Community for Asia?," *Asian Survey* 42, no. 3 (2002).

[109] Notable exceptions include Tumo Lekhooa, "Security Community Building? An Assessment of Southern African Regional Integration in the Post-Apartheid Era," (2005), Theo Neethling, "Pursuing a Functional Security Community in Southern Africa: Is It Possible after All?," *Strategic Review for Southern Africa* 25, no. 1 (2003), Naison Ngoma, *Prospects for a Security Community in Southern Africa: An Analysis of Regional Security in the Southern African Development Community* (Pretoria: Institute for Security Studies, 2005), Naison Ngoma, "SADC's Mutual Defense Pact: A Final Move to a Security Community?," *The Round Table* 93, no. 375 (2004), Naison Ngoma, "SADC: Towards a Security Community?," *African Security Review* 12, no. 3 (2003), M. Schoeman, "Imagining a Community: The African Union as an Emerging Security Community," *Strategic Review for Southern Africa* 24, no. 1 (2002).

[110] See Hammerstad, "Domestic Threats, Regional Solutions? The Challenge of Security Integration in Southern Africa.", Nathan, "Security Communities and the Problem of Domestic Instability."

[111] Charles Tilly, "International Communities, Secure or Otherwise," in *Security Communities*, ed. Emanuel Adler and Michael Barnett (Cambridge: Cambridge University Press, 1998), 410. See A Bjuner, "Security and the Next Century: Towards a Wider Concept of Prevention," in *Preventing Violent Conflicts: Past Record and Future Challenges*, ed. P Wallensteen (Uppsala: Department of Peace and Conflict Research, 1998), 285.

[112] Acharya, "Collective Identity and Conflict Management in Southeast Asia," 198.

[113] For the idea of "democratic security communities" see, for example, John Vasquez, ed., *Classics of International Relations*, 3rd ed. (Upper Saddle River: Prentice Hall, 1966), 288-289. In the 1970s, neo-functionalists like Ernst Haas pointed out that the absence of domestic pluralism was a major reason why European Community-style regional integration did not flourish in the developing world. A high dose of authoritarian politics and relatively low levels of intra-regional economic interdependence render the developing world inhospitable for the emergence of regional security communities. Ernst Haas, "The Study of Regional Integration: Reflections on the Joy and Anguish of Pretheorising," in *Regional Politics and World Order*, ed. Richard Falk and Saul Mendlovitz (San Francisco: W.H. Freeman and Company, 1973).

[114] See, for example, Ken Booth and Peter Vale, "Security in Southern Africa: After Apartheid, Beyond Realism," *International Affairs (Royal Institute of International Affairs 1944-)* 71, no. 2 (1995).

[115] Arie Kacowicz, *Zones of Peace in the Third World: South America and West Africa in Comparative Perspective* (Albany: State University of New York Press, 1998), Ole Waever, "Insecurity, Security and Asecurity in the West European Non-War Community," in *Security Communities*, ed. Emanuel Adler and Michael Barnett (Cambridge: Cambridge University Press, 1998).

[116] The definitional difference corresponds to Lynn Miller's distinction between the peace and security role of regional organizations. The peace role refers to the potential of an organization for controlling the forceful settlement

of conflicts among its own members. The security role, which is integral to the new definition, denotes the potential of the organization to present a common solution to a specific security problem, be it internal or external to the community and/or its constitutive members. See Lynn Miller, "The Prospects for Order through Regional Security," in *Regional Politics and World Order*, ed. Richard Falk and Saul Mendlovitz (San Francisco: W.H. Freeman and Company, 1973), 51.

[117] Björn Hettne and Fredrik Söderbaum, "Theorizing the Rise of Regioness," in *New Regionalisms in the Global Political Economy*, ed. S Breslin, et al. (London: Routledge, 2002), 45.

[118] Ernst Haas, "Why Collaborate? Issue-Linkage and International Regimes," *World Politics* 32, no. 3 (1980), Philippe Schmitter, "A Revised Theory of Regional Integration," *International Organization* 24, no. 4 (1970).

[119] Andrew Hurrell, "Regionalism in Theoretical Perspective," in *Regionalism in World Politics: Regional Organizations and International Order*, ed. L Fawcett and A Hurrell (Oxford: Oxford University Press, 1995).

[120] Buzan and Waever, *Regions and Powers - the Structure of International Security*.

[121] Fulvio Attina, "The European Security Partnership, NATO and the European Union," *Jean Monnet Working Paper*, no. 29 (2001).

[122] Arie Kacowicz, "Explaining Zones of Peace: Democracies as Satisfied Powers?," *Journal of Peace Research* 32, no. 3 (1995), Kacowicz, *Zones of Peace in the Third World: South America and West Africa in Comparative Perspective*.

[123] Amitav Acharya, "Regional Approaches to Security in the Third World: Lessons and Prospects " in *The South at the End of the Twentieth Century*, ed. L Swatuk and T Shaw (London: St. Martin's Press, 1994), 79-94.

[124] Stephen Walt, "International Relations: One World, Many Theories," *Foreign Policy* 110 (1998): 44. For an extended discussion of the regrettable prevalence of "false dichotomies" in international relations theory, see Michael Brecher, "International Studies in the Twentieth Century and Beyond: Flawed Dichotomies, Synthesis, Cumulation," *International Studies Quarterly* 43, no. 2 (1999).

3
The Early Quest for Continental Security Cooperation

Even though the type of continental security cooperation that is the main subject of this book is a relatively recent phenomenon (see chapter five), its conceptual roots reach back into the colonial period. Initially inspired by the struggle against imperial domination and a growing thirst for liberation, the quest for some sort of alliance between the continent's peoples was based as much on Pan-African ideology as on practical military concerns. Once liberation was achieved, the perceived need to defend the newly won sovereignty against neo-imperialist attempts to re-colonize the continent became the driving rationale for seeking military cooperation. It was only after the end of the Cold War that the proliferation of violent intra-state conflicts and the simultaneous disengagement of the international community combined with a renewed wave of Pan-Africanist idealism to shift the focus from liberation and continental defense to conflict prevention, management and resolution as the primary purpose of inter-African security cooperation. The following chapters will track the quest for continental security cooperation through the last century, covering the feeble attempts of Africa's freedom fighters to join forces, the repeated failures to establish an African High Command in the early years of decolonization, the subsequent inability of the OAU Defense Commission to agree on a continental defense structure, the devolution of security cooperation to the regional level in the late 1980s and, lastly, the revival of continental security cooperation in the late 1990s.

Pan-Africanism and the Evolution of an Idea

Originally rooted in opposition to the Atlantic slave trade and its consequences, Pan-Africanism is both a system of ideological beliefs and an organizational framework.[1] As a socio-political worldview, Pan-Africanism sought (and still seeks) to unify and uplift both native Africans and those of the African Diaspora as part of a global African community. As an organizational framework and movement, Pan-

Africanism has evolved substantially over the years from its abolitionist roots and political acquiescence to being a spearhead of nationalist agitation, which placed primary value on immediate national independence for the African territories and, ultimately, total unification thereof.[2]

Originating outside the African continent, the Pan-African movement initially merely meant to mitigate and reverse the impact of European colonialism on peoples of African descent, without questioning the colonial system in itself. Heavily influenced and promoted by Martin Delany (who championed voluntary re-emigration to Africa with the aim of building up a modern nation on African soil),[3] Henry Sylvester Williams (who founded the Pan-African Association and organized the first Pan-African Conference in 1900),[4] Edward Wilmot Blyden (who sought to prove that Africa and Africans have a worthy history and culture),[5] Marcus Garvey (who founded the powerful United Negro Improvement Association to produce a sense of collective identity among Africans),[6] George Padmore (who built up the Pan-African Federation and later wrote the book *Pan-Africanism or Communism?*),[7] and William Edward Burghardt (W.E.B) Du Bois (who organized and presided over five Pan-African congresses),[8] the movement gained momentum between 1900 and 1945. The sixth Pan-African Conference held in Manchester in October 1945 finally adopted Pan-Africanism as a rallying cry for Africa's independence from colonial rule and fostered African leadership of the movement, most notably in the persons of Kwame Nkrumah (who was to become the first President of Ghana) and Jomo Kenyatta (who was to become Kenya's first president).

The conference marked a watershed in many ways. Not only was the connection between Pan-Africanism and African nationalism discussed fully for the first time, but the participants also stressed the necessity for well-organized, firmly-knit movements as a primary condition for the success of the national liberation struggle in Africa.[9] By the end of the congress, it had become clear that, as Adekunle Ajala phrased it, "Pan-Africanism was growing from a protest movement by people of African descent in the West Indies and the United States into an instrument of African nationalist movements fighting colonial rule".[10]

As such, the concept of Pan-Africanism essentially evolved around five distinctive sets of ideas. According to Charles Andrain, the first set comprised those beliefs emanating from the French revolution and its credo *Liberté, Egalité, Fraternité* with an emphasis on the rights of man, especially the right of Africans to have the same opportunities for social and political development as the white race.[11] This set was reinforced by the experiences of the Second World War where Africans fought alongside whites for the principles of democracy and national sovereignty.[12] A second set was formed by the ideas of Garvey who sought to "advance the redemption of Africa as the home for the Negro race".[13] The influence of Ghandi on the Pan-African movement constituted a third set of beliefs (it became particularly evident in Nkrumah's peaceful resistance to colonial rule).[14] A fourth set identified by Andrain was Wilsonian idealism and especially its emphasis of right over might. The fifth set consisted of some of the ideas arising from Marxism and the Russian Revolution, most notably concepts such as the organization of the masses and the idea of being a vanguard movement.

Following the Manchester Conference, the Pan-African movement seemed to dissolve into its diverse national constituent parts as Kenyatta returned to Kenya (1946) and Nkrumah went back to the Gold Coast (1947), each to work towards the liberation of his country. The Pan-African idea, however, endured without further congresses and conferences. Even though not all independence movements of the continent necessarily subscribed to the underlying idea of African oneness, the ideologically charged rhetoric of Pan-Africanism served them well by carrying the anti-colonial message and finally creating a feeling of self-assertion. In addition, the concept held the promise of mutual support and assistance in the face of obvious vulnerability and an omnipresent fear of neo-colonial suppression.

As the struggle for liberation from colonial rule intensified, so did the calls for uniting Africa's military resources in order to achieve its independence. The idea for a Pan-African military force seems to have grown out of communist revolutionary propaganda for as early as 1922 an article in the *Communist Review* demanded that "no opportunity should be lost for propagandizing the native soldiers in the colonial armies and for organizing secretly a great Pan-African army in the same way as the Sinn Fein built up the Irish Army under the very nose of England".[15] The topic was discussed at Pan-African conferences across the world, but did not receive serious political support until Nkrumah, who had become Africa's leading exponent of continental independence and unity, voiced the idea of an African High Command (AHC) and the establishment of an African legion during the first All-African Peoples Conference in 1958.[16] According to him, the objectives of such a military construct were threefold, namely, (1) to defend the increasing number of independent African states from imperialist aggression, (2) to offer African states a feasible alternative to disadvantageous military pacts with the Cold War powers and (3) to spearhead the liberation of areas under colonial and white supremacist control.

Liberation and the Quest for an African High Command

Despite its popular appeal, Nkrumah's radical proposal encountered passionate opposition from the growing number of nationalists among Africa's leading politicians such as President Tubman of Liberia who saw the centralization of military power as a first (and irreversible) step towards the political unification of the continent. While this was exactly what fervent Pan-Africanists such as Nkrumah or Guinea's Sékou Touré had hoped, preached and worked for, many other African leaders believed in a more gradual approach to continental unity that would not infringe upon the newly-won sovereignty of their states. This irreconcilable difference in perspectives eventually combined with divergent views on ongoing developments like the international intervention in the Congo crisis and the war in Algeria to polarize Africa's states into opposing groups.

The so-called Casablanca group consisted of countries who proposed the immediate creation of a political union for Africa in which economic, cultural and military activities would be coordinated centrally in order to advance much-needed development and make the African voice in world politics both more effective and respected. The states in the rival Brazzaville group (later to be called Monrovia group) considered themselves more conservative and gradualist.[17] Instead of a close organic identification within some form of constitutional Union of Africa, they advocated a unity that was not "political integration of sovereign states, but unity of aspirations and of action".[18]

Given this divergence in objectives, it is hardly surprising that the two groups attempted to institutionalize two very different conceptions of military cooperation and integration. While the Brazzaville states opted for a simple Joint Defense Command (with a purely advisory role) to be based in Ougoudougou, the capital of Upper Volta (now Burkina Faso), the Casablanca states were far more ambitious. Article 2 of the African Charter of Casablanca not only created a Joint African High Command as one of four specialized committees, but also charged it with the setting up of a viable unified military structure capable of freeing all African territories that were still under foreign rule.[19]

For several reasons, among them most states' increasing preoccupation with domestic issues, neither group's concept was realized before a general *rapprochement* culminated in the establishment of the OAU in May 1963 (and the groups' subsequent dissolution). Far from marking the end of his quest for an AHC, this re-organization of Africa's institutional landscape tempted Nkrumah to renew his calls for the establishment of a unified military structure to ensure the stability and security of Africa. In a book distributed at the OAU's founding conference in Addis Ababa, Nkrumah wrote:

> We should aim at the establishment of a unified military and defense strategy. I do not see much virtue or wisdom in our separate efforts to build up or maintain vast military forces for self-defense, which, in any case, would be ineffective in any major attack upon our separate states. [...] If we do not unite and combine our military resources for common defense, individual states, out of a sense of insecurity, may be drawn into making defense pacts with foreign powers which may endanger the security of us all. [...] Also, the maintenance of large military forces imposes a heavy financial burden on even the most wealthy states. For young African states, who are in great need of capital for internal development, it is ridiculous – indeed suicidal – for each state separately to assume the heavy burden of self-defense, when the weight of this burden could be easily lightened by sharing it among themselves. Some attempt has already been made by the Casablanca Powers and the Afro-Malagasy Union in the matter of common defense, but how much better and stronger it would be if, instead of two such ventures, there was one over-all (land, sea and air) Defense Command for Africa.[20]

However, despite this passionate plea, Nkrumah failed to get the idea of an African High Command or indeed a common defense strategy entrenched in the OAU Charter and a far less authoritative Defense Commission was created in its stead as one of the new organization's five specialized commissions.[21]

The OAU Defense Commission

The central purpose of the Defense Commission was to work out a formula for coordinating and harmonizing the defense policies of member states to enable the OAU to execute the defense role it assumed under Article 2c of its charter. Even though the proposal for an AHC had been rejected by the majority of founding members as premature, the idea was repeatedly re-introduced to the meetings of the commission and discussed under ever new names such as African Defense Organization, African Defense Force or African Peace Force.[22] It also remained a popular topic with the continent's academics.[23] However, no matter how often or under what name and parameters the idea was discussed, the increasingly entrenched concepts of territoriality and sovereignty that had already plagued continental politics before the inception of the OAU continued to prevent the establishment of a supra-national military organization.[24] Nonetheless, the issue never quite disappeared. Instances of insecurity such as mutinies (for example, Tanzania in 1964), mercenary raids (for example, the seizure of Kisangani in 1967) as well as attacks by colonial powers and white supremacist regimes (for example, the Portuguese invasion of Guinea in 1970) occasionally reminded Africa's states of their own vulnerability and generally led to renewed discussions on the need to join forces. In that way, the quest for some kind of Pan-African military force as possible organ for the preservation of Africa's territorial integrity and spearhead for the continent's liberation served as constant background music to inter-African relations until the end of the Cold War changed many of the underlying dynamics. The following examples present some of the evolutionary concepts and milestones on the long and winding road towards continental security cooperation during that period.

During the Defense Commission's first meeting in Accra in late 1963, Nkrumah's Ghanaian delegation presented yet another elaborate proposal for a unified military structure, including the strategic siting or re-siting of military bases throughout Africa and the drawing up of actual plans for the immediate liberation of the dependent territories of Africa.[25] The proposal provided for the establishment of a military organization controlled by one military authority and a Supreme Command Headquarters to be responsible to the Assembly of Heads of State and Government. Besides the setting up of a Union Joint Services Supreme Military Command Headquarters, the plan also included four Joint Services Regional Headquarters to be responsible for the defense of the four "free" regions of Africa (North, East, Central and West) and an extremely ambitious Union Joint Services Strategic Reserve Command which (very much like today's conceptual ASF) would be in a state of readiness to counter any military threat that might arise anywhere in Africa. In addition to a union army, union navy and union air force, there would also be a union strike force and even a union military intelligence organization, union military research and development organization and union military planning organization.[26]

This proposal was strongly opposed by the Nigerian delegation which raised three main objections to it, namely, that (1) it involved a substantial loss of sovereignty, (2) the cost of having such a military structure was prohibitive and (3) it was inevitably bedeviled by other problems such as manpower, equipment and weapon standardization, problems of logistics, unified training, deployment of troops, and the appointment of the Supreme Commander.[27] To underline its argument, the Nigerian delegation repeatedly alluded to the failure of the Casablanca group's Joint African High Command to achieve any practical results as an indication of the difficulties.[28] The majority of delegations subsequently voted against the Ghanaian proposal and instead recommended the establishment of an insignificantly staffed permanent military headquarters within the OAU Secretariat.

At the second meeting of the Defense Commission at Freetown in February 1965, the delegation from Sierra Leone submitted a somewhat more moderate proposal calling for the establishment of an African Defense Organization (ADO).[29] Instead of advocating a permanent standing army as Nkrumah and his Ghanaians had done, the Sierra Leonean delegates suggested a continental clearinghouse for national armed forces (which would later serve as a model for the ASF Regional Headquarters) supported by a committee of military experts. Under this clearinghouse, each OAU member state would have been asked to earmark one or more units of its armed forces to be placed at the disposal of the OAU for specific operations. These forces would have remained stationed in their own countries and would have been mobilized and used under the aegis of the OAU only at the express request of one or more member-states attacked from outside Africa or suffering from serious internal trouble, or in conflict with other OAU member-states.[30]

Despite its more moderate character, the Sierra Leonean proposal was also opposed by the majority of delegations. While the Nigerian delegations saw it as "yet another clever maneuver to skip in the concept of an AHC by the back door",[31] many other delegations expressed concerns about capabilities, financing and security implications as well as the possible role of ADO forces in maintaining oppressive and unpopular governments in power. Following this fruitless discussion, the Defense Commission was not revived until December 1970 when it gathered in Addis Ababa in order to examine the growing threat posed by Portugal and the white regimes in South Africa and Rhodesia.

In an ironic reversal of positions, the Nigerians finally came to embrace the idea of an AHC when their civil war ended in January 1970, while the Ghanaians, having expelled the leading advocate of the idea, President Nkrumah, seemed less and less enthusiastic. However, even with the strong support of the Nigerians and continental attention redrawn to the need for common action by the OAU's inability to respond to the Portuguese invasion of Guinea in November 1970, the Defense Commission rejected the formation of a centralized High Command and in its stead recommended the creation of regional defense units. Based on the original division of the continent into four zones proposed by Nkrumah nearly a decade earlier, these units were supposed to consist of national armed forces which could be placed at the disposal of the OAU for specific operations. An executive secretariat for defense composed of one regional chief of staff, his deputy and representatives from the national armed forces was to coordinate the regional units.[32] Just like the previous plans, this one was not implemented, once again confirming OAU Secretary-General Diallo Telli's lamentation that "nowhere is the sense of urgency so lacking in the majority of member-states as towards the idea of an African High Command whose creation is the outstanding task of the Defense Commission".[33]

The call for a Pan-African force which had flared up occasionally since the debate in the early 1970s (especially during the height of the civil war in Angola in 1975), became particularly loud again during the Council of Ministers 31st ordinary session in Khartoum in July 1978. By then, events such as the increasingly frequent attacks by South Africa and Rhodesia on the so-called Frontline States – a loose anti-apartheid association of Angola, Botswana, Mozambique, Tanzania, Zambia and Zimbabwe – or the Zaire government's use of transport provided by non-African powers (most of all, Belgium) to deploy troops from Morocco and other African countries within its borders, had driven even Tanzania's previously so skeptical President Julius Nyerere to declare that "it might be a good thing if the OAU was sufficiently united to establish an African High Command and a Pan-African Security Force".[34] Following a heated debate, the Council called for the reactivation of the OAU Defense Commission to consider "the desirability of establishing an inter-African military force under the aegis of the OAU".[35] In April 1979, the sixth ordinary session of the Defense Commission agreed that it was both desirable and necessary that the OAU should finally set up an OAU Defense Force whose role was to be fourfold, namely, to (1) support member-states in the event of an aggression from non-African powers, (2) assist liberation movements in their struggles, (3) provide peacekeeping and observer forces in the event of conflict between member-states and (4) cooperate with the UN in matters of defense and security affecting member states.

Even though the chances for the establishment of a Pan-African military force thus seemed better than ever before, the OAU summit held in Sierra Leone in July 1980 avoided a decision on the Defense Commission's proposal and simply referred the OAU Defense Force scheme back for further study (something that would be happening regularly over the next ten years).[36] Once again, as soon as the states' shock over their vulnerability and thus the felt need for action had receded, so had their enthusiasm for tackling all the political obstacles and severe practical, structural, technical, logistical, financial and operational difficulties associated with continental security cooperation.

While it is certainly true that various leaders' personal conceptions of African unity played an important role in the repeated attempts to establish a common defense structure, the security situation on the continent at any one time was the all-important determinant. Every serious discussion on the topic since 1965 had been triggered by an incident of insecurity (and had eventually ebbed away again with the memory of that incident and its particular imminence). Without such an accompanying unifying threat to overcome the enormous introversion of African states, a proposal for military cooperation or even integration did not stand a chance against the continent's many vested interests.[37]

The OAU Mission in Chad

Despite not being able to agree on a common security structure, the OAU occasionally undertook or endorsed less complex ceasefire monitoring missions such as the Bamako Ceasefire Commission in 1963 or the miniature peacekeeping operation in the Shaba Province of Congo in 1978-79.[38] In December 1981, following a mediatory process that had lasted since 1977, the OAU decided to deploy its first (and only) true military operation in order to quell the decade-long civil war in Chad and, in the words of OAU Chairman and President of Kenya Daniel Arap Moi, "enable the people of Chad to decide on a national government in elections supervised by the OAU with the help of an African peacekeeping mission".[39] For the first time ever, an African force was mandated by an African organization to conduct peacekeeping operations within one of its member states and many saw this as a first step towards the eventual institutionalization of continental military cooperation. However, the OAU force soon encountered immense difficulties and was hastily withdrawn in June 1982.[40]

The many problems that beset the OAU peacekeeping force in Chad, ranging from logistical and financial shortages to an unclear mandate and a lack of interoperability, were a practical demonstration of all that the opponents of the Pan-African high command or any other form of Pan-African military force had been saying all along.[41] Not surprisingly, the operation's unmitigated failure had a great impact on the general willingness to contemplate further Pan-African security initiatives as the ensuing institutional frustration and growing disillusion amongst the regions led to the devolution of such initiatives away from the continental level.

Notes

¹   In his 1962 article on Pan-Africanism, George Shepperson has argued for a greater conceptual separation between Pan-African ideology and the various movements. While there is some validity to his argument, for the purpose of this book both concepts will remain subsumed under the term "Pan-Africanism". See George Shepperson, "Pan-Africanism And "Pan-Africanism": Some Historical Notes," *Phylon* 23, no. 4 (1962). See also Kwame Nantambu, "Pan-Africanism Versus Pan-African Nationalism," *Journal of Black Studies* 28, no. 5 (1998).

²   See, for example, Adekunle Ajala, *Pan-Africanism: Evolution, Progress and Prospects* (London: André Deutsch, 1973), Imanuel Geiss, *The Pan-African Movement*, trans. Ann Keep (London: Methuen & Co, 1968), Colin Legum, *Pan-Africanism; a Short Political Guide*, Rev. ed. (New York: F.A. Praeger, 1965), Vincent Thompson, *Africa and Unity: The Evolution of Pan-Africanism* (London: Longmans, 1969). For an excellent overview see P. Olisanwuche Esedebe, *Pan-Africanism : The Idea and Movement, 1776-1991*, 2nd ed. (Washington, D.C.: Howard University, 1994).

³   Cyril Griffith, *The African Dream: Martin R. Delany and the Emergence of Pan-African Thought* (London: The Pennsylvania State University Press, 1975).

⁴   Owen Mathurin, *Henry Sylvester Williams and the Origins of the Pan-African Movement, 1869-1911* (Westport: Greenwood Press, 1976).

⁵   Hollis Lynch, *Edward Wilmot Blyden: Pan-Negro Patriot, 1832-1912* (Oxford: Oxford University Press, 1970).

⁶   Rupert Lewis and Patrick Bryan, eds., *Garvey: His Work and Impact* (Trenton: Africa World Press, 1991), Tony Martin, "International Aspects of the Garvey Movement," *Jamaica Journal* 20, no. 3 (1987), Randolph Persaud, "Re-Envisioning Sovereignty: Marcus Garvey and the Making of a Transnational Identity," in *Africa's Challenge to International Relations Theory*, ed. Kevin Dunn and Timothy Shaw (Basingstoke: Palgrave, 2001).

⁷   J Hooker, *Black Revolutionary: George Padmore's Path from Communism to Pan-Africanism* (London: Pall Mall Press, 1967).

⁸   Francis Broderick, *W.E.B. Dubois: Negro Leader in a Time of Crisis* (Stanford: Stanford University Press, 1959). Also see Elliot Rudwick, *W.E.B. Dubois: A Study in Minority Group Leadership* (Philadelphia: University of Pennsylvania Press, 1960).

⁹   Hakim Adi and Marika Sherwood, *The 1945 Manchester Pan-African Congress Revisited*, ed. George Padmore (London: New Beacon Books, 1995).

¹⁰   Ajala, *Pan-Africanism: Evolution, Progress and Prospects*, 11.

¹¹   See Charles F. Andrain, "The Pan-African Movement: The Search for Organization and Community," *Phylon* 23, no. 1 (1962): 10-13.

¹²   The politicizing effect World War II had on participating Africans and their subsequent commitment to the Pan-African cause must not be underestimated. Returning veterans played a significant part in various nationalist movements on the continent. For example, it was the February 1948

demonstration of war veterans in Accra that sparked off the political and constitutional process that led to the independence of Ghana nine years later. See Geiss, *The Pan-African Movement*, 363-366.

[13] See Persaud, "Re-Envisioning Sovereignty: Marcus Garvey and the Making of a Transnational Identity."

[14] Bill Sutherland and Matt Meyer, *Guns and Gandhi in Africa: Pan-African Insights on Non-Violence, Armed Struggle and Liberation in Africa* (Trenton: Africa World Press, 2000).

[15] Anonymous, Program of the African Blood Brotherhood, *Communist Review*, 2(6), 1922, 449-454.

[16] The complete proceedings of the conference have been reproduced in *Current History* 37, no. 215 (1959).

[17] The Casablanca group consisted of Egypt, Algeria, Morocco, Libya, Ghana, Guinea and Mali. The Brazzaville group comprised Cameroon, Congo-Brazzaville, Cote d'Ivoire, Dahomey (Benin), Gabon, Upper Volta (Burkina Faso), Madagascar, Mauritania, Niger, the Central African Republic, Senegal and Chad. Eventually, the Brazzaville group merged into the Monrovia group resulting in an increased membership of 24 (including Nigeria, Liberia and Togo).

[18] C Chimelu, *Integration and Politics among African States* (Uppsala: Scandinavian Institute of African Studies, 1977), 164. For a more detailed discussion of the disagreement between the two groups see Guy Arnold, *Africa: A Modern History* (London: Atlantic Books, 2005), 95-107, Benedikt Franke, "Competing Regionalisms in Africa and the Continent's Emerging Security Architecture," *African Studies Quarterly* 10, no. 1 (2007), Erasmus Kloman, "African Unification Movements," *International Organization* 16, no. 2 (1962).

[19] Several bilateral attempts at military integration among the newly independent states predated these group efforts. Noteworthy is the establishment of a *Conseil de l'Entente* by the four West African states Niger, Upper Volta, Dahomey and the Ivory Coast which included provisions for a common army and the 1960 creation of a *Union des Républiques d'Afrique Centrale* by the governments of the Central African Republic, Chad and the former French Congo who had agreed on a common external defense policy. See Andrain, "The Pan-African Movement: The Search for Organization and Community," 7.

[20] Kwame Nkrumah, *Africa Must Unite* (New York: F.A. Praeger, 1963), 219-220.

[21] For more details on the discussions during the OAU's founding conference see Ajala, *Pan-Africanism: Evolution, Progress and Prospects*, 47-64.

[22] For a more detailed discussion of the various proposals see C. O. C. Amate, *Inside the OAU : Pan-Africanism in Practice* (New York: St. Martin's Press, 1986), 170-189. Also see OAU, *Resolving Conflicts in Africa: Implementation Options*, OAU Information Services Publication Series (II), 1993, para. 81-106.

[23] See, for example, B. Ijomah, "The African Military Interventions: A Prelude to Military High Command," *Journal of African Activist Association* 5, no. 5 (1974), Thomas Imobighe, "An African High Command: The Search for a Feasible Strategy of Continental Defense," *African Affairs* 79, no. 315 (1980).

24   For a good discussion of the problems involved in the creation of an OAU force see S. Agbi, *The OAU and African Diplomacy, 1963-1979* (Ibadan: Impact Publishers, 1986), 114-131.

25   See O Fasehun, "Nigeria and the Issue of an African High Command: Towards a Regional and/or Continental Defense System," *Afrika Spektrum* 80, no. 3 (1980).

26   See OAU Proceedings of the 1st Meeting of the Defense Commission, Proposal by Ghana Def.1/Memo 3 (31 October 1963, Accra, Ghana)

27   See O Aluko, *Ghana and Nigeria 1957-70. A Study in Inter-African Discord* (London: Rex Collings, 1976), 130.

28   See W Gutteridge, *Military Institutions and Power in the New States* (London: Pall Mall Press, 1964), 161.

29   Jon Woronoff, "The Case for an African Defense Organization," *Africa Report* 16, no. 6 (1971): 23-25.

30   See Amate, *Inside the OAU : Pan-Africanism in Practice*, 174.

31   See Aluko, *Ghana and Nigeria 1957-70. A Study in Inter-African Discord*, 137.

32   Michael Wolfers, *Politics in the Organization of African Unity* (London: Methuen & Co, 1976), 96.

33   Diallo Telli, *Report to the Seventh Ordinary Session of the Assembly of Heads of State*, September 1970.

34   *Daily Times* (Lagos), 19 June 1978: 7.

35   OAU Council of Ministers 31st Ordinary Session, CM/Res. 635, Sudan, July 1978.

36   See OAU Council of Ministers 35th Ordinary Session, CM/Res.815, Sierra Leone, June-July 1980 and OAU Council of Ministers 50th Ordinary Session, CM/Res. 1216(L), Ethiopia, July 1989. Both times the text of the resolution reads "The Council reaffirms the decision in principle to establish an African Defense Organ and requests the Defense Commission to pursue its studies on the modalities of establishing such an Organ, by analyzing and assessing the budgetary implications". Also see Esedebe, *Pan-Africanism : The Idea and Movement, 1776-1991*, 232-233.

37   Two specific proposals were the African Task Force and the Collective African Intervention Force. The African Task Force was proposed by Nigeria at the 1972 OAU Ministerial Council Meeting and was to be a joint force to which all OAU member states would contribute and was to be based in independent African states bordering on the Portuguese colonies in an effort to hasten their liberation. The Collective Intervention Force was suggested by OAU Secretary-General, William Eteki Moumoua, in his report to the OAU ministerial meeting in Libreville, Gabon in 1977. The aim was to create a force which could be rapidly mobilized to move against any attacks on the frontline states.

38   See Gino Naldi, "Peacekeeping Attempts by the Organization of African Unity," *The International and Comparative Law Quarterly* 34, no. 3 (1985).

39   Ibid.: 594.

40   For more detailed information on the OAU Peacekeeping Operation in Chad see Sam Amoo, "Frustrations of Regional Peacekeeping: The OAU in Chad, 1977-1982," *Carter Center Working Paper* (2001), Terry Mays, *Africa's First Peacekeeping Operation: The OAU in Chad, 1981-1982* (New York:

Praeger, 2002), Ahmadu Sesay, "The Limits of Peacekeeping by a Regional Organization: The OAU Peacekeeping Force in Chad," *Conflict Quarterly* 11, no. 1 (1991), Margaret Vogt and S. Aminu, eds., *Peacekeeping as a Security Strategy in Africa: Chad and Liberia as Case Studies*, vol. 1 (Enugu (Nigeria): Fourth Dimension Publishing, 1996).

[41] See Sesay, "The Limits of Peacekeeping by a Regional Organization: The OAU Peacekeeping Force in Chad," 21. Also see Thomas Imobighe, "The Analysis of Political Issues Raised by OAU Peacekeeping in Chad," in *Peacekeeping as a Security Strategy in Africa: Chad and Liberia as Case Studies*, ed. Margaret Vogt and S. Aminu (Enugu (Nigeria): Fourth Dimension Publishing, 1996).

4
The Devolution of Security Cooperation

While it was the failure of the Chad operation that sounded the obvious death knell to the OAU's cautious efforts, the devolution of security cooperation from the continental to the regional level(s) had long been in the making. Regional initiatives such as the Economic Community of West African States or the Front Line States' Inter-State Defense and Security Committee (ISDSC) had gradually begun to fill the void created by the OAU's inability to set up an integrated defense mechanism since the mid-1970s.

By that time, African states had already had more than ten years experience with regional cooperation which had quickly become a notable feature of inter-African relations following decolonization.[1] While the first wave of regionalization and the emergence of cooperative schemes like the *Conseil de l'Entente* (1959), the Union of African States (1960) or the African and Malagasy Union (1961) was mainly a result of Pan-African euphoria and the fear of neo-colonial interference, the second wave beginning in the early 1970s was characterized by more practical considerations.

Firstly, Africa's disappointing economic performance during the 1960s – the continent had emerged from the UN's first Development Decade (1960-1970) as the region registering the lowest rate of growth among developing countries – provided an obvious motivation for increasing regional cooperation as states began to feel the negative consequences of the extreme segmentation and the intrinsically problematic viability of the political divisions and economic circuits inherited from the colonial period. In addition to overcoming the effects of the continent's balkanization, Africa's leaders also hoped that regional cooperation would lessen their states' disadvantageous dependency on the economies of the industrialized Western countries and thus fortify their independence.[2]

Another reason for the growth of regionalism in the 1970s was the failure of the OAU to provide a true continental framework for cooperative ventures. Although Article XX of the OAU Charter had established several Specialized Commissions (Economic and Social,

Educational and Cultural, Health, Sanitation and Nutrition, Defense as well as Scientific, Technical and Research) these never really materialized and plans for continental action were rarely translated into concrete activities.[3] Instead, the OAU's failure "to coordinate and intensify member states' cooperation and efforts to achieve a better life for the people of Africa" left a sizeable vacuum in the continent's perceived potential which the states themselves ventured to fill.[4] They did so by expanding and intensifying regional cooperation.

While regional cooperation during the 1970s and 1980s largely centered on economic issues, a third wave of regionalization broadened the cooperative agenda in the early 1990s when five principal reasons caused the continent's regional economic communities to add security and conflict management initiatives to their original (economic) purpose, namely (1) the drastic deterioration in Africa's security landscape following the end of the Cold War, (2) waning superpower interest and the international community's apparent unwillingness to get involved in the continent's proliferating conflicts, (3) the OAU's equally obvious inability to provide continental solutions to the latter, (4) the successful precedent set by the 1990 intervention of the ECOWAS Cease-Fire Monitoring Group (ECOMOG) in Liberia's civil war,[5] and (5) the growing acceptance of regional approaches to security by the UN and other international actors.[6] The following sections will briefly introduce the main regional security initiatives and the role of non-African actors in their evolution.

The Economic Community of West African States

The Economic Community of West African States (ECOWAS) was founded on May 28, 1975 with the signing of the Treaty of Lagos in order to unite West Africa's states into a collective political and economic bargaining bloc.[7] Going back to an initiative President William Tubman of Liberia started in 1964, the creation of ECOWAS was also supposed to heal the rift between the region's former French and British colonies by crossing the language barrier and incorporating previous initiatives such as the *Union Monétaire Ouest Africaine* and the *Communauté de l'Afrique de l'Ouest* (CEAO) into one overarching organization.[8]

Even though the Community was mainly founded for the purpose of economic cooperation, the increasingly unstable political and military situation in West Africa and the OAU's aforementioned inability to do anything about the underlying spate of *coups d'Etat* and mercenary attacks soon led to attempts to formulate a regional approach to security.[9] In June 1977, the seven CEAO member states (that is, Burkina Faso, Côte d'Ivoire, Mali, Mauritania, Niger and Senegal) and Togo blazed the trail when they signed an Agreement on Non-Aggression and Defense Assistance – the *Accord de Non-Aggression et d'Assistance en Matière de Défense* (ANAD).[10] ECOWAS, increasingly aware that it would not be able to attain its (economic) objectives save in an atmosphere of peace, followed suit and adopted its own Protocol on Non-Aggression in April 1978. This protocol sought to outlaw aggression by member states and provided for the peaceful resolution of conflicts in the region. In May 1981, it was supplemented by a more elaborate Protocol on Mutual Assistance on Defense which spelt out three situations that would call for joint military action by member states. First, any armed threat or aggression directed against any member state, which shall constitute a threat or aggression against the entire community. Second, any armed conflict between two or more member states in which the settlement procedure of the Non-Aggression Protocol has proven ineffective. Third, any internal armed conflicts within a member state that have been engineered and supported from outside and are likely to endanger the peace and security of the entire community. In addition, the protocol also provided for organs of collective action such as a Defense Council and Committee, an Allied Armed Force of the Community and a Deputy Executive Secretary for Military Matters to be positioned in the Secretariat.

While the protocol, for reasons reaching from fear of Nigerian domination to a general lack of political will, only became effective in 1986, it provided the basis for the highly successful intervention of the Community's Cease-Fire Monitoring Group (ECOMOG) in Liberia's civil war several years later. When state authority disintegrated in Liberia in 1990, ECOWAS invoked Article 16 of the protocol and formed a five-member Standing Mediation Committee (SMC) to steer the parties toward a cease-fire and national reconciliation. As the conflict escalated, ECOWAS extended its mandate by establishing ECOMOG in August 1990 with the task of keeping the peace, restoring law and order and ensuring respect for the cease-fire.[11] Named Operation Liberty, this intervention under Nigerian leadership and control received widespread praise as "the first real attempt by African countries to (re)solve an African conflict" and OAU Secretary-General Dr. Salim A. Salim anticipated that the experience would make Africans finally realize the need for the establishment of an African High Command and greater military cooperation.[12]

While the ECOMOG intervention did not result in the establishment of a High Command, it certainly reinforced the trend towards regionalized military cooperation by establishing a pattern of norm-building and setting a remarkable precedent which dealt a crushing blow to the OAU's founding principle of non-intervention among member states.[13] It also increased the international community's attention to and support for the concept of African solutions to African problems and thereby set the stage for the proliferation of African security initiatives in the 1990s, and thus eventually also for the realization of a continental security framework under the aegis of the AU.

Following its relatively successful ECOMOG interventions in Liberia, ECOWAS increasingly sought to institutionalize its security cooperation. This process began in earnest in July 1993 when the region's Heads of State endorsed a revised ECOWAS Treaty and adopted a declaration of political principle to promote mutual collaboration in defense and security issues. It culminated in an extraordinary ECOWAS summit in Togo in December 1997 that established the Mechanism for Conflict Prevention, Management, Resolution, Peacekeeping and Security. Following the successful ECOMOG intervention in Sierra Leone in February 1998 which restored the democratically elected government of Ahmed Tejan Kabbah to power as well as two further meetings by the relevant ministers and experts in March and July 1998, this mechanism was finally accepted and ratified by the Heads of State at the Abuja summit in August 1999. On 10 December 1999 at Lomé, Togo, the protocol relating to the mechanism was finally signed, thus effectively replacing the earlier ECOWAS Protocols Relating to Non-Aggression (1978) and Mutual Assistance and Defense (1981).

Composed of thirteen chapters, the protocol is an elaborate framework document that set out to institutionalize structures and processes that would ensure consultation and collective management of regional security issues (see Figure 4.1).[14] It provided for the establishment of the following institutions and supporting organs: a Mediation and Security Council that would take decisions on issues of peace and security in the region on behalf of the Authority of Heads of State and Government and implement all the provisions of the protocol, a Defense and Security Commission charged with advising the council on technical and operative details and a Council of Elders.[15] In addition, the protocol also provided for the institutionalization of ECOMOG as brigade-sized standby force for regional intervention and the creation of an Early Warning System that would detect, monitor, analyze and make reports on conflict indicators within or between member states.[16]

Figure 4.1: ECOWAS Mechanism for Conflict Prevention, Peacekeeping and Security[17]

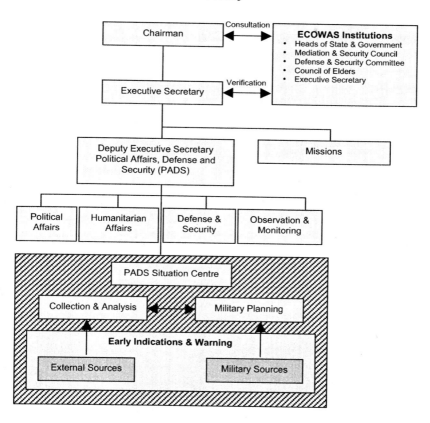

With the swift implementation of the mechanism in 1999, ECOWAS reinforced its role as trendsetter in regional security cooperation. Now, it was not only the first African organization to have successfully conducted military interventions to halt a civil war (Liberia) and restore a democratically elected government to power (Sierra Leone), but it was also the first organization to have formally codified the underlying doctrines of humanitarian intervention and the legitimate use of force.[18] Despite the many shortcomings which its military operations undoubtedly suffered, the overly dominant role of Nigeria and the often merely lukewarm endorsement by its francophone members, ECOWAS thus became a role model for many of the other regional security initiatives and, indeed, the AU itself.[19]

From Frontline States to Development Community

Today's Southern African Development Community (SADC) was preceded by two regional groupings, the Frontline States (FLS) and the Southern African Development Coordination Conference (SADCC), neither of which made serious attempts at security cooperation. The primary purpose of the FLS was the coordination of liberation struggles and negotiations, while SADCC was set up to reduce the economic dependence of other Southern African states on South Africa. However, both organizations were instrumental in creating and fostering a sense of community and belonging among these states, which contributed as much to the formation of SADC's current security architecture as did some of their surviving institutions, such as the Inter-State Defense and Security Committee (ISDSC). Consequently, it seems appropriate to outline the evolution of both organizations, and to point out important milestones on the way towards structured security cooperation in the region.[20]

What became known as the Front Line States can hardly be described as a formal organization. Instead it offered an informal forum in which respected heads of state could discuss the political difficulties of the newly independent governments in Angola, Mozambique and Zambia and, to a lesser extent, the military problems of the region's liberation movements. However, despite its lack of official structure and institutional procedure (no agendas for meetings were published, and no minutes were taken), the FLS played an important role in bringing about the dramatic shifts in the regional balance of power that occurred after 1975.[21] It did so by offering political support and a platform for negotiation to liberation movements, rather than by coordinating military support for their guerrilla forces, as is sometimes postulated.[22] In fact, there was hardly any military interaction between the members of the FLS, even though it created an Inter-State Defense and Security Committee to improve the synchronization of defense activities in the region. Daunted by the looming military might of their racist neighbor, the FLS states had to confine themselves to informal military collaboration, such as the exchange of information on defense and security matters, the training of newly-established armed forces like those of Mozambique, or occasional joint operations undertaken to combat national resistance movements. Nonetheless, the FLS, and the ISDSC in particular, sowed the seeds for increased military interaction by institutionalizing regular meetings (which were held at least twice a year) and fostering a relatively open dialogue among the top political and military leaders of the region.

Realizing the dangers inherent in their collective economic dependence on South Africa, the FLS passed the Lusaka Declaration in 1980, which set up the Southern African Development Coordination Conference. This was done to promote their economic liberation and integration and to provide the economic pillar of the anti-colonial and anti-apartheid struggle in the region. SADCC was in essence a politically-motivated response to the idea of a "constellation of states" in the region proposed by the South African Prime Minister PW Botha. As long as some states remained under colonial or minority rule, SADCC and the FLS remained separate forums, accepting responsibility for economic coordination and for mutual political and military support respectively.

When the anti-colonial struggle finally ended and apartheid was abolished in South Africa in the early 1990s, the security and political concerns of Southern Africa changed dramatically. Since the 1960s, the region's alliance patterns had been determined by South Africa's military and economic pre-eminence. Even though this dominance did not wane with the institution of majority rule, it was considered much less threatening. With their original *raison d'être* (to counter white minority rule and promote political and economic liberation) nullified by events, the institutions described above could turn their attention towards addressing the region's many and deep-seated political, economic and military challenges. They did so by increasing their integrative efforts in accordance with the 1991 Abuja Treaty, which aimed to establish a continent-wide economic community by 2025. To this end, SADCC was transformed into the more formal Southern African Development Community at the 1992 Windhoek Summit,[23] while the ISDSC continued to retain responsibility for matters of defense and security under the nominal guidance of the FLS.

However, it was not until Southern Africa's leaders created the Organ for Politics, Defense and Security (OPDS) in 1996 – as a result of very much the same pressures that had caused the ECOWAS region to formalize its collaboration – that the region began to institutionalize security cooperation in earnest.[24] The OPDS was modeled on the OAU's Central Organ of the Mechanism for Conflict Prevention, Management and Resolution founded in 1993 and, working in conjunction with the ISDSC, was intended to provide a special forum for political, defense and security cooperation, with a focus on conflict management. Over the years, the ISDSC had become an institution of some complexity. It consisted of three primary sub-committees which were in turn divided into various specialist sub-committees. In the defense domain, for example, there were some 15 sub-committees, which covered areas of common interest to SADC defense ranging from sport and chaplains' affairs on the one hand to maritime and operational issues on the other. The OPDS was to complement the ISDSC activities and fulfill 16 broad objectives, among them the protection of the region and its member states against instability, the development of a collective security capacity, the conclusion of a Mutual Defense Pact and the development of a regional peacekeeping capacity.[25] To this purpose, the OPDS was to be positioned within the institutional structure of SADC.

However, even though the OPDS was meant to "promote political cooperation among member states" and "develop a common foreign and security policy" growing tensions over its form and functions threatened to pull the region apart.[26] In fact, the organ did not become operational until the SADC Summit of Blantyre in 2001. The reason for this delay was a single sentence in the final communiqué of the founding summit in Gaborone, which stated that the OPDS would "function independently of other structures".[27] These words were interpreted in very different ways. President Robert Mugabe of Zimbabwe took them to mean that he, as chairman of the OPDS, could act independently of the SADC decision-making process, while President Nelson Mandela of South Africa believed that SADC should be in firm control of the organ.

As Theo Neethling quite rightly argued, this institutional infighting would have earned little more than a footnote in SADC's history of security cooperation had it not been directly responsible for the organization's inability to respond meaningfully to the conflicts in the Democratic Republic of Congo and Lesotho.[28] Far from showcasing regional cohesiveness, the initially un-mandated excursions of Zimbabwe, Angola and Namibia (in the case of the DRC) and South Africa (in the case of Lesotho) under the banner of the so-called SADC Allied Armed Forces (AAF) revealed such deep divisions within Southern Africa that both the memories of previous collaborative efforts by the region's states and its hopes for creating a viable security architecture could not but fade away.[29]

It was the realization of the disastrous effects of their disharmony that finally galvanized the region's states into action in August 2001 when they adopted the Protocol on Politics, Defense and Security Cooperation. This protocol clarified the nature of the region's institutional structure for security and opened the way for further interaction on matters related to defense and security.

The climax of the slow evolution towards institutionalized regional security in Southern Africa occurred at SADC's 2003 Summit, where the region's states signed a Mutual Defense Pact.[30] Despite being a considerably watered-down version of the earlier drafts, it entails a clear commitment by the signatories to permanent military cooperation and integration.[31] Article 9, for example, calls for increased interaction among the region's armed forces in such areas as training, exchange of military intelligence, joint research, development and production of military equipment. Together with the 2004 Strategic Indicative Plan for the Organ (SIPO) which contains instructions relating to the development of a regional defense capability and the formulation of a doctrine that will make the region's armed forces interoperable, the pact provides the legal foundation for SADC's security cooperation.[32]

Similarly to ECOWAS, SADC had evolved from an economic venture to a regional security provider in order to safeguard its development objectives and fill the security gap left by the OAU's ineffective approach.[33] While by the end of the 1990s tensions between certain member states still ran high, the memories of SADC's divisive interventions in the DRC and Lesotho remained fresh and a fear of South African hegemony often dampened enthusiasm for regional cooperation, the creation of the OPDS (now occasionally referred to as Organ for Politics, Defense and Security Cooperation, OPDSC) was an important step towards a Southern African security community and, together with the aforementioned precedents set by ECOWAS, provided a clear signal to the continent's other regional organizations.[34]

The Intergovernmental Authority on Development

The origins and genesis of the Intergovernmental Authority of Development (IGAD) differ from those of Africa's other regional organizations.[35] Instead of evolving from an economic purpose, IGAD grew out of the attempts in the mid-1980s to confront the region's recurring environmental catastrophes. Following the devastating droughts between 1974 and 1985, Djibouti, Ethiopia, Kenya, Somalia, the Sudan and Uganda formed the Inter-Governmental Authority on Drought and Development (IGADD) in 1986 in order to improve their responses to natural disasters. Actively encouraged by the United Nations Environment Program, IGADD concentrated on cooperation in areas such as drought, desertification and food security, while military security and defense were viewed as the prerogative of individual states and thus remained outside the arena of collective action.[36]

IGADD first ventured into the realms of security cooperation in the early 1990s when it began to host and facilitate negotiating sessions between the Sudanese government in Khartoum and the rebel forces from southern Sudan in an attempt to end the country's long-running civil war.[37] Almost as a logical consequence of this diplomatic initiative, chaired by Kenya's President Daniel Arap Moi, an extraordinary summit was convened in Addis Ababa in April 1995 to discuss ways to revitalize the organization and expand its cooperative activities permanently into spheres such as politics, economics and security. At this summit, the six original IGADD member states and Eritrea, which had joined following its independence in 1993, resolved to broaden the mandate of IGADD and expand cooperation among member states just like SADC and ECOWAS had done earlier in the 1990s. At another extraordinary summit held in March 1996, IGADD was then renamed the Intergovernmental Authority on Development and the original agreement establishing IGADD was amended accordingly.[38] The new IGAD was finally launched in Djibouti in November 1996.

The name change was not merely cosmetic as the new agreement expanded the mandate of IGAD to include peace and security, economic cooperation, infrastructural development and political and humanitarian affairs. Article 18a of the agreement, for example, called on member states to (1) take effective collective measures to eliminate threats to regional cooperation, peace and stability, (2) establish an effective mechanism of consultation and cooperation for the pacific settlement of differences and disputes and (3) accept to deal with disputes between member states within this regional mechanism before they are referred to other regional or international organizations.

In 1998, IGAD embarked on a five point program on Conflict Prevention, Resolution and Management which aimed at (1) building a institutional capacity, (2) documenting peacemaking initiatives in the region, (3) promoting a culture of peace and tolerance, (4) developing an early warning mechanism and (5) establishing a peace fund to complement the activities of other actors engaged in humanitarian and peacebuilding work.

The Khartoum summit in November 2000 finally endorsed the establishment of a "mechanism in the IGAD sub-region for the prevention, management and resolution of inter-state and intra-state conflicts".[39] This security mechanism was conceived within the Office of Political and Humanitarian Affairs and structured into three divisions: Conflict Prevention, Management and Resolution (CPMR), Humanitarian Affairs and Political Affairs.

In October 2003 the summit of Heads of State and Government endorsed yet another IGAD Program on Conflict Prevention, Management and Resolution and a 5-year implementation plan. Both foresee CPMR programs as one of the priority areas for IGAD and envisage the setting up of a CPMR strategy. In addition to the existing programs, some of which have been going on since the revitalization of IGAD in 1996, the newly renamed Division of Peace and Security was tasked to coordinate the development of a regional peace and security strategy for the Eastern and Southern African region that would bring together IGAD and other regional groupings such as SADC, the East African Community (EAC) and the Common Market for Eastern and Southern Africa (COMESA).

As a system of security cooperation, Eastern Africa differs markedly from Western and Southern Africa. Not only is there no clearly defined regional leader with sufficient resources to give overarching direction in security issues (like Nigeria in Western Africa or South Africa in Southern Africa), but the array of debilitating civil wars, sustained hostilities and mutual suspicions is also even more depressing than in the other regions. Nonetheless, IGAD has established itself as noteworthy political forum and central framework for efforts in the area of peace and security and some of its initiatives like its attempts to broker peace deals in the Sudanese and Somali civil wars or the establishment of a Central Early Warning System (CEWARN), which will be discussed in detail in chapter nine, have even developed into models for the rest of the continent.[40]

Other Regional Security Initiatives

Besides ECOWAS, SADC and IGAD, at least three other regional security initiatives need to be mentioned briefly in order to provide the necessary context for the following chapters, namely, the East African Community (EAC), the Economic Community of Central African States (ECCAS) and the Arab-Maghreb Union (AMU).

The East African Community was originally founded in 1967 by Tanzania, Kenya and Uganda with the ultimate aim of political unification. However, due to increasing tensions between the leaders of all three member states and the incompatibility of their political ideologies, the EAC collapsed less than ten years after its creation.[41] Once Tanzania had ousted Uganda's dictator Idi Amin in 1979 and the political standoff between socialist Tanzania and capitalist Kenya began to normalize in the 1980s, regional cooperation returned onto the agenda. Accordingly, the Mediation Agreement on Sharing the Assets and Liabilities of the Community which officially disbanded the EAC in 1984 already bore the fruit for its reconstitution. Article 14.2, for example, urged states to explore and identify areas for future cooperation and to make arrangements for such cooperation.

Pressured by the same economic and political dynamics as their counterparts in the western and southern regions of the continent, East Africa's Presidents Moi (Kenya), Mwinyi (Tanzania) and Museveni (Uganda) finally re-institutionalized regional cooperation by signing a Treaty for East African Cooperation in November 1993. In March 1996, they re-established the Tri-partite Commission for Cooperation and began a process of re-integration which involved tri-partite programs of cooperation in political, economic, social and cultural fields, research and technology, defense, security, legal and judicial affairs.

While the focus of the East African Cooperation certainly lay on economic affairs, it differed significantly from its unlucky predecessor in also devoting considerable attention to security-related matters. Following the examples of IGAD, SADC and ECOWAS, the countries of East Africa began to consider all sorts of military and defense cooperation in the second half of the 1990s. In November 1997 and January 1998, for example, Kenya, Tanzania and Uganda held high-level meetings to discuss possible peace support operations and the creation of a joint-training minister.[42] In April 1998, the three countries' armed forces signed a Memorandum of Understanding (MoU) on defense matters which addressed a wide range of issues such as the mutual use of communication facilities, sharing of intelligence, the coordination of military research and production measures.[43] In June 1998, the East African Cooperation held a highly successful joint peacekeeping exercise (Natural Fire) in Kenya which was conceived as a springboard for further cooperation in peacekeeping activities and complex emergency operations.[44]

Increasing cooperation among the three countries eventually led to the official revival of the EAC in July 2000.[45] The revised East African Treaty on Cooperation of November 1999 defined cooperation as an agent for regional peace, established a Sectoral Committee on Cooperation in Defense as well as an Inter-State Security Committee and called on all member states to cooperate closely in defense and security affairs.[46] Over the years, the EAC has indeed made substantial progress in developing a Conflict Early Warning System and a Conflict Prevention, Management and Resolution Mechanism. The EAC is important to the ensuing analysis, however, not only for its successes in regional security cooperation, but also for a practical demonstration of the negative effects of overlapping institutional memberships.

The Economic Community of Central African States was founded in 1981 by the members of the *Communauté Économique des États de l'Afrique Centrale* (Burundi, Rwanda and Zaire), the members of the *Union douanière et économique de l'Afrique centrale* (Cameroon, the Central African Republic, Chad, Congo Brazzaville and Gabon) as well as Equatorial Guinea and Sao Tome and Principe in order to advance economic cooperation in the region.

Even though the organization's initial mandate did not provide for political and security issues to be addressed, the recurrent political crises, military hostilities and *coups d'Etat* in Central Africa soon generated the desire for such cooperation. In 1986, ECCAS Chairman and President of Cameroon Paul Biya asked the UN to support his organization in identifying and implementing programs to promote peace and security in the region.[47] The UN Regional Centre for Peace and Disarmament subsequently held a workshop with ECCAS member states in February 1988.[48] As result of this workshop and a related UN General Assembly resolution, UN Secretary-General Boutros Boutros-Ghali established the United Nations Standing Advisory Committee on Security Questions in Central Africa in May 1992.[49]

Through this UN Committee, ECCAS member states have undertaken a number of ambitious initiatives to promote regional peace and security. During the fifth meeting of the Committee in September 1994, for example, the states of Central Africa adopted a Non-Aggression Pact which was signed during the Committee's first Summit of Heads of State and Government in July 1996.[50] In the same year, the Committee also assisted ECCAS with the establishment of an early warning mechanism (*mécanisme d'alerte rapide*) based in Libreville. In February 1999, it supported the ECCAS member states in institutionalizing an organizational and legal framework for their security efforts.[51] The *Conseil de Paix et de Sécurité de l'Afrique Centrale* (COPAX) was to prevent, manage and resolve conflicts in Central Africa and to undertake all and any necessary action that could deal effectively with political conflicts.[52] In June 2002, the 10th Ordinary Summit of ECCAS adopted an important protocol relating to COPAX which clarified the rules of procedures for its three technical organs, namely, (1) the Early Warning System, (2) a Defense and Security Commission which is to advise the decision-making bodies on the initiation of military operations and (3) a multi-national, non-permanent military force. While most of these elaborate initiatives have yet to be implemented, ECCAS has managed to position itself as one of the AU's seven officially sanctioned regional security actors.[53]

As Eric Berman and Katie Sams have pointed out, the very creation of the Arab-Maghreb Union (AMU) in February 1989 represented a notable achievement given the level of distrust that had characterized the relations among some of its members ever since decolonization.[54] The organization's five member states – Algeria, Libya, Mauritania, Morocco and Tunisia – however, soon froze their cooperation again when Morocco fell out with Algeria over Western Sahara in 1995.[55] The AMU has lain virtually dormant ever since.

Despite the organization's lackluster history and the fact that its security mechanism is the least developed among Africa's regional organizations – Article 14 of its treaty addresses peace and security matters only very briefly – it deserves attention because North African states were significant players in the deliberations concerning the development of a continental security management arrangement.

The International Component of Devolution

Having briefly introduced the various regional security initiatives that have sprung up on the continent in the early 1990s, it is important to highlight the role of the international community in their evolution. This role was twofold. First, the increasing financial and capacity-building support, which the Western world gradually substituted for its direct involvement in the continent's conflicts, was crucial to the growth of organizations such as ECOWAS, ECCAS or SADC.[56] Second, the obvious overstretch of the United Nations system following the end of the Cold War fostered a new approach to collective security which accepted regional organizations as legitimate actors and partners and institutionalized a new division of labor in international conflict management.[57]

For the major powers of the Western world, the close of the Cold War necessitated a re-definition of their strategic interests. With the ideological battle for Africa won and no other significant economic or political issues at stake, international attention quickly shifted away from the continent and towards seemingly more important regions such as the Middle East or Eastern Europe.[58] In the process, the international community gradually substituted the promotion of home-grown African initiatives for its own physical involvement. The tragic (and, arguably, preventable) events in Somalia and Rwanda in the early 1990s amplified the pressures on the international community to specify the concepts for such a promotion and advance their speedy implementation. The three most notable concepts to emerge were (1) the United States' African Crisis Response Force/Initiative, (2) the French program *Renforcement des Capacités Africaines de Maintien de la Paix* and (3) the so-called P-3 Initiative.[59]

Contrary to what is often postulated, the United States did not disengage from Africa immediately following the Cold War. Instead, its initial policy reassessment in form of the *National Security Review 30: American Policy towards Africa in the 1990s* (NSR 30) concluded that post-Cold War developments in Africa provided both "significant opportunities for and obstacles to US interests" and that the United States had to remain militarily engaged on the continent.[60] The US thus continued with a proactive strategy towards the continent until October 3, 1993, when 18 US soldiers were killed and at least 75 more seriously injured in the streets of Mogadishu. It was only then that a radical review of its African peacekeeping policies, and what might be construed as a distinct desire to divorce itself from any UN-led missions after Somalia, led the US government under President Clinton to issue Presidential Decision Directive 25 (PDD 25), which sought to strictly limit US deployments abroad.

PDD 25 heralded a shift towards isolationism that was characterized by greater reluctance to become involved in further deployments in Africa. Even though this shift was partially reversed once the scale of the tragedy in Rwanda was revealed and the international community developed a sense of collective guilt over the its inaction, the United States did not revert to direct military intervention when fear of an imminent genocide in neighboring Burundi broke out in 1996. Instead, the American government launched a series of initiatives to support indigenous African conflict resolution.[61] While this was far from a serious re-engagement, indeed some called it "virtual engagement",[62] it did represent recognition that the US could not afford complete disengagement from Africa, or as Letitia Lawson put it:

> The lesson of Somalia, Rwanda and Liberia taken together was that the US could not engage directly, could not do nothing and could not expect African forces to contain instability on their own. And so the search began for alternatives that would combine US financial resources and African human resources for conflict resolution/peacekeeping, political reform and economic development.[63]

In order to shift more of the military conflict management burden on Africa's shoulders, US Secretary of State Warren Christopher fell back on the United Kingdom's suggestion to create a regional peacekeeping force for Africa organized along the lines of the Organization for Security and Cooperation in Europe (OSCE).[64] In an address to the OAU in October 1996, Christopher stated that due to the Burundi crisis and its potential impact on other states, "we must develop the capacity for an effective response in any future crisis, and we must find new ways for Africans to work together and for the international community to support you".[65] Christopher suggested the creation of an African Crisis Response Force (ACRF), an indigenous African military force, trained and equipped with the help of the US military, available for deployment to trouble spots on the continent. While the concept held many attractions for its American sponsors – it could help prevent another Somalia or Rwanda without necessitating the direct involvement of the US military – and even though it was very much in line with the goal enunciated in the UN Secretary-General's peacekeeping report of November 1995, the ACRF proposal was not well received by most African states.[66] It was subsequently reformulated into the African Crisis Response Initiative (ACRI) and later morphed into Operation Focus Relief, all of which essentially aimed at establishing and training an African peacekeeping force.[67]

The French RECAMP program, on the other hand, did not focus on the establishment of such a force, but intended to enhance African capacities on a non-discriminatory basis in order to facilitate their participation in peacekeeping operations within the framework of, for example, the UN Stand-by Arrangements System (UNSAS). Presented to the public at the Africa-France Summit at the Louvre in 1997, RECAMP has since been extraordinarily active in training and supplying various African armies for peacekeeping operations.[68]

Britain, another key player by virtue of its major colonial legacies and post-colonial cultural and trade links, to some extent duplicated the American and French initiatives. In April 1997, for example, it sponsored a joint peacekeeping exercise (Blue Hungwe) involving troops and observers from Angola, Botswana, Swaziland, South Africa, Lesotho, Malawi, Mozambique, Namibia, Tanzania and Zimbabwe while France conducted a similar exercise (Operation Nangbeto) in West Africa. In late 1997, realizing their increasingly wasteful duplication of effort, France, the United Kingdom and the United States announced a joint "P-3 Initiative" which was to harmonize their various peacekeeping capacity-building programs in Africa. This initiative was to generate an overarching umbrella for a broad range of valuable individual programs and to seek out areas of possible cooperation.[69]

While they were certainly not the only international capacity building programs, the initiatives of the US, France and Britain did much to foster the development of regional security ventures. Other instrumental initiatives in this respect included the UN's assistance to ECCAS via its Standing Advisory Committee on Security Questions in Central Africa as well as the capacity building support Italy and others gave to IGAD via the IGAD Partners Forum.

The second external factor fostering the growth of Africa's regional organizations was the changing attitude of the United Nations towards regionalizing the responsibility for peace and security.[70] Even though Articles 52 and 53 of the UN Charter signed in June 1945 already envisioned a noteworthy role for regional arrangements in the pacific settlement of local disputes as well as in enforcement action, it was only with the end of the Cold War and the concomitant surge in ever more complex UN peace operations that the global body became seriously interested in the concept of burden-sharing.[71] As early as 1992, UN Secretary-General Boutros Boutros-Ghali's *Agenda for Peace* reaffirmed that "regional actions as a matter of decentralization, delegation and cooperation with United Nations efforts could lighten the burden of the Security Council".[72] In his 1995 report on *Improving Preparedness for Conflict Prevention and Peace-keeping in Africa*, the Secretary-General was even more specific:

> The founders of the United Nations, in Chapter VIII of the Charter of the United Nations, envisaged an important role for regional organizations in the maintenance of international peace and security. It is increasingly apparent that the United Nations cannot address every potential and actual conflict troubling the world. Regional or sub-regional organizations sometimes have a comparative advantage in taking the lead role in the prevention and settlement of conflicts and to assist the United Nations in containing them.[73]

As the mandates of UN peace operations continued to increase in complexity (including holding elections, protecting civilians and building government institutions) in the second half of the 1990s, the gap between the demand for UN services and the possible supply widened even further.[74] In Africa, regional organizations like ECOWAS offered one way to fill this growing gap by providing an initial muscle to UN peace operations. This led Boutros-Ghali's successor Kofi Annan to recommend building up their capabilities in order to make them effective partners in his 1998 report on *The Causes of Conflict and the Promotion of Durable Peace.*

> Within the context of the United Nations' primary responsibility for matters of international peace and security, providing support for regional and sub-regional initiatives in Africa is both necessary and desirable. Such support is necessary, because the United Nations lacks the capacity, resources and expertise to address all problems that may arise in Africa. It is desirable because wherever possible the international community should strive to complement rather than supplant African efforts to resolve Africa's problems.[75]

The UN's once critical attitude to Africa's RECs had thus turned into an attempt to nurture them so that they could ease the UN's growing burden.[76] The legitimization inherent in this support did much to boost the growth of the continent's various regional security initiatives.

Notes

[1]   For excellent histories of regional cooperation in Africa see Daniel Bach, *Regionalization in Africa: Integration & Disintegration* (Oxford: Bloomington, 1999), Morten Bøås, *Regions and Regionalization: A Heretic's View* (Uppsala: Nordiska Afrikainstitutet, 2001).

[2]   While some may not accept dependency theory as an accurate description of Africa's economic situation in the 1970s, it is beyond doubt that African states perceived systemic inequality as reason for cooperation. See Patrick McGowan and Dale Smith, "Economic Dependency in Black Africa: An Analysis of Competing Theories," *International Organization* 32, no. 1 (1978).

[3]   OAU, *Charter of the OAU*, Article XX, 1-5 (Addis Ababa, 1963).

[4]   Ibid.: Article II, 1b.

[5]   See Comfort Ero, *ECOMOG: A Model for Africa?*, Monograph Series No. 46 (Pretoria: Institute for Security Studies, 2000).

[6]   While Chapter VIII of the UN Charter acknowledges a major role for regional organizations, it was only under Secretary-General Boutros Boutros-Ghali that regional organizations were encouraged to play such role in order to ease the growing burden on the UN system. See *Agenda for Peace: Preventive Diplomacy, Peace Making and Peacekeeping: Report of the Secretary-General* (UN Document A/47/277-S/24111, 17 June 1992), paragraph 64; see also *Improving Preparedness for Conflict Prevention and Peacekeeping in Africa,"* *Report of the Secretary-General* (UN Document A/50/711 and S/1995/911, 1 November 1995), paragraph 4. Also see Ademola Abass, *Regional*

Organizations and the Development of Collective Security - Beyond Chapter VIII of the UN Charter (Oxford: Hart Publishing, 2004).

[7] ECOWAS initially comprised 16 member states, but membership fell to 15 when Mauritania withdrew in protest in 2002. ECOWAS member states are Benin, Burkina Faso, Cape Verde, Côte d'Ivoire, The Gambia, Ghana, Guinea, Guinea-Bissau, Liberia, Mali, Niger, Nigeria, Senegal, Sierra Leone and Togo.

[8] For a more detailed account of the foundation of ECOWAS see Adebayo Adedeji, "ECOWAS: A Retrospective Journey," in *West Africa's Security Challenges - Building Peace in a Troubled Region*, ed. Adekeye Adebajo and Ismail Rashid (Boulder: Lynne Rienner, 2004).

[9] Among the many events that fostered the growing desire for a regional conflict management mechanism were the mercenary attack on the Republic of Guinea in 1971, the border conflict between Burkina Faso and Mali in 1974 and the *coups d'Etat* in the 1960s. See Patrick McGowan and T. Johnson, "Sixty Coups in Thirty Years - Further Evidence Regarding African Military Coups," *Journal of Modern African Studies* 24, no. 3 (1984).

[10] The impulse for conclusion of the Accord was the same as led to the creation of the CEAO in the first place, that is the creation of a francophone security arrangement particularly after the border war between Burkina Faso and Mali in 1974 had shown that defense links with France could not necessarily deter all forms of local threats. The accord sets out the general principles of the commitment of the parties not to use force to settle any dispute among them and to come to each others assistance in defense against aggression. It was the first multilateral African mutual defense mechanism to be established, and, remarkably, considerable effort was made for its implementation. The Protocol of Application was adopted in 1981 and all the envisaged institutions including the Secretariat were made functional. Between 1981 and 1987, 12 other Protocols and 7 related instruments were adopted. ANAD was eventually integrated into ECOWAS in 2001. See Oluyemi Adeniji, "Mechanisms for Conflict Management in West Africa: Politics of Harmonization " Journal of Humanitarian Assistance, no. 27 (1997).

[11] For more detailed information on the ECOMOG intervention in Liberia see Adekeye Adebajo, *Liberia's Civil War: Nigeria, ECOMOG and Regional Security in West Africa* (Boulder: Lynne Rienner, 2002), Mourtada Déme, *Law, Morality, and International Armed Intervention: The United Nations and ECOWAS in Liberia* (London: Routledge, 2005), Thomas Jaye, *Issues of Sovereignty, Strategy, and Security in the Economic Community of West African States (ECOWAS) Intervention in the Liberian Civil War* (Edwin Mellen Press, 2003), W. Ofuatey-Kodjoe, "Regional Organizations and the Resolution of Internal Conflict," *International Peacekeeping* 1, no. 3 (1994), Margaret Vogt, ed., *The Liberian Crisis and ECOMOG: A Bold Attempt at Regional Peacekeeping* (Lagos: Gabumo Press, 1992), Klaas van Walraven, *The Pretence of Peacekeeping: ECOMOG, West Africa and Liberia, 1990-1998* (The Hague: Netherlands Institute of International Relations, 1999), D Wippman, "Enforcing the Peace: ECOWAS and the Liberian Civil War," in *Enforcing Restraint: Collective Intervention in Internal Conflicts*, ed. L Fisler-Damrosch (New York: Council on Foreign Relations, 1993), 261-302.

[12]   See N Echezons and E Duru, "Conflict Prevention, Management and Resolution: Establishing a Regional Force for Africa," *European Journal of Scientific Research* 8, no. 3 (2005): 39.

[13]   See Ero, *ECOMOG: A Model for Africa?*

[14]   For more detailed information on the Mechanism see Adekeye Adebajo, "The ECOWAS Security Mechanism: Toward a Pax West Africana," in *CODESRIA General Assembly Meeting* (Kampala: 2002), Dorina Bekoe and Aida Mengistu, *Operationalizing the ECOWAS Mechanism for Conflict Prevention, Management, Resolution, Peacekeeping and Security* (New York: International Peace Academy, 2002).

[15]   ECOWAS, *Protocol Relating to the Mechanism for Conflict Prevention, Management, Resolution, Peacekeeping and Security*, Articles 9-14.

[16]   Ibid., Articles 21-22 (for the standby force) and 23-24 (for the early warning system).

[17]   Figure adapted from Funmi Olonisakin, "African Peacekeeping at the Crossroads: An Assessment of the Continent's Evolving Peace and Security Architecture," (New York: United Nations Peacekeeping Best Practices, 2004), Annex I.

[18]   Ademola Abass, "The New Collective Security Mechanism of ECOWAS: Innovations and Problems," *Journal of Conflict and Security Law* 5, no. 2 (2000): 211.

[19]   See Festus Aboagye, "The ECOWAS Security Regime and Its Utility for Africa," in *Peace in Africa - Towards a Collaborative Security Regime*, ed. Shannon Field (Johannesburg: Institute for Global Dialogue, 2004).

[20]   For a more detailed account of the importance of the FLS and SADCC to the development of SADC see W. Breytenbach, "Conflict in Sub-Saharan Africa: From Frontline State to Collective Security," in *The Arusha Paper 2* (1995).

[21]   A good assessment of this role can be found in Gilbert Khadiagala, *Allies in Adversity: The Frontline States in Southern African Security, 1975-1993* (Athens: Ohio University Press, 1994).

[22]   See Robert Jaster, "A Regional Security Role for Africa's Front Line States: Experience and Prospects," in *Adelphi Paper No. 180* (London: International Institute for Strategic Studies, 1983).

[23]   SADC member states are Angola, Botswana, the Democratic Republic of Congo (since 1997), Lesotho, Malawi, Mozambique, Madagascar (since 2005), Mauritius (since 1995), Namibia, South Africa (since 1994), Swaziland, the Seychelles (since 2007), Tanzania, Zambia, and Zimbabwe.

[24]   Previous attempts at institutionalization include the 1995 proposal to create an Association of Southern African States (ASAS). For more details on the establishment of the OPDS see Jakkie Cilliers, "The SADC Organ for Defense, Politics and Security," *ISS Occasional Papers*, no. 10 (1996), L. Fisher and Naison Ngoma, "The SADC Organ: Challenges in the New Millennium," *ISS Occasional Papers*, no. 114 (2005), Hans-Georg Schleicher, "Regionale Sicherheitskooperation Im Südlichen Afrika: SADC and OPDSC," *University of Leipzig Papers on Africa*, no. 78 (2006).

[25]   See Extraordinary SADC Heads of State and Government Summit Communiqué, Gaborone, 28 June 1996

[26] For more information on the OPDS and the difficulties in its implementation see, for example, W. Breytenbach, "Failure of Security Cooperation in SADC: The Suspension of the Organ for Politics, Defense and Security " *South African Journal of International Affairs* 7, no. 1 (2000).

[27] See Extraordinary SADC Heads of State and Government Summit Communiqué, Gaborone, 28 June 1996

[28] Theo Neethling, "Pursuing a Functional Security Community in Southern Africa: Is It Possible after All?," *Strategic Review for Southern Africa* 25, no. 1 (2003): 37.

[29] For more information on the Congo crisis and SADC's involvement see Mark Malan, "Regional Power Politics under Cover of SADC - Running Amok with a Mythical Organ," *ISS Occasional Papers*, no. 35 (1998), Naison Ngoma, "Hawks, Doves or Penguins? A Critical Review of the SADC Military Intervention in the DRC," *ISS Occasional Papers*, no. 88 (2004). For more information on the Lesotho intervention see Fako Likoti, "The 1998 Military Intervention in Lesotho: SADC Peace Mission or Resource War?," *International Peacekeeping* 14, no. 2 (2007), Theo Neethling, "Military Intervention in Lesotho: Perspectives on Operation Boleas and Beyond," *The Online Journal of Peace and Conflict Resolution* 2, no. 2 (1999), Sehoai Santho, "Lesotho: Lessons and Challenges of the SADC Intervention, 1998," in *Sustainable Security in Africa*, ed. Diane Philander (Pretoria: Institute for Security Studies, 2000).

[30] For a good history of this slow evolution see Laurie Nathan, "SADC's Uncommon Approach to Common Security, 1992-2003," *Journal of Southern African Studies* 32, no. 3 (2006). For an alternative view on SADC's evolution see James Sidaway, *Imagined Regional Communities: Integration and Sovereignty in the Global South* (London: Routledge, 2002).

[31] SADC, *Mutual Defense Pact*, Article 9.

[32] For more information on the Strategic Indicative Plan see Anthoni van Nieuwkerk, "Wither SIPO? Gains and Challenges of Implementing RISDP and SIPO," ISS Presentation (4 May 2006). See also J. Ndlovu, "New SADC-ICP Partnership for the implementation of the SIPO," Briefing note delivered at the SADC Consultative Conference, 27 April 2006, Windhoek.

[33] Mwesiga Baregu and Christopher Landsberg, eds., *From Cape to Congo: Southern Africa's Evolving Security Challenges* (Boulder: Lynne Rienner, 2003).

[34] See Naison Ngoma, *Prospects for a Security Community in Southern Africa: An Analysis of Regional Security in the Southern African Development Community* (Pretoria: Institute for Security Studies, 2005), Naison Ngoma, "SADC's Mutual Defense Pact: A Final Move to a Security Community?," *The Round Table* 93, no. 375 (2004), Naison Ngoma, "SADC: Towards a Security Community?," *African Security Review* 12, no. 3 (2003).

[35] IGAD started with six member states, namely, Djibouti, Ethiopia, Kenya, Somalia, the Sudan and Uganda. Eritrea joined after attaining independence in 1993 and withdrew again in protest in 2007.

[36] For an excellent discussion of the establishment of IGADD see Dirk Spilker, *Regional Security am Horn von Afrika im Rahmen der IGAD: Bisherige Entwicklung, Probleme und Perspektiven*, unpublished study (Potsdam: University of Potsdam, 2005). Also see Monica Juma, "The Intergovernmental

Authority on Development and the East African Community," in *From Cape to Congo: Southern Africa's Evolving Security Challenges*, ed. Mwesiga Baregu and Christopher Landsberg (Boulder: Lynne Rienner, 2003).

[37] Francis Deng, *Mediating the Sudanese Conflict: A Challenge for IGADD, CSIS Africa Notes No. 169* (Washington DC: Centre for Strategic and International Studies, 1995), 5.

[38] See IGAD, *Agreement Establishing the Intergovernmental Authority on Development (IGAD)*, Nairobi, 21 March 1996.

[39] IGAD, Khartoum Declaration of the 8th Summit of Heads of State and Government, Khartoum, 23 November 2000, Article 3a.

[40] See Kasaija Apuuli, *IGAD's Protocol on Conflict Early Warning and Response Mechanism (CEWARN): A Ray of Hope in Conflict Prevention* (Utrecht: Arbeitsgruppe Internationale Politik, 2004).

[41] For more information on the first EAC and its collapse see H. Heimsoeth, "Die Auflösung Der Ostafrikanischen Gemeinschaft," *Verfassung und Recht in Übersee* 13 (1980), D. Kappeler, "Causes Et Conséquences De La Désintegration De La Communauté Est-Africaine," *Politique Étrangère* 43 (1978), Agrippah Mugomba, "Regional Organizations and African Underdevelopment: The Collapse of the East African Community," *The Journal of modern African studies* 16, no. 2 (1978), Christian Potholm and Richard Friedland, eds., *Integration and Disintegration in East Africa* (Washington DC: University Press of America, 1980).

[42] See "East African Military Chiefs Discuss Ties," *Panafrican News Agency*, 20 January 1998; "East African Armies for Joint Training-Minister", *New Vision* (Kampala), 23 February 1997

[43] Eric Berman and Katie Sams, *Peacekeeping in Africa: Capabilities and Culpabilities* (Geneva: United Nations Institute for Disarmament Research, 2000), 199-200.

[44] Willy Faria, "Ministers Hail Joint Military Operations," *Kenya Times*, 21 June 1998, 2.

[45] For more information on the revival of the EAC see Diodorus Kamala, "The Achievements and Challenges of the New East-African Community Cooperation," *University of Hull Research Memoranda*, no. 58 (2006), Sam Tulya-Muhika, "Revival of the East African Cooperation and Its Institutional Framework," in *EAC, Perspectives on Regional Integration and Cooperation in East Africa* (Arusha: EAC, 2000).

[46] EAC, *Treaty Establishing the East African Community*, Articles 124 and 125.

[47] United Nations, *United Nations Concern for Peace and Security in Central Africa: Reference Document*, New York (1997), 2.

[48] United Nations, *Conférence sur la promotion de la confiance de la sécurité et du développement dans le cadre de la Communauté Économique des États de l'Afrique Centrale*, New York (1988).

[49] UN Document A/RES/46/37 B, 6 December 1991.

[50] UN Document A/51/274 – S/1996/631, Annex, *Final Declaration of the First Summit of Heads of State and Government of Countries Members of the United Nations Standing Advisory Committee on Security Questions in Central Africa, 8 July 1996*, 6 August 1996, para. 4.

[51] For a good historical discussion of the creation of COPAX see Musifiky Mwanasali, "Politics and Security in Central Africa," *African Journal of Political Science* 4, no. 2 (1999). For the original text of the agreement see UN Document A/53/868 – S/1999/303, Annex I, *Decision on the creation of a mechanism for promotion, maintenance and consolidation of peace and security in Central Africa, adopted on 25 February 1999*, 17 March 1999.

[52] Ibid.: Article 2.

[53] Mwanasali, "Politics and Security in Central Africa.", Bellarmin Ndongui, "Central Africa: Collective Security and Regional Integration," *African Geopolitics*, no. 23 (2006).

[54] Berman and Sams, *Peacekeeping in Africa: Capabilities and Culpabilities*, 193.

[55] Ian Lesser, *Security in North Africa: Internal and External Challenges* (Santa Monica: Rand, 1993), Mohammed-Mahmoud Mohamedou, "The Arab Maghreb Union of North Africa: The Challenge of Regional Integration and Mediterranean Cooperation," *The Ralph Bunche Institute of the United Nations Occasional Paper Series*, no. 26 (1997).

[56] See Adebayo Oyebade, "The End of the Cold War in Africa: Implications for Conflict Management and Resolution," in *Africa after the Cold War: The Changing Perspectives on Security*, ed. Adebayo Oyebade and Abiodun Alao (Trenton: Africa World Press, 1998), 166-176.

[57] For more detail see Thomas Weiss, ed., *Beyond UN Subcontracting: Task-Sharing with Regional Security Arrangements and Service-Providing NGOs* (Basingstoke: Macmillan Press, 1998).

[58] See, for example, Michael Clough, "The United States and Africa: The Policy of Cynical Disengagement," *Current History* 91 (1992): 193-198, Marguerite Michaels, "Retreat from Africa," *Foreign Affairs* 72, no. 1 (1993): 93-108.

[59] For a detailed discussion of these initiatives see Eric Berman, *French, UK and US Policies to Support Peacekeeping in Africa: Current Status and Future Prospects, Paper No. 622* (Oslo: Norwegian Institute of International Affairs, 2002), Eric Berman and Katie Sams, *Constructive Disengagement: Western Efforts to Develop African Peacekeeping, Monograph Series No. 33* (Pretoria: Institute for Security Studies, 1998).

[60] NSR 30 as quoted in Emmanuel Aning, "African Crisis Response Initiative and the New African Security (Dis)Order," *African Journal of Political Science* 6, no. 1 (2001): 45.

[61] For a more detailed review of US efforts see Benedikt Franke, "Enabling a Continent to Help Itself: US Military Capacity Building and Africa's Emerging Security Architecture," *Strategic Insights* VI, no. 1 (2007).

[62] Chris Alden, "From Neglect to 'Virtual Engagement': The United States and Its New Paradigm for Africa," *African Affairs* 99, no. 396 (2000): 355-371.

[63] Letitia Lawson, "US Africa Policy since the Cold War," *Strategic Insights* VI, no. 1 (2007): 3.

[64] Financial Times, 21 September 1994: 4

[65] Warren Christopher, *Speech to the OAU*, Addis Ababa, 11 October 1996.

---

[66]   See Report of the Secretary-General on Standby Arrangements for Peacekeeping (UN Document S/1995/943, 10 November 1995).

[67]   For more information on ACRF/ACRI see Mark Malan, "US Response to African Crises: An Overview and Preliminary Analysis of ACRI," in *ISS Occasional Paper No. 24* (Pretoria: 1997), Marshall McCallie, "ACRI: Positive Engagement with Africa," *USIA Electronic Journal* 3, no. 2 (1998).

[68]   For more information on RECAMP see Oliver de Cevins, "Pour Que RECAMP Ne Rime Plus Avec Décampe," *Défense Nationale* 59, no. 3 (2003), Herve Giraud, "Efforts at Conflict Prevention and Resolution: The French Experience," in *Sustainable Security in Africa*, ed. Diane Philander (Pretoria: Institute for Security Studies, 2000).

[69]   See Alice Walpole, "A British Perspective on the P3 Initiative for Enhancing African Peacekeeping Capability," in *Resolute Partners: Building Peacekeeping Capacity in Southern Africa*, ed. Mark Malan (Pretoria: Institute for Security Studies, 1998).

[70]   See Jane Boulden, *Dealing with Conflict in Africa: The United Nations and Regional Organizations* (Basingstoke: Palgrave Macmillan, 2003).

[71]   See Abass, *Regional Organizations and the Development of Collective Security - Beyond Chapter VIII of the UN Charter.*

[72]   See *Agenda for Peace: Preventive Diplomacy, Peace Making and Peacekeeping* (UN Document A/47/277-S/24111, 17 June 1992) para. 64.

[73]   See *Improving preparedness for conflict prevention and peace-keeping in Africa: Report of the Secretary-General* (UN Document A/50/711-S/1995/911, 1 November 1995) paragraph 4.

[74]   Berman and Sams, *Peacekeeping in Africa: Capabilities and Culpabilities*, 379-380.

[75]   See *The Causes of Conflict and the Promotion of Durable Peace and Sustainable Development in Africa: Report of the Secretary-General* (UN Document A/52/871-S/1998/318, 13 April 1998) paragraph 41. Also see UN Press Release SC/6575, *Security Council urges SG to aid African Organizations*, 18 September 1998.

[76]   For critiques of this development see Eric Berman, "The Security Council's Increasing Reliance on Burden-Sharing: Collaboration or Abrogation," *International Peacekeeping* 4, no. 1 (1998), David Francis et al., *Dangers of Co-Deployment - UN Cooperative Peacekeeping in Africa* (Aldershot: Ashgate, 2005).

5

The Revival of Continental Security Cooperation

In the early 1990s, many observers believed that the increasing devolution of security initiatives described in the previous chapter would inevitably mean the end to any continental peace and security scheme. However, quite to the contrary, this devolution actually turned out to be one of the developments facilitating the revival of continental security cooperation at the end of the 1990s, others being the galvanizing proliferation of conflicts following the Cold War, the diminishing interest of the international community and a twofold change in the continental self-conception. Before analyzing these developments in detail, this chapter will track the steps that led to the institutionalization of the AU's current peace and security architecture via the OAU's establishment of a Mechanism for Conflict Prevention, Management and Resolution in June 1993, the Sirte Declaration of September 1999, the Durban Summit of July 2002 and the AU's subsequent efforts to realize Kwame Nkrumah's dream of permanent and structured continental security cooperation.

The OAU's Conflict Management Mechanism

As with the regional organizations, the end of the Cold War, the concomitant proliferation of violent conflicts throughout the continent and the simultaneous disengagement of the international community quickly forced the OAU to reconsider its own role with regard to Africa's security. As early as July 1990, the OAU Summit in Addis Ababa noted the urgent need for collective action to tackle the continent's manifold security problems. The outcome of this summit was a *Declaration on the Political and Socio-Economic Situation in Africa and the Fundamental Changes Taking Place in the World* in which the Heads of State and Government stated that:

> We realize that the possibilities of achieving the objectives we have set [socio-economic transformation and integration, democratization] will be constrained as long as an atmosphere of lasting peace and stability does not prevail in Africa. We therefore renew our determination to work together towards the peaceful and speedy resolution of all the conflicts on our continent.[1]

The next important step was made in May 1991 at the landmark African Leadership Conference on "Security, Stability, Development and Cooperation" in Kampala during which the continent's leaders finally appeared willing to overcome many of the hindrances that had plagued previous attempts at continental security cooperation.[2] Acknowledging that "there is a link between security, stability, development and cooperation in Africa", they deliberated on a proposal to launch a permanent Conference on Peace, Security, Stability, Development and Cooperation in Africa (CSSDCA) modeled on the Conference for Security and Cooperation in Europe (CSCE, later OSCE) in order to institutionalize the increasing efforts at continental security cooperation. The resultant Kampala Document was subsequently discussed by the OAU Council of Ministers and the June 1991 OAU Summit in Abuja both of which recognized the importance and necessity of replacing the OAU's obviously inadequate *ad hoc* approach to security and conflict management with an institutionalized framework.

Having been tasked to work out implementation options for such a framework, OAU Secretary-General Salim Ahmed Salim proposed the creation of a Mechanism for Conflict Prevention, Management and Resolution in his 1992 report *Resolving Conflicts in Africa: Proposals for Action*.[3] The African leaders endorsed the report and the OAU finally began to conceptualize the structure and process by which it could effectively manage conflicts in Africa. Hardly a year later in June 1993, the 29th OAU Assembly of Heads of State and Government assembled in Cairo to announce the creation of the OAU's Mechanism for Conflict Prevention, Management and Resolution. Following a foreign ministers meeting in Addis Ababa in November 1993 which approved the principles that would guide its establishment, the Mechanism was eventually inaugurated at the June 1994 OAU summit.

While the establishment of the Mechanism marked the beginning of the OAU's second generation peace and security agenda, it was still lagging far behind the proactive stance towards conflict management of regional organizations such as ECOWAS. In fact, the Mechanism's focus explicitly lay on conflict prevention rather than conflict management and resolution. According to Said Djinnit, OAU Secretary-

General Salim's Director of Cabinet, during negotiations at the Dakar Summit in July 1992, "a clear consensus emerged against the involvement of the OAU in peacekeeping".[4] The Secretariat's proposal that the OAU Defense Commission be tasked with performing an advisory function within the Mechanism to strengthen and harmonize member countries' peacekeeping policies also received little support. This emphasis on prevention is clearly spelt out in the Declaration of the Assembly of Heads of State and Government establishing the Mechanism, which states:

> The Mechanism will have, as a primary objective, the anticipation and prevention of conflicts; in circumstances where conflicts have occurred it will be its responsibility to undertake peacemaking and peacebuilding functions in order to facilitate the resolution of those conflicts. In this respect, civilian and military missions of limited scope and duration may be mounted and deployed. [...] Emphasis on anticipatory and preventive measures and concerted action in peacemaking and peacebuilding will obviate the need to resort to the complex and resource-demanding peacekeeping operations, which our countries will find difficult to finance.[5]

Despite this somewhat artificially constrained focus, the OAU Mechanism was a significant improvement on previous structures.[6] Besides incorporating the four units of the OAU Conflict Management Centre which was created in March 1992,[7] it provided for a new decision-making body called the Central Organ and a separate source of funding for peace and security initiatives called the Peace Fund.

The Central Organ which was modeled on the Bureau of the Assembly of Heads of State and Government was to be the primary decision-making body regarding peace and security on the continent.[8] It was composed of 15 member states elected annually according to geographical and rotational criteria as well as the states of the old and new OAU presidencies. The General Secretariat, with the help of the Conflict Management Centre and its four divisions, was to be the executive arm of the Central Organ ensuring that all political decisions were implemented as directed. In its work, the General Secretariat was supported by the OAU Peace Fund which was designed specifically to finance initiatives of the Central Organ, and more generally, to develop the Conflict Management Division. Divided into a General Peace Fund and a Special Contributions Fund, it initially provided for five per cent of the OAU's annual regular budget to be earmarked for peace and security initiatives, which netted about $2 million a year as the money was to be taken regardless of the state of arrears.[9]

Continental Security Cooperation until the Sirte Summit

The time between June 1993 and September 1999 was characterized by two independent developments in continental security cooperation. The first was the transformation of the OAU into a more credible organization with an increased visibility and an elevated profile in the conflict management arena. This was mainly due to the mechanism's activism.[10] The second development was the resurgence of attempts to create a Pan-African peacekeeping force.[11]

Immediately following its creation in June 1993, the Mechanism for Conflict Prevention, Management and Resolution began to transform the conflict management role of the OAU.[12] Finally overcoming its institutional paralysis, the OAU increasingly engaged in the quiet and preventive diplomacy of mediation and conflict resolution through the good offices of the OAU Secretary-General, special envoys and representatives, fact finding as well as observation and monitoring missions. In July 1993, for example, the OAU helped to broker the Arusha Peace Agreement for Rwanda and, in its first intervention since the debacle in Chad in 1981, quickly deployed the Neutral Military Observer Group (NMOG) with 50 observers to monitor its implementation.[13] In late 1993, the OAU Special Envoy Mohamed Sahnoun helped to de-escalate dangerous political tensions in Congo-Brazzaville.[14] In February 1994, the OAU send a 67-observer strong mission to Burundi (OMIB) in order to restore peace through confidence building measures. The OAU also supported the activities of ECOWAS and the UN in Liberia and later in Sierra Leone, helped to broker the Lusaka Protocol in Angola in November 1994, aided the resultant UN Verification Mission in Angola (UNAVEM III) and assisted with the mediation efforts of IGAD in the Sudanese civil war. In 1997, the OAU and the UN send a joint special envoy (Mohamed Sahnoun) to mediate the crises in the Great Lakes region. In the same year, the OAU also deployed an observer mission to the Comoros (OMIC) to monitor the security situation and build confidence among the parties after the island of Anjouan had sought secession. Simultaneously, it supported the deployment of the Inter-African Mission to Monitor the Implementation of the Bangui Agreement (MISAB) to the Central African Republic which was hailed by UN Secretary-General Kofi Annan as a worthy example of preventive diplomacy that has sent a "positive and important signal to the region and to Africa as a whole".[15]

This extraordinary activism contrasts starkly with the OAU's lackluster performance in the first three decades of its existence. Constrained by its mantra of the respect for its member's territorial integrity, the OAU's Commission on Mediation, Arbitration and Reconciliation had been moribund for much of its existence and did not get involved in the civil wars in Nigeria, Sudan, Angola, Mozambique, Ethiopia and Uganda. When the OAU finally intervened in the Chadian civil war in 1981, its operation was marred by severe logistical and financial difficulties and had to be withdrawn quickly. The resultant disappointment about the OAU's inability and unwillingness to provide continental solutions to Africa's most pressing problems was summed up memorably by its Secretary-General during the 1992 Dakar negotiations on the establishment of an OAU Mechanism for Conflict Prevention, Management and Resolution:

> Many times, we have looked around for the OAU to intervene constructively in a conflict situation only to find that it is not there, and when present, to realize that it is not adequately equipped to be decisively helpful.[16]

However, while the Mechanism for Conflict Prevention, Management and Resolution certainly increased the OAU's visibility and elevated its profile in the conflict management arena, its creation did not lead to a paradigm shift. Despite its operations in Rwanda, Burundi and the Comoros and its increasingly numerous efforts at mediation and conflict prevention, the OAU remained a peripheral actor compared to the UN and regional organizations like ECOWAS. It did so because it proved unable to overcome the financial, organizational and mandate-related limitations that had already prescribed its conflict management role in the pre-1993 period.[17] Its Peace Fund did not generate sufficient financial resources,[18] its mechanism, according to Christopher Bakwesegha, former head of the OAU's Conflict Management Division was not operationalized properly and its shortcomings not resolved timely enough,[19] and its actions continued to be hampered by key provisions in its charter such as the non-interference in member states' internal affairs and the inviolability of the territorial status quo (Articles III 2 and 3 respectively). Nonetheless, the establishment of the mechanism in 1993 and its subsequent activities until 1999, however limited they may have been, gave an important impetus to the OAU's efforts to assume responsibility for peace and security on the continent. They also lay the technical foundation for later operations through the building of administrative know-how and the development of standard operation procedures and rules of engagement.

The second notable development characterizing continental security cooperation in the period between the establishment of the OAU

Mechanism for Conflict Prevention, Management and Resolution in June 1993 and the Sirte Summit of September 1999 was the recurrence of attempts to establish a Pan-African peacekeeping force that could be rapidly deployed in times of crisis. Unlike the attempts described in chapter three, the renewed efforts at continental military integration did not spring from Pan-African euphoria but were mostly motivated by pragmatic considerations such as the inability of African forces to react to the crises in Somalia and Rwanda and the growing disinterest of the international community. As part of the resultant quest for "African solutions to African problems", many of the continent's states began to explore seriously the question of establishing a joint force that could intervene in crises as ECOMOG had done in Liberia. In fact, the establishment of such a force had already been recommended by the same 1992 report of OAU Secretary-General Salim which had also proposed the creation of the Mechanism for Conflict Prevention, Management and Resolution.

> The Defense Commission can assist the Bureau [that is, the Central Organ] in the peacekeeping process by ensuring the standardization of the training and the harmonization of the different components of a possible inter-African peacekeeping force which may be identified at national level for possible deployment in conflict situations. In this context, it is recommended that within the Armed Forces of each OAU Member State there should be earmarked a unit or units which, in addition to performing regular functions, will also be trained in peacekeeping.[20]

The idea of a Pan-African peacekeeping force was discussed at length during the meetings in Dakar and Cairo, but in the end the expected costs were considered prohibitive and the mechanism's focus was restricted to conflict prevention rather than conflict management or resolution.[21] However, Western powers, most notably the United States, the United Kingdom and France, anxious to see an African alternative to their own involvement in the continent's messy conflicts, continued to pressure for the establishment of such a force. In November 1994, for example, France invited 34 African nations to a conference in Biarritz in order to discuss the formation of an African peacekeeping force and its logistical requirements. According to the *Washington Post*, France proposed to train, equip and finance such a force in conjunction with other European powers and the United States,[22] aiming, as Adebayo Oyebade wrote, "to put squarely on Africa's shoulders the responsibility of keeping the peace in the continent, therefore absolving the West from any entanglement in African conflicts".[23]

Another two-day conference was held in Cairo in January 1995 at which military and political experts from the United Kingdom, Canada, France, the United States and Japan joined their counterparts from 14 African states and representatives from the OAU and the UN to discuss the formation of such a force.[24] At a subsequent week-long meeting of 20 African states held in Harare in February 1995 and attended by Britain, France and the United States the creation of an African standby arrangement was proposed as potential solution to the huge problems still confronting the deployment of African forces in a peacekeeping context.[25] During the meeting much stress was laid upon Africa's chronic lack of military assets and the resultant undignified "begging syndrome" and "humiliating reliance upon donor countries".[26] Participants were reminded that the OAU's peacekeeping operation in Chad was totally reliant upon French logistic support, that the OAU's Neutral Military Observer Group, deployed to Rwanda in 1993, was paralyzed by a lack of vehicle support and that the OAU Mission in Burundi was emasculated by an almost total failure of communications with a lack of contact with Bujumbura lasting "sometimes almost for a month".[27] The co-host of the meeting, Field Marshal Lord Peter Inge, Chief of the British Defense Staff, subsequently suggested that the establishment of OAU standby forces along the model of the OSCE and financed by the international community might be able to resolve these critical shortcomings.[28]

The OAU debated this suggestion at its summit in June 1995 during which African leaders agreed to place their armed services on standby for a possible intervention in increasingly unstable Burundi.[29] They also discussed a plan to create two standby centers, one in Cairo and one in Harare, as hubs for a continental rapid deployment force. Troops for such a force would be drawn from national armies, trained and deployed from either center and would operate under the aegis of the UN.[30]

The idea of an earmarked standby as opposed to a standing force received mixed responses from the African states. While some states were in favor of a standing multinational force, like the African High Command advocated by Kwame Nkrumah in the early 1960s, others were deterred by the high costs and political implications. Several states put forward their own suggestions for an African peacekeeping force, most notably Togo whose proposal was deemed to "have all the legal and administrative ingredients needed to bolster action on the formation of the much vaunted Pan-African peacekeeping force".[31] The Togolese proposal envisaged a force nucleus of 3,000 troops accompanied and monitored by a flexible, military-dominated, military-controlled but not-permanent body with the declared aims of preventing conflicts, keeping and restoring peace, consolidating peace and carrying out humanitarian missions for refugees and displaced persons, and, if necessary, enforcing or imposing peace. Even though the plan benefited from South African support and came in the wake of the US-sponsored African Crisis Response Initiative, it was rejected by the majority of OAU member states as premature.

At their first meeting in June 1996, the OAU chiefs of defense staff instead agreed that "the concept of standby arrangements and earmarked units may be expensive but is absolutely necessary" and that "each country should inform the OAU General Secretariat of what it is capable of earmarking in terms of the number and type of troops".[32] At their second meeting, in October 1997, they took the issue further in recommending that

> ...the OAU could earmark a brigade-sized contribution to standby arrangements from each of the five African sub-regions as a starting point, which could then be adjusted upwards or downwards according to evolving circumstances. If the prevailing situation in a given sub-region does not allow for this, bilateral agreements should be reached with the countries of the region individually. The OAU should identify about 500 trained military and civilian observers (100 from each sub-region) as an appropriate starting point for a standby capacity. OAU member states, individually or as part of sub-regional organizations, should supply the conflict management division with the same data on strengths, tables of equipment, etc. as that which they provide to UN DPKO.[33]

In March 1998, the OAU Council of Ministers finally agreed that an eventual African peacekeeping force should be made up of sub-regional brigades under the OAU's command and control, within the framework of the OAU Central Organ.[34] This decision provided the basis for the conceptual development of the ASF in the early years of the African Union.

While the activism of the OAU's Mechanism on Conflict Prevention, Management and Resolution and the attempts to create a Pan-African peacekeeping force were the most prominent developments characterizing continental security cooperation in the period between June 1993 and September 1999, they were far from the only ones. The OAU efforts to establish a continental early warning system for conflict prevention since 1994, for example, should also be mentioned as should the attempt by Nigeria's President Olusegun Obasanjo to re-launch the Kampala Document and its Conference on Peace, Security, Stability, Development and Cooperation in Africa in July 1999.

All these developments were, however, overtaken by the events of September 1999. Colonel Muammar al-Gaddafi had used the discussions on a reform of the OAU initiated by the newly elected Presidents of South Africa and Nigeria, Thabo Mbeki and Olusegun Obasanjo during the Algiers Summit of July 1999 to invite Africa's leaders to an extraordinary summit on this topic to Libya. The OAU Heads of State and Government accepted this invitation and assembled for their 4th Extraordinary Summit in September 1999 in al-Gaddafi's home town, the Libyan sea resort of Sirte, in order to review the OAU Charter and "discuss ways and means to increase the organization's effectiveness".[35] At the summit themed "Strengthening OAU capacity to enable it to meet the challenges of the new millennium", the Libyan leader surprisingly revived Kwame Nkrumah's vision of Pan-African unity and called for the creation of a "United States of Africa" with a single army, currency and powerful leadership. Whether he did so because he wanted to overcome his pariah image by redeeming himself as international statesman or simply because he had really internalized the Pan-African ideology of Nkrumah,[36] his proposal for a total overhaul of OAU structures fell on fertile soil. With its original task, that is, the total liberation of the African continent, completed and discontent over its inability to provide its members with a cooperative platform to effectively confront Africa's economic and political marginalization growing, calls for structural reforms of the OAU had become increasingly frequent in the second half of the 1990s. Several states such as South Africa and Nigeria had already tabled their own proposals for such reforms when Libya's bold move and promise to initially bankroll any new organization opened a unique window of opportunity. While not prepared to accept the total political and economic unification inherent in Gaddafi's United States of Africa, the continent's leaders did agree on the need for greater political cooperation and economic integration to overcome Africa's problems and the resultant imperative for institutional reform,[37] especially as the repeated hijacking of ECOWAS and SADC by powerful lead states had begun to nourish doubts about the wisdom of solely relying on regional organizations to work towards peace and security.[38] To this purpose, they adopted the Sirte Declaration which called for the transformation of the OAU into a structurally more promising African Union, the creation of a Pan-African Parliament as well as the acceleration of the economic integration process mapped out in the 1991 Abuja Treaty.

From the Sirte Declaration to the Durban Summit

The Sirte Declaration was followed by the summit at Lomé in July 2000 which adopted the Constitutive Act of the African Union and the summit at Lusaka in July 2001 which approved the implementation plan and formally established the AU. In July 2002, the Assembly of the Heads of State and Government of the AU met for their first ordinary session in Durban. These events and their genesis have been described in great detail elsewhere and so this section will concentrate on those developments of that period that were of direct relevance to the evolution of continental security cooperation.[39]

The Sirte Declaration itself contained rather little on issues of peace and security. While the OAU Heads of State and Government did, in fact, pledge to "eliminate the scourge of conflicts" and to convene an African Ministerial Conference on Security, Stability, Development and Cooperation as soon as possible, no specific mention was made of the Mechanism for Conflict Prevention, Management and Resolution or its Central Organ.[40] Even though the Lomé Declaration, adopted by the Heads of State and Government at their summit in July 2000, did refer to the mechanism and pledged to strengthen it and other African capacities for conflict management,[41] the AU's Constitutive Act, adopted at the same summit, again failed to mention it. In fact, despite the contribution that the mechanism, the associated Conflict Management Centre and the Peace Fund had made to the OAU's organizational profile over much of the previous decade, the act did not make any reference to an institutionalized framework for security cooperation and conflict management at all. To be sure, the act did contain a number of very relevant provisions, most notably the groundbreaking Articles 4(h) and (j). The former allowed for the AU to intervene in a member state in case of war crimes, genocide and crimes against humanity. The latter accorded member states the right to request intervention from the AU to restore peace and security. Both articles represented a clear departure from the constraining principles of the OAU Charter and have since been covered in great detail in the literature.[42] For this reason, it should suffice to point to the end of this chapter for a discussion of the conceptual mitigation of the OAU's norm of non-intervention and the concomitant shift from regime security to human security during the 1990s. The Constitutive Act entered into force on May 26, 2001 after Nigeria had become the 36th OAU member state to deposit its instrument of ratification.

It was not until the Lusaka Summit in July 2001 that the Assembly of the OAU Heads of State and Government made an explicit decision on the fate of the Mechanism for Conflict Prevention, Management and Resolution. Besides the establishment of the four principle organs of the AU (that is, the Assembly of the Union, the Executive Council, the Permanent Representatives' Committee and the Commission) and the creation of the New Partnership for African Development (NEPAD) as development program of the new Union, the summit finally also provided for the incorporation of the Mechanism with the possibility of changing the name of the Central Organ.[43] While this was an important first step towards an AU conflict management capability, the parallel creation of a security agenda within NEPAD complicated the situation. A meeting of the NEPAD Implementing Committee of Heads of State and Government in Abuja in October 2001 decided to make capacity building on peace and security a NEPAD responsibility. The same communiqué announced a Sub-Committee on Peace and Security to focus on conflict management, prevention and resolution in Africa, to be chaired by President Mbeki.[44]

Following long debates on the rules of procedure, the second meeting of the OAU Permanent Representatives and Experts held in Addis Ababa from 14 to 21 February 2002 was charged with deliberating on the incorporation of the OAU Mechanism for Conflict Prevention, Management and Resolution into the structures of the AU.[45] The ECOWAS countries supported by Algeria, Libya, Egypt and South Africa proposed the transformation of the Central Organ into an AU Peace and Security Council (PSC) with 17 member states, ten of which would be permanent members. This proposal was strongly opposed by the delegation of Tanzania which, along with several others, rejected the idea of permanent membership and any potential veto power conferred upon individual states. As no agreement could be reached, the Draft Protocol Relating to the Establishment of the PSC forwarded to the Special Session of the OAU Council of Ministers that directly preceded Durban Summit entailed three different options for the composition of the Council. The first option provided for fifteen members elected by the Assembly for a term of two years. In the second option, the PSC would consist of five permanent members and ten non-permanent members elected by the Assembly for two years. In the third option, ten members of the PSC would be elected for a term of two years and five members would be elected for a term of three years. After a lengthy debate on the matter, the special session adopted the third option, stating that the second category of elected members would ensure continuity while avoiding permanence.[46]

Another controversial issue surrounding the PSC Protocol was the inclusion of a reference to a Pan-African military force. Having already followed the discussions on this concept through nearly five decades, it should not come as a surprise that its eventual realization was not an easy affair. On the contrary, despite the aforementioned agreement by the OAU Council of Ministers from March 1998 to base an eventual African peacekeeping force on regional standby brigades under the OAU's command, there were such serious disagreements on the composition and purpose of the future force in the run-up to the Durban Summit that the entire concept was at risk. While old-guard leaders including Colonel Gaddafi (who actually called for an amendment of the Constitutive Act to include a single standing army for Africa), Robert Mugabe and former Kenyan President Daniel Arap Moi saw the primary purpose of the force as that of defending Africa from external threats, many of the younger leaders, including Thabo Mbeki, saw its main purpose as a peacekeeping force for intervention in the continent's internal conflicts.[47] In the end, the younger leaders were able to build on the 1998 compromise and their version of an African Standby Force was included in the protocol.

Following these decisions, the protocol was finalized in great haste in time for approval by the Heads of State and Government during the inaugural summit of the African Union on 9 July 2002. Once ratified by a simple majority of member states, (27 out of 53), the Peace and Security Council would replace the Central Organ and the Mechanism and serve as the "standing decision-making organ for the prevention, management and resolution of conflicts [...] a collective security and early warning arrangement to facilitate timely and efficient response to conflict and crisis situations in Africa".[48]

Besides the ASF, the Protocol Relating to the Establishment of the Peace and Security Council adopted by the Durban Summit also provided for an eminent Panel of the Wise, a Continental Early Warning System, a Military Staff Committee and a special Peace Fund as the main pillars of the new African Peace and Security Architecture (APSA).[49] Within this framework, the PSC was given six principal functions by the protocol ranging from the promotion of peace and the provision of early warning and preventive diplomacy to disaster management and the conduct of humanitarian interventions.[50] In order to be able to fulfill these functions, the PSC was accorded eighteen specific powers by the protocol including the authority to mount and deploy peace operations and to implement the common defense policy of the Union.[51]

While the Constitutive Act initially did not provide for the post of a Commissioner for Peace and Security, Article 10(4) of the PSC Protocol remedied this surprising omission. The same article also established a PSC Secretariat within the Department for Peace and Security to support the Commissioner's work.

Despite its comprehensiveness and scope – the Commission for Peace and Security was to be by far the largest of the ten AU commissions in terms of manpower and funding – the AU's peace and security structure described above was only one of three continental security initiative promoted at the time, the others being Olusegun Obasanjo's Conference on Security, Stability, Development and Cooperation in Africa (CSSDCA) and Thabo Mbeki's New Partnership for Africa's Development (NEPAD).

The initial session of the CSSDCA was timed to coincide with the launch of the AU at Durban in July 2002. At it, the Heads of State and Government agreed to subscribe to "a set of core values and key commitments to buttress the process of security and stability in Africa".[52] Even though the memorandum of understanding signed stated that "the CSSDCA process forms part and parcel of the work program of the AU Commission", many critics feared that it would lead to an unnecessary duplication of effort in the security sphere.

The same was true for NEPAD. While primarily conceived to eradicate poverty and place African countries on a path of sustainable growth and development, NEPAD also included a peace and security initiative which focused on institutional capacity building for conflict early warning, peacemaking and post-conflict reconciliation, rehabilitation and reconstruction. At a Heads of State and Government NEPAD Implementation Committee Meeting in Abuja in March 2002, six priorities were identified for the sub-committee on peace and security which included enhancing capacity to conduct strategic assessments of conflict situations and assisting in resource mobilization for the African Peace Fund.[53]

Before elaborating on the implementation and operationalization of this array of initiatives and structures, it is important to point out that while the deliberations about its transformation were ongoing the OAU did continue to engage in notable conflict management efforts in the period between the Sirte Declaration and the Durban Summit. The two most prominent certainly were its complex mediation attempts during the war in the Democratic Republic of Congo and the OAU Liaison Mission in Ethiopia and Eritrea (OLMEE).[54] While the former were a reaction to the outbreak of the largest war in modern African history which directly involved eight African states and more than twenty-five armed groups, the latter was created as part of the OAU-brokered Agreement on the Cessation of Hostilities signed by Ethiopia and Eritrea in June 2000. Its purpose was to facilitate the implementation of the agreement in a pioneering partnership with the United Nations Mission in Ethiopia and Eritrea (UNMEE).[55] Both efforts contributed in their own way to the consolidation of the OAU's role in continental conflict management.

The Birth of the African Union and the Realization of an Idea

On 9 July 2002 the African continent entered a new era when the African Union was formally inaugurated in Durban. Its Constitutive Act and the PSC Protocol substantially enhanced the institutional basis for continental security cooperation. This section will briefly describe the gradual implementation and operationalization of this basis and thus provide the institutional context for the in-depth analysis of the architecture and two of its pillars (that is, the ASF and the CEWS) in chapters seven, eight and nine.

Following the Durban Summit, many critics had voiced their fear that Africa would once again prove to be better at conceiving cooperative structures than implementing them.[56] These fears, however, were mostly misplaced. As set out in Article 33 of the AU's Constitutive Act, an interim period began with effect from 9 July 2002 to last for the duration of one year. During this time the OAU Charter was to remain operative in order to "enable the OAU to undertake the necessary measures regarding the devolution of its assets and liabilities to the Union".[57] Following the end of the interim period in July 2003, the 2nd Ordinary Session of the Assembly held in Maputo elected the Chairperson (Alpha Konare, a former President of Mali) and the Deputy Chairperson (Patrick Mazimhaka from Rwanda) of the Commission. The Executive Council appointed the other commissioners. The new commission assumed office on 1 September 2003.

The Maputo Summit also approved the so-called Maputo Structure, that is, the detailed organizational structure of the AU Commission. Once fully established, the Department for Peace and Security was to have a staff complement of 53, including the PSC Secretariat and a Peace Support Operations Division (PSOD). This number excluded the various Special Envoys, Special Representatives, AU Field Missions and other initiatives that the department would technically support. The fact that the Department of Peace and Security was granted four times as much staff as the Department for Political Affairs (with responsibility for human rights, emergence of democratic institutions, transparency and accountability, monitoring of elections) reflected the primary focus of the AU on conflict prevention and management.

By the time of the Maputo Summit, most of the groundwork for the operationalization of the Peace and Security Council and its pillars had already been laid.[58] In May 2003, for example, the third meeting of the African Chiefs of Defense Staff (ACDS) had been convened in Addis Ababa in order to discuss the implementation of the military aspects of the PSC Protocol. At the end of this meeting – which came almost six years after the previous ACDS meeting was held in Harare – the participants adopted the "Policy Framework for the Establishment of the African Standby Force and the Military Staff Committee". This framework was subsequently tabled at the meeting of the Executive Council of the Union that was held in Sun City (South Africa) in late May 2003. Having thus been "noted" by African foreign ministers, the document served as the common African position during the Africa – G8 meeting in Evian in June 2003. At that meeting, the G8 reconfirmed their commitment to help Africa establish a standby peacekeeping force by 2010.

Besides the adoption of the Policy Framework, the meeting of the Chiefs of Defense Staff also strongly recommended the involvement of Africa's Ministers of Defense and Security. To this end, the participants proposed that their recommendations be discussed sequentially by regional and continental meetings of Defense and Security Ministers in order to deepen the process and expedite efforts towards the establishment of the military components of the PSC.

The PSC Protocol entered into force on 26 December 2003, after ratification by the required 27 of the AU's 53 member countries. In March 2004, the AU's Executive Council elected 15 member states to serve on the PSC.[59] Even before that, the ACDS held their fourth meeting in Addis Ababa from 17-18 January 2004. The meeting was followed by the first meeting of the African Ministers of Defense on 20 January 2004.[60] The purpose of this meeting was to follow-up efforts to institutionalize the structures requisite for the African security architecture.

At their Extraordinary Session held in Sirte at the end of February 2004, the AU Heads of State and Government adopted the "Solemn Declaration on a Common African Defense and Security Policy" (CADSP). The CADSP, which is largely premised on the concept of human security, identifies the common security threats to the continent; the objectives and goals of such a policy;[61] as well as the implementing organs and mechanisms and the building blocks of the CADSP.[62] Together with the integration of NEPAD into the AU structures – something that had been decided by the NEPAD Implementation Committee in November 2002 but had been implemented only very slowly – the formulation of the CADSP completed the conceptual African Peace and Security Architecture and underscored the new-found vitality of continental security cooperation.

Analyzing the Revival of Continental Security Cooperation

As with many developments, there were root and trigger causes as well as facilitating factors for the revival of continental security cooperation in the late 1990s. This section will briefly elaborate on all three, identifying the end of the Cold War as "master variable" that helps to explain many of the root causes of the phenomenon such as the proliferation of conflict, Africa's political and economic marginalization and the resultant changes in the continental self-conception. These root causes prepared the ground for events like the OAU reform discussions in Algiers in July 1999 and Colonel Gaddafi's forceful foray into Pan-Africanism to trigger the revival of continental security cooperation in Sirte in September 1999.

The end of the Cold War was crucial in many respects.[63] First, the sudden breakdown of the bipolar system of order that had kept African conflicts in check led to a proliferation of violent crises throughout the continent. Awash with weapons delivered by their respective sponsors (US$ 65 billion worth of weapons had been transferred to Africa during the last twenty years of the Cold War alone), client states like Somalia descended into chaos once superpower support ceased to prop up their regimes. Second, the end of superpower competition meant that Africa's geopolitical and strategic importance declined drastically. With the ideological battle for Africa won and no other significant economic or political issues at stake, international attention quickly shifted away from the continent and towards seemingly more important regions such as the Middle East or Eastern Europe.[64] As a result, the amount of international aid given to African states fell by more than 21 percent between 1990 and 1996 despite the fact that conflict and humanitarian crises increased manifold over the same period.[65] This and the negative effects of globalization further consolidated Africa's economic marginalization and added to the continent's long list of pressing problems.

These post-Cold War developments initiated a discernable change in the continental self-conception. In what Uganda's President Museveni had called a "decade of awakening" in the face of an increasingly-felt impact of globalization on Africa's desolate economies, waning superpower interest and the proliferation of horrific humanitarian catastrophes on the continent, Africa began to experience a new wave of cooperative Pan-Africanism.[66] Driven by a growing sense of urgency and a feeling of disappointment and distrust in the international community and its motives, capabilities and willingness to get involved in African affairs, the continent's leaders realized that if they wanted to break the cycle of violence, poverty and underdevelopment they had to cooperate with each other and together take charge of Africa's destiny.[67] The positive effect of this galvanizing realization was further compounded by the end of Apartheid in South Africa and the rise and relative success of regional organizations like ECOWAS and SADC.

The ensuing (fifth) wave of Pan-Africanism differed markedly from the preceding ones.[68] Previous attempts at continental cooperation were dominated by the Westphalian notion of sovereignty entrenched in the OAU's Charter since Africa's Heads of State pledged non-interference in each other's internal affairs at the organization's founding conference in 1963. The new wave, however, was characterized by a (slow) conceptual shift from regime security and its sacrosanct principles of sovereignty and territorial integrity to the notion of human security.[69] Increasingly aware of the negative effects of an unconditional insistence on the *status quo*, leaders like Olusegun Obasanjo and Yoweri Museveni called for the redefinition of security and sovereignty as precondition for the continent's development. As early as 1991, they noted at the African Leadership Conference in Kampala that "sovereignty had become a sacred cow and many crimes have been committed in its name [...] If the European countries can surrender some of their sovereignty for greater development, African states should similarly surrender some of their sovereignty for greater security, both at the intra and interstate levels".[70] The shift from non-interference to non-indifference underlying this sentiment grew stronger as the humanitarian catastrophes in places like Liberia, Somalia and Rwanda began to overshadow any progress the continent had made following the end of the Cold War. Forced into action, the continent's leaders were increasingly ready to overcome the conceptual hurdles that had prevented meaningful and effective cooperation in the past.

This new found readiness and the emergence of common values nourished the hopes for an African Renaissance.[71] First introduced by Thabo Mbeki in his famous "I am an African" speech to South Africa's

Constitutional Assembly in May 1996, the notion of renaissance had a galvanizing effect on imaginations because of the emancipatory imagery and potential it offered.[72] Whether originally a strategy aimed at gaining electoral success as some cynical critics have suggested or an honest call for modernization and the reconstruction of African identity, it provided a useful counterpoint to the Afropessimism of the days.[73] Once situated within other attempts at forging African identities such as *La Négritude*, Pan-Africanism or Kwame Nkrumah's "African personality",[74] the concept of African Renaissance proved extremely useful to rally the continent's population behind what Benedict Anderson would call an "imagined African community" ready to overcome the continent's problems by working together.[75] This idealistic undercurrent found expression in renewed interest in African institutions and African solutions to African problems and eventually paved the way for a reappraisal of continental unity. As a result, the institutional inadequacies of the OAU became painfully obvious and calls for ist reform grew increasingly louder.

The end of the Cold War, the concomitant proliferation of conflicts, the disengagement of the international community, the resultant sense of urgency on part of the continent's leaders and the hopes for an African Renaissance thus set the stage for Colonel Gaddafi's reform proposals in September 1999 to trigger the revival of continental security cooperation. While several other states had called for substantial reforms, it remains doubtful whether such a radical change as that from OAU to AU would have been realized without his generous financial contributions and personal commitment.[76]

Two factors greatly facilitated this revival. First, the increasing devolution of inter-African cooperation to the regional level, seemingly dealing a deathblow to continental-level cooperation, actually provided an important basis for its reorganization. Proponents of Pan-African integration realized that, if properly managed, devolution was not necessarily detrimental to continental cooperation, but was, in fact, offering a way to circumvent many of the problems that had crippled previous continental initiatives. By basing continental cooperation on regional pillars in which member states seemed to have more confidence, stakes and (perceived) direct control than in the OAU, competition between the levels could be avoided, resources could be channeled to a common objective and direct ownership of the process of continental integration would continue to rest with Africa's states.[77] With this in mind, the 1991 Abuja Treaty first stressed the constitutive character of Africa's regional organizations and the AU has retained this organizational structure ever since. Within the realm of peace and security, Article 16 of the PSC Protocol and the Common African Defense and Security Policy stress that the regional mechanisms will form the building blocks of the AU's peace and security architecture, including the ASF and the CEWS. The PSC Protocol reinforces this relationship by emphasizing the importance of harmonization, coordination and cooperation between the AU and the regional mechanisms and ensuring effective partnerships between the regional mechanisms and the PSC.[78] Without this explicit inclusion of regional frameworks and thus those powers that would have continued to oppose any centralization had they not felt any direct ownership in the process, nothing like the AU would have ever made it past the proposal stage.[79]

The second factor that greatly facilitated the revival of continental security cooperation was the level of international support for home-grown African initiatives. Whether in order to absolve themselves of the obligation of direct involvement in the continent's affairs or in order to build up potent partners for burden-sharing, many international actors began to engage in capacity building activities in the mid 1990s. Ever since then, international support has kept African security cooperation alive at both, the regional and the continental level.

Summary

The struggle for continental security cooperation has come a long way since Kwame Nkrumah's call for an African High Command in the early 1960s. The last three chapters have tracked the conceptual evolution of continental security cooperation from its ideological roots in Africa's liberation movements to today's African Peace and Security Architecture. While the idea of establishing such an architecture had found nothing but a lone and idealistic voice in the Ghanaian President in the early post-colonial years and only occasionally attracted attention thereafter, today's efforts are based on a broad consensus among Africans and the international community alike. Changes in the geo-political security situation, the continent's organizational landscape and self-conception as well as the level of international support have finally allowed the African Union to centralize the responsibility for peace and security on the continent and institutionalize an appropriate framework that differs from its feeble predecessors in two important ways.

First, the AU distinguishes itself through its underlying acceptance of the normative commitment to protect. Where Articles II and III of the OAU Charter had placed a premium on mutual preservation through unconditional adherence to the principles of sovereignty, territorial integrity and non-interference in member states' internal affairs, the AU's Constitutive Act imposes important limitations on state sovereignty.[80] Under the AU, member states enjoy the privileges of sovereignty such as the non-interference in its internal affairs only as long as they fulfill their responsibility to protect their citizens.[81] If, however, states fail, for whatever reasons, to honor this responsibility, the AU reserves itself "the right to intervene pursuant to a decision of the Assembly in respect of grave circumstances, namely war crimes, genocide and crimes against humanity".[82] The significance of this shift from non-interference to what is now generally referred to as "non-indifference" cannot be overstated even though critics have rightly pointed out that it has not yet resulted in a visible change to the AU's dealings with autocratic leaders like Zimbabwe's Robert Mugabe or Sudan's Omar al-Bashir.[83] Nonetheless, by defining sovereignty in the conditional terms of a state's capacity and willingness to protect its citizens, the AU's Constitutive Act is the first international treaty to recognize the right of an organization to intervene militarily in its member states' affairs.[84] It thereby not only takes the idea of collective security to a new level, but also provides the AU with a powerful legal foundation on which to anchor its emerging conflict management mechanism. While not exactly an intervention according to Article 4(h), the ongoing trial of the former Chadian president Hissène Habré by an AU-mandated Senegalese court shows that the AU has begun to move away from the OAU's infamous "culture of impunity" and towards the "culture of accountability" that must necessarily go along with its newfound commitment to non-indifference.[85]

The second prominent feature of the new peace and security architecture is its multi-layered and symbiotic approach to security cooperation. Likened by some to a "peace pyramid", the continental security structure rests firmly on Africa's existing regional security mechanisms, which act both as pillars of and implementation agencies for continental security policy.[86] This structural interdependence not only contrasts starkly with the OAU's often uneasy relationship with the continent's regional organizations, but also helps to focus the plethora of African security initiatives onto one common objective. Moreover, it allows the AU to profit from the regional organizations' comparative advantage in military and security matters, their experience with peace operations and – in the case of western, eastern and southern Africa – their established frameworks and mechanisms for conflict prevention, management and resolution. At the same time, the cooperative structure does not deny the regional organizations a significant stake and central role in all processes and respects their regional authority and responsibility. Under this system of decentralized collective security, the primary responsibility for peace and security remains squarely with the regional organizations while the AU serves as the clearinghouse and framework for all initiatives, thus filling the conceptual and institutional gap between the global level (the United Nations) and the regional level. The resultant symbiosis ensures that the regional organizations feel ownership in the process of establishing a continental security architecture and virtually eliminates the risk of competition between the various levels of inter-African security cooperation. Furthermore, it increases the stakes all actors have in the process and thereby reduces the chances of failure.[87]

While some critics argue that this decentralized approach merely creates or reinforces additional layers of bureaucracy and thus slows down responses to crises and conflicts, there is ample evidence that the symbiotic relationship between the continental and regional levels is already beginning to bear fruit. Over the past six years, the ambitious dream of a comprehensive security architecture has been taking shape at a remarkable pace and the AU has become deeply involved in the continent's manifold security problems by building on the experiences and relying on the resources of the regional organizations.

Of course a brief discussion such as this one runs the risk of oversimplifying what is a long and complex history, but it seems safe to say that while still far from Nkrumah's dream of a "United States of Africa", the African Union has made great strides in advancing continental cooperation. Ever since its foundation in Durban in July 2002, it has based its political legitimacy squarely on Pan-Africanist ideology and has shown a new willingness to overcome the continent's many perils. Aware that willingness must be paralleled with capacity, the next four chapters of this book will assess the surge in African-led peace operations that accompanied the revival of continental security cooperation, the institutional setup of the security architecture as well as two of the AU's most prominent security instruments, namely the African Standby Force and the Continental Early Warning System.

Notes

[1]   OAU, Declaration of the Assembly of Heads of State and Government of the OAU on the Political and Socio-Economic Situation in Africa and the Fundamental Changes Taking Place in the World, 11 July 1990, para. 11.

[2]   For more information on the Kampala Conference see Francis Deng and William Zartman, A Strategic Vision for Africa: The Kampala Movement (Washington DC: Brookings Institution Press, 2002).

[3]   For a full text of the Report of the Secretary-General on the Establishment of a Mechanism for Conflict Prevention, Management and Resolution see *Resolving Conflicts in Africa: Proposals for Action*, OAU Information Services Publication Series II, Addis Ababa, 1993.

[4]   Said Djinnit, Speech delivered at the "Meeting on Enhancing Africa's Peacekeeping Capacity", 5 December 1997 as quoted in Eric Berman and Katie Sams, Peacekeeping in Africa: Capabilities and Culpabilities (Geneva: United Nations Institute for Disarmament Research, 2000), 61.

[5]   See Declaration of the Assembly of Heads of State and Government on the Establishment within the OAU of a Mechanism for Conflict Prevention, Management and Resolution (OAU Document AHG/Decl. 3, (XXIX), Rev. 1, Cairo, 28-30 June 1993).

[6]   For a detailed exposition of the modalities of the mechanism see Method of Work of the Central Organ of the OAU Mechanism for Conflict Prevention, Management and Resolution (OAU Document Central Organ/Mec/AHG.2.1).

[7]   For more information on the establishment of the OAU Conflict Management Division see OAU General Secretariat, Resolving Conflicts in Africa: Implementation Options, OAU Information Services Publication – Series (II) 1993, para. 153 as reprinted in Refugee Survey Quarterly 13, no. 2 (1994), pp. 174-178.

[8]   For more information on the various proposals put forth and the reasons behind the eventual decision to opt for this model see OAU General Secretariat, Resolving Conflicts in Africa: Implementation Options, OAU Information Services Publication – Series (II) 1993, para. 135-149.

[9]   This figure was changed to six percent in OAU FY 1998/1999.

[10]   Joram Biswaro, Perspectives on Africa's Integration and Cooperation from OAU to AU: Old Wine in New Bottles? (Dar es Salaam: Tanzania Publishing House, 2005), 52. For more detailed discussions of the OAU Mechanism see M. Muyangwa and M. Vogt, "An Assessment of the OAU Mechanism for Conflict Prevention, Management and Resolution, 1993-2000," (New York: International Peace Academy, 2000).

[11]   Elton Nzaou, Vers La Création D'une Armée Panafricaine: La Force Africaine De Paix (Paris: L'Harmattan, 2004).

[12]   Chris Bakwesegha, "The Role of the Organization of African Unity in Conflict Prevention, Management and Resolution in the Context of the Political Evolution of Africa," African Journal on Conflict Prevention, Management and Resolution 1, no. 1 (1997): 90, Cedric de Coning and Hussein Solomon,

"Enhancing the OAU Mechanism for Conflict Prevention, Management and Resolution," Politeia 8, no. 4 (1999), Winrich Kühne, Afrika auf dem Wege zu eigenen Kapazitäten für Konfliktprävention und Peacekeeping? Geschichte, Organisation und Perspektiven des OAU Mechanismus von 1993 (Ebenhausen: Stiftung Wissenschaft und Politik, 1998), 41.

[13] Amare Tekle, "The OAU: Conflict Prevention, Management and Resolution," in The Path of a Genocide: The Rwanda Crisis from Uganda to Zaire, ed. Howard Adelman and Astri Suhrke (London: Transaction Publishers, 1999), 111-130.

[14] William Zartman and Katharina Vogeli, "Prevention Gained and Prevention Lost: Collapse, Competition and Coup in Congo," in Opportunities Missed, Opportunities Seized: Preventive Diplomacy in the Post-Cold War World, ed. Bruce Jentleson (Lanham: Rowman & Littlefield, 2000), 265-292.

[15] Report of the UN Secretary-General, 13 April 1998. See also Fiona MacFarlane and Mark Malan, "Crisis and Response in the Central African Republic: A New Trend in African Peacekeeping?," African Security Review 7, no. 2 (1998).

[16] OAU Secretary-General Salim Ahmed Salim in an address at the Dakar Summit of the Organization of African Unity, Dakar, Senegal, July 1993.

[17] See Muyangwa and Vogt, "An Assessment of the OAU Mechanism for Conflict Prevention, Management and Resolution, 1993-2000," 7.

[18] The OAU arguably remained the poorest regional organization in the world for much of the 1990s. Its Peace Fund was directly affected by this parlous financial state. For example, the total contribution received from 1 June 1995 to 25 March 1996 was just over seven million US$ ($7, 439723.28). Total expenditure over the same period amounted to over seven million seven hundred thousand US$ ($ 7,759366.73) which resulted in a deficit of about three hundred thousand US$ ($ 319643.45) at the end of March 1996. See Cedric de Coning, "The Role of the OAU in Conflict Management in Africa," ISS Monograph, no. 10 (1997): 5.

[19] Bakwesegha, "The Role of the Organization of African Unity in Conflict Prevention, Management and Resolution in the Context of the Political Evolution of Africa," 14.

[20] See OAU, Resolving Conflicts in Africa: Proposals for Action, OAU Information Services Publication Series (I), 1992, part I, section D.

[21] See OAU, Resolving Conflicts in Africa: Implementation Options, OAU Information Services Publication Series (II), 1993, para. 165-171.

[22] The Washington Post, 10 November 1994

[23] Adebayo Oyebade, "The End of the Cold War in Africa: Implications for Conflict Management and Resolution," in Africa after the Cold War: The Changing Perspectives on Security, ed. Adebayo Oyebade and Abiodun Alao (Trenton: Africa World Press, 1998), 169.

[24] See Ibid., 173.

[25] Africa Research Bulletin, no. 11707, 1-31 January 1995.

[26] See "International efforts to establish collective security mechanisms for Africa", Collected Papers, Zimbabwe Peacekeeping Workshop, Harare, 23-27 January 1995: 2.

[27] Ibid., 3.

[28]   Africa Research Bulletin, no. 11707, 1-31 January 1995. Interview with Lord Peter in Geneva, September 2008.

[29]   See Report on the OAU's position towards the various initiatives on conflict management: enhancing the OAU's capacity in preventive diplomacy, conflict resolution and peacekeeping (OAU Document Central Organ/MEC/MIN/3(IV), July 1995).

[30]   "OAU Discusses Rapid Deployment Force", Agence France Press, Addis Ababa, 27June 1995.

[31]   E Godwin, "Blueprint for Enforcement," West Africa, 6-12 October 1997. See also John Brookes, "A Military Model for Conflict Resolution in Sub-Saharan Africa," Parameters 27, no. 4 (1997): 108-120.

[32]   "Military Chiefs Meet," Africa Research Bulletin, 1-30 June 1996: 12289.

[33]   See Report of the Second Meeting of Chiefs of Defense Staff of the Central Organ of the OAU Mechanism for Conflict Management and Resolution (OAU Document OAU/CHT/CO/RPT(II), Harare, 2-25 October 1997), pp. 11-21. For more information see Mark Malan, "New Tools in the Box? Towards a Standby Force for Africa," in Peace in Africa - Towards a Collaborative Security Regime, ed. Shannon Field (Johannesburg: Institute for Global Dialogue, 2004), 200-201.

[34]   See "OAU wants Sub-Regional Brigades for African Force," Pan-African News Agency, 9 March 1998.

[35]   See OAU Document AHG/Decl. XXXV.

[36]   For the debate on Gaddafi's motivation see, for example, Dallas Browne, "Libya and the African Union," in History Behind the Headlines, ed. Megan O'Meara (New York: Gale Cengage, 2003).

[37]   See Thomas Tieku, "Explaining the Clash of Interests of Major Actors in the Creation of the African Union," African Affairs 103, no. 411 (2004): 249-267.

[38]   Nigeria used ECOWAS as a vehicle to respond to the conflicts in Liberia, Sierra Leone and Guinea-Bissau while South Africa used SADC to defend its national interests in Lesotho and the DRC.

[39]   For detailed discussions of the transition of the OAU to the AU see, for example, Biswaro, Perspectives on Africa's Integration and Cooperation from OAU to AU: Old Wine in New Bottles? , 68-109, M Mwanasali, "From the Organization of African Unity to the African Union," in From Cape to Congo: Southern Africa's Evolving Security Challenges, ed. Mwesiga Baregu and Christopher Landsberg (Boulder: Lynne Rienner, 2002).

[40]   See OAU, Declaration of the 4th Extraordinary Summit of the Assembly of the Heads of State and Government of the OAU, Sirte, 9 September 1999, para. 6 and 8(v).

[41]   See Lomé Declaration (OAU Document AHG/Decl.2 (XXXVI), 12 July 2000).

[42]   See, for example, Ademola Abass and M. Baderin, "Towards Effective Collective Security and Human Rights Protection in Africa: An Assessment of the Constitutive Act of the New African Union," Netherlands International Law Review 49, no. 1 (2002), Tiyanjana Maluwa, "The Constitutive Act of the African Union and Institution-Building in Postcolonial Africa," Leiden Journal of International Law, no. 16 (2003), C. Packer and D. Rukare, "The New

African Union and Its Constitutive Act," American Journal of International Law 96, no. 365 (2002).

[43] For these decisions see OAU Document AHG/Dec. 160(xxvii).

[44] See Communiqué issued at the End of the Meeting of the Implementation Committee of Heads of State and Government on the New Partnership for African Development, Abuja, 23 October 2001.

[45] Report of ad hoc Ministerial Committee on AU-CM/2242(LXXXV).

[46] See PSC/Draft Protocol of the AU Art.5(1)

[47] P Kagwanja, "Power and Peace: South African and the Refurbishing of Africa's Multilateral Capacity for Peacemaking," Journal of Contemporary African Studies 24, no. 2 (2006): 172.

[48] See Protocol Relating to the Establishment of the Peace and Security Council, Article 2(1).

[49] Protocol Relating to the Establishment of the Peace and Security Council, Article 2(2).

[50] Ibid., Article 6.

[51] Ibid., Article 7.

[52] CSSDCA, Memorandum of Understanding on Security, Stability, Development and Cooperation in Africa, Durban, 8 July 2002.

[53] NEPAD, Communiqué issued at the end of the Second Meeting of the Heads of State and Government Implementation Committee of the New Partnership For Africa's Development, Abuja, 26 March 2002, para. 7.

[54] For more information on the war in the DRC and the role of the OAU see John Clark, ed., The African Stakes of the Congo War (Basingstoke: Palgrave Macmillan, 2004), Michael Nest, Francois Grignon, and Emizet Kisangani, The Democratic Republic of Congo: Economic Dimensions of War and Peace (Boulder: Lynne Rienner, 2005), Thomas Turner, The Congo Wars: Conflict, Myth and Reality (London: Zed Books, 2007).

[55] See Festus Aboagye, "Towards New Peacekeeping Partnerships in Africa? The OAU Liaison Mission in Ethiopia-Eritrea," African Security Review 10, no. 2 (2001).

[56] See, for example, Jakkie Cilliers, "From Acronyms to Action: The Seminal Assembly of the African Union," African Security Review 11, no. 1 (2002).

[57] AU, Constitutive Act of the AU, Lomé, July 2000, Article 33.

[58] Jakkie Cilliers, "From Durban to Maputo: A Review of the 2003 Summit of the African Union," ISS Occasional Papers, no. 76 (2003).

[59] Gabon, Ethiopia, Algeria, South Africa and Nigeria were elected for the first three-year term, while Cameroon, Congo, Kenya, Sudan, Libya, Lesotho, Mozambique, Ghana, Senegal and Togo were elected to serve the two year term.

[60] AU Document MIN/Def.&Sec. 2(1), Report of the Chairperson on the Establishment of the African Standby Force and the Military Staff Committee, Addis Ababa, 20-21 January 2004.

[61] AU, Solemn Declaration on a Common African Defense and Security Policy, Sirte, February 2004, Article I (16).

[62] O. A. Touray, "The Common African Defense and Security Policy," African Affairs 104, no. 417 (2005): 635-656.

[63]   Oyebade, "The End of the Cold War in Africa: Implications for Conflict Management and Resolution," 169. Also see William Hale and Eberhard Kienle, eds., After the Cold War: Security and Democracy in Africa and Asia (London: IB Tauris, 1997), Edmond Keller, "African Conflict Management and the New World Order," Institute on Global Conflict and Cooperation Policy Paper, no. 13 (1995), Winrich Kühne, Africa and the End of the Cold War (Ebenhausen: Stiftung Wissenschaft und Politik, 1990), Scott Thomas, "Africa and the End of the Cold War: An Overview of Impacts," in Africa in the Post-Cold War International System, ed. Sola Akinrinade and Amadu Sesay (London: Pinter, 1998), 3-27.

[64]   See, for example, Michael Clough, "The United States and Africa: The Policy of Cynical Disengagement," Current History 91 (1992): 193-198, Marguerite Michaels, "Retreat from Africa," Foreign Affairs 72, no. 1 (1993): 93-108.

[65]   Guy Arnold, Africa: A Modern History (London: Atlantic Books, 2005), 772.

[66]   Yoweri Museveni, Address to the South African Parliament, Cape Town, 27 May 1997.

[67]   Jane Perlez, "After the Cold War: Views from Africa; Stranded by Superpowers, Africa seeks an Identity," New York Times, 17 May 1992.

[68]   Christopher Landsberg, "The Fifth Wave of Pan-Africanism," in West Africa's Security Challenges: Building Peace in a Troubled Region, ed. Adekeye Adebajo and Ismail Rashid (Boulder: Lynne Rienner, 2004), 117.

[69]   For an interesting constructivist discussion of the notion of human security see Edward Newmann, "Human Security and Constructivism," International Studies Perspectives 2, no. 3 (2002): 239-251. Also see Jakkie Cilliers, Human Security in Africa: A Conceptual Framework for Review (Pretoria: African Human Security Initiative, 2004).

[70]   Yoweri Museveni, Speech at the Conference on Peace, Security, Stability, Development and Cooperation in Africa, Kampala, May 1991.

[71]   For more on the concept of the African Renaissance see Bernard Magubane, "The African Renaissance in Historical Perspective," in African Renaissance, ed. M Makgoba (Cape Town: Mafube & Tafelberg, 1999), Eddy Maloka, "The South African "African Renaissance" Debate: A Critique," Polis 8 (2001).

[72]   Peter Vale and Sipho Maseko, "South Africa and the African Renaissance," International Affairs 74, no. 2 (1998).

[73]   Ian Liebenberg, "The African Renaissance: Myth, Vital Lie or Mobilizing Tool?," African Security Review 7, no. 3 (1998).

[74]   Pal Ahluwalia, "The African Renaissance: Reinventing African Identity," in Africa Beyond 2000: Essays on Africa's Political and Economic Development in the Twenty-First Century, ed. S. Saxena (Delhi: Kalinga Publications, 2001).

[75]   Benedict Anderson, Imagined Communities (London: Verso, 1992).

[76]   During the Sirte Summit Gaddafi paid US$ 4.5 million to the OAU in order to ensure the participation of the seven member states that were under sanctions at the time. Following the Sirte Summit, Gaddafi continued to pay for defaulting member states to enable them to participate in the deliberations, and consequently, sign, ratify and accede to the Constitutive Act. In Tripoli in

March 2001, Libya paid for: Burundi (US$ 201,164.17), the Central African Republic (US$ 400,556.47), Equatorial Guinea (US$ 274,355.31), Guinea Bissau (US$ 324,409.95), Liberia (US$ 497,564.79), Niger (US$ 369,723.70), Sao Tome and Principe (US$ 485,896.23), Seychelles (336,106.36) and Sierra Leone (US$ 647,322.50). At the Lusaka Summit in July 2001, Libya again paid for Burundi (US$ 43,469.29), the Central African Republic (US$ 358,307.81), Guinea Bissau (US$ 297,355.32), Niger (US$ 528,027.00) and Cape Verde (US$ 265,000). See Biswaro, Perspectives on Africa's Integration and Cooperation from OAU to AU: Old Wine in New Bottles?, 111.

[77]   See UNECA, Sub-Regional Blocs as Regional Building Blocks in Assessing Regional Integration in Africa, Addis Ababa, 2004, 39-55.

[78]   AU, Protocol Relating to the Establishment of the Peace and Security Council, Durban, 9 July 2002, Article 7(j).

[79]   See Benedikt Franke, "In Defense of Regional Peace Operations in Africa," Journal of Humanitarian Assistance, no. 185 (2006).

[80]   Articles II and III, Charter of the Organization of African Unity, 25 May 1963, reprinted in International Legal Materials 2, no. 4 (July 1963), pp. 767-78.

[81]   "The Responsibility to Protect," Report by the International Commission on Intervention and State Sovereignty, December 2001, para. 6.1-6.12.

[82]   AU, The Constitutive Act of the African Union, July 2002, Article 4 (Principles), para. h.

[83]   For an excellent discussion of this shift see Paul Williams, "From Non-Intervention to Non-Indifference: The Origins and Development of the African Union's Security Culture," African Affairs 106, no. 423 (2007): 253-279.

[84]   Kristiana Powell, The African Union's Emerging Peace and Security Regime - Opportunities and Challenges for Delivering on the Responsibility to Protect, Monograph Series No. 119 (Pretoria: Institute for Security Studies, 2005), 1.

[85]   See Bruce Baker, "Twilight of Impunity for Africa's Presidential Criminals," Third World Quarterly 25, no. 8 (2004): 1497-1498. In 2000, Habré was indicted for atrocities by the state of Senegal; the first time this had happened to a former African head of state who traditionally have not been held to account for their time in office. Following initial problems within the Senegalese legal system which did not feel authorized to try Habré, the AU Assembly decided in July 2006 that Habré's crime fell within the competence of the Union and mandated Senegal to try him "on behalf of Africa" (see AU document Assembly/AU/Dec.127(VII) adopted at the 7th Ordinary Session of the AU Assembly, 1-2 July 2006, Banjul). Following the AU's decision, Senegal's president announced that Habré would be tried by a special commission under an AU mandate in Senegal. At the time of writing, the constitution of Senegal had been amended to allow for the prosecution of non-Senegalese citizens in the country's courts (April 2008) and four special judges had been appointed to oversee this landmark trial (July 2008).

[86]   For the concept of "peace pyramid" see, for example, Mark Malan, "The OAU and African Sub-Regional Organizations - a Closer Look at the Peace Pyramid," (Pretoria: Institute for Security Studies, 1999).

---

[87]   See AU Document AU-RECs/EXP/2(II) Rev.3, Draft Memorandum of Understanding on Cooperation in the Area of Peace and Security between the African Union, the Regional Economic Communities and the Coordinating Mechanisms of the Regional Standby Brigades of Eastern Africa and Northern Africa, 2 September 2007.

6

The Peace Operations of the
African Union

The revival of continental security cooperation did not only find an expression in the renewed efforts to institutionalize an elaborate security architecture, but also in a notable surge in AU-led peace operations. Even though both processes were driven by the same considerations and despite the important structural interrelations between them – the PSC was the mandating authority for all operations but AMIB and the PSOD was in charge of running the operations – it makes sense to analyze them separately. While this may be an obvious point, some academics continue to treat the two processes as one and the same or, even worse, infer the particulars of one process from an analysis of the other. A common tendency, for example, is to equate the shortcomings of the AU's *ad hoc* operations with the quality of the emerging security institutions. However, just because the six operations described in this chapter were conducted under the aegis of the AU, it does not necessarily mean that they are a sign of what to expect from the organization's emerging peace and security architecture. On the contrary, the latter should be seen as a deliberate attempt to institutionalize structures and processes to overcome many of the difficulties for which makeshift operations like AMIS or AMISOM have (rightly) been criticized. Whatever their flaws though, a brief discussion of the AU's operations in Burundi, Darfur, the Comoros and Somalia helps to demonstrate the growing sense of responsibility among many of Africa's states as well as their increasing readiness to cooperate militarily (both of which are essential foundations for the success of the emerging institutions).

The African Union Mission in Burundi

The African Union Mission in Burundi (AMIB) was the first operation wholly initiated, planned and executed by AU members and thus represented a milestone for the AU in terms of self-reliance.[1] While the mission was officially launched in April 2003, its origins lie in a long series of African attempts to broker a peace settlement in Burundi. Sparked by the assassination of the country's first democratically elected President, Melchior Ndadaye, by Tutsi extremists in October 1993, Burundi's civil war quickly drew in neighbouring states eager to prevent the spill-over of ethnic violence.[2] First led by Tanzania's founding president Julius Nyerere, the resultant African mediation efforts (and the supporting diplomacy of the UN's special envoy Ahmedou Ould-Abdallah) proved fruitless for years.[3] It was only with Nyerere's death in October 1999 and the subsequent selection of Nelson Mandela as new chief mediator that real progress was achieved.[4] Under his stewardship, several parties finally signed a peace agreement – the Arusha Accord for Peace and Reconciliation – in August 2000. The remaining groups and rebel movements, however, continued to fight out their grievances and the deteriorating security situation eventually led Mandela to deploy 750 troops to protect those Hutu politicians who had returned from exile to participate in the political process. Partly owing to the success of this South African Protection Support Detachment (SAPSD), another cease-fire agreement was signed in Arusha between Burundi's transitional government and Pierre Nkurunziza's Hutu Forces for the Defence of Democracy (CNDD-FDD) in early December 2002. Amongst other things this agreement called for the rapid deployment of an African cease-fire monitoring mission until the end of December.

While they could not but miss this unrealistic timeline, the AU's heads of state and government – still enthusiastic about the revival of continental cooperation and eager to put an end to the long-running crisis in Burundi – approved the deployment of such a mission less than two months later. As the PSC had not yet been established, the Central Organ of the OAU Mechanism for Conflict Prevention, Management and Resolution was given the task of devising the details of the organization's first peace operation.[5] At its 91st ordinary session on 2 April 2003, the Central Organ mandated the deployment of AMIB as a holding operation[6] with four specific objectives, namely to (1) oversee the implementation of the ceasefire agreements, (2) support the disarmament, demobilization and reintegration of an expected 20,000 ex-combatants, (3) strive towards ensuring that conditions were created for the establishment of a UN peacekeeping mission and (4) contribute to political and economic stability in Burundi so as to allow the considerable number of internally displaced persons as well as the refugees living in three camps in Tanzania to return to their homes. In order to achieve these ambitious objectives, AMIB was mandated to comprise 3,335 personnel with military contingents from South Africa

(1,600), Ethiopia (858) and Mozambique (228) as well as an observer element (43) drawn from Burkina Faso, Gabon, Mali, Togo and Tunisia.

At the end of April 2003, the AU appointed the experienced Guinean ambassador Mamadou Bah as Head of Mission and Special Representative of the Chairperson of the AU Commission and Ambassador Welile Nhlapo from South Africa and Martin Mwakalindile from Tanzania as his deputies. At the same time, Major-General Sipho Binda from South Africa was appointed as force commander of AMIB's military component. The initial phase of AMIB looked promising enough as South Africa managed to deploy all of its 1,600 troops by early May (900 troops deployed from South Africa, the rest was made up of members of the SAPSD which was integrated into AMIB on 1 May). Concerned about the fragility of Burundi's ceasefire and plagued by a lack of funds, the Ethiopian and Mozambican contingents, however, did not arrive until late September and mid-October respectively forcing the South African troops to operate alone for several months. It then took another two months until AMIB finally reached its envisaged strength of 2,645 troops.[7]

Substantial delays in force deployment were not the only problem that beset the AU's first peace operation. Militarily, AMIB had difficulties to maintain its neutrality and occasionally even had to engage in combat activities (for example, on 30 June AMIB forces killed several CNDD-FDD rebels while defending their cantonment zone in Muyange). In addition, AMIB lacked the military resources and organization to disarm what turned out to be more than three times the anticipated number of rebel fighters. Its financial problems, however, were even more severe. As Mamadou Bah pointed out in late 2003, of the $120 million required to fund AMIB's operations for a year, only $20 million had been made available.[8] Without adequate funds in its special peace fund (see next chapter for a detailed description of this fund), the AU had expected to fund AMIB's budget from redeemed pledges and donations from its international partners, who had given indications of sufficient goodwill towards the peace efforts of the AU. However, many of these pledges never materialized.

Despite the problems that beset AMIB, the security situation in Burundi improved during its deployment and in February 2004 a UN evaluation team concluded that conditions were sufficiently stable for establishing a follow-up UN peacekeeping operation in the country. By the time of its decommissioning in June 2004 (when it was re-hatted as *Opération des Nations Unies au Burundi*, ONUB),[9] AMIB had overseen a return of stability to most provinces in Burundi, with the notable exception of the rural area outside the capital Bujumbura where Agathon

Rwasa and his *Forces Nationales de Libération* (FNL) continued to offer armed resistance. While it had little success in ensuring political and economic stability in Burundi, AMIB managed to facilitate the delivery of humanitarian assistance through its Civil Military Coordination Centre and provided much-needed protection to the designated returning leaders.[10] It also began work on the disarmament, demobilization and reintegration of combatants and reached an agreement with the transitional government on a first pre-assembly and disarmament area (at Muyange).

Most critics tend to agree that, given its pioneering character, AMIB actually did very well. There is, however a danger to overestimate AMIB's contribution to the amelioration of conditions in Burundi at the expense of simultaneously ongoing mediation efforts like the Pretoria peace talks. While the mission on the ground did provide the mediators with a helpful show of force and commitment, there is no doubt that peace in Burundi was made at the negotiation table. However small AMIB's final contribution was though, its first peace support operation taught the African Union a number of valuable lessons. Most importantly, it clearly showed the need for alternative funding arrangements as AMIB had been hampered by a lack of resources from the very start. The absence of sufficient support from within Africa as well as the unwillingness of the UN and the international community to defray the mission's costs reverberated throughout the entire operation and crippled its effectiveness. According to Festus Agoagye, "different languages inside the mission's command structures, a weak concept of operation, the absence of a standardized doctrine and operating procedures, force generation difficulties, an incomplete disarmament, demobilization and reintegration process as well as logistic limitations" added to the challenges.[11] However, there were also a number of practices that seemed worthy of replication, most notably, the exemplary use of good offices, the reliance on a lead nation (South Africa in this case) as well as the collaboration with the UN on the basis of Chapter VIII of its charter.

The African Union Missions in Sudan

Much has already been written about the African Mission in Sudan (AMIS).[12] For many, this operation represented the biggest test case of the AU's new peacekeeping ambitions, not only because of its sheer size but also because of the complexities of the conflict it was meant to solve.[13] As part of a much larger conflict network, the war in Darfur defies easy historical analysis.[14] Its most recent episode began in February 2003 when two mainly non-Arab rebel groups, the Justice and Equality Movement (JEM) and the Sudan Liberation Movement/Army (SLM/A) attacked government installations in El-Fasher to protest against the social and economic marginalization of Darfurians by the ruling regime in Khartoum. The government retaliated with a combination of its own military offensive and a proxy fighting force that became known as the *Janjaweed*.[15] These semi-regularized Arab militias were provided training, arms and air cover by the government's Popular Defence Forces and were soon committing massive human rights abuses throughout Darfur.[16] By early 2004, the escalating violence had already left tens of thousands dead and millions displaced from their homes.

As the government of Sudan under Omar al-Bashir at the time did not consent to a UN peace operation on its territory, it was left to African actors to play the leading role. Consequently, just as the mission in Burundi was winding down, the AU began to face the possibility of having to launch another operation. This possibility became reality when the Government of Sudan, the SLM/A and the JEM signed the so-called N'Djamena Humanitarian Ceasefire Agreement on 8 April 2004 and in the subsequent Addis Ababa Ceasefire Agreement (signed on 28 May 2004) called on the AU to monitor its implementation. Eager to sharpen its emerging profile as a serious conflict management actor, the AU was quick to heed this call and, in early June, deployed 80 observers and a small protection force of 300 Nigerian and Rwandan troops (later referred to as AMIS I) to monitor, verify, investigate and report transgressions of the ceasefire agreement. The latter, however, broke down as soon as the AU observers had arrived in Darfur.

As the violence escalated once more, international calls on the AU to increase its commitment grew louder by the day.[17] On 20 October 2004 the PSC finally agreed to increase the number of AMIS personnel to 3,320 including a civilian police component of 815.[18] This larger force became known as AMIS II and quickly faced many of the same problems that had already hampered the performance of AMIB. For example, it took over six months to deploy and, due to a lack of sound logistical planning, had nowhere near enough vehicles and communication equipment. While the logistical situation improved somewhat when the AU established the so-called Darfur Integrated Task Force (DITF) in January 2005 and called in the US firm Pacific Architectural Engineers to provide logistical support, the AU had to acknowledge that the situation in Darfur continued to worsen despite its engagement.[19]

Based on the recommendations of an AU-led assessment mission, the PSC authorized a further increase in the strength of AMIS to 6,170 military personnel and 1,560 civilian police in April 2005.[20] Referred to as AMIS IIE, the enhanced force was to "encourage improved compliance with the N'djamena Humanitarian Ceasefire Agreement and create a secure environment for the IDPs in and around the camps as well as for humanitarian relief services".[21] Once again, however, the increase in numbers did not translate into a discernible improvement in the conditions on the ground. By January 2006, a report of the Chairperson of the AU Commission had to conclude that there had been an escalation in the number of ceasefire violations since August 2005 and that the security situation had further deteriorated with attacks on AMIS becoming more frequent.[22] The same report also asked the members of the Peace and Security Council to consider possible alternatives to AMIS IIE given the increasing difficulties in securing sufficient funding for the operation.[23] As a result of this request and further encouraged by a collective *démarche* the AU's international partners had presented to the commission on 5 January 2006, the PSC used its 45th meeting on 12 January 2006 to express its support for a transition from AMIS to a UN operation.[24]

In February 2006, the UN Security Council asked Secretary-General Kofi Annan to initiate contingency planning for a range of options for such a transition and, following the conclusion of the Abuja Peace Talks and the signing of the Darfur Peace Agreement (DPA) in May 2006,[25] the PSC reaffirmed its decision to end the mandate of AMIS at the earliest possible time. Two months later, the UN Security Council decided to expand the mandate of its mission in Sudan (UNMIS), launched in March 2005 to monitor the implementation of the Comprehensive Peace Agreement in the southern part of the country, to cover Darfur and "invited" the consent of the Sudanese authorities to this move.[26] However, as the Sudanese government strongly opposed the spread of what it called "UN imperialism",[27] it took over a year of negotiations until UN Security Council Resolution 1769 could finally authorize and mandate the establishment of an AU/UN hybrid operation in Darfur on 31 July 2007. The United Nations African Mission in Sudan (UNAMID) was to incorporate AMIS and, despite an envisaged force strength of up to 26,000 personnel, remain "African in character". After more than three years on the ground, AMIS was officially replaced by UNAMID on 31 December 2007. More than a year later, little has changed in Darfur as UNAMID continues to be plagued by many of the problems that had already undermined the effectiveness of AMIS.

In line with some of the assessments of the African Mission in Burundi, a number of critics have argued that, in light of the unfavourable operational circumstances and limitations inherent in its mandate and access to financial and military resources, the performance of AMIS on the ground should not be judged too harshly. Seth Appiah-Mensah, for example, pointed out that despite undeniable operational difficulties, the presence of AMIS personnel did bring some measure of security to the vulnerable civilian populations in selected camp areas and helped to "achieve a semblance of stability in much of Darfur".[28] While this may be true to some extent, AMIS was not able to provide security corridors for humanitarian aid or protect humanitarian convoys, nor did it disarm the Janjaweed as "demanded" by UN Security Council Resolution 1556 of July 2004. The critics are, however, right that the troops on the ground cannot be blamed for these failures. Rather, the problems were caused by a combination of structural conditions like a severe lack of financial, military and institutional resources and a dangerous defiance of well-established peacekeeping principles like the need for diligent planning, a workable political settlement and a clear mandate.

Beginning with the latter, the *ad hoc* nature of AMIS and its rapid evolution from a simple observer mission to a full-blown peacekeeping operation led to what peacekeeping professionals were quick to label "beginners' mistakes". Firstly, driven by political imperatives of various sorts, every single phase of AMIS (that is, AMIS I, AMIS II and AMIS IIE) was put together in a rush. As a result, there was little time for proper planning, or, in the memorable words of a participant in a lessons-learned workshop organized by the International Peace Institute (IPI) in Ghana, "AMIS was never planned, it just happened".[29] Together with a notable absence of strategic guidance – the AU PSOD had hardly been formed at the time and the Special Representative of the Chairman of the Commission responsible for the overall coordination of the mission was only nominated several months into the operation – this lack of planning caused widespread problems ranging from the implementation of inefficient structures to the absence of a clear division of labour between mission components. While the quality of planning did improve somewhat with the creation of the DITF in January 2005 and the subsequent augmentation of AU headquarters staff with international experts, AMIS was never able to shed its quintessentially reactive character and assume the initiative.

Secondly, by not basing AMIS on a viable political settlement, the AU forced its troops to engage in what Alex Bellamy and Paul Williams refer to as "wider peacekeeping tasks" in the midst of a live war-zone.[30]

Literally caught in the crossfire of constantly shifting factions, AMIS soon began to suffer its first casualties as it was increasingly seen (and treated) as just another participant in the war rather than as the neutral facilitator of peace it should have been according to standard peacekeeping doctrine.

Thirdly, the constantly changing nature and imprecise formulation of its mandates led to substantial confusion within AMIS. A frequently-used example is the uncertainty created by the first expansion of the AMIS mandate in October 2004. The new mandate stated that AMIS should "protect civilians whom it encounters under imminent threat and in the immediate vicinity, within resources and capabilities, it being understood that the protection of the civilian population is the responsibility of the Government of Sudan".[31] This formulation, however, did not provide AMIS with any guidance as to what kind of protection initiatives were to be considered within its already overstretched resources and capabilities or how it was to react to Sudanese soldiers threatening the civilian population (something that happened quite frequently). While eventually even the Chairperson of the AU Commission, Alpha Konare, had to admit that the new AMIS mandate "was not clearly understood by commanders at all levels",[32] the second major revision of the operation's mandate ran into similar problems. Following the signing of the DPA in late May 2006, AMIS was asked to monitor and verify the implementation of the agreement's security provisions. When the DPA broke down shortly afterwards, the commanders found themselves once again without a clear point of reference and unsure of how to react to the various signatories and non-signatories of the now defunct agreement.

The negative effects of these three violations of important peacekeeping principles were compounded by a severe lack of financial, military and institutional resources.[33] Like AMIB before it, AMIS was under-funded from the very start. The shortfalls in funding went hand in hand with a lack of critical force enablers such as vehicles, strategic transport and communication equipment. Given the sheer size of Darfur (comparable to the whole of France) and the absence of a road network and other infrastructure, the lack of sufficient air assets proved particularly detrimental to the mission's overall effectiveness. While AMIS did receive an unprecedented degree of attention from the international community[34] – also due to what Tim Murithi had termed the "celebrification" of the Darfur conflict resulting from the public engagement of international celebrities like George Clooney and Angelina Joly[35] – the AU was unable to secure the type of long-term (that is, sustained) funding that would have allowed it to address these critical shortfalls, leaving its Chairman to conclude that "the AMIS experience has demonstrated the difficulty to mount large peace support operations for a long period of time without reliable sources of funding".[36]

Given the size of the operation as well as the political and military complexities of the conflict at hand, the lack of institutional capacity at the AU-level was a much bigger problem for AMIS than it had been for AMIB. According to Adekeye Adebajo, only one full-time professional staff member of the AU Commission was dedicated to Darfur at the beginning of the mission and this number only increased very slowly.[37] This lack of institutional capacity did not only lead to numerous control and coordination problems on the ground, but also prevented the AU from deriving the maximum benefit from the multitude of capacity-building programmes that partners brought to the mission. The absence of strategic-level guidance also left much space for the blossoming of personal and national rivalries throughout the mission hierarchy and often led to severe disagreements over resource allocation.[38] Although many of the problems were directly related to the lack of sufficient personnel within the AU's Peace and Security Department (including the DITF), the general management structures of the Union also proved quickly overburdened with the administrative requirements of AMIS. The shortage of trained accountants and financial managers, for example, resulted in substantial delays in donors' disbursements and troop contributing countries' reimbursements leaving the majority of AMIS troops unpaid for months.

During its three and a half years in the field, AMIS demonstrated the growing willingness of the African Union to get involved in the continent's conflicts. For all the above reasons, however, it proved unable to bring peace to Darfur. Its enduring legacy thus lies in the wealth of lessons that the AU learned from its planning and conduct as well as in the increasingly sophisticated division of labour that has emerged between the AU and the United Nations.

The African Union Missions in the Comoros

Largely in the shadow of its mission(s) in Darfur, the AU also conducted three peace support operations in the Comoros between March 2006 and October 2008. Consisting of an archipelago of three islands (that is, Grande Comore, Mohéli and Anjouan), the Union of the Comoros has been poisoned by political instability ever since its independence from

France in July 1975. Following almost 20 coups and counter-coups, the islands of Anjouan and Mohéli finally seceded from the Union in 1997 in protest against the increasing centralization of power on Grande Comore. This unilateral declaration of independence led the OAU – keen as ever to prevent the precedent of successful secession – to initiate a mediation process and deploy three small observer missions to the Comoros known as OMIC (1997-1998), OMIC 2 (2001-2002) and OMIC 3 (2002). Heavily supported by South Africa, the OAU managed to broker the so-called Antananarivo Agreement in April 1999 which granted the individual islands a greater degree of autonomy within the framework of the Union of the Comoros. Far from marking the end of the traditional inter-island rivalry, however, the agreement merely sparked another coup on 30 April 1999.

Led by Colonel Azali, the military junta reopened the negotiations with the OAU and, on 26 August 2000, signed the so-called Fomboni Accords which prepared the ground for a constitutional reform. The new constitution granted each island further political privileges such as its own president, parliament and local government and turned the Comoros into a federation with a rotating presidency. Even though these substantial political concessions were further complemented by a revenue sharing agreement in 2003, secessionist sentiments continued to exist on the islands, particularly on Anjouan, and there were widespread fears that these would eventually lead to another conflict. When allegations of insufficient revenue sharing halted all cooperation between the islands in the run-up to the 2006 elections for the Union presidency, the government of the Comoros turned to the AU for assistance.

The AU Mission for Support to the Elections in the Comoros

At its 47th meeting on 21 March 2006, the PSC authorized "the deployment of an African Union Mission for Support to the Elections in the Comoros (AMISEC) comprising election observers and monitors as well as 462 military and civilian police personnel".[39] AMISEC was to monitor and secure the elections, ensure that the Comorian security forces were not involved in the electoral process, protect civilians within the proximity of the polling station and support the reconciliation process.[40]

Led by the Mozambican diplomat Francisco Madeira, AMISEC quickly established itself on the Comoros. In order to be able to secure all 624 polling stations, the initial 462-strong contingent made up of troops from South Africa, Rwanda, Nigeria, Mozambique, Congo-Brazzaville and Egypt was reinforced by 700 additional South African troops when the first round of voting took place in mid-April. Both this and the second round held on 14 May went relatively smoothly and, except for the arrest of a small number of individuals for fraud, AMISEC did not have to intervene in the electoral process. On 9 June 2006, the last AMISEC troops left the archipelago "with pride and satisfaction".[41]

Even allowing for its comparatively easy task, AMISEC is generally seen as a success. Its presence was undoubtedly instrumental in the smooth running of the first democratic elections in the Comoros, its deployment was swift and its conduct remarkable. While constantly overshadowed by the operations in Darfur, it also made a valuable contribution to the AU's learning process. It not only reconfirmed the utility of the lead nation concept, but also reminded everyone that there were certain instances in which the AU could make a substantial contribution to Africa's security without large expenditures (AMISEC merely cost US$ 19 million), something that had almost been forgotten over the financial quagmire in Darfur.

The African Union Electoral and Security Assistance Mission

Following the success of AMISEC, the AU was quick to authorize another electoral assistance mission to the Comoros when the President of Anjouan, Colonel Mohamed Bacar, rejected a degree from the central government to postpone the holding of the island's presidential elections because of the unfavourable conditions on the ground. At its 77th meeting on 9 May 2007, the PSC mandated the African Union Electoral and Security Assistance Mission (known by its French acronym MAES) to create the conditions for free and fair elections and facilitate the regaining of authority of the Union government on Anjouan.[42] Made up of troops from South Africa (which once again assumed the lead) as well as Senegal, Sudan and Tanzania and financed with the help of the League of Arab States, MAES, however, could not prevent President Bacar from holding an illegal election on 10 June 2007 which confirmed him in office.

Following fruitless protests by the Constitutional Court of the Comoros which had declared the elections to be "null and void" and a number of equally ineffective negotiation attempts by a South African-led ministerial delegation, the PSC decided to impose sanctions on the illegal authorities in Anjouan in October 2007. These sanctions included travel bans as well as the freezing of the economic resources of Bacar and his supporters.[43] The PSC also reviewed the mandate of MAES in order to enable it to deploy to Anjouan, facilitate the organization of a new round of elections, supervise the Anjouanese security forces during the elections and assist with the restoration of the Union's authority on the island. Bacar, however, refused to grant MAES access to Anjouan.

After more than half a year of negotiation, the head of state of the Union of the Comoros used his speech before the 10th Ordinary Session of the AU Assembly to ask for AU support in forcefully re-establishing the authority of his government on the island of Anjouan. This request was supported by the assembly and on 20 February 2008 the Foreign Minister of Tanzania, Bernard Membe, convened a meeting of the Foreign and Defence Ministers as well as other senior officials of the countries that had expressed a readiness to contribute to a military intervention on Anjouan.[44] The meeting considered the modalities of implementing the Assembly decision and agreed on practical, military and security measures to assist the Comorian government in restoring its authority. As a result, a team of military planners from Tanzania, the Sudan, Senegal and Libya visited the Comoros from 25 February to 5 March 2008 to put the finishing touches to the plan of what came to be known as "Operation Democracy".

Operation Democracy

Following a series of smaller forays into the island (on 14, 15 and 17 March), the invasion of Anjouan began in the early morning of 25 March 2008. Five boats carried a force of about 1,800 soldiers (approximately 1,350 AU troops and 450 from the Union of the Comoros) from neighbouring Mohéli to the shores of the renegade island. The main towns were quickly overrun and Anjouan was declared under the control of the invading forces the next day. While the Anjouanese security forces suffered a couple of casualties (reports vary from three to ten), none of the AU or Comorian soldiers were killed or wounded in the mission. Largely thanks to the timely announcement of the operation to the island's residents through air-dropped leaflets, there were also no civilian casualties.

With the reinstatement of the Union government's authority, the mandate of MAES was once again amended and extended until the end of October 2008. Its new tasks included the collection of arms and ammunition on Anjouan and the re-organization of the Anjouanese security forces.[45] Now consisting of 356 military and civilian personnel from Tanzania and the Sudan, MAES was also to provide organizational assistance and security to a new round of presidential elections in June 2008. Following the successful holding of these elections, MAES was withdrawn from the Comoros and an AU liaison office was established in its stead to support the inter-Comorian dialogue.

Some analysts have suggested that the AU has only taken on the operation in Anjouan to distract from its faltering missions in Sudan and Somalia, or in the cynical words of Chrysantus Ayangafac, "there is nothing in the Comoros – it is an easier pig to slaughter than Chad or Somalia".[46] Whatever the reasons for the AU's increasing engagement in the Comorian conflict, however, both MAES and Operation Democracy deserve some credit for the return of peace and stability to the archipelago. They also point towards a number of improvements in the AU's conflict management capacities. A recent report from the Swedish Defence Research Agency, for example, comes to the conclusion that "Operation Democracy has been a breakthrough for the AU when it comes to planning and conducting peace operations".[47] The same report also praises the quick force generation process and the fact that the operation achieved its objective with only very limited support from partner countries and despite the non-involvement of usual key players like South Africa, Kenya and Nigeria.[48]

The African Union Mission in Somalia

The African Union Mission in Somalia (AMISOM) is the only AU-led operation that is still ongoing. As such it has not yet received much academic attention.[49] This is unfortunate given that the mission appears to be the exemplification of the challenges the AU continues to face in the execution of complex peace operations.

While it was officially launched on 19 January 2007, AMISOM had its roots in the 2005 attempt by IGAD to assemble a 10,500 strong regional peacebuilding force in support of Somalia's Transitional Federal Government (TFG). IGAD had been trying to mediate in the long-running civil war since 2000 and had helped to establish the TFG in 2004. In response to a request by the TFG's president, Abdullahi Yusuf, IGAD decided to deploy a peace support operation (IGASOM) to Somalia on 31 January 2005.[50] The PSC endorsed the mission a week later and on 12 May 2005 called on AU member states and the UN to provide IGASOM with political, financial and logistical support.[51] Another two months later, the PSC announced that it was envisaging the deployment of an AU peace operation to take over from IGASOM.[52] However, the reluctance of IGAD member states to contribute troops to the operation, disagreements over the composition of the force and the military advances of the Union of Islamic Courts (UIC) inside Somalia delayed the deployment of IGASOM and the mission never materialized.

The UIC continued its military advances throughout 2006 and by the autumn had extended its control over most of the Somali territory. At this time the TFG turned to neighbouring Ethiopia for help. Eager to prevent the UIC rebellion from spilling over into its notoriously unstable Ogaden region, Ethiopia chose Christmas Eve to intervene in Somalia and, with some assistance of the United States, quickly routed the UIC forces. Once the TFG had relocated to Mogadishu, it called for the deployment of a multinational peace support operation to fill the security vacuum that would inevitably result from a withdrawal of the Ethiopian forces.[53] This request led the PSC to revive the idea of an African peacekeeping force at a special meeting on 8 January 2007.[54] Following the deployment of a technical evaluation mission from 13 to 15 January, the council authorized the deployment of AMISOM at its 69th meeting on 19 January with the intent that the mission would be taken over by the UN within six months.[55]

AMISOM was to "comprise 9 infantry battalions of 850 personnel each supported by maritime, coastal and air components as well as an appropriate civilian component, including a police training team".[56] Its stated objectives were to support the TFG in its efforts to stabilize the situation in the country and further dialogue and reconciliation, to assist in the implementation of a national security and stabilization plan, particularly, the effective reestablishment and training of Somali security forces and to provide security for key infrastructure and the delivery of humanitarian aid. Importantly, the concept of logistical support for AMISOM was to be based on the AMIB-model which relies on the self-sustenance of national contingents.[57]

While the decision-making process for the AMISOM deployment had been rather rapid (less than four weeks passed from the beginning of the Ethiopian invasion until the authorization of the AU operation), the force generation and actual deployment of the mission turned out to be even slower than that of AMIS. In fact, the AU failed to secure pledges for almost half the envisaged 8,000 troops as only Uganda (1,800), Burundi (1,600), Nigeria (850), Ghana (350) and Malawi seemed prepared to contribute to AMISOM[58] – the prospect of having to maintain themselves in Somalia's hostile environment being one reason why so few states responded to the AU's request for troops.[59] Whilst Uganda deployed its battalions relatively swiftly, the other contingents lacked the resources and logistical capacity to sustain a deployment. It thus took until December 2007 before a company of 192 Burundian soldiers could finally join the forces from Uganda. By the time of writing, the total troop strength had still not surpassed 3,400.[60]

This lack of boots on the ground is certainly one reason why AMISOM has had such limited effect on the prevailing situation in Somalia. There are, however, plenty of other reasons as well, which – just as in the case of AMIS – can be divided into structural conditions like a lack of institutional capacities and a complete disregard for established peacekeeping principles. Once again the latter include a problematic mandate, the deployment in a zone of ongoing conflict and the lack of a viable political settlement that could have provided a point of reference to the operation.

AMISOM's mandate has proved problematic in two important ways. First, the mission was mandated to support a weak, divided and (in the view of many Somalis) illegitimate government that is totally reliant on the presence of foreign forces.[61] In combination with its close association with the Ethiopian occupying forces, this stigmatized AMISOM as party to the conflict rather than as a neutral arbiter and it soon came to be treated as such by the anti-government insurgency. As a result, attacks on AMISOM have become increasingly frequent since the first Ugandan peacekeeper was killed in April 2007.[62] The second problem with the mandate was that AMISOM was initially deployed with the intention that the UN would take over the responsibility after a period "ideally not exceeding six months".[63] As a swift take-over by the UN became increasingly unlikely, the AU failed to adapt AMISOM's transitory mandate to the complexities on the ground.[64]

Very much like AMIS, AMISOM has been forced to operate in a zone of ongoing conflict. Although the forces of the Islamic Courts had been driven from Mogadishu in December 2006, they soon reorganized and, with the help of Eritrea, began to launch increasingly sophisticated attacks on the Ethiopian forces, TFG soldiers and AMISOM peacekeepers. In addition to worsening the already precarious humanitarian situation in and around Mogadishu, the resulting circle of violence and counter-violence also fuelled the growing anti-AMISOM feelings of the Somali population.

The absence of any sort of political process between the various conflict parties has further undermined the position of AMISOM. Left without a peace to keep or an agreement to monitor, the mission has been confined to infrastructure protection and minor patrol activities for over two years and there is no real end in sight. While the TFG has signed what has come to be known as the Djibouti Agreement in June 2008, neither the ceasefire mentioned in it nor the international force it has called for have materialized thus far. The problems encountered by AMISOM as a result vindicate the refusal of the UN to re-hat the operation in the absence of a political settlement.

Contrary to AMIS where the defiance of peacekeeping principles was mainly a result of insufficient planning capacities and inexperience at the AU level, many of the conceptual shortcomings of AMISOM can be blamed on Ethiopia's (and the TFG's) forceful insistence on the rapid deployment of an AU-led peace operation to Somalia. This notwithstanding, the AU PSOD is not free from guilt. For example, it took several months until it had established and staffed a rudimentary planning cell – the so-called Support Management and Planning Unit (SMPU) which consisted of ten experts crammed into a single room within the DITF premises in Addis Ababa. It took even longer to establish a working force headquarters within Somalia.[65] Given that the AU was at the time still expecting the UN to take over the mission after a couple of months, these delays are particularly distressing.

As every AU operation before it, AMISOM has also been hampered by a severe lack of financial and military resources. Even though the United States (US$ 78.7 million), the European Union (€15 million), Italy (€10 million), the UK (£1.3 million), Sweden, China and the League of Arab States provided substantial support to the initial phase of AMISOM, the total pledges fell far short of the US$ 622 million required for the first year of deployment (2007).[66] This shortfall in funding has continued throughout 2008 and has gone hand in hand with a lack of critical force enablers such as helicopters, armoured personnel carriers and IT equipment. As it currently appears as if AMISOM will have to remain in Somalia for quite some time to come – the plan to create an UN-led Mogadishu International Stabilization Force (MISF) to replace AMISOM has fallen through after only two out of the fifty countries approached have indicated a willingness to contribute[67] – one can only hope that the international community increases its commitments to AMISOM in line with its new-found desire to curb the surge in piracy along Somalia's coast.

Summary

Beyond the specifics of each operation, the preceding analysis allows for at least four general conclusions about the nature, quality and problems of AU-led peace operations. First, the missions have generally been defined by what is probably best described as an ambition-resources gap.[68] The increasing willingness of the AU to intervene in violent conflicts throughout the continent should not conceal the fact that the organization continues to have enormous difficulties in mobilizing sufficient funds, troops and military equipment to sustain even relatively small-scale peace operations. While there have been some notable improvements in areas such as peacekeeping training over the last few years, the operations in Darfur and Somalia have clearly shown how dependent the AU remains on the continuation of the international community's financial support. The same operations can also serve to demonstrate the current insufficiencies of Africa's military capabilities. Without the logistical assistance of outside partners, the African contingents would not have been able to deploy to Darfur and Somalia. Without planning support from the UN, NATO and the EU, African commanders would have encountered even greater difficulties in putting the missions together and lastly, without the vehicles, food, medical facilities and inter-operable equipment provided by the international community, neither AMIS nor AMISOM could have been sustained in the field. This lack of financial and military resources is compounded by a lack of institutional capacity at the AU-level where the merely nine staff members of the PSOD are responsible for the planning, deploying and managing of all operations, as well as for conflict mediation and post-conflict reconstruction (as compared to the 630 personnel employed by the UN's Department of Peacekeeping Operations for similar tasks).[69] Given this small number of staff, it is not surprising that the tasks at hand have generally outweighed the available capacities.

The second conclusion to be drawn concerns the operations' mandates. These have generally been less than perfect, one often-cited reason being that all operations thus far have been conducted with the consent or even at the invitation of the *de jure* authorities of the country in which the conflict was taking place. This has accorded these authorities which often are parties to the conflict with considerable influence over the terms of the mission mandate, particularly so when they simultaneously held a seat in the PSC (as was the case with Sudan and Ethiopia during the authorization processes of AMIS and AMISOM). As a result, the mandates have usually either been weakened by political compromises or forced to ignore established peacekeeping maxims like the crucial importance of an accompanying political process at the expense of overall operational effectiveness.

The third issue to note is what is increasingly referred to as the "emerging division of labour" between the AU and the United Nations. With the exception of the operations in the Comoros, all of the AU's peace operations have followed a similar pattern in which the AU intervention was supposed to create the conditions for a follow-up UN operation in accordance with the principle of subsidiarity as set out in Chapter VIII of the UN Charter.[70] While the operation in Burundi has demonstrated that this sequencing can work, both AMIS and AMISOM have also shown that many issues still require clarification. For example, there is not yet any arrangement to prevent UN operations from competing with AU operations for African troops as has been the case with UNAMID. Many AU member states decided to opt out of AMISOM in order to participate in the new hybrid mission because the UN reimbursement scheme was perceived to offer more immediate (and reliable) financial benefits than that of the AU.[71]

The fourth conclusion concerns the improvised nature of all six operations. While it is true that, given the unpredictability and variety of conflict dynamics across the continent, a certain element of improvisation is unavoidable, the AU has demonstrated a particularly remarkable lack of institutional learning with respect to the planning and conduct of its peace support operations.[72] Planning cells, for example, had to be painfully re-created from scratch for every operation and structures and procedures had to be constantly re-invented. The enormous loss of effectiveness that has resulted from such improvisation proves the vital importance of institutionalized instruments like the ASF.

The relatively early stage of the AU's development means that it is difficult to pass any more than a preliminary judgement on the organization's peace support efforts. This notwithstanding, it is already evident that the AU's ability to intervene in intra-state conflicts has surpassed that of most other regional organizations in Asia, South America and the Middle East.[73] Its experience in Burundi, Darfur and Somalia, however, also suggests that the organization has much to do to improve its ability to deliver peace and security to the African people. The institutionalization of an elaborate security architecture and the operationalization of instruments like the African Standby Force and the Continental Early Warning System that will be described in the following chapters are important steps in this respect.

Notes

[1] Tim Murithi, "The African Union's Evolving Role in Peace Operations: The African Union Mission in Burundi, the African Union Mission in Sudan and the African Union Mission in Somalia," *African Security Review* 17, no. 1 (2008): 75.

[2] For more information on the civil war in Burundi see Rene Lemarchand, *Burundi: Ethnic Conflict and Genocide* (Cambridge: Cambridge University Press, 1996).

[3] For good summaries of the mediation efforts see Patricia Daley, "The Burundi Peace Negotiations: An African Experience of Peacemaking " *Review of African Political Economy* 34, no. 112 (2007): 333-352, Gilbert Khadiagala, "Burundi," in *Dealing with Conflict in Africa: The United Nations and Regional Organizations*, ed. Jane Boulden (Basingstoke: Palgrave Macmillan, 2003). For more detailed information on the Nyerere mediation see Gaudens Mpangala and Bismarck Mwansasu, eds., *Beyond Conflict in Burundi* (Dar es Salaam: Mwalimu Nyerere Foundation, 2004). For UN efforts see Ahmedou Ould-Abdullah, *Burundi on the Brink, 1993-1995: A UN Special Envoy Reflects on Preventive Diplomacy* (Washington, DC: US Institute of Peace, 2000).

[4] For more information on the South African mediation attempts see Roger Southall and Kristina Bentley, *An African Peace Process: Mandela, South Africa and Burundi* (London: Human Science Research Council, 2005).

[5] For details of the planning process see Henri Boshoff and Dara Francis, "The AU Mission in Burundi: Technical and Operational Dimensions," *African Security Review* 12, no. 3 (2003): 41-44. See also Emma Svensson, *The African Mission in Burundi: Lessons Learned from the African Union's First Peace Operation* (Stockholm: Swedish Defense Research Agency, 2008), 11-17.

[6] See Communiqué of the 91st Ordinary Session of the Central Organ of the OAU Mechanism for Conflict Prevention, Management, and Resolution at Ambassadorial Level, Addis Ababa, Ethiopia, 2 April 2003.

[7] The force comprised 866 troops from Ethiopia, 228 from Mozambique, 1,508 from South Africa, and 43 military observers from Benin, Burkina Faso, Gabon, Mali, and Tunisia. Ethiopia later indicated a willingness to expand its contingent to 1,300. See UN Document S/2003/1146, p. 7.

[8] Festus Agoagye, "The African Mission in Burundi: Lessons Learned from the First African Union Peacekeeping Operation," *Conflict Trends*, no. 2 (2004): 13.

[9] For more information on ONUB see Stephen Jackson, *The United Nations Operation in Burundi (ONUB) - Political and Strategic Lessons Learned* (New York: UN Peacekeeping Best Practices Unit, 2006).

[10] Agoagye, "The African Mission in Burundi: Lessons Learned from the First African Union Peacekeeping Operation," 14.

[11] Agoagye, Festus as quoted in Hannes, Rebekka and Angela Unkrüer. 2008. Global and Regional Approaches to Peacekeeping in Africa. Conference Report, Potsdam Spring Dialogues, 4-5 April 2008, pp. 9-10.

[12]   See, for example, Seth Appiah-Mensah, "The African Mission in Sudan: Darfur Dilemmas," *African Security Review* 15, no. 1 (2006), William O'Neill and Violet Cassis, *Protecting Two Million Internally Displaced: The Successes and Shortcomings of the African Union in Darfur* (Washington DC: Brookings Institution Press, 2005), Paul Williams, "Military Responses to Mass Killing: The African Union Mission in Darfur," *International Peacekeeping* 13, no. 2 (2006).

[13]   Adekeye Adebajo, "The Peacekeeping Travails of the AU and the Regional Economic Communities," in *The African Union and Its Institutions*, ed. John Akokpari, Angela Ndinga-Muvumba, and Tim Murithi (Auckland Park: Fanele, 2008), 136.

[14]   For a more detailed discussion of the war in Darfur see Julie Flint and Alex de Waal, *Darfur: A New History of a Long War* (London: Zed, 2008), Gerard Prunier, *Darfur: The Ambiguous Genocide*, Revised and updated edition ed. (London: Hurst, 2007), Alex de Waal, ed., *War in Darfur and the Search for Peace* (Cambridge: Global Equity Initiative, Harvard University, 2007). For information on the root causes of the war see Douglas Johnson, *The Root Causes of Sudan's Civil Wars* (London: James Currey, 2003).

[15]   For more information on the Janjaweed see Ali Haggar, "The Origins and Organization of the Janjawiid in Darfur," in *War in Darfur and the Search for Peace*, ed. Alex de Waal (Cambridge: Global Equity Initiative, Harvard University, 2007), 113-139.

[16]   International Commission of Inquiry on Darfur, Report to the Secretary-General, Pursuant to Security Council Resolution 1564 (2004) of 18 September 2004 (UN Document S/2005/60, Annex).

[17]   The US House of Representatives, for example, voted unanimously to describe the situation in Darfur as "genocide" in July 2004 and called for action to stop the massacres.

[18]   See *Report of the Chairperson of the Commission on the Situation in the Darfur Region of the Sudan* (AU Document PSC/PR/2 (XVII), 20 October 2004), para. 64.

[19]   See Report of the Chairperson of the Commission on the Situation in the Darfur Region of the Sudan (AU Document PSC/PR/2 (XXVIII), 28 April 2005), para. 103.

[20]   Ibid., para. 3.

[21]   Ibid., para. 126.

[22]   See *Report of the Chairperson of the Commission on the Situation in the Darfur Region of the Sudan* (AU Document PSC/PR/2 (XLV), 12 January 2006), p. 4.

[23]   Ibid., pp. 29-30.

[24]   *Report of the Chairperson of the Commission on the Situation in the Darfur Region of the Sudan* (AU Document PSC/MIN/2 (LXIII), 18 September 2006), para. 88.

[25]   For more information on the Abuja Peace talks and the DPA see Laurie Nathan, "The Making and Unmaking of the Darfur Peace Process," in *War in Darfur and the Search for Peace*, ed. Alex de Waal (Cambridge: Global Equity Initiative, Harvard University, 2007), 245-266, Dawit Toga, "The African Union Mediation and the Abuja Peace Talks," in *War in Darfur and the*

Search for Peace, ed. Alex de Waal (Cambridge: Global Equity Initiative, Harvard University, 2007), 214-244.

[26] See *UN Security Council Resolution 1706*, 31 August 2006.

[27] See Associated Press (AP), *Bashir accuses UN of meddling in Darfur*, 25 September 2006.

[28] See Appiah-Mensah, "The African Mission in Sudan: Darfur Dilemmas," 19.

[29] See "AU Multi-Dimensional Missions: Lessons Learned from the African Mission in Sudan (AMIS) for the African Standby Force (ASF)" Conference Report. International Peace Academy/Institute Seminar. Accra, 10-12 October 2006, p. 9.

[30] For an interesting discussion of the concept of "wider peacekeeping" see Alex Bellamy and Paul Williams, *Understanding Peacekeeping*, 2nd ed. (Oxford: Polity, 2009).

[31] AU Communiqué (AU Document PSC/PR/Comm.(XVII), 20 October 2004).

[32] See *Report of the Chairperson of the Commission on the Situation in the Darfur Region of the Sudan* (AU Document PSC/PR/2 (XLV), 12 January 2006), para. 105.

[33] It is important to note that there is a direct relationship between the defiance of well-established peacekeeping principles and structural conditions like a lack of institutional capacity as the latter increases the likelihood of the former.

[34] Many countries provided material and/or financial assistance to AMIS. Canada and the Netherlands, for example, provided 28 helicopters and several fixed-wing aircraft. Canada also donated 150 armored personnel carriers. Besides providing substantial financial support, the US also flew in a battalion from Burundi and France provided air transport to the Senegalese contingent. Germany and the UK also provided transport and other assistance to AMIS.

[35] Murithi, "The African Union's Evolving Role in Peace Operations: The African Union Mission in Burundi, the African Union Mission in Sudan and the African Union Mission in Somalia," 78.

[36] See *Report of the Chairperson of the Commission on the Situation in the Darfur Region of the Sudan* (AU Document PSC/PR/2 (XLV), 12 January 2006), p. 16.

[37] Adebajo, "The Peacekeeping Travails of the AU and the Regional Economic Communities," 138.

[38] See "AU Multi-Dimensional Missions: Lessons Learned from the African Mission in Sudan (AMIS) for the African Standby Force (ASF)" Conference Report. International Peace Academy/Institute Seminar. Accra, 10-12 October 2006, pp. 10-13.

[39] *Communiqué on the Situation in the Comoros* (AU Document PSC/PR/Comm.1 (XLVII), 21 March 2006), para. 9.

[40] Ibid.

[41] Francisco Madeira, *Concluding Remarks on AMISEC*, Moroni, 8 June 2006.

[42] See *Communiqué on the Situation in the Comoros* (AU Document PSC/MIN/Comm.1 (LXXVII), 9 May 2007).

---

⁴³   See *Communiqué on the Situation in the Comoros* (AU Document PSC/PR/Comm (XCV), 10 October 2007).

⁴⁴   *Report of the Chairperson of the Commission on the Situation in the Comoros since the 10ᵗʰ Ordinary Session of the Assembly of the African Union* (AU Document PSC/PR/2 (CXXIV), 30 April 2008).

⁴⁵   Ibid.

⁴⁶   Chrysantus Ayangafac cited in Africa Research Bulletin: Political, Social, and Cultural Series, 1-31 March 2008, 17464A.

⁴⁷   See Emma Svensson, *The African Union's Operations in the Comoros* (Stockholm: Swedish Defense Research Agency, 2008), 23.

⁴⁸   Helmoed-Römer Heitman, "Comoros Operation: The Positives and Negatives " *Jane's Defense Weekly* 45, no. 15 (2008): 33.

⁴⁹   A notable exception is Cecilia Hull and Emma Svensson, *African Union Mission in Somalia (AMISOM): Exemplifying African Union Peacekeeping Challenges* (Stockholm: Swedish Defense Research Agency, 2008).

⁵⁰   IGAD, *Communiqué on Somalia*, 31 January 2005.

⁵¹   *Communiqué of the 24ᵗʰ Meeting of the Peace and Security Council* (AU Document PSC/PR/Comm. (XXIV), 7 February 2005) and *Communiqué of the 29ᵗʰ Meeting of the Peace and Security Council* (AU Document PSC/PR/Comm. (XXIX), 12 May 2005)

⁵²   *Communiqué on the Situation in Somalia* (AU Document PSC/Min/Comm. (XXXIV) – (i), 3 July 2005).

⁵³   *Report of the Chairperson of the Commission on the Situation in Somalia* (AU Document PSC/PR/2 (LXIX), 19 January 2007).

⁵⁴   Ibid.

⁵⁵   *Communiqué of the 69ᵗʰ Meeting of the Peace and Security Council* (AU Document PSC/PR/Comm. (LXIX), 19 January 2007). For more information on how the AU became involved see Hull and Svensson, *African Union Mission in Somalia (AMISOM): Exemplifying African Union Peacekeeping Challenges*, 22-25.

⁵⁶   Ibid., para. 9.

⁵⁷   Ibid.

⁵⁸   *Report of the Chairperson of the Commission on the Situation in Somalia* (AU Document PSC/PR/2 (LXXX), 18 July 2007).

⁵⁹   Other reasons cited in the literature include the widespread perception that Ethiopia had succeeded in directly shaping the AU's position on the conflict in Somalia as well as the decreasing likelihood of a speedy take-over of the mission by the UN.

⁶⁰   Phone interview with Colonel Reinhard Linz, EU Military Liaison Officer to the AU, 11 January 2009.

⁶¹   International Institute for Strategic Studies, "Conflict in Somalia: Faint Hope of Resolution," *Strategic Comments* 15, no. 4.

⁶²   K Andrew and Victoria Holt, *United Nations - African Union Coordination on Peace and Security* (Washington DC: Henry L. Stimson Centre, 2007), 8.

⁶³   *Report of the Chairperson on the Situation in Somalia* (AU Document PSC/PR/2 (CV), 18 January 2008).

[64] As early as November 2007, UN Secretary-General Ban Ki-Moon stated that the idea of deploying UN peacekeepers to Somalia was "neither realistic nor viable". "Somalia peacekeepers not viable", *BBC News Online*, 9 November 2007.

[65] Interview with Major-General Benon Biraro, AMISOM Force Commander, Addis Ababa, August 2007.

[66] For more information on the shortfall in pledges for 2007 see *Report of the Chairperson on the Situation in Somalia* (AU Document PSC/PR/2 (CV), 18 January 2008)

[67] *Letter from the Secretary-General to the President of the Security Council* (UN Document S/2008/804, 19 December 2008), Annex, para. 1.

[68] This term is a variation on the phrase "capability-expectation gap" coined by Christopher Hill. See Christopher Hill, "The Capability-Expectations Gap or Conceptualizing Europe's International Role," *Journal of Common Market Studies* 31, no. 3 (1993): 305-328.

[69] Hull and Svensson, *African Union Mission in Somalia (AMISOM): Exemplifying African Union Peacekeeping Challenges*, 35.

[70] For more information on idea of regional peace operations and Chapter VIII of the UN Charter see Ademola Abass, *Regional Organizations and the Development of Collective Security - Beyond Chapter VIII of the UN Charter* (Oxford: Hart Publishing, 2004), Benedikt Franke, "In Defense of Regional Peace Operations in Africa," *Journal of Humanitarian Assistance*, no. 185 (2006).

[71] For a more detailed discussion of the emerging AU-UN cooperation see chapter ten of this book.

[72] There are two obvious reasons for the AU's inability to create a knowledge base. First, there simply has not been enough institutional capacity to create one. Second, there is not yet any effective process for evaluating an operation while it is ongoing or after it is completed. Furthermore, the AU does not debrief the personnel returning from missions and has no institutional memory on the PSO it has been involved in.

[73] This fact, however, has to be noted with care. One reason for Africa's "superiority" in this respect may simply be that the other regions either did not have a comparable need for conflict management capabilities (Asia, South America) or the structural conditions to allow regional cooperation in this area (the Middle East). I am grateful to Michael Møller from the Kofi Annan Foundation for bringing this point to my attention and to Paul Williams for clarifying my thoughts on this topic.

7
The Security Institutions of the African Union

It is certainly true that the operations covered in the previous chapter have shown that the AU has not yet reached the institutional capacities that would allow it to bridge the wide gap between its ambitions and actual abilities. Nonetheless, a discussion of its emerging organizational structures helps to illustrate the increasing extent and quality of inter-African security cooperation that is the subject of this book.[1]

The institutional structures of the AU have evolved substantially since the organization was inaugurated in 2002. At present, the AU consists of ten organs, namely, the Assembly of Heads of State and Government, the Executive Council, the Commission, the Permanent Representatives Committee, the Pan-African Parliament, the Specialized Technical Committees, the Economic, Social and Cultural Council, the Court of Justice, the African Central Bank, the African Investment Bank and the African Monetary Fund.[2] These organs, though not yet all fully operational, provide the institutional framework within which the organization's conflict management structures must be situated. In sum referred to as the AU's "security architecture",[3] they include the Peace and Security Council, the Panel of the Wise, the Military Staff Committee (MSC), the Special (Peace) Fund, the African Standby Force and the Continental Early Warning System (see Figure 7.1).[4] While leaving the ASF and the CEWS to be discussed separately in chapters eight and nine, this chapter also covers the Common African Defense and Security Policy (CADSP) which provides the conceptual basis for the entire architecture as well as the AU Commission's Peace and Security Directorate (PSD) which functions as its implementation agency.

Figure 7.1: The AU Peace and Security Architecture

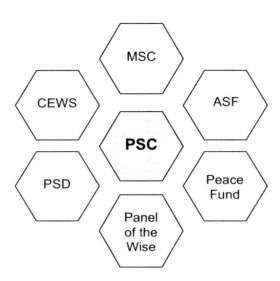

The Peace and Security Council

As illustrated by the figure above, the AU structures and mechanisms for peace and security revolve around the PSC.[5] Modeled on the UN Security Council, it is supposed to be the AU's "standing decision-making organ for the prevention, management and resolution of conflicts".[6] As such it is mandated to promote peace, security and stability, anticipate and prevent conflicts, promote and implement peace-building and post-conflict reconstruction activities, coordinate and harmonize continental efforts in the prevention and combating of international terrorism, develop a common defense policy for the Union, encourage democratic practices, good governance and the rule of law, as well as protect human rights and fundamental freedoms.[7] To be able to do all the above, the PSC has been granted eighteen specific powers which range from the provision of humanitarian assistance to the authorization of military intervention in AU members states.

Of the many interesting aspects of the PSC, five deserve particular attention, namely, (1) its membership, (2) the formal rules that govern its conduct, (3) its relationship with the UN Security Council, (4) its relationship with civil society actors, and (5) its performance to date.

During OAU times, substantive debates about peace and security involved all member states in an open and unstructured fashion. This lack of clear rules and procedures severely hampered the organization's ability to agree on effective security measures, especially so as its membership increased from just above thirty in 1963 to more than fifty in the early 1990s. To avoid this pitfall, the designers of the new African Union agreed that its conflict management efforts should no longer be guided by the totality of its members but rather by what one official referred to as a "smaller committee of big minds".[8] After some debate it was decided that the membership of this new committee should be limited to fifteen states to guarantee effective decision-making. The *Protocol Relating to the Establishment of the Peace and Security Council of the African Union* specified that the AU Executive Council is to elect these fifteen members, five of them for terms of three years and ten for terms of two years.[9] Besides the principles of "equitable regional representation and rotation", the Executive Council is also to consider criteria such as a country's "contribution to the promotion and maintenance of peace and security in Africa" as well as its "respect for constitutional governance, the rule of law and human rights" when making decisions about membership.[10] In addition to the elected members, selected member states of the AU and officials from both inside and outside the AU apparatus may participate in the open sessions of the PSC.

The meetings of the PSC, whether open or closed, are governed by strict rules and procedures. These are set out in Article 8 of the PSC Protocol and regulate the number of votes each member has (one), the way in which decisions are to be reached ("generally by consensus",[11] but if consensus cannot be reached by a two-thirds majority for all matters except for procedural ones where a simple majority is enough) as well as the meeting schedule (at least twice a month at ambassadorial level, once a month at ministerial level and once a year at the Head of State and Government level). There are three different types of meetings, namely, (1) formal meetings, (2) briefing sessions at which the PSC is updated on specific issues, and (3) consultations with experts. All these meetings are led by a monthly rotating chairperson who also plays a role in the selection of agenda items.

The relationship between the PSC and the United Nations Security Council has been marred by disagreements over which body has the primary legal authority to sanction the use of military force. Partly, this disagreement arose out of accidental ambiguities within the PSC Protocol which states in one article (16.1) that the AU has the "primary responsibility for promoting peace, security and stability in Africa" and in another (17.1) that the UN has the "primary responsibility for the maintenance of international peace and security".[12] Partly, it sprung from the increasing disappointment many African states were feeling towards the UN and a resultant disregard for its principles, in the words of the AU's legal advisor, Ben Kioko:

> When questions were raised as to whether the Union could possibly have an inherent right to intervene other than through the Security Council, they were dismissed out of hand. This decision reflected a sense of frustration with the slow pace of reform of the international order, and with instances in which the international community tended to focus attention on other parts of the world at the expense of more pressing problems in Africa. Furthermore, the process of drawing up the Constitutive Act took place not long after the OAU Assembly of Heads of State and Government had adopted the Ouagadougou decision defying the sanctions imposed by the UN Security Council on Libya in connection with the Lockerbie crisis. [...] African leaders have shown themselves willing to push the frontiers of collective stability and security to the limit without any regard for legal niceties such as the authorization of the Security Council.[13]

It was only in March 2005 that the AU agreed on a common position with the UN in this regard. The so-called Ezulwini Consensus specified that, in general, interventions of regional organizations necessitate the approval of the UN Security Council, but that "in certain situations, such approval could be granted *post hoc* in circumstances requiring urgent action".[14] As the interaction of both bodies grew as a result of the AU's increasing activism in peace and security affairs, such debates on principles eventually gave way to more practical discussions about force re-hatting, support arrangements and capacity-building cooperation. Today, the two bodies have a good working relationship. They occasionally hold joint sessions in New York and have already issued several joint communiqués on a range of security-related topics, particularly so since the transformation of AMIS into the first AU-UN hybrid operation institutionalized their partnership in December 2007.

The relationship between the PSC and civil society actors has traditionally been rather sporadic and inconsequential. While Article 20 of the PSC Protocol requests the PSC to encourage civil society organizations to "participate actively in the efforts aimed at promoting peace, security and stability",[15] in practice little interaction has taken place between the PSC and civil society. However, in light of the increasingly important and prominent role of the latter in Africa, the PSC held a retreat in December 2008 at which it agreed on a formula for interaction with civil society organizations.[16] The so-called Livingstone formula designates the AU's Economic, Social and Cultural Council (ECOSOCC) as the focal point of this interaction and specifies areas in which civil society organizations can make a valuable contribution to the efforts of the PSC. Such areas include technical support to AU field and fact-finding missions, early warning reporting and situation analysis, mediation assistance and the implementation of peace agreements, post-conflict confidence-building, environmental rehabilitation, the provision of training and humanitarian assistance as well as public advocacy of PSC decisions.[17] Given the identification of such a wide range of potential areas of cooperation, the Livingstone Formula is as much an attempt to narrow the ambition-resources gap as an acknowledgement of the growing role of civil society actors.

When the PSC was launched in May 2004, its creation was hailed as "an historic watershed in Africa's progress towards resolving its conflicts and the building of a durable peace and security order".[18] Almost five years later, the PSC has held over 170 meetings, issued over 100 communiqués and authorized sanctions against several African states as well as peace operations in Sudan, the Comoros and Somalia. An evaluation of the PSC's performance to date, however, needs to go beyond these facts. Paul Williams, for example, suggests adapting Edward Luck's framework for assessing the performance of the UN Security Council by asking a set of questions, including (1) whether African states are displaying an interest in the PSC, (2) whether the PSC is abused for political grand-standing, (3) whether the PSC elicits sufficient support from the continent's states, (4) whether the PSC carries out its operational activities and missions competently and efficiently, and (5) whether, ultimately, the PSC makes a real difference to the maintenance of peace and security in Africa.[19] While Williams' answers to these questions are generally positive, he also points to a number of remaining problems which range from member states' lack of financial contributions and the occasional disregard for the council's procedures to delays in establishing a sufficiently staffed secretariat.[20] His concerns are echoed both by other academics covering the PSC such as Jeremy Levitt as well as by the general audit report of the African Union presented in early 2008. The latter also criticizes the lack of fact-finding efforts by the PSC as well as its unwillingness to establish working groups and advisory bodies to support its work.[21] In general, however, there seems to be consensus that despite these shortcomings, the PSC has developed into an increasingly effective centerpiece of the continental security architecture.

The Panel of the Wise

Article 11 of the PSC Protocol calls for the establishment of a Panel of the Wise to support the work of the council in the area of conflict prevention and act as a general advisory mechanism.[22] Its main task is the use of personal mediation, discreet diplomacy and good offices to avoid the escalation of conflicts and facilitate the conclusion of viable peace agreements.[23] As such it is the institutionalization of Africa's long tradition of high-level and personal mediation within the AU's security architecture.[24] To fulfill its purpose, the panel is composed of five eminent African personalities who on the basis of their good standing and expertise are suited for personal mediation on behalf of the AU.[25]

For a number of reasons ranging from disagreements about its composition and purpose to financial concerns, it took the AU over four years to agree on the first panel. During its 10th Ordinary Session in January 2007, the AU Assembly finally appointed the following personalities to serve on the inaugural Panel of the Wise: Salim Ahmed Salim, former Secretary-General of the OAU (for Eastern Africa), Brigalia Bam, Chairperson of the Independent Electoral Commission of South Africa (for Southern Africa), Ahmed Ben Bella, former President of Algeria (for Northern Africa), Elisabeth Pognon, President of the Constitutional Court of Benin (for Western Africa) and Miguel Trovaoda, former President of Sao Tome and Principe (for Central Africa).

With these appointments made, the AU Commission began to draw up the modalities for the functioning of the panel in accordance with Article 11.7 of the PSC Protocol. At its 100th meeting held on 12 November 2007, the PSC agreed on these modalities and specified the panel's mandate and procedures. In addition to advising the PSC and the AU Commission, the panel was mandated to carry out fact-finding missions, shuttle diplomacy between parties not yet ready to engage in formal talks, adopt confidence-building measures, assist and advise mediation teams in formal negotiations and develop and recommend ideas that can promote peace and security.[26] The PSC also called for the establishment of a dedicated secretariat for the panel within the Conflict Management Division of the Peace and Security Department and identified five criteria which should guide the panel members in setting their priorities for any given year, namely, (1) the degree to which a conflict situation already receives regional or international attention or not, (2) whether the PSC is already seized with a particular conflict situation and whether additional attention by the panel may add further value to existing efforts, (3) whether a given situation has remained in conflict for a considerable amount of time or is in danger of descending into conflict despite multiple ongoing mediation and negotiation efforts, (4) whether a conflict situation has experienced a sudden and speedy decline, and (5) whether a conflict situation has experienced difficulties in implementing a peace agreement and, therefore, faces the risk of reverting to conflict.[27]

Little more than a month after the PSC had adopted these modalities, the Panel of the Wise was formally inaugurated and the 91-year old Ahmed Ben Bella was elected as its first chair. During the ceremony, Ben Bella summarized his expectations for the panel's work:

> Our common wish is that wherever we may be called on to intervene, the Panel of the Wise will be prepared to lend its interlocutors the benefit of the ancestral African values of wisdom and dialogue and ensure that peaceful solutions prevail, regardless of the nature of the crisis or conflict. [...] By working together, we will be able to realize the hopes we all cherish of an Africa that is once and for all at peace, permanently reconciled with itself and effectively engaged on the road to development and integration.[28]

Since its inauguration, the panel has held six ordinary meetings covering issues ranging from the adoption of work plans and the problems associated with recent electoral processes in Kenya and Zimbabwe to the indictment of Sudan's President Omar al-Bashir by the prosecutor of the International Criminal Court. However, it has not yet engaged in mediation.

The Military Staff Committee

The Military Staff Committee is the second advisory body established by the PSC Protocol. According to Article 13.8, the MSC shall "advise and assist the Peace and Security Council in all questions relating to military and security requirements for the promotion and maintenance of peace and security in Africa".[29] For this purpose, it is composed of senior military officers of the fifteen PSC member states.[30] In addition to their advisory role, the members of the MSC also act as liaison officers between the PSC, the African Chiefs of Defense Staff and the regional conflict management mechanisms.

Even though the MSC has met regularly to discuss ongoing peace operations as well as the development of the African Standby Force and the Continental Early Warning System, it has not been very influential. At their second meeting in March 2008, the Ministers of Defense and

Security of the AU member states stressed the importance of enhancing the capacity and effectiveness of the MSC as a critical advisory structure to the PSC and in the development of the ASF. Accordingly, they urged the member states concerned to take the necessary steps to be appropriately represented in the MSC by deploying Defense Attachés who should be actively involved in the evolving process to establish the ASF and offer assistance to the AU Commission in order to ensure African ownership. They also recommended that reflection should be initiated on the purely military composition of the MSC to reflect the multi-dimensional nature of the ASF and peace support operations.[31]

The Special (Peace) Fund

The Special Fund is the continental financial mechanism created to support the AU's operational activities in the area of peace and security. According to Article 21 of the PSC Protocol, the fund is specifically meant to collect and administer the funds needed for AU-led peace operations. As such it is the continuation of the OAU's Peace Fund which had been created as part of the Mechanism for Conflict Prevention, Management and Resolution in 1993. Just like this fund, the Special Fund is financed through an annual contribution from the organization's regular budget,[32] by voluntary contributions from member states and donations from international partners. Given the merely cosmetic nature of the name change, it is not surprising that the Special Fund is plagued by two all too familiar problems. Firstly, the total contributions to the fund have remained far below the required levels. Secondly, the total contributions of AU member states have never made up more than two percent of the fund's total income (see Table 7.1).

Table 7.1: Summary of the Peace Fund (off-budget, in US$ '000s)[33]

Year	Contributions from AU members	Donors' contributions	Total income received
2004	1,794	107,652	109,446
2005	2,737	122,892	125,629
2006	2,786	179,622	182,408
2007	2,940	142,350	145,290

While these problems certainly raise important questions regarding the overall effectiveness of the fund as well as the quality of African ownership thereof, the AU's Peace and Security Department is actively trying to overcome them. On the one hand, it is lobbying for an increase of the annual contribution to ten percent of the AU's regular budget as well as the creation of a revolving trust fund to generate reliable financial flows, on the other hand it is cooperating with the UN in identifying new funding mechanisms for AU peace operations.[34]

The AU Commission

Similar in role to the UN Secretariat, the commission is both a preparatory and an executive body. It runs the organization in-between summits, prepares and implements policy decisions and manages the donor funds. Within the commission there are several departments that are theoretically dealing with security issues, but in reality the Department for Political Affairs is heavily marginalized by the Department for Peace and Security. The latter not only receives the most donor attention, but with 53 full-time staff members it is also by far the largest of the commission's eight substantive departments (that is, peace and security, political affairs, infrastructure and energy, social affairs, human resources, science and technology, trade and industry, farming and agricultural economics, and economic affairs).[35] The department is run by a commissioner and essentially consists of a Peace and Security Directorate with four separate divisions (see Figure 7.2).

The Peace and Security Directorate is the body that follows up the policy decisions taken by the Peace and Security Council. In addition, it coordinates the establishment of the African Standby Force and the Continental Early Warning System, plans and conducts peace operations and maintains the relations with international partners, particularly the UN and the EU, in the area of peace and security. To this purpose, it is split into a PSC Division, a Conflict Management Division, a Peace Support Operations Division and a Defense and Security Division.

The Peace and Security Council Division is the permanent secretariat of the council. It is meant to provide continuous administrative and planning support to the rotating membership of the PSC. Even though the PSC Protocol provided for such a division as early as 2003, it took over 15 months for the AU to recruit the first staff member and nearly two years for it to hire the head of the division (who finally started in September 2006).[36] While the process of establishing a secretariat for the PSC dragged on, the Conflict Management Division managed the affairs of the PSC on an *ad hoc* basis.

Figure 7.2: The Structure of the Peace & Security Directorate[37]

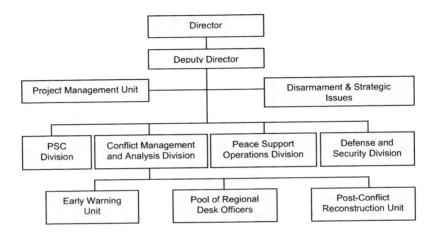

The Conflict Management Division is the operational policy arm of the PSC. It consists of an Early Warning Unit and a Post-Conflict Reconstruction Unit both of which are developing policy options in their area of expertise and coordinate activities to support the prevention, management and resolution of inter- and intra-state conflicts in Africa. The AU's permanently staffed situation room is also part of the Conflict Management Division.

The Peace Supports Operations Division is also divided into two units.[38] The Operations and Support Unit is in charge of planning and conducting AU peace operations and thus has a role similar to that of the UN's Department for Peacekeeping Operations (DPKO). The African Standby Force and Military Staff Committee Unit is in charge of planning and managing the establishment of the ASF and providing the rotating membership of the MSC with a permanent secretariat. As such it is the central coordinating authority for the operationalization of the regional standby brigades and the hub of military expertise within the AU. While the previous chapter has shown that with less than a dozen full-time staff members the PSOD is woefully understaffed and unable to cope with its tasks, there are increasing attempts to improve the institutional capacities of this division. The most recent reform proposal championed by the UN recommends the complete reorganization of the PSOD, including upgrading it to the status of a department and increasing the number of its full-time staff to 207.[39]

The Defense and Security Division facilitates disarmament initiatives, promotes defense cooperation and coordinates African efforts in preventing and combating terrorism.[40] Except for some joint initiatives with the African Centre for the Study and Research on Terrorism (ACSRT), its role has been limited thus far. At the present time there is only one full-time staff member assigned to the division.

Summary

While serious capacity problems remain, the AU's security institutions described above are a significant improvement on the structures of the OAU especially so as they are embedded in an emerging consensus on their role in continental conflict prevention, management and resolution. This consensus is enshrined in the Solemn Declaration on a Common African Defense and Security Policy (CASDP) that was signed on 28 February 2004 in Sirte.[41] The CASDP provides the conceptual basis for the AU's security architecture by defining key terms such as *Defense*, *Security* and *Common Security Threats* and stating the principles which are to guide inter-state security cooperation in Africa within the AU framework.[42] This means that the institutions described in this chapter are in the words of Gambia's Secretary of State, Omar Touray, "implementation agencies of a broader policy framework" and as such less susceptible to the kind of partisan politics that had crippled the OAU's security institutions.[43]

Even though it is true that the AU security architecture is currently unable to fulfill the high expectations placed on it, the elaborateness of the structures described in this chapter as well as the existence of a continent-wide consensus on the architecture's design and purpose testify to the increasing quality of inter-state security cooperation in Africa. The following chapters will describe two particularly telling examples of this improved cooperation, namely, the ongoing efforts to operationalize the African Standby Force and the Continental Early Warning System.

Notes

¹   There is a growing body of works on this important topic. See, for example, John Akokpari, Angela Ndinga-Muvumba, and Tim Murithi, eds., *The African Union and Its Institutions* (Auckland Park: Fanele, 2008), Karin Bogland, Robert Egnell, and Maria Lagerström, *The African Union - a Study Focusing on Conflict Management* (Stockholm: Swedish Defense Research Agency, 2008).

²   There are currently discussions on how to integrate NEPAD into the structures of the AU. It is not yet clear whether a separate organ will be established.

³   This term has become increasingly popular over the last few years. See, for example, Ulrich Golaszinski, *Africa's Evolving Security Architecture*, *Hintergrundinformation Aus Der Internationalen Entwicklungszusammenarbeit* (Bonn: Friedrich Ebert Stiftung, 2004), Funmi Olonisakin, "African Peacekeeping at the Crossroads: An Assessment of the Continent's Evolving Peace and Security Architecture," (New York: United Nations Peacekeeping Best Practices, 2004), Lindsay Scorgie, "Building African Peacekeeping Capacity: Donors and the African Union's Emerging Peace and Security Architecture," *KAIPTC Paper*, no. 16 (2007).

⁴   Some also count the African Commission on Human and Peoples' Rights (ACHPR) and NEPAD's African Peer Review Mechanism (APRM) towards this security architecture. See Sam Makinda and Wafula Okumu, The African Union: Challenges of Globalization, Security and Governance (London: Routledge, 2008).

⁵   For more information on the PSC see Jackie Cilliers and Kathryn Sturman, "Challenges Facing the AU's Peace and Security Council," *African Security Review* 13, no. 1 (2004), Delphine Lecoutre, "Les Premiers Pas Du Conseil De Paix Et De Sécurité De L'union Africaine," *Géopolitique Africaine*, no. 19 (2005), Jeremy Levitt, "The Peace and Security Council of the African Union: The Known Unknowns," *Transnational Law & Contemporary Problems* 13, no. 1 (2003), Paul Williams, "The Peace and Security Council of the African Union: Evaluating an Embryonic International Institution," in *ISA Annual Convention* (San Francisco: 2008).

⁶   *Protocol Relating to the Establishment of the Peace and Security Council of the African Union*, Article 2(1).

⁷   Ibid., Article 3.

⁸   Unnamed AU-official as quoted in Williams, "The Peace and Security Council of the African Union: Evaluating an Embryonic International Institution," 4.

⁹   *Protocol Relating to the Establishment of the Peace and Security Council of the African Union*, Article 5(1).

¹⁰   Ibid., Article 5(2).

¹¹   Given that to date all decision within the PSC have been taken by consensus, Paul Williams argues that the body can be understood as a "social environment within which the micro-processes of socialization (persuasion and

social influence) operate both among the PSC members and between them, the wider group of AU member states and the AU Commission". Williams, "The Peace and Security Council of the African Union: Evaluating an Embryonic International Institution," 8. See also Alastair Johnston, "Treating International Institutions as Social Environments," *International Studies Quarterly* 45, no. 4 (2001): 487-515.

[12] Levitt suggests that this ambiguity may be explained by the fact that the PSC Protocol was never formally reviewed by a committee of legal experts. See Levitt, "The Peace and Security Council of the African Union: The Known Unknowns."

[13] Ben Kioko, "The Right of Intervention under the African Union's Constitutive Act," *International Review of the Red Cross* 85, no. 852 (2003): 821.

[14] *The Common African Position on the Proposed Reform of the United Nations: "The Ezulwini Consensus"* (AU Document Ext/EX.CL/2(vii), 7-8 March 2005), p. 6.

[15] *Protocol Relating to the Establishment of the Peace and Security Council of the African Union*, Article 20.

[16] See *Conclusions on a Mechanism for Interaction between the Peace and Security Council and Civil Society Organizations in the Promotion of Peace, Security and Stability in Africa* (AU Document PSC/PR/(CLX), 5 December 2008, Livingstone), Annex 3.

[17] Ibid., Article D(i-ix).

[18] *Statement of Commitment to Peace and Security in Africa, issued by the Heads of State and Government of the Member States of the Peace and Security Council of the African Union* (AU Document PSC/AHG/St.(X), 25 May 2004), para. 1.

[19] Williams, "The Peace and Security Council of the African Union: Evaluating an Embryonic International Institution," 10. See also Edward Luck, *UN Security Council: Practice and Promise* (London: Routledge, 2006).

[20] Williams, "The Peace and Security Council of the African Union: Evaluating an Embryonic International Institution," 10-17.

[21] General Audit of the African Union, 18 December 2007, para. 270, para. 275 and para. 302.

[22] *Protocol Relating to the Establishment of the Peace and Security Council of the African Union*, Article 11(1) and 11(3).

[23] See Laurie Nathan, "Mediation and the AU's Panel of the Wise," in *Peace in Africa - Towards a Collaborative Security Regime*, ed. Shannon Field (Johannesburg: Institute for Global Dialogue, 2004), 63-80.

[24] For the role of mediation in African conflicts see, for example, Cameron Hume, *Ending Mozambique's War: The Role of Mediation and Good Offices* (Washington DC: United States Institute of Peace Press, 1994), Gilbert Khadiagala, "Mediating Civil Conflicts in Eastern Africa," *Politeia* 24, no. 3 (2005): 295-314, Roger Southall and Kristina Bentley, *An African Peace Process: Mandela, South Africa and Burundi* (London: Human Science Research Council, 2005).

[25] PSC Protocol, Article 11

[26] AU PSC, *Modalities for the Functioning of the Panel of the Wise*, adopted on 12 November 2007, Addis Ababa, Article III (a)-(h).

---

27   Panel of the Wise, *Work Program for 2008*, Article 16 (i)-(v).

28   Ahmed Ben Bella, *Speech on the Occasion of the Inauguration of the Panel of the Wise*, 18 December 2007, Addis Ababa, p. 3.

29   *Protocol Relating to the Establishment of the Peace and Security Council of the African Union*, Article 13(8).

30   See *Policy Framework fort he Establishment of the African Standby Force and the Military Staff Committee* (AU Document Exp/ASF-MSC/2 (I), 16 May 2003, Addis Ababa).

31   *Declaration by the Ministers of Defense and Security of the Members of the African Union*, 2nd Meeting, 28 March 2008, Addis Ababa, para. 8.

32   While this contribution was five percent for the OAU Mechanism, it is six percent for the Special Fund. The PSD would like to increase this number to ten percent.

33   The table covers off-budget income and expenditure. It does not capture unanticipated income such as that raised and spent on peacekeeping operations. See Audit of the African Union, 18 December 2007, p. 146.

34   UN Security Council Resolution 1809(2008), UN Document SC/9301, 16 April 2008.

35   While the so-called Maputo Structure has approved 53 staff for the Peace and Security Department, the latter has not yet managed to fill all positions. There are currently renewed efforts to reform the Maputo Structure.

36   Williams, "The Peace and Security Council of the African Union: Evaluating an Embryonic International Institution," 16.

37   Figure adapted from Jakkie Cilliers, "Towards a Continental Early Warning System for Africa," *ISS Occasional Papers*, no. 102 (2005).

38   The section on the PSOD is based largely on several interviews with the former head of the PSOD, Bereng Mtimkulu, in Addis Ababa in 2007-8.

39   *Report by a Consultancy, Facilitated by the UN and Funded by the Government of Canada on the Organizational Structure of the Peace Support Operations Department of the African Union*, January 2009, Addis Ababa.

40   For more information on inter-African cooperation in counterterrorism see Andre Le Sage, ed., *African Counterterrorism Cooperation: Assessing Regional and Subregional Initiatives* (Dulles: Potomac Books, 2007).

41   For a very informative discussion of the CADSP see Omar Touray, "The Common African Defense and Security Policy," *African Affairs* 104, no. 417 (2005): 635-656.

42   *Solemn Declaration on a Common African Defense and Security Policy*, 28 February 2004, Sirte, paragraphs 4-9.

43   Touray, "The Common African Defense and Security Policy," 654.

8

The African Standby Force

This chapter examines the quality and extent of inter-African security cooperation within the framework of the African Standby Force currently being established by the African Union. To this purpose, it details the essential characteristics and current status of the envisaged force before it reviews and measures the progress at the regional level where component standby brigades are in varying stages of development. While the chapter goes into great detail to demonstrate the complexity of this undertaking, it does not seek to provide an ultimate description of the ASF. Rather it focuses on those aspects that help to highlight the state of contemporary inter-African security cooperation and thus provide valuable insights for the analysis in chapter ten.

As described in chapters three and four, many attempts at establishing some sort of Pan-African military force preceded the creation of the ASF.[1] In fact, the current attempt is very similar to the proposal made by the delegation from Sierra Leone at the 3rd Ordinary Session of the OAU Defense Commission in 1965. As envisioned over forty years ago, it does not entail the establishment of a standing multinational force, but is built around a standby arrangement whereby states earmark and train specific units for joint operations and then keep these units ready for rapid deployment at appropriate notice.[2] Such standby systems have become increasingly popular over the last decade as they do not force member states to permanently surrender parts of their armed forces to a supra-national body while still giving such a body the possibility to deploy an interoperable and readily trained force at relatively short notice. As the conceptualization and operationalization of the ASF have been very much informed by five standby models, namely, (1) the United Nations Standby Arrangement System, (2) the UN Standby High Readiness Brigade, (3) the ECOWAS Standby Arrangement, (4) NATO's Response Force, and (5) the EU's Battlegroups, the following section will briefly provide an overview of their essential characteristics and relevance to the ASF before turning to the details of the latter.

The history of the United Nation's Standby Arrangement System (UNSAS) reaches back to the beginnings of the UN itself. When the organization was founded in the 1940s, several proposals for UN military force arrangements were discussed by the Informal Political Agenda Group.[3] The Group eventually agreed that the idea of a standing force presented "general difficulties of maintaining and operating such forces ... and of more particular constitutional hazards in the United States".[4] Upon a referral from the Agenda Group to the US Joint Chiefs of Staff, the latter endorsed the "system of national contingents in which the forces would be used only as occasion demanded by virtue of specific agreement" which provides the basis for today's UNSAS.[5]

In brief, UNSAS consists of arrangements negotiated between the UN and individual member states which detail conditional commitments of specified resources by the latter to UN peacekeeping operations. These resources can be military formations, specialized personnel (civilian and military), services as well as material and equipment. The resources agreed-upon remain on "stand-by" in their home country, where necessary preparation, including training, is conducted to prepare them to fulfill specified tasks or functions in accordance with UN guidelines. When specific needs arise, stand-by resources are requested by the Secretary-General and, if approved by participating member states, are rapidly deployed to set up new peacekeeping missions or to reinforce existing ones. The system is based on three components, namely, (1) standby arrangements for formed units, (2) a separate on-call list, and (3) a system of matching offers of equipment with troop contributions.

The standby arrangement for formed units comprises varying levels of increasing participation in the system that may be made available by a member state to UN operations. Levels 1-3 provide broad information regarding what may be made available. At Level 3 a Memorandum of Understanding (MoU) is signed, but it does not define capability in a level of detail that would be necessary to deploy a unit. In addition, information is not verifiable. The level with the most utility is the Rapid Deployment Level (RDL), which seeks to speed up deployment times by obtaining detailed information from a member state about a unit that may be made available at short notice, and by providing information to the member state as to exactly what is required and the amount of reimbursement that can be expected. At this level, the UN and the member state exchange information to the degree that a detailed MoU for the capability that may be deployed is drafted (but not signed). The MoU details personnel, contingent-owned equipment and self-sustainment capacity. This level may also involve visits to a member state by a DPKO staff assistance team in order to verify the equipment pledged, the training of personnel, and the level of self-sustainment.

The on-call list comprises a number of key posts on which member states can bid at three levels. Level one involves bids against nine headquarters posts on seven days notice to move. Personnel bid on this level can either be deployed to New York to assist in planning prior to deployment or directly to a concentration area. Level two involves bids against the remaining headquarters posts on 14 days notice to move. Level three involves individuals that can be used as military observers, staff officers and military experts.

As lack of suitable equipment is often a reason for member states not to contribute troops to UN operations, UNSAS has developed a system that links offers of equipment from one member state or organization with personnel or units from another. In addition, UNSAS maintains significant amounts of materiel as part of its Strategic Deployment Stocks (SDS) in its logistics base in Brindisi, Italy.

All three components were closely examined by AU staff prior to the establishment of the ASF and a copy of the UNSAS Handbook was handed over to the AU's Peace and Security Department. Particularly the RDL concept (and its possibility to determine shortfalls), the use of logistics depots and the mechanism for linking equipment from one nation with potential troop contributions from another were seen as helpful.[6]

The UN Standby High Readiness Brigade (SHIRBRIG) is a multinational brigade-sized force created to provide the UN with a coherent rapid deployment capability. It has its origins in the Secretary-General's 1995 "Supplement to an Agenda for Peace" which recommended that the UN should consider the idea of a rapid deployment force, consisting of units from a number of member states, trained to the same standard, using the same operating procedures and inter-operable equipment, and taking part in combined exercises at regular intervals.[7] In December 1996, seven states (Austria, Canada, Denmark, The Netherlands, Norway, Poland and Sweden) signed a letter of intent to cooperate in the establishment of such a force which was eventually declared operational in January 2000. By the time of writing, the number of participating states had grown to sixteen with seven more taking part as observers.[8]

The SHIRBRIG concept has three key components. First, a small permanent Planning Element (PLANELM) of 15 staff officers provided for free by member states which coordinates troop contributions, training requirements and verification. Second, an on-call list which details non-permanent staff provided by the member states to fill up the remaining HQ posts whenever the need arises. Third, a sufficient number of identified units on standby in member states which meet UN standards as regards equipment and self-sustainment (the so-called Force Pool).

The Policy Framework for the Establishment of the ASF has identified the organizational structure of SHIRBRIG – especially the use of a permanently staffed PLANELM – and its scheme of management including its legal framework and system of certification as important to the operationalization of the ASF.[9] In acknowledgement of its model character, SHIRBRIG has become heavily involved with ASF capacity-building. Currently, it supports ECOWAS, the Eastern African Standby Brigade (EASBRIG) as well as the PSD through workshops and the organization of joint training exercises.[10]

ECOWAS is the only African organization that has any experience with developing a military standby arrangement. Based to a large extent on the knowledge gained from its Cease-Fire Monitoring Group (ECOMOG) and its interventions in Liberia and Sierra Leone, ECOWAS agreed on the establishment of a standby force of brigade size consisting of specially trained and equipped units of national armies ready to be deployed at short notice in 1999. All fifteen ECOWAS member states have since pledged one battalion each to the proposed force.[11] While the ECOWAS standby mechanism as such has been of little relevance to the conceptualization and operationalization of the ASF, ECOMOG's experience has shed light on the importance of the lead nation concept.[12] Even though this concept is often criticized for undermining the very idea of collective action and burden sharing, it has been realized that in certain parts of the continent the reliance on lead nations may provide the only way to pull together and finance a regional standby brigade for the ASF.

Both, NATO and the EU also maintain their own military standby arrangements. While most aspects of these highly complex and advanced systems are not applicable to the African context, their doctrines, standard operating procedures, legal frameworks and technical agreements have often provided the basis for the development of key ASF documents. The EU's Rapid Response concept, for example, was crucial to the discussion about the development of an ASF Rapid Deployment Capability.[13] Together with the input from the United Nations, SHIRBRIG and ECOWAS, the NATO Rapid Response Force and the European Union's Battlegroups thus provide some of the context in which the conceptualization and operationalization of the African Standby Force needs to be seen and assessed.

The Concept and Structure of the ASF

Ever since the African Union agreed on the establishment of the ASF, the latter's concept has been subject to intense academic and professional scrutiny.[14] Over the years, the resultant studies have varied widely in their conclusions ranging from enthusiastic endorsements to unveiled skepticism. This section does not seek to pass any such judgment on the ASF, but to provide a detailed description of its concept and envisaged structure in order to highlight the extraordinary level of inter-state cooperation involved.

In July 2002, the Protocol Relating to the Establishment of the Peace and Security Council formally concluded a long process of discussion on the purpose and shape of a continental military force that, in one form or the other, had been ongoing since decolonization. Article 13 of the Protocol provides for the establishment of an African Standby Force "in order to enable the Peace and Security Council to perform its responsibilities with respect to the deployment of peace support missions and intervention pursuant to Article 4(h) and (j) of the Constitutive Act".[15] While it does specify seven functions for the proposed force (ranging from the conduct of observation and monitoring missions to full-blown humanitarian interventions),[16] the often-cited article provides only very little information about its concept and structure except that it shall be composed of "standby multi-disciplinary contingents with civilian and military components in their countries of origin and ready for rapid deployment at appropriate notice".[17] It was only with the adoption of the Policy Framework for the Establishment of the African Standby Force and the Military Staff Committee by the 3rd Meeting of the African Chiefs of Defense Staff (ACDS) in May 2003 and its subsequent approval by the Heads of States in July 2004 that the idea of the envisaged standby arrangement was somewhat clarified.[18]

In its introduction, the Policy Framework refers to the recommendations made by the 2nd Meeting of the ACDS in Harare in 1997 which, amongst others, included the earmarking of five brigade-sized contributions to a common standby force by the continent's regions.[19] On the basis of these recommendations, the final document adopted by the Heads of State details an elaborate structure for the planned force that consists of five regionally-managed standby brigades supported by civilian police and one continentally-managed permanent body responsible for final oversight, coordination and harmonization. Conceptually, the ASF is thus based on three levels, namely, the continental level (that is, the AU Commission), the regional level (that is, the RECs or specifically dedicated coordinating mechanisms) and the national level (that is, the contributing countries).

At the continental level, the Policy Framework envisages the establishment of a permanent 15-person Planning Element within the AU's Peace and Security Department to provide for a multi-dimensional, strategic-level management capability. The core function of this unit is to supervise the system of regional standby arrangements to ensure standardization, interoperability and currency of information. In addition, the AU PLANELM is in charge of (1) developing and, if necessary, updating key documents such as the ASF doctrine, standard operating procedures and training manuals, (2) coordinating the efforts to establish a logistical infrastructure consisting of a central and five regional depots, (3) coordinating the efforts to mobilize, harmonize and focus external support activities such as RECAMP, (4) developing and maintaining relationships with the UN Standby Arrangement System and other relevant organizations such as SHIRBRIG and (5) establishing and maintaining central standby arrangement systems including roosters for individual AU HQ staff, up to 240 civilian police and 300-500 military observers. In a mission situation, the continental PLANELM provides the basis for an AU Strategic HQ capable of planning, managing and conducting all necessary arrangements for the effective employment of the ASF.

At the regional level, each of the continent's five geographic regions has one REC or specifically dedicated coordinating mechanism in charge of setting up and administering a standby component for the ASF. [20] Each standby component is to be between 3,000 and 4,000 troops strong, giving the ASF an overall strength of 15,000 to 20,000 troops, and provide a number of predefined military capabilities.[21] Regional PLANELMs, similar in form to the one at the continental level and ideally co-located with the regional brigade headquarters, are responsible for the planning, preparation and training, including the verification of the standby elements and the brigade headquarters. In addition, the regional PLANELMs coordinate with the AU headquarters and each other and administer designated regional training centers as well as the envisaged regional logistics infrastructure including the regional military depots.

At the national level, member states contributing contingents to the regional brigades are expected to train the individuals and units that form part of the standby brigades in basic military tasks as well as in the standardized doctrine and operating procedures developed by the AU.[22] Accordingly, all designated regional training centers as well as national military schools have to follow the guidelines set by the AU in consultation with the regional PLANELMs and coordinate their training cycles. Member states are also required to allow access to the units and personnel that form part of the ASF by the relevant authorities from the regional planning and management organs or the AU Commission for the purpose of periodic reviews including the verification of training standards and interoperability as well as the identification of possible shortfalls.

This three-level structure, according to the Policy Framework, allows the continent's decision-makers to employ the ASF effectively in all likely mission scenarios, reaching from simply providing military advice to a political mission to full-blown military peace enforcement operations to halt an ongoing genocide or grave violations against human rights (see Figure 8.1).

Figure 8.1: Mission Scenarios for the ASF[23]

Scenario 1	AU/Regional military advice to a political mission
Scenario 2	AU/Regional observer mission co-deployed with UN mission
Scenario 3	Stand-alone AU/Regional observer mission
Scenario 4	AU/Regional peacekeeping force for Chapter VI missions
Scenario 5	AU peacekeeping force for multi-dimensional peacekeeping mission
Scenario 6	AU intervention and peace enforcement mission

The Policy Framework has set very ambitions timelines for deployment in the above scenarios. It envisages that the ASF can deploy within 30 days for scenarios one to four, within 90 days for scenario five and within 14 days for scenario six, all beginning from the decision of the AU Assembly and the Peace and Security Council to carry out the operation. Such tight deployment timelines necessitate highly-trained and interoperable units, an established and fully stocked logistics infrastructure as well as a sophisticated command and control system. Both, the Policy Framework as well as the ASF Roadmap have called on expert working groups to discuss these requirements in more detail.

With respect to training, the relevant workshops conducted between 2004 and late 2007 reiterated the importance of ensuring the universal adherence to AU and UN training standards. To this purpose, they recommended the use of approved regional training centers such as the Kofi Annan International Peacekeeping Centre in Accra (for West Africa), the Regional Peacekeeping Training Centre in Harare (for

Southern Africa) and the Peace Support Training Centre in Nairobi (for Eastern Africa). The workshops also decided that while training is to remain primarily a national responsibility, the joint nature of the ASF inevitably means that both the regional and the continental level have to stay closely involved in the training process. Besides the determination of the training curriculum and the harmonization of training cycles, this involvement should include a continuous evaluation and validation process informed by lessons learned from previous operations and best practices from other organizations and operations.[24]

With respect to logistics, the ASF Policy Framework provides that missions deployed for scenarios one to three should be self-sustainable for up to 30 days, while those deployed for scenarios four to six should even be self-sustainable for up to 90 days after which the AU takes responsibility for mission sustainment. Together with the ambitious deployment timelines mentioned above these goals present enormous logistical challenges. A Logistics Working Group has developed an ASF Logistics Support Concept as well as a 177-page Logistics Manual to help overcome the challenges associated with the deployment and sustainment of the ASF.[25] Regarding deployment, these documents state the importance of pre-deploying equipment into regional logistics depots and negotiating standing arrangements with lead nations, international donors or commercial contractors regarding strategic sea and airlift to ensure the ability of the ASF to deploy within the set timelines. Regarding sustainment in theater, they draw attention to the UN system in which troop contributing countries must be prepared to sustain their units from national sources from the time of arrival in the mission area until the mandating authority's logistics and reimbursement systems have been established. In addition, they recommend that the ASF be given the ability to negotiate support agreements with host nations and commercial contractors.

In addition to standardized and continuously monitored training and elaborate logistics, an effective ASF also necessitates a clearly defined Command and Control (C^2) structure in which commands and instructions can flow from a higher level to all levels of the hierarchy and control can be executed through specified feedback. While the Policy Framework is relatively silent on this matter, subsequent workshops have developed detailed C^2 systems for force generation and force utilization.[26] During force generation, that is the process of setting up and administering the standby force, command and control lies with the national authorities of the contributing nations or with the regional authorities whenever the national contributions are preparing or exercising jointly. During force utilization, that is the use of ASF forces for military purposes by the AU or the RECs, C^2 lies with the mandating authority. With regard to the AU, the Policy Framework states that "the PSC as the decision-making institution should be the sole authority for mandating and terminating AU peace missions and operations" and that "the political command and control of missions mandated by the PSC should be vested in the Chairperson who should then submit periodic reports on the progress of implementation of the relevant mandates".[27] The Chairperson also appoints the Head of Mission, Force Commander, Police Commissioner and the Head of the Civilian Component while delegating the political direction and administrative control to the AU Commissioner for Peace and Security. The Peace Support Operations Division is thus responsible for the strategic planning of ASF operations. As such it conducts all the staff work related to any mission, be it the organizing of reconnaissance missions, the drafting of mandates, concepts of operations and rules of engagement or the preparation of reports. In the field, the Head of Mission establishes the relationship between the military, police and political elements of the operation, assigns areas of responsibility and establishes mechanisms to integrate the activities of all involved parties and organizations (see Figure 8.2).[28]

Figure 8.2: AU Chain of Command in ASF Operations[29]

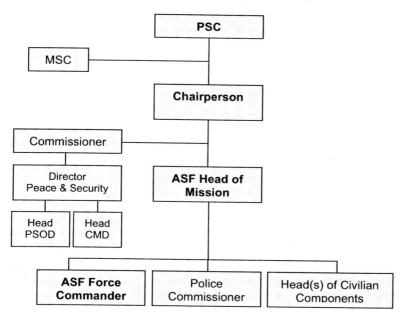

If a mission is mandated by one of the RECs or coordinating mechanisms, this chain of command is replicated on the regional level, that is, the regional political authority appoints the Head of Mission, Force Commander, Police Commissioner and Head of the Civilian Component through its peace and security mechanism. The AU should be kept informed through close contact between the regional and the continental PLANELM, but does not have any political authority over the conduct of the mission.[30] The following section will discuss to what extent this elaborate concept has been operationalized thus far.

The Operationalization of the African Standby Force

When the 3rd Ordinary Session of the AU Assembly approved the Policy Framework for the Establishment of the African Standby Force it also requested the Chairperson of the AU Commission "to take all steps required for the implementation of the Policy Framework document".[31] In line with this request and the recommendation of the Policy Framework that the ASF should be established in two phases, the Commissioner for Peace and Security, Ambassador Said Djinnit, convened a meeting of experts in March 2005 that provided a roadmap for the operationalization of Phase I.[32] In this phase, which the Policy Framework originally intended to be achieved by the end of June 2005, the plan was to establish a strategic management capacity at the level of the AU for scenarios one and two while the regions would establish standby components ready for scenarios one to four. In the second phase which is intended to be completed by June 2010, the AU should then continue to develop its management capacity to be able to deal with scenario five while the regions should increasingly focus on their rapid deployment capability.[33]

Given the ambitious scale of the project, it is not surprising that this original timeline for the establishment of the ASF has not been adhered to. Phase I was only completed at the end of 2006 and some aspects of it will carry over to Phase II which is now going to end in late 2009 and will be followed by a third phase which is expected to end in late 2010.[34]

Even though the first phase has taken substantially longer than originally planned, its outputs have surpassed many expectations.[35] Not only have most of the regions made remarkable progress in establishing their standby brigades, but there have also been several promising developments at the continental level. First, the five central documents that will regulate the functioning of the ASF, that is, the ASF Doctrine, a

Training Policy, an ASF Logistics Concept, a Command and Control Plan and the Standard Operating Procedures have been finalized through a painstaking series of workshops and seminars and subsequently approved by the ACDS at their 5th meeting in March 2008.[36] These documents along with the results of the workshops on financial and legal matters provide the basic tools for operationalizing the ASF.

Second, the Peace Support Operations Division of the AU has managed to foster a wide base of international support for the operationalization of the ASF. Besides many national donors such as the US, the UK, Canada or Germany which have helped to build up the necessary infrastructure in Addis and have organized and financed many of the aforementioned workshops and experts meetings, the PSOD can count on the support of several institutional donors. The UN's Department for Peacekeeping Operations, for example, has established a liaison team to the PSOD in order to offer expertise and tailored support to the operationalization of the ASF.[37] The EU has financed many aspects of the emerging force through its €250 million African Peace Facility (APF) and has taken over the French capacity building programme *Renforcement des capacités africaines au maintien de la paix* (RECAMP) and adapted it to suit the training needs of the ASF.[38] Both organizations are extremely keen to bolster the capacities of the AU in the area of peace and security and ensure a smooth and sustainable operationalization of the ASF.

Third, the AU has managed to develop the strategic management capacity to deal with scenarios one to three.[39] Together with the regions, the AU is thus already able to deploy observer missions throughout the continent and, with substantial help from international partners, might even be able to conduct limited scenario four operations. Even though the PSOD has still not reached the staff level mandated by the 2003 Maputo Summit and no replacement for the deceased Chief of ASF Staff, the late Major-General Ishaya Hassan, has yet been found, the AU has recruited a number of highly-qualified staff to guide and support the operationalization of the ASF following its temporary move into a office building outside the AU compound in Addis.[40] The number of personnel is to increase further once the new purpose-built PSOD building (financed by Germany) will be completed in late 2009.

Fourth, the AU has established itself as the unquestionable authority in the operationalization of the ASF. Not only have all contributing states signaled their intention to adhere to and train their troops according to the documents developed by the AU in conjunction with the regions and external experts, but they have also acknowledged the leadership role of the PSOD in other matters such as the development of a logistics concept and the development of a rapid deployment capability (that is, the entry forces of the first regional brigade to deploy). Article IV of the MoU between the AU and the RECs regarding security cooperation reconfirms the "primary responsibility of the AU in the maintenance and promotion of peace, security and stability in Africa".[41]

While these are all promising signs, much remains to be done at the continental level. Following the approval of the five central documents of Phase I by the Ministers of Defense at their second meeting in March 2008, Phase II now focuses on the development of a policy guiding document that addresses the political and legal aspects of mandating and deploying the ASF and the development of a concept of operation, capability development and force generation.[42] Besides these conceptual issues, the workshops conducted in Phase I have identified six other areas in need of further development, namely, (1) the communications and information system, (2) a training directive and needs analysis, (3) a logistics supply system to facilitate rapid deployment and sustainability, (4) the civilian aspects of the ASF, (5) the validation of key ASF documents such as the doctrine or the SOPs through exercises and lessons learned, and (6) a sustainable finance mechanism.[43]

Once these issues have been dealt with, Phase III envisages a validation command post exercise (CPX) "Joint Brigades" that will test the ASF structures. The CPX will be developed around the AU Peace and Security Architecture decision-making process and will be based on the EU's adapted RECAMP format.[44] It will validate legal and financial aspects and involve the deployment of one or more of the regional brigades to deliver trained and equipped individuals and units to meet a contingency requiring rapid reaction. This will allow validation of ASF command and control, force generation, mobilization and deployment, training, logistics, standard operating procedures and communication systems. It will also test the AU's ability to cooperate with the UN and other international partners in tackling a rapidly developing crisis.

However, before the ASF capabilities can be evaluated in such an exercise, the regions must follow the continental example and build up their capacities in accordance with the roadmap for Phase II. In order to gauge the extent of this challenge and to get an impression of the regional aspect of inter-African security cooperation, the following three sections will briefly assess the progress of the three RECs (SADC, ECOWAS and ECCAS) and two coordinating mechanisms (EASBRICOM and NARC) currently establishing component standby brigades at the regional level.

Eastern Africa's Regional Brigade (EASBRIG)

In February 2004, the Intergovernmental Authority of Development (IGAD) which had been nominated by the region's states as the REC responsible for the interim coordination of efforts towards the establishment of a standby brigade in the East African region convened a meeting of experts in Jinja (Uganda) in order to discuss the process of operationalizing such a brigade. This meeting was followed by the 1st Meeting of Eastern Africa Chiefs of Defense Staff on the Establishment of the Eastern Africa Standby Brigade (EASBRIG) which adopted a Draft Policy Framework for the Establishment of the Eastern Africa Standby Brigade.[45] This Policy Framework was subsequently approved by a Council of Ministers meeting held in Kigali in September 2004 and the 1st Assembly of EASBRIG Heads of State and Government held in Addis in April 2005. It reconfirmed IGAD's interim coordination role and committed the 13 EASBRIG member states (Comoros, Djibouti, Eritrea, Ethiopia, Kenya, Madagascar, Mauritius, Rwanda, Seychelles, Somalia, Sudan, Tanzania and Uganda) to the by then still two-phased approach to the operationalization of the ASF. In addition to the Policy Framework, the Assembly also adopted a Memorandum of Understanding on the Establishment of EASBRIG and approved the necessary budget.[46]

In July 2005, the Chiefs of Defense Staff met again and operationalized the regional Planning Element in Nairobi. Faced with the refusal of some member states to pay for the establishment of EASBRIG as long as the question of coordination was not finally resolved, they also appointed a Technical Committee of Experts to study the issue of coordination and make appropriate recommendations to resolve the matter once and for all. The committee reported to the 4th Meeting of the Chiefs of Defense Staff in August 2005 and recommended the creation of an independent coordination mechanism to account for the non-IGAD member states involved in the establishment of EASBRIG. Other topics discussed by the Chiefs of Defense Staff included the hosting agreements for the PLANELM in Nairobi and the Brigade HQ in Addis as well as the operationalization of the regional logistics base.

The 3rd Council of Ministers met in September 2005 in Kigali and adopted the recommendations of the Chiefs of Defense Staff on the operationalization of the PLANELM, the skeleton Brigade HQ, the establishment of an independent coordination mechanism (EASBRICOM) and the deferment of the operationalization of the logistics base until the AU had finalized its logistics concept.[47]

Following another meeting of the Council of Ministers in April 2006, the 1st Extraordinary Meeting of the Heads of State and Government of Eastern Africa approved the operationalization of the independent coordination mechanism in January 2007 and the 2nd Extraordinary Meeting of the Council of Ministers held in Nairobi in March 2007 implemented this decision by mandating EASBRICOM to serve as the Secretariat of EASBRIG. In addition, the Council of Ministers commissioned several studies to make recommendations on (1) the duplications in functions and inconsistencies in the EASBRIG structures, (2) the harmonization of the Policy Framework and the MoU on the establishment of EASBRIG, and (3) the development of policy documents for EASBRIG including a Procurement Manual, Financial Regulations and an Employment Policy.[48] In August 2007, the 5th Meeting of the Council of Ministers accepted the experts' recommendations and asked EASBRICOM to take all necessary actions. The meeting also approved the membership request of Burundi and agreed on the formation of a Friends of EASBRIG Committee in order to offer international partners a forum for support and consultation.

Since its inauguration in January 2007, the new EASBRIG structure (see Figure 8.3) has made substantial progress in achieving the milestones set by the AU's roadmap for the operationalization of the ASF. Both the PLANELM and the Brigade HQ are fully operational and the Logistics Depot is currently being built up in Addis.[49] Several of the member states have begun to earmark and train units for EASBRIG and Kenya is currently in the process of establishing a rapid deployment capability for the standby brigade.[50]

In November 2007, EASBRICOM adopted a Strategic Development Plan for the period 2007 to 2015 which specifies eight objectives to help it achieve its vision of an initial operational capability by 2010 and full operational capability by 2015.[51] These objectives include the development of (1) cohesive political decision-making structures by 2010, (2) a command, control and communications (C^3) structure capable of preparing, planning for, and commanding the deployed forces by the end of 2009, (3) an initial operational capability of a trained force of brigade size on standby and maintained in member states to the required readiness level by the end of 2010, (4) a trained civilian police element on standby and maintained in member states to the required readiness level by the end of 2010, (5) a roster of trained civilian experts available for deployment by the end of 2010, (6) a logistics system capable of supporting the deployment and sustainment of EASBRIG by 2010, and (7) an integrated training system able to provide individual and collective training for regional forces by the end of 2010. In order to achieve these objectives EASBRICOM relies heavily on the continuing support of its international partners which have organized themselves into an EASBRIG Development Support Committee (EDSC) to coordinate their donor support.[52]

Figure 8.3: EASBRIG Decision-Making Structure[53]

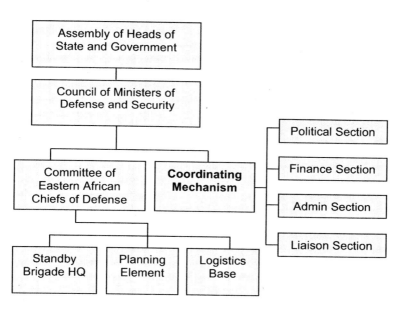

While Eastern Africa's progress in operationalizing its regional standby brigade is encouraging, several formidable challenges remain. First, the rise of violent conflict in the region, ranging from Ethiopia's invasion of Somalia to combat Islamic extremism and the resultant independence struggles in Somaliland and Puntland to the escalation of the situation in Darfur and the recent electoral crisis in Kenya, diverts vital attention and resources, both financial and military, away from the EASBRIG process. States like Burundi and Uganda, for example, are currently too preoccupied with their participation in the AU Mission in Somalia to earmark and prepare units for the regional standby force. Another example is the smoldering border conflict between Ethiopia and Eritrea which limits both states' ability (and willingness) to commit military capabilities to EASBRIG.

Second, this effect is further compounded by the fact that not all 14 EASBRIG member states are currently contributing to its operationalization. Eritrea, Madagascar and Mauritius have yet to join EASBRICOM and in conjunction with the preoccupation of other states described above, this means that the burden of establishing the regional brigade for the moment rests on only a few states such as Tanzania, the Seychelles and Djibouti. Given these and other problems such as the fact that member states increasingly drag their political tensions into the EASBRIG process,[54] implementing the EASBRIG strategy and achieving its eight objectives will certainly be difficult.

However, the increasing institutionalization of EASBRICOM, the formulation of a detailed EASBRIG strategy and the inception of training cycles at the Regional Peace Support Training Centre (PSTC) in Nairobi are promising signs that the region's states will continue to overcome their inhibitions and cooperate on the establishment of their standby brigade. In addition, the high level of focused partner support and the region's heartfelt ambition to prove its skeptics wrong are powerful assets for the operationalization of EASBRIG.[55]

West Africa's Regional Brigade (ESF)

Several years before the AU decided on the establishment of the ASF, the ECOWAS Security Protocol of 1999 already called for the institutionalization of its Cease-Fire Monitoring Group (ECOMOG) in the form of a standby force of brigade-size consisting of specially-trained and equipped units of national armies ready for deployment at short notice.[56] This force was to be used in the case of (1) aggression or conflict within a member state, (2) a conflict between two or more member states, and (3) internal conflicts that threaten to trigger a humanitarian disaster, pose a serious threat to regional peace and security, result in serious and massive violations of human rights and/or follow the overthrow or attempted overthrow of a democratically elected government. Even though all 15 ECOWAS states pledged one battalion each to the proposed force, the implementation of the Protocol's provisions was delayed by the need for emergency responses to the armed conflicts in Liberia and Côte d'Ivoire and the political crisis in Togo.

By April 2004, all ECOMOG interventions had transitioned to UN operations and ECOWAS military planners were finally able to concentrate on developing the proposed standby force.[57] As the AU had agreed on the establishment of the ASF in the meantime, the 9th Meeting of the ECOWAS Defense and Security Commission (DSC) formulated a military strategy that provided some guidance to the establishment of the so-called ECOWAS Standby Force (ESF) as a regional component of the ASF. According to the strategy, the ESF was to consist of 6,500 troops divided into a Task Force of 1,500 troops (deployable within 30 days) and a Main Brigade of 5,000 troops (deployable within 90 days) all of whom to be highly trained, equipped and prepared to deploy as directed in response to a crisis or threat to peace and security.[58] In order to coordinate the establishment of this force and adhere to the AU's call for the establishment of regional PLANELMs, ECOWAS (with Canadian support) set up a permanent Mission Planning and Management Cell (MPMC) in early 2005 to be responsible for strategic and operational planning.

In February 2005, the MPMC and a number of international military advisors formulated an operational framework which specified activity strands and benchmarks for the operationalization of the ESF. This framework was approved by the 12th Meeting of the DSC in April 2005. It contains the strategic and operational guidance to assist ECOWAS to sequence and coordinate its activities with the AU and its international partners. The operational framework bases the ESF force generation process on a tiered system in line with the AU Policy Framework for the Establishment of the ASF (see Figure 8.4).

Figure 8.4: The ESF Readiness Model[59]

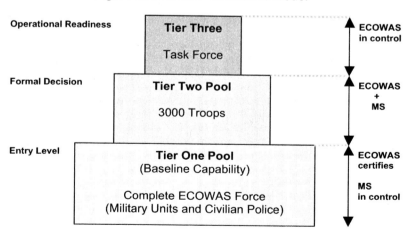

On the ESF readiness model Tier One represents the baseline capability of member states and incorporates their military forces and civilian police elements. For pledges from this pool to be acceptable to ECOWAS, they must be able to achieve an entry level of operational readiness in line with UN standards. Tier Two consists of a pool of 3,000 soldiers from which the Task Force of 1,500 troops (Tier Three) will be drawn on a case-by-case basis, depending on the specifics of the mission and the political situation at the time. Rotation from Tier One to Tier Two is be coordinated by the MPMC in consultation with the member states and is for a minimum period of two years which allows extensive training. Tier Two units are under the direct authority of the ESF, but remain under the operational command of member states while held in readiness for ESF deployment.[60]

In July 2005, the 13th Meeting of the DSC endorsed the selection criteria for staff for the Task Force HQ as well as the site for the ECOWAS Peace Support Operations Logistics Depot at the Hastings Airfield in Freetown, Sierra Leone.[61] A second depot is to be established in Mali.

In November 2005, the 14th Meeting of the DSC approved a five-year training plan for the ESF in order to enable it to meet the challenges of peace support operations in the region.[62] Based on training modules consistent with UN standards, the endorsed program is categorized into individual, collective and specialized components and is to be executed at three regional training centers, the so-called Centers of Excellence. These centers are the Nigerian War College in Abuja (for strategic training), the Kofi Annan International Peacekeeping Training Centre (KAIPTC) in Accra (for operational training) and the *Ecole Maintien de la Paix* in Bamako (for tactical training). In addition, the DSC urged all ECOWAS member states to participate in international exercises such as those provided by RECAMP or ACOTA.

In June 2006, the Task Force HQ was operationalized and it is currently envisaged that the Task Force itself will become operational following its certification at the end of 2009 while the Main Brigade will follow the AU timetable for the operationalization of the ASF. The first joint exercise of the Task Force took place in Senegal in December 2007 and proved a great success for the participating countries.[63] While the ESF is thus certainly among the more advanced regional standby brigades, many challenges remain. As in Eastern Africa, the continuing presence of violent conflicts in Nigeria's River Delta, in Mali and the Manu River Union as well as political tensions between many of the region's states endanger the progress achieved thus far. Despite the optimism spread by the publication of an ECOWAS Strategic Vision in

June 2007 which envisions a borderless West Africa by 2020, not all historic suspicions between Anglophone and Francophone states and between the region's smaller states and the unquestionable hegemon Nigeria have yet been overcome so as to guarantee the smooth functioning of the ESF decision-making structures in times of crises.

Another problem relates to the financing of the ESF. Even though Article 16 of the ECOWAS Protocol Relating to the Mechanism for Conflict Prevention, Management and Resolution, Peacekeeping and Security provides for one percent of the annual levy of member states (0.5 percent of GDP) to be used for an ECOWAS Peace Fund, financing the ESF remains a critical issue as not all member states pay their dues.

Despite these challenges, however, the operationalization of the ESF appears well on track.[64] Due to its extensive experience in force generation gained from the ECOMOG operations as well as the substantial partner support from the US, the EU, France, Germany and the Scandinavian countries, ECOWAS has been able to earmark and train most of the necessary troops (6,200 out of 6,500) and has held several exercises throughout the region.[65] In addition, it has begun with the building of a Task Force HQ in Abuja and has almost finalized its logistics concept. By all indications, ECOWAS has thus already come a long way in establishing its regional standby brigade.

Southern Africa's Regional Brigade (SADCBRIG)

In the case of Southern Africa's regional standby brigade, the region's relatively long history of security cooperation and its institutional set-up within the framework of SADC simplified the initial stages of the establishment process considerably. Rather than having to go through the tedious process of conceiving, approving and implementing new structures for inter-state collaboration, the SADC members could use the forum provided by the Inter-State Defense and Security Committee (ISDSC) and its associated bodies to coordinate their activities and harmonize their policies. Following an ISDSC staff meeting in Lesotho in 2004, a Ministerial Defense Sub-Committee was mandated by the ISDSC to set up a technical team that would plan the establishment of a SADC Standby Force (SADCBRIG) as part of the ASF.

This technical team was able to build on previous attempts to set up a regional peacekeeping force in Southern Africa. As early as 1998, a SADC military delegation had visited the SHIRBRIG Headquarters in Denmark in order to discuss ways to establish a SADC peacekeeping force In March 1999, the ISDSC approved a roadmap for the establishment of such a force which was to consist of a mobile headquarters, three infantry battalions, one reconnaissance company, an engineer squadron, a logistical support company, a military police company, a civilian police component and an air and naval component.[66] The brigade was supposed to be established over a period of five years and include a standing brigade headquarters. Little, however, happened until the Strategic Indicative Plan of the Organ (SIPO) was eventually approved in August 2003. It provided for the development of a regional peace support operations capability based upon the standby arrangements of individual member states.[67]

With this background, the technical team quickly developed a roadmap for operationalization that was in line with the AU schedule for the ASF. By the end of 2005, SADC had established an interim PLANELM (see Figure 8.5 for SADC's strategic management structure for SADCBRIG), approved a logistics support and financial management system and held its first combined military exercise.[68] In addition, member states had pledged over 6,000 troops to the proposed force and the Regional Peacekeeping Training Centre in Harare had developed training standards in line with the standards developed by the AU. Despite these successes, however, financial and logistical reasons forced the ISDSC during its meeting in Windhoek in July 2006 to postpone the official launch of SADCBRIG by one year. Consequently, SADCBRIG was officially launched by the SADC Summit on 17 August 2007 in Lusaka. At this summit the SADC Heads of States and Government also signed a Memorandum of Understanding in order to establish and provide a legal basis for the operationalization of SADCBRIG.[69]

The MoU provides for a permanent and autonomous PLANELM headquartered at the SADC Secretariat in Gaberone (Article 6) as well as a Main Logistics Depot (MLD) also to be based in Botswana (Article 9). It also regulates member states' contributions to SADCBRIG (Article 7) as well as issues regarding command and control (Article 12), training and exercises (Article 13) and deployment, movement and transportation (Article 14). By November 2007, many of the provisions of the MoU had already been implemented.

None of the above could have been achieved without the constant capacity-building support of the international community and its agencies (especially the UN and the EU). Acknowledging the great potential of the standby force as well as the importance of the region's determination to implement it, international assistance programs have actively supported SADC's efforts. The United States' Global Peace

Operations Initiative, the French RECAMP program and the United Kingdom's African Peacekeeping Training Support Program, for example, have provided vital funding, training and surplus military equipment and conducted a range of important peacekeeping exercises over the years such as exercises Tanzanite (2003), Nicuzy (2004) and Thokgamo (2005).

Figure 8.5: Strategic Management Structure for SADCBRIG[70]

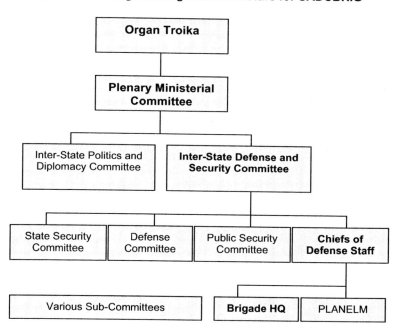

However, despite the wealth of international support and the encouraging progress made so far, not all of the obstacles endangering the success of the project have yet been overcome. For example, at the moment the standby brigade is too dependent on the regional hegemon, South Africa (whose military forces are over-stretched and eroded by a spiraling HIV crisis).[71] This dependence not only runs the risk of creating the impression that the force may become subservient to South Africa's national interest, but also detracts from what is supposed to be a collective effort and thus an expression of regional unity. It may also discourage increasingly constructive actors like Angola from further vital concessions.

Other potential problems include the political estrangement between SADC and its international donors over the role of Mugabe's Zimbabwe in the region, increasing tensions with the AU over the distribution of funds and competencies and a decline in the political will of member countries due to shifts in their cost-benefit considerations. The latter would have especially detrimental consequences for SADC's hopes of having its brigade ready for deployment by 2010, as political will is based less on the region's impressive-looking institutional arrangements and structures than on the collective commitment of its member states to the idea of permanent military cooperation.

Despite the many challenges outlined above, the prospects for effective military collaboration and integration in Southern Africa have never looked better. The region's states have made enormous progress toward creating a Southern African standby brigade by building on already-existing patterns of military cooperation and firmly anchoring the emerging entity within the stabilizing framework of SADC. Given that the region was characterized by deep divisions and rivalries until relatively recently, today's level of security cooperation in Southern Africa is a major achievement.

The Other Regional Brigades

While EASBRIG, the ESF and SADCBRIG are generally ahead of the ASF operationalization timeline, both the northern and central region are lacking behind. However, contrary to prevailing opinion, both regions have quietly begun to catch up.

As in Eastern Africa, the existence of overlapping regional organizations forced the states of Northern Africa to establish an independent coordination mechanism outside of existing RECs for the operationalization of their standby brigade. In November 2005, the Chiefs of Defense Staff of Algeria, Egypt, Libya, Mauritania, Western Sahara and Tunisia met in Tripoli in order to sign a Memorandum of Understanding on the Establishment of the North Africa Region Capability (NARC) in the African Standby Force.[72] The MoU not only provides for the establishment of a permanent PLANELM (Article 13), a logistics base (Article 14) and a Brigade HQ (Article 16), but Appendix 2 also already details some offers of contributions by member states. Libya, for example, offered a light infantry battalion, a signal company and 30 military observers. Egypt reiterated its previous offer of a supported infantry battalion, a reconnaissance unit, a signal unit, an engineering unit and up to 30 military observers. Algeria offered to participate with two light infantry battalions, a signal unit, a military police unit, a reconnaissance group and up to 40 military observers.[73]

Since the signing of the MoU in late 2005, the Northern African states have participated in the AU's central workshops, set up the Brigade HQ in Egypt and the PLANELM in Libya and have designated the Cairo Centre for Conflict Resolution and Peacekeeping as regional training centre. Even though the progress of establishing the standby brigade is definitely slower than in all other regions, the operationalization of NARC and the joint participation in continental ASF initiatives such as the African Peace Support Training Association (APSTA) are promising steps for the notoriously rivalrous states of North Africa.[74]

In Central Africa, the process of establishing a regional peacekeeping capability has been ongoing since the formation of the Council for Peace and Security in Central Africa (COPAX) in February 1999. The COPAX Protocol also provided for the establishment of a non-permanent *Force Multinational d'Afrique Central* (FOMAC) "to accomplish missions of peace, security and humanitarian relief".[75] In June 2002, the ECCAS Ministers of Defense and Security finally agreed on the Standing Orders for FOMAC.[76] These orders defined the force in more detail as "composed of national inter-service, police and gendarmerie contingents from ECCAS member states" (Article 1). Annex A detailed the military composition of the force and put its total strength down as 3,171 troops. In October 2003, the ECCAS Chiefs of Defense Staff met in Brazzaville in order to discuss the incorporation of FOMAC into the ASF concept proposed by the AU. They agreed on the establishment of several working groups to work out the details of the force as well as on a joint peacekeeping training centre and the organization of joint military exercises every two years.

From July 2003 to December 2004, ECCAS held six meetings at the levels of experts, Chiefs of Defense Staff and Ministers of COPAX. At these meetings four issues were adopted, namely (1) the structure of the ECCAS PLANELM, (2) the structure and tables of equipment for the standby brigade as well as its revised strength of 2,177 troops, (3) an action plan for the establishment of the PLANELM and the standby brigade, and (4) the exercise paper for the multinational training exercise known as Bahl El Ghazel 2005.[77] In April 2005, the Chiefs of Defense Staff met again and in light of the volatile security situation in the region revised the strength of the brigade back up to 3,600 troops. Since then, ECCAS has made remarkable progress in establishing its standby force even though Rwanda had to withdraw from the community in order to reduce its integration engagements to fewer regional blocs. FOMAC not only participated in several peacekeeping missions in the Central African Republic (FOMUC I-III), but in November 2006 also led the fifth RECAMP cycle peacekeeping exercise in Cameroon and in 2007 finally operationalized a permanent Brigade HQ in Gabon. In January 2009, ECCAS held a three day seminar in Kinshasa to discuss possible ways to further speed up the operationalization of its brigade.

Inter-African Cooperation within the ASF Framework

However brief this introduction to the ASF and its regional components has been, it nonetheless allows for a number of tentative conclusions with respect to the extent and quality of contemporary inter-African security cooperation. First, the establishment of the regional brigades and their continental coordination mechanism necessitates an extraordinarily high level of inter-state cooperation including difficult decisions regarding political processes and military details. The list of tasks associated with the establishment of such a brigade is daunting. The *Guidelines for the Establishment of a Regional Peace Support Operations Standby Brigade* compiled by the AU's PSOD detail 84 specific tasks to be completed during the operationalization. They range from the creation of a funding mechanism and an early warning system (Tasks 6 and 7) to the establishment of a standby roster of at least 240 police officers (Task 72) and the development of a regional training policy (Task 78). In addition to these region-specific duties, each region also has to participate in collective (that is, continental) tasks, such as developing a joint command and control structure and synchronizing logistical infrastructure. These requirements place a heavy burden on the regions and the states within them. Even though some of them have a history of military cooperation and, in the case of ECOMOG, of military integration, the creation of a compatible standby brigade requires new levels of military interaction as well as considerable political will and financial commitment. In order to ensure that the various national contingents follow standardized operational procedures, for example, states not only have to raise the level of interaction between their military decision-makers and institutionalize some sort of working relationship, but also to collaborate in extremely sensitive areas such as Command, Control, Communication, Intelligence and Surveillance (C^3IS) systems.

Second, despite these difficulties and even though the five regional brigades are at widely varying stages of development, reaching from SADC's already fully operational force to Northern Africa's nascent capability, it appears as if most of the continent's states have overcome their inhibitions to cooperate with each other in military matters and have joined the collective effort. The basic factors responsible for the failures of pre-ASF initiatives as well as the reasons for the success of the current attempt are easy to discern. Whether one talks of a high command, a military standby system or any of the other known appellations referring to some joint African force, it seems that the underlying problem is the inevitable tension between states' perceived need to maintain full control over national capabilities in order to keep peace at home and project strength abroad and the necessity of relinquishing al least certain aspects of their national command authority to a supra-national body like the OAU inherent in the principle of a Pan-African force. Many of the aforementioned attempts at establishing such a force failed because their institutional setup was not able to resolve this and similar tensions and was thus considered a threat by many states. Through its unique reliance on regional frameworks, the ASF's likelihood of failure in this area is significantly lower than that of its predecessors. The decentralized character of the ASF ensures that the states feel ownership in the process of establishing a continental peacekeeping capability and allows the AU to incorporate all states into a common framework without infringing on their national and regional authority or responsibilities. This almost symbiotic relationship which is discussed in more detail in chapter ten not only reduces the risk of competition between the continental, regional and national levels of inter-African security cooperation, but also increases the stakes all actors have in the process, builds up helpful peer group pressure and thus reduces the chances of failure.[78]

Nonetheless, tensions continue to exist and are not likely to disappear any time soon. Consequently, the AU and its international supporters need to ensure that the bridges built over the past five years are not torn down in a moment of crisis, but are instead continuously reinforced. In addition, the AU still has to find persuasive answers to many of the arguments raised against previous Pan-African security initiatives, namely, the difficulty of agreeing on a workable funding arrangement (in order to decrease and eventually erase the ASF's dependence on international financial aid) and ensuring the force's interoperability. However, given the level of cooperation achieved thus far, these objectives do not seem out of reach.

Notes

[1]   For a detailed history of these attempts see Benedikt Franke, "A Pan-African Army: The Evolution of an Idea and Its Eventual Realization in the African Standby Force," *African Security Review* 15, no. 4 (2006): 2-16.

[2]   Cedric de Coning, "Refining the African Standby Force Concept," *Conflict Trends*, no. 2 (2004): 21.

[3]   See R Russell, *A History of the United Nations Charter: The Role of the United States 1940-45* (Washington DC: Brookings Institution Press, 1958).

[4]   Ibid., 258. The discussion about the wisdom of creating a standing UN force continues to the present day. See Olivia Ward, "United Nations Army Proposed," *Toronto Star*, June 15 2006.

[5]   Russell, *A History of the United Nations Charter: The Role of the United States 1940-45*, 258-259.

[6]   See African Union, *Policy Framework for the Establishment of the African Standby Force and the Military Staff Committee*, Part II, Annex E (Models of Standby Arrangements).

[7]   See *Supplement to an Agenda for Peace: Position Paper of the Secretary-General on the Occasion of the Fiftieth Anniversary of the United Nations* (UN Document A/50/60-S/1995, 13 January 1995), Part III.

[8]   At the time of writing (Spring 2009) the future of SHIRBRIG had been called into doubt as the Scandinavian countries sought to shift their support towards the EU and NATO. For up-to-date information on SHIRBRIG see www.shirbrig.dk.

[9]   See African Union, *Policy Framework for the Establishment of the African Standby Force and the Military Staff Committee*, Part II, Annex E (Models of Standby Arrangements), Annex H.

[10]   See SHIRBRIG, *Work Plan 2008*, 4 January 2008, Vienna.

[11]   Adekeye Adebajo, "Pax West Africana? Regional Security Mechanisms," in *West Africa's Security Challenges - Building Peace in a Troubled Region*, ed. Adekeye Adebajo and Ismail Rashid (Boulder: Lynne Rienner, 2004), 307.

[12]   With or without regional consensus, Nigeria bore over 70 percent of the collective manpower, logistical and financial burden of ECOWAS's interventions in Liberia and Sierra Leone. In the process, the cohesion of ECOWAS was ruptured owing to apprehensions of Nigerian hegemony in the region. Similarly, the lack of consensus on SADC intervention in Lesotho (1998) and DRC in the same year also spelled further strategic conflicts in the SADC and IGAD regions.

[13]   See EU Military Rapid Response Concept (5641/1/03 REV 1). Also see EU Battlegroup Concept, 13618/06 (EU-Restricted), agreed upon by the European Union Military Committee on 2 October 2006. Interview with Colonel Reinhard Linz, EU Military Liaison Officer to the African Union, Addis Ababa, 18 May 2007.

[14]   See, for example, Jakkie Cilliers and Mark Malan, *Progress with the African Standby Force*, *ISS Papers No. 98.* (Pretoria: Institute for Security

Studies, 2005), Coning, "Refining the African Standby Force Concept.", Mark Malan, "New Tools in the Box? Towards a Standby Force for Africa," in *Peace in Africa - Towards a Collaborative Security Regime*, ed. Shannon Field (Johannesburg: Institute for Global Dialogue, 2004), James Shircliffe, "Tip of the African Spear: Forging an Expeditionary Capability for a Troubled Continent," *The Royal United Services Institute Journal* 152, no. 4 (2007): 58-62.

[15]   AU, *Protocol Relating to the Establishment of the Peace and Security Council*, 9 July 2002, Durban, Article 13, para 1.

[16]   Ibid., para 3.

[17]   Ibid.

[18]   See *Policy Framework for the Establishment of the African Standby Force and the Military Staff Committee* (AU Document EXP/ASF-MSC/2(I), 16 May 2003, Addis Ababa).

[19]   AU, *Policy Framework for the Establishment of the African Standby Force and the Military Staff Committee*, Part II, Annex I.

[20]   It is important to note that the idea of the ASF is built on geographic regions rather than the RECs. Thus, a contingent of the ASF can be established by regional states in an independent arrangement that has little or no connection with any REC (this has been the case in Eastern Africa, see section on EASBRIG). If member states in a region are unable to come together to establish their branch of the ASF, the Policy Framework provides that "encouragement be given to potential lead nations to form coalitions of the willing as a stop-gap arrangement, pending the establishment of a regional standby forces arrangement". See AU, *Policy Framework for the Establishment of the African Standby Force and the Military Staff Committee*, 17.

[21]   See AU, *Policy Framework for the Establishment of the African Standby Force and the Military Staff Committee*, Annex 3. The Roadmap for the Operationalization of the ASF specifies the following capabilities in its Annex 3: A brigade HQ and support unit of up to 65 personnel and 16 vehicles; a HQ company and support unit of up to 120 personnel; four light infantry battalions, each composed of up to 750 personnel and 70 vehicles; an engineer unit of up to 135 personnel; a light signals unit of up to 135 personnel; a reconnaissance company of up to 150 personnel; a helicopter unit of up to 80 personnel, 10 vehicles and 4 helicopters; a military police unit of up to 48 personnel and 17 vehicles; a light multi-role logistical unit of up to 190 personnel and 40 vehicles; a level 2 medical unit of up to 35 personnel and 10 vehicles; a military observer group of up to 120 officers; a civilian support group consisting of logistical, administrative and budget components.

[22]   AU, *Policy Framework for the Establishment of the African Standby Force and the Military Staff Committee*, 23.

[23]   Ibid., 3.

[24]   Report of the Training and Evaluation ASF Pre-Workshop held from 31 January to 2 February 2006.

[25]   For an early discussion of logistical and capacity considerations surrounding the ASF see Tsepe Motumi, "Logistical and Capacity Considerations Surrounding a Standby Force," in *Peace in Africa - Towards a Collaborative Security Regime*, ed. Shannon Field (Johannesburg: Institute for Global Dialogue, 2004). For an alternative view on ASF Logistics see Rick

Thompson, "Afloat Depots for the African Standby Force," *Canadian Military Journal* 8, no. 4 (2007): 37-44.

[26]   See Final Report of the Expert Workshop on Command and Control held in Cairo, 5-12 April 2006.

[27]   AU, *Policy Framework for the Establishment of the African Standby Force and the Military Staff Committee*, para. 3.17.

[28]   In large and complex operations (scenarios five and six), involving major civilian elements, the Head of Mission is called Special Representative of the Chairperson of the AU Commission. See ASF Peace Support Operations Doctrine, Sect 8, para 68.

[29]   Figure adapted from Final Report of the Expert Workshop on Command and Control, Annexure E.

[30]   AU Working Paper, *The African Standby Force Command and Control System*, Annexure B

[31]   See *Decision on the African Standby Force and the Military Staff Committee* (AU Document EX.CL/110(V), 6-8 July 2004, Addis Ababa).

[32]   See *Experts' Meeting on the Relationship between the AU and the Regional Mechanisms for Conflict Prevention, Management and Resolution* (AU Document Exp/AU-RECS/ASF/4(I), 22-23 March 2005 Addis Ababa).

[33]   *Policy Framework for the Establishment of the ASF and the MSC*, 40.

[34]   Figure based on AU, *Roadmap for the Operationalization of the African Standby Force Phase II*.

[35]   See *Report of the Chairperson of the Commission for the Period July to December 2006*, Executive Council, 10th Ordinary Session, 25-26 January 2007, Addis Ababa, 13.

[36]   Correspondence with Colonel Reinhard Linz, EU MIL LO AU, 25 November 2008.

[37]   Interview with Dr. Abdel-Kader Haireche, Team Leader DPKO-AU Peace Support Team, 12 June 2007, Addis Ababa.

[38]   EURO-RECAMP will provide the basis for the ASF Command Post Exercise (CPX) in early 2010. Interviews with Dr. Genoveva Hernandez-Uriz, Administrator for Civilian Crisis Management, Council of the European Union and Mr. Sébastien Bergeon, Defense Expert, Council of the European Union, 5-7 September 2007, Addis Ababa.

[39]   Interview with Mr. Bereng Mtimkulu, Head of the AU PSOD, 20 September 2007, Addis Ababa.

[40]   Interview with Mr. Hartwig Bretenitz, Consultant to the AU PSOD, 29 September 2007, Addis Ababa.

[41]   See *Memorandum of Understanding on Cooperation in the Area of Peace and Security between the African Union, the Regional Economic Communities and the Coordinating Mechanisms of the Regional Standby Brigades of Eastern Africa and Northern Africa* (AU Document AU-RECs/EXP/2(II) Rev. 3, 2 September 2007, Kampala) Article IV, para (ii).

[42]   Interview with Captain (SA Navy) John Potgieter, Military Expert, AU PSOD, 12 June 2007, Addis Ababa.

[43]   For a good though somewhat outdated discussion on the financing of the ASF see Roger Kibasomba, "Financing a Credible Standby Force Via the AU's Peace Fund " in *Peace in Africa - Towards a Collaborative Security Regime*, ed. Shannon Field (Johannesburg: Institute for Global Dialogue, 2004).

⁴⁴ The Peace Support Training Centre (PSTC) in Nairobi has volunteered to develop the scenario for the ASF CPX until the end of April 2008.

⁴⁵ See Proceedings of the 1ˢᵗ Meeting of Eastern Africa Chiefs of Defense Staff on the Establishment of the Eastern African Standby Brigade (EASBRIG), 16-17 February 2004, Jinja, Uganda.

⁴⁶ See *Decision of the 1ˢᵗ Assembly of Heads of State and Government on the Establishment of the Eastern Africa Standby Brigade* (EASBRIG Document AHG/1/05).

⁴⁷ See Report of the 3ʳᵈ Ordinary Meeting of the Council of Ministers of Defense and Security, September 2005, Kigali.

⁴⁸ See Report of the 5ᵗʰ Ordinary Meeting of the Council of Ministers of Defense and Security, 17 August 2007, Nairobi, para 2.

⁴⁹ Interviews with Colonel Moustapha Handouleh, Deputy Chief of Staff, EASBRIG Planning Element, 28 August 2007, Addis Ababa and Mr. Simon Mulongo, Director EASBRICOM, 29 August 2007, Addis Ababa.

⁵⁰ Interview with Colonel Reinhard Linz, EU MIL LO AU, 1 September 2007, Addis Ababa.

⁵¹ EASBRICOM, *Eastern Africa Standby Force Strategic Development Plan 2007-2015*, November 2007, Nairobi.

⁵² The EDSC has met five times since its inaugural meeting in June 2007. The author was present at the second meeting.

⁵³ Figure adapted from presentation on the EASBRIG Strategic Development Plan 2007-2015 to the Friends of EASBRIG Meeting by the Director of EASBRICOM, Mr. Simon Mulongo, 10 December 2007, Nairobi.

⁵⁴ The struggle between Ethiopia and Kenya for regional hegemony, for example, has had a substantial impact on the location of EASBRIG elements, the appointment of EASBRICOM staff as well as the concept of a regional rapid deployment capability.

⁵⁵ For more information on the operationalization of EASBRIG see www.easbrig.org.

⁵⁶ See ECOWAS, *Protocol Relating to the Mechanism for Conflict Prevention, Management, Resolution, Peacekeeping and Security*, 1999, Chapter III.

⁵⁷ See Cilliers and Malan, *Progress with the African Standby Force*, 5.

⁵⁸ See Proceedings of the 9ᵗʰ Ordinary Session of the Defense and Security Committee, September 2004.

⁵⁹ Figure adapted from Richard Amponsem-Boateng, "Prospects of the Economic Community of West African States Standby Force" (US Army Command and General Staff College, 2006), Appendix B.

⁶⁰ ECOWAS Secretariat, *ECOWAS Standby Force (ESF) Operational Framework*, 10 April 2005, para 16.

⁶¹ See Proceedings of the 13ᵗʰ Meeting of the Defense and Security Committee, 10 July 2005, Yamoussoukro.

⁶² See Proceedings of the 14ᵗʰ Meeting of the Defense and Security Committee, 9 November 2005, Lome.

⁶³ Agence France-Press (AFP), *West African Troubleshooting Force starts Military Maneuvers*, 6 December 2007.

⁶⁴ Official Report and Update by the German Military Advisor to ECOWAS, Colonel Klaus-Peter Koschny, 6 February 2008. Also, interview

with Colonel Werner Rauber, Head of the Peacekeeping Study Section, Kofi Annan International Peacekeeping Training Centre, 2 February 2008.

[65]   See Report of the ECOWAS Workshop, *Lessons from ECOWAS Peacekeeping Operations: 1990-2004*, 11-12 February 2005, Accra.

[66]   See Cilliers and Malan, *Progress with the African Standby Force*, 12.

[67]   SADC, *Strategic Indicative Plan for the Organ on Politics, Defense and Security*, August 2003, para 8.3.1

[68]   Statement by Brigadier-General Les Rudman to a Center for International Political Studies Seminar, 19 September 2005, Pretoria.

[69]   SADC, Memorandum of Understanding amongst the Southern African Development Community Member States on the Establishment of a Southern African Development Community Standby Brigade, 17 August 2007, Lusaka.

[70]   Figure adapted from Cilliers and Malan, *Progress with the African Standby Force*, 10.

[71]   Stephan Elbe, "Strategic Implications of HIV/AIDS," *Adelphi Papers*, no. 357 (2003).

[72]   See NARC, *Memorandum of Understanding on the Establishment of the North Africa Region Capability in the African Standby Force*, 16 November 2005, Tripoli.

[73]   See NARC, *Memorandum of Understanding on the Establishment of the North Africa Region Capability in the African Standby Force*, 16 November 2005, Tripoli, Appendix 2.

[74]   Interview with Captain (SA Navy) John Potgieter, Military Consultant to the AU PSOD, 21 September 2007, Addis Ababa.

[75]   ECCAS, *Protocol Relating to the Council for Peace and Security in Central Africa (COPAX)*, 25-26 February 2007, Yaoundé, Articles 25 and 26.

[76]   ECCAS, *Standing Orders for the Central African Multinational Force (FOMAC)*, 17 June 2002, Malabo.

[77]   Cilliers and Malan, "Progress with the African Standby Force", 16.

[78]   For a detailed discussion of the impact of competing regionalism(s) on Africa's emerging security architecture see Benedikt Franke, "Competing Regionalisms in Africa and the Continent's Emerging Security Architecture," *African Studies Quarterly* 10, no. 1 (2007).

9
The Continental Early
Warning System

This chapter examines the quality and extent of inter-African security cooperation within the framework of the Continental Early Warning System currently being developed by the African Union. To this purpose, it details the essential characteristics and current status of the continental system before it reviews and measures the progress at the regional level where component early warning systems are in varying stages of development. While the chapter goes into great detail to demonstrate the complexity of this undertaking, it does not seek to provide an ultimate description of the CEWS. Rather it focuses on those aspects that help to highlight the state of contemporary inter-African security cooperation and thus provide valuable insights for the analysis in the next chapter.

In June 2001, the UN Secretary General issued his Report on the Prevention of Armed Conflict. Central to the report was the argument that "prevention should be initiated at the earliest possible stage of a conflict cycle in order to be most effective".[1] Early warning and early response systems are considered central pillars of such operational conflict prevention. As such, they have generated a substantial body of literature over the past couple of years.[2] Despite the ongoing academic debate about many of the key terms and concepts, a general consensus seems to have emerged that early warning can be defined as the systematic collection and analysis of information coming from areas of potential crises for the purposes of (1) anticipating the escalation of violent conflict, (2) developing strategic responses to these crises, and (3) presenting preventive or mitigating options to critical decision-makers. The *Berghof Handbook for Conflict Transformation* accordingly defines an early warning system as "any initiative that focuses on systematic data collection, analysis and/or formulation of recommendations, including risk assessment and information sharing".[3]

Early warning systems have long been in use. Beginning in the 1950s, the longstanding efforts to predict environmental disasters such as droughts and famines began to inform attempts to foresee crises arising out of political causes. Building on the advances in information technology and statistical analysis, many governments funded projects which sought to build models for understanding political behavior and warn of impending crises.[4]

In the UN system, early warning was initially associated with traditional intelligence gathering to detect, deter, prevent or counter hostile acts against UN peacekeepers in the Congo.[5] As Howard Adelman has pointed out, the roots of its contemporary conception, however, are to be found in the humanitarian area. Intent on enabling the UN to prepare for and perhaps even mitigate the causes of forced migration, a 1981 study by Prince Sadrunnin for the UN Commission on Human Rights set forth a number of push and pull factors which contributed to forced migration. Sadrunnin recommended the creation of an early warning system within the UN to study and track these factors. His recommendation was reinforced when the Group of Government Experts to Avert New Refugee Flows formally requested the UN Secretary-General to establish an office to gather more complex information in a timely fashion.[6]

With the spread of conflict following the end of the Cold War, multilateral early warning efforts expanded beyond natural disasters, refugee flows and food security to include the prediction of crisis escalation. According to Kumar Rupesinghe, the resultant conflict early warning systems evolved in three stages:

> The first generation early warning systems were the systems where the entire early warning mechanism (including conflict monitoring) was based outside the conflict region (namely, in the West). The second generation amended this approach by basing the monitoring mechanism in the conflict zones, namely by having the field monitors to gather primary event data. The analysis, however, continued to be conducted outside the conflict region. The third generation early warning systems are entirely located in the conflict regions. They integrate early warning and response as simultaneous processes.[7]

The best-known current conflict early warning systems include the *Internationales System für die Früherkennung von Spannungen und Tatsachenermittlung* (FAST) of the Swiss Peace Foundation and the *Crisis Watch* of the International Crisis Group.[8] Until its bankruptcy in 2004, the UK-based Forum on Early Warning and Early Response (FEWER) also played a prominent role. Whether they rely on quantitative or qualitative methods, these systems are generally based on the same principles. They use a wide variety of open sources and a network of local data gatherers to identify relevant conflict indicators ranging from structural preconditions (systemic indicators) and specific situational circumstances (proximate indicators) to immediate catalysts (trigger indicators).[9] Through constant monitoring of these indicators and evaluation against predefined thresholds, the early warning systems hope to be able to predict potential crises and provide decision-makers with specific recommendations as to their prevention or mitigation (see Figure 9.1 for a graphical representation).

Figure 9.1: The Early Warning Process[10]

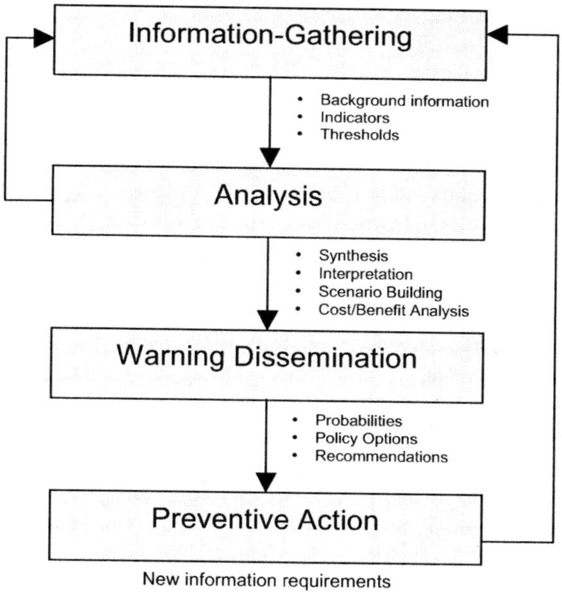

While the early warning processes are becoming increasingly more sophisticated and proponents like Sean O'Brien argue that some of the current systems can even predict country-specific instabilities with an astonishing overall accuracy of up to 80 percent,[11] skepticism about the real value of early warning systems is not an uncommon reaction.[12] Criticism generally revolves around five issues, namely, (1) the inability of such systems to predict crises beyond the obvious trends, (2) their inherently biased and unmistakably political nature, (3) their general failure to produce actionable results and to generate timely responses, (4) the reluctance of governments to react to their warnings and (5) the lack of political will and/or resources to ensure effective responses. Despite such criticism, however, conflict early warning systems have multiplied over the last couple of years and organizations such as the AU or ASEAN are increasingly eager to operationalize their own mechanisms in order to improve their capacity to prevent or mitigate conflicts in their respective regions.

The establishment of a continental early warning system in Africa was formally initiated in June 1992 when the Assembly of the OAU decided at its 28th Meeting in Dakar to establish the Mechanism for Conflict Prevention, Management and Resolution. This decision was put into effect in June 1993 with the adoption of the Cairo Declaration that established the Central Mechanism. The Mechanism was charged with the anticipation and prevention of situations of armed conflict as well as with undertaking peacemaking and peace-building efforts during conflicts and in post-conflict situations. However, despite the proliferation of violent conflicts in places like Somalia and Rwanda little happened until a June 1995 OAU Council of Ministers meeting in Addis Ababa endorsed a proposal for the establishment of a continent-wide early warning system submitted by the Secretary General.

In January 1996, the OAU held a high-level seminar on the establishment of an early warning system on conflict situations in Addis Ababa. The objective of the seminar was to "provide a forum for the exchange of information, with a view to bringing conceptual clarity and coherence on the measures to be undertaken, as well as the modalities for putting in place an early warning system on conflict situations in Africa".[13] The seminar concluded that the establishment of an early warning capacity by the OAU was "imperative" and it made 13 specific recommendations to this end. These recommendations resulted in the first specific reference to the establishment of an early warning system at the level of OAU Heads of State in the Yaounde Declaration of 1996:

> We welcome the creation in June 1993 of the OAU Mechanism for Conflict Prevention, Management and Resolution which is already contributing significantly towards improving the Organization's capacity to prevent conflicts and maintain peace in Africa. We hail in advance the imminent institution within the said Mechanism of our early warning system on conflict situations in Africa, convinced that its establishment should be able to further improve the action of the Organization in the area of preventive diplomacy by making it possible, notably through pre-emptive action in gathering and analyzing pertinent data, not only to establish the existence of a threat to the peace, but also to look for a quick way to remove the threat. We exhort all potential data collectors to communicate same information in time and provide the OAU Mechanism regularly with any at their disposal on warning signs of imminent conflict.[14]

Following the Yaounde Declaration, the Central Organ devoted considerable energies to preventive diplomacy and the establishment of a working early warning system. In early 1998 it heeded the proposal of a second high-level seminar to establish a rudimentary early warning system consisting of an Internet-linked situation room based in Addis Ababa and to develop a system of early warning focal points around the continent. Financed by a $11 million aid package which the US government had granted to this purpose in 1995,[15] the OAU finally set up a "news-gathering centre whose purpose is to alert the Secretary-General of looming crises". Around the time the OAU gave way to the AU, the staff of this situation room had grown to six people who were supported by a unit for conflict prevention, management and reconciliation staffed by eight analysts and an early warning unit staffed by two experts.[16] The OAU's experience with the establishment of an early warning system provided the basis for the AU's Continental Early Warning System as described below.[17]

The Concept and Structure of the CEWS

Article 12 of the Protocol Relating to the Establishment of the Peace and Security Council of the AU provides that, in order to facilitate the anticipation of conflicts in Africa, a Continental Early Warning System shall be established as one of the five pillars of the PSC. It shall consist of (1) a situation room as observation and monitoring centre located at the Conflict Management Directorate of the Union, and responsible for data collection and analysis on the basis of an appropriate early warning indicators module with "clearly defined and accepted political, economic, social, military and humanitarian indicators"; and (2) regional observation and monitoring units under the supervision of the RECs which are to be linked directly to the situation room, and which shall collect and process data at their level and transmit the same to the situation room (for a graphical representation of the resultant structure see Figure 9.2).[18]

Similar to the structure of the ASF, the CEWS is thus based directly on the component early warning mechanisms of the regions. While the central management and coordination tasks as well as the strategic analysis of incoming information are conducted at the AU headquarters in Addis, the responsibility for data collection rests firmly with the RECs.

Figure 9.2: Schematic Representation of the CEWS[19]

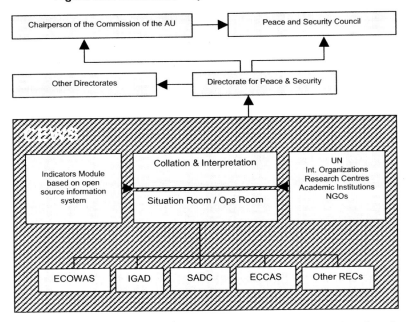

This structure is meant to enable the CEWS to fulfill its five key objectives as specified by the roadmap for its operationalization, namely, (1) to collect, compile, archive and distribute information, (2) to continuously monitor the socio, political, economic and other situations across the continent, to analyze data and to articulate policy and preventive responses in real-time, (3) to support the AU's management of acute situations of conflict and instability, disruptions and disasters, (4) to systematize the engagement of the PSC with potential conflict situations and issues, and (5) to develop strategies for engaging decision-makers on the effective use of specific reports.[20]

The fulfillment of these objectives is to be firmly embedded in the so-called Strategic Conflict Analysis and Response Framework (SCARF) which consists of a three step process. The first step is the continuous monitoring of developments across the continent and information-gathering on relevant settings, that is, on potential or acute conflicts via open sources and the regional mechanisms.[21] The data collection focuses on three categories, namely (1) contextual indicators, (2) profiles of individual and group actors, and (3) event baselines.

In the second step, this data will be analyzed. Experts of the AU's Conflict Management Division will examine the situation(s) and evaluate structural factors (that is, the so-called root causes of conflict), the interests, motivations and relations of the actors involved as well as the conflict dynamics and trends.

In the third step, this analysis will be turned into specific policy recommendations which are distributed to the AU's political decision-makers in the form of tailored reports. These reports include potential conflict scenarios as well as a list of policy options which are open to the AU at the particular moment in time and/or the near future. It is planned that the CEWS will produce a wide variety of such reports once fully operational, including news highlights, daily and weekly reports, mission reports, background papers, briefing notes, PSC situation reports, flash reports, early warning reports and reports to the Chairperson.

As specified by Article 12 of the Protocol Relating to the Establishment of the PSC, these reports are to "inform the Chairperson of the Commission in a timely manner so that he/she can advise the Council on potential conflicts and threats to peace and security and recommend the best courses of action".[22] The following section will assess to what extent the above concept and structure has been operationalized thus far.

The Operationalization of the CEWS

The PSC Protocol that specified the CEWS concept and structure as described above also mandated the Chairperson of the Commission, in consultation with member states, the regional mechanisms, the UN and other relevant organizations, to work out the practical details for the establishment of the early warning system and to "take all the steps required for its effective operationalization".[23] Even though several expert workshops were held following the adoption of the PSC Protocol in July 2002, little concrete happened over the next three years. In mid 2005, however, the political pressure on the AU had mounted to the extent that it organized another expert workshop in June 2005 in order to finalize a roadmap for the operationalization of the CEWS. This workshop was followed by a meeting on technical issues in November 2005 which focused on the selection of appropriate early warning indicators. In April 2006, the AU held a consultative meeting with the RECs and other partners with the aim of involving them more closely in the establishment of the continental early warning system on the basis of the roadmap.[24] Two months later, the PSC agreed on the modalities for the establishment of the African Peace and Security Architecture (which includes the CEWS) and, in December 2006, the AU member states finally adopted the roadmap for the operationalization of the CEWS. This provided the AU Conflict Management Division with the political mandate necessary to begin the implementation of the CEWS concept.

This implementation began in earnest in March 2007 when the AU CMD and the German GTZ as its main international partner with respect to early warning and conflict prevention agreed on a detailed work plan to operationalize the CEWS until the end of 2009.[25] The formulation of the Strategic Conflict Analysis and Response Framework was given highest priority for 2007 with the aim of specifying the basic instruments and processes for monitoring, analysis and reporting until the end of the year. To this purpose, the GTZ organized three working meetings between May and December 2007 which were attended by about 15 AU representatives such as situation room staff, early warning officers and analysts. The outcomes of these meetings was subsequently amalgamated into a CEWS Manual which now serves as authoritative reference guide as well as a list of standing operational procedures which formalizes the various CEWS processes.[26]

Following the production of these two documents, the AU and the GTZ will now continue to operationalize the CEWS according to the aforementioned work plan. The focus will thereby lie on a sustainable improvement of the analytical capacities of the CMD (it is currently envisaged to use the conflict prevention and management programs of the Universities of Bradford and Leipzig to provide train-the-trainers instruction in social science methods), the installation of a reliable information technology infrastructure analogous to the European Media Monitoring System (EMM) of the European Commission and the development of the regional early warning mechanisms.[27] Given that the latter are not only based on differing premises such as the type of conflict they attempt to predict or the way in which they rely on the input of civil society actors, but are also at widely varying stages of development, the coordination and harmonization of the regional efforts at early warning will be a key issue in the implementation of the CEWS.[28] In order to gauge the extent of this challenge and get an impression of the regional aspect of inter-African security cooperation, the following three sections will briefly assess the progress of the RECs in establishing component early warning mechanisms at the regional and sub-regional levels.

Eastern Africa's Regional Mechanism (CEWARN)

CEWARN is the Conflict Early Warning and Response Mechanism of the seven member states (Djibouti, Eritrea, Ethiopia, Kenya, Somalia, Sudan and Uganda) of the Intergovernmental Authority on Development (IGAD) in the Horn of Africa sub-region. In clear contrast to the other African early warning mechanisms, CEWARN has already featured prominently in the conflict prevention and management literature because of its innovative approach and model character.[29]

Originally founded to coordinate responses to the environmental disasters in the region, IGAD began to broaden its mandate to issues of conflict prevention, management and resolution following its revitalization in November 1996. Article 18(a) of the Agreement Establishing the Intergovernmental Authority on Development called on member states to "take effective collective measures to eliminate threats to regional cooperation, peace and stability".[30] In 1998, IGAD embarked on a five point program on conflict prevention, management and resolution which included the development of a regional early warning mechanism. A Council of Ministers meeting in Khartoum in November 2000 approved the establishment of such an early warning mechanism within the Peace and Security Division of the IGAD Secretariat.[31] After focused research, consultations and assessments in all IGAD member states, the Council of Ministers endorsed the Protocol on the Establishment of a Conflict Early Warning and Response Mechanism in another meeting in Khartoum in January 2002, providing CEWARN with a legal entity and operational framework.[32] The protocol entered into force in July 2003 having been ratified by Eritrea, Kenya, Ethiopia and Sudan. Djibouti ratified the Protocol in April 2005.

The protocol mandates CEWARN to (1) receive and share information concerning potentially violent conflicts as well as their outbreak and escalation in the IGAD region, (2) undertake and share analyses of that information, (3) develop case scenarios and formulate realistic options for response, (4) share and communicate information, analyses and response options, and (5) carry out studies on specific types and areas of conflict in the IGAD region.[33] The CEWARN Protocol lays down a wide range of areas on which CEWARN can collect information. These include livestock rustling, conflicts over grazing and water points, nomadic movements, smuggling and illegal trade, refugees, landmines and banditry.[34] However, CEWARN was mandated by the member states to commence with the monitoring of cross-border pastoral conflicts. The focus on cross-border pastoral conflicts was chosen as a trust-building entry point for CEWARN because it was a project all IGAD member states had an interest in and could agree on. Arid and semi-arid cross-border areas with a livelihood system of pastoralists and agro-pastoralists run along all the borders of IGAD, with similar ethnic groups along the boundaries.

In operationalizing its early warning and response mechanism, IGAD adopted a bottom-up and process-oriented approach that builds upon existing efforts, mechanisms and skills within the sub-region. To lay the foundation for data collection and analysis eight workshops with different stakeholders of the IGAD member states were realized over a period of 18 months. In November 2002, the indicators to frame the collection of dynamic behavioral (events) data on pastoral conflicts were developed by local and regional experts and practitioners who had an intimate knowledge of pastoral conflicts. In June 2003, the CEWARN Unit was established in Addis Ababa to act as central point of coordination, monitoring and quality control. Field data collection in the first pilot area, the so-called Karamoja Cluster located in the border region of Kenya, Uganda, Sudan and Ethiopia began in July 2003. The second pilot area, the so-called Somali Cluster located in the border region of Somalia, Kenya and Ethiopia followed in June 2005.

In order to be able to monitor the situation in these two clusters, collect relevant data, analyze this data and make specific policy recommendations on this analysis, IGAD has devised a sophisticated early warning and early response mechanism which works on three geographical levels (for a graphical representation of the organizational structure of this mechanism see Figure 9.3). At the local level, CEWARN has established a system of information collection networks to collect and document relevant information and data on cross-border and related pastoral conflicts. Each network is composed of several field monitors (FMs), trained in collecting information, categorization and reporting formats and procedures. Initially, fourteen FMs were deployed in the Karamoja Cluster and eight FMs in the Somali Cluster, but this number has since increased.[35] Each FM submits incident reports as violent incidences occur and situation reports based on observable events submitted on a weekly basis. Incident reports document violent events and record key attributes that describe *who did what, to whom, when, where, why and how*. More specifically, these incident parameters include the type of violence used, initiator, recipient, location, and date. The incident reports also record the consequences of the incidents. Human deaths and livestock losses are the two most central of these outcomes.[36]

At the national level, IGAD identified appropriate research institutes and contracted them as partner organizations for the Mechanism. Each research institute includes a CEWARN country coordinator, supported by an assistant, who is responsible to (1) organize and supervise the required field monitoring, (2) coordinate the information and data collection, and (3) to analyze the data and submit early warning reports. The country coordinators use the CEWARN Reporter – a network software program specifically designed for early warning purposes – to enter and store the standardized field reports submitted to them by the field monitors. The Reporter enables users to analyze the reports and provides them with a system for data management and a graphic display of incident frequency over time. It also allows for qualitative and quantitative analysis of field data with a view to identifying emerging trends. It thereby assists in the understanding and analysis of how changes in pastoral behavior are likely to lead to more tension and conflict, or cooperation. Based on the data gathered in the field, the country coordinators produce regular reports including (1) country updates based on the peace and security situation of the areas of reporting, (2) alerts based on impeding or existing conflict which requires immediate action, and (3) situation briefs to inform on existing events or events that may affect the dynamics of the conflicts being monitored including natural disasters such as floods or drought.

Also at the national level, the CEWARN Mechanism builds upon so-called Conflict Early Warning and Early Response Units (CEWERUs) as focal coordinating units integrated to operate within the relevant ministries of IGAD member states. These units are directed and managed by CEWERU Heads who are nominated by the member states themselves. Each CEWERU is mandated to form a Steering Committee including representatives of relevant ministries and provincial administration, security bodies such as police, intelligence and military, legislative bodies, civil society organizations, academia, religious organizations or other influential members of societies. Bringing together governmental decision makers and civil society representatives, the CEWERUs are the responsible bodies for response initiatives on a country level to be implemented in close cooperation with local committees or sub-regional peace councils.

At the regional level, the CEWARN Unit in Addis Ababa is the hub for data collection, conflict analyses, information sharing and communication of response options. It acts as a clearing house and is responsible for quality control.[37] It supports CEWARN stakeholders in capacity-building (including training), coordinates the different CEWARN organs, assists in developing regional cooperation structures and is the driving force for the political process behind the Mechanism. Moreover, the CEWARN Unit produces early warning reports that focus on cross-border or regional nature of conflicts including regional cluster reports and annual risk assessments capturing the evolution of trends of cross-border pastoral and related conflicts. The reports generated by CEWARN are shared with each national Conflict Early Warning and Early Response Unit. Ideally, when early warning information is relayed to the CEWERUs, response actions would be initiated to mitigate or prevent an imminent conflict.

Figure 9.3: Organizational Structure of the CEWARN Mechanism[38]

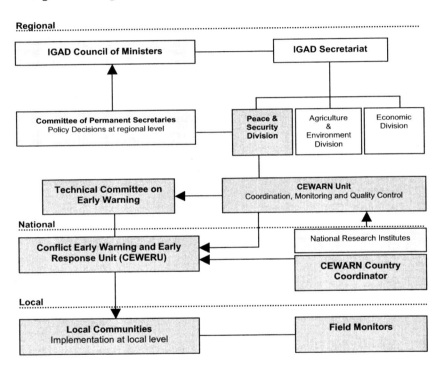

A Technical Committee for Early Warning (TCEW) and a Committee of Permanent Secretaries (CPS) complement the regional coordination structure. At the intermediate level, the Heads of the CEWERUs collectively form the Technical Committee which convenes twice a year to run technical consultations on the CEWARN Mechanism including the discussion of early warning reports and response options. The TCEW submits its recommendations to the CPS comprised of senior governmental representatives designated by IGAD member states. The CPS is the policy-making organ of CEWARN and it reports to the Council of Ministers which in turn reports to the Assembly of Heads of State and Government. The Executive Secretary, the Director of Peace and Security Division and the Director of the CEWARN Unit are *ex-officio* members of the CPS.

At a meeting in May 2006, the CPS agreed on a programmatic focus for CEWARN and spelt out a detailed five-year strategy.[39] The latter set six strategic objectives which CEWARN hopes to achieve until 2011, namely, to (1) expand the monitoring and reporting of pastoral and related conflicts in all IGAD member states, (2) strengthen the early response side of the mechanism by fully operationalizing CEWERUs in all IGAD member states, (3) widen sources of information, enhance the information collection system, and strengthen the data analysis capacity of CEWARN, (4) develop a public relations and communication strategy and promote awareness on CEWARN's work, (5) strengthen the institutional and functional capacity of the CEWARN Mechanism using all enabling means, including research and training as well as administrative and financial support, and (6) implement a sustainable long-term funding strategy that will ensure CEWARN's access to adequate resources to fulfill its mandate. [40]

While this may seem a tall order, IGAD has proven over the past five years that it is serious about establishing a working conflict early warning and response mechanism and it has already made great strides towards this goal.[41] Since it became operational in 2003, CEWARN has managed to bring together state and non-state actors to collaborate and adopt strategies toward addressing violent cross-border pastoral conflicts and it has successfully developed a state of the art field monitoring and data analysis tool along with the necessary capacity building and training structure. As early as 2004, Howard Adelman acknowledged CEWARN's model character and its status as the most developed data-based regional early warning system in Africa:

> CEWARN is cutting edge and even in its infant state shows greater strength than virtually any other early warning system extant with respect to data collection... The documentation function alone that has been achieved in the pilot study of the Karamoja Cluster is absolutely remarkable, and, reveals horrifying devastation of human and livelihood resources.[42]

However, while CEWARN is certainly the most advanced regional early warning system on the continent, much remains to be done. First, it has yet to link its successful primary source early warning capacity with an effective mechanism for preventing or mitigating conflicts. The slow development within national CEWERUs – so far operational only in Uganda, Kenya and Ethiopia – vital to initiation and implementation of responses has further impaired linking the early warning to early response.[43] The delayed reactions to build the response devices such as information sharing, communication and cooperation between various actors that could enable the Mechanism to assess capacities and use available resources have contributed to those failures. CEWARN's experiences in trying to prevent conflict have shown that it requires much more cooperation and input of stakeholders – at the local, national and regional levels – both in information provision and implementation of responses. The complexity and depth of conflicts require multi-faceted approaches to address and mitigate them.

Second, CEWARN has to broaden its sources of information and improve its ability to interpret and analyze the information it collects. The current mechanism depends solely on the field monitors and individual knowledge of the country coordinators for its information and analysis. The tool does not yet integrate structural data (on ethnicity or culture, for example) that is required to contextualize and interpret the field events data and, in future, could also be used to analyze critical events other than pastoralist conflicts.

Third, CEWARN also has to broaden its geographical focus. Even though a third cluster (located in the border region between Ethiopia and Djibouti) has now been added, the geographical coverage is still extremely limited.[44] Not all member states have yet operationalized the necessary structures and Eritrea has even stalled its CEWARN activities completely following its withdrawal from IGAD.

Fourth, CEWARN needs to develop a comprehensive communications strategy. At the moment, save for some development partners with an interest in the development of CEWARN and a few academics and researchers, its efforts to provide early warning and early response remain largely unknown in the member states, in the region and, most importantly, among local communities who are supposed to be the direct beneficiaries of its work. Moreover, apart from occasional workshops or seminars organized by the AU, its linkages with other regional bodies like ECOWAS, SADC or the EAC remain limited and uncoordinated. In order to actively place the CEWARN Mechanism within its larger political context CEWARN needs to develop an effective PR and communication strategy spelling out CEWARN's achievements and contribution to conflict prevention, management and resolution in the region. Such a strategy could raise awareness of the Mechanism's "value added", build and strengthen sustainable relations among stakeholders and ultimately inspire member states to endorse the expansion of CEWARN's early warning functions to cover other types of conflicts.

Given these and other challenges such as the poor infrastructure, remoteness and inaccessibility of the pilot areas, the complexity of conflicts in the region and the absence of a sustainable funding mechanism, the implementation of CEWARN's five-year strategy will certainly be difficult.[45] However, whatever happens, CEWARN has already shown that meaningful inter-state security cooperation, even if it is only to jointly monitor pastoralist conflicts in selected areas, can be initiated in areas as unstable and conflictual as the Horn of Africa. CEWARN's incremental approach is thereby consistent with the process-orientated argumentation of constructivist theory as described in chapter two. As Ciru Mwaura and his colleagues have pointed out, CEWARN began with the monitoring and reporting on pastoral and related conflicts because it was something each member state could agree upon.[46] While it was accepted that full regional coverage was the ultimate end goal, it had to be acknowledged that this was unlikely to occur in the short term. It was hoped that based on the successful application of the CEWARN model to an identified entry point, confidence to move towards this system of full coverage would gradually build up in the member states. In that way, the current mechanism is conceived as merely the first step to developing a comprehensive early warning and response system to cover all types of conflicts in the region. However, even at its present stage of development, the CEWARN Mechanism is a model of cooperation to many of the other regional early warning systems. It is a unique kind of multilateral government-civil society partnership that thrives on open sources and transparent tools, and most importantly, participation by all stakeholders. In the words of Douglas Bond and Patrick Meier, "the CEWARN Mechanism is truly collective in spirit as well as its operations, both locally and internationally".[47]

Western Africa's Regional Mechanism (ECOWARN)

The second fairly advanced regional early warning system is the West African ECOWARN. Its origins reach back to the 1990 ECOMOG intervention in Liberia in the aftermath of which several processes were initiated to improve and increase the effectiveness of future interventions.[48] These and the continuing outbreaks of conflicts and other security challenges in the region led to a call for the creation of a permanent peace and security framework including a "regional peace and security observation system" in the revised ECOWAS Treaty of 1993.[49] Little, however, happened until an extraordinary summit was held in Lomé in December 1997 in order to discuss the establishment of a mechanism for conflict prevention, management and peacekeeping that could replace ECOWAS's ad hoc conflict resolution procedures. The summit quickly reached consensus on the need for such a mechanism and an experts meeting was convened less than six months later in order to outline its modalities. The conclusions of the July 1998 meeting resulted in the drafting of a Protocol Relating to the Mechanism for Conflict Prevention, Management, Resolution, Peacekeeping and Security which was finally signed in December 1999.[50]

Chapter IV of the Protocol established an early warning system that was to "detect, monitor and analyze signs of threats or break-down in relations within or between member states (conflict indicators) in accordance with Article 58 of the revised ECOWAS Treaty and make reports for use by the Executive Secretariat now transformed into the Commission".[51] The Protocol also called for the establishment of an Observation and Monitoring Centre (OMC) located at the ECOWAS Secretariat in Abuja and four Observation and Monitoring Zones (OMZs) located within the region.

The OMZs are to gather information from their focal area through contact with governmental authorities, local citizens, public media and other news agencies and report this information to the OMC. There are four zonal headquarters based in Banjul (to cover Cape Verde, Gambia, Guinea-Bissau and Senegal), Cotonou (to cover Benin, Nigeria and Togo), Monrovia (to cover Ghana, Guinea, Liberia and Sierra Leone) and Ouagadougou (to cover Burkina Faso, Côte d'Ivoire, Mali and Niger). From these four zonal headquarters, officials are expected to assess political (human rights, democracy), economic (food shortages), social (unemployment), security (arms flow, civil-military relations) and environmental (drought, flooding) indicators on a daily basis and report these to the OMC via the so-called ECOWARN Reporter.[52] This software allows the OMZs and a selected number of civil-society organizations to submit, view and edit field situation and incident reports online.[53]

The OMC is responsible for data collection and analysis, the drafting of up-to-date reports that identify and outline possible emerging crises as well as the monitoring of ongoing crises and post-crisis transition.[54] The Director of the Centre is expected to compile daily situation reports, occasional situation reports and country profiles which are meant to provide the situational context and background for analysis.[55] These reports are then to inform the ECOWAS decision-making bodies, that is, the ECOWAS Commission and the Mediation and Security Council (MSC), in their efforts to bring peace and security to the region. Besides collecting and analyzing data and then reporting on it, the OMC also has responsibilities for maintaining contact with the 15 ECOWAS member states, the other RECs, the AU, the UN, research centers, major NGOs active in the region and all other relevant regional and international bodies. It is also the focal point for civil society input into the early warning process (for a graphical representation of the ECOWAS early warning structure see Figure 9.4).

Figure 9.4: Early Warning and Response Processes within ECOWAS[56]

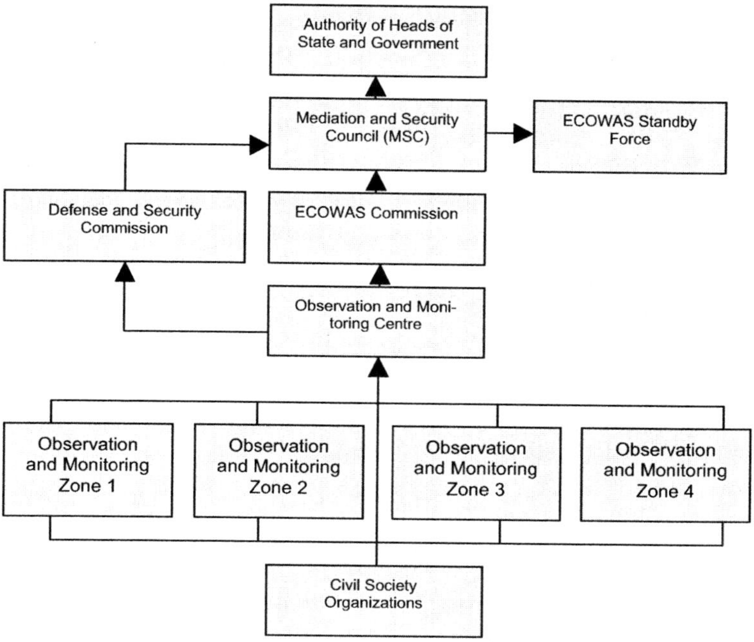

While the ECOWARN system is still at an early stage of development, it has made remarkable progress over the last eight years. In early 2001, the EU gave a grant that kick started the operationalization with the recruitment of zonal bureau officers and the purchase of limited office equipment. By April 2002, the zonal bureaus had been established. Programmers and analysts had been recruited, equipment purchased and the US European Command was helping ECOWAS to establish an effective communications system with a US$ 500.000 grant.[57]

However, the development that was to prove the most consequential in many ways was the growing involvement of civil society actors in the operationalization of ECOWARN. Following a series of consultations in the aftermath of the adoption of the Protocol Relating to the Mechanism for Conflict Prevention, Management, Resolution, Peacekeeping and Security, the US Agency for International Development (USAID) provided a grant for a two year project aimed at increasing the capacity of the ECOWAS Conflict Prevention Mechanism through partnership with existing network organizations in the region. The West Africa Network for Peacebuilding (WANEP), a network organization with knowledge of early warning and peacebuilding was chosen to partner with ECOWAS through a Memorandum of Understanding to reinforce its capacity to operationalize the planned early warning system.[58]

WANEP first met in Abuja in March 2001 to discuss the potential contributions of civil society groups to ECOWARN. The follow-up consultations between member states and civil society organizations (including think tanks and research institutions) and the subsequent series of review workshops organized by WANEP and ECOWAS proved to be landmark developments.[59] They not only laid down the modalities for database collection, processing and access, but also determined 93 region-specific indicators which were to be used in the monitoring of peace and security. A computer based data base for systematic tracking and monitoring of peace and conflict trends was designed and has been in its testing phase since June 2006.[60] In addition to these developments, an information exchange bulletin has also been created to allow for comments, suggestions and additional input and information from key stakeholders. In late 2006, ECOWAS decided to broaden the data collection base by eliciting the services of 15 so-called national focal points in its member states and WANEP has hired another 15 civil society network monitors in order to complement the work of these national monitors. A total of 30 staff thus feeds the system with information, in addition to the four heads of the zonal bureaus and the four civil society zonal coordinators who are responsible for quality control.

In November 2007, a regional experts meeting endorsed a Conflict Prevention Framework (CPF) as basis for the further operationalization of the ECOWAS Mechanism. The CPF is designed to mainstream conflict prevention into ECOWAS's policies and programs and enhance the community's anticipation and planning capabilities, especially in relation to regional tensions.[61] It also seeks to strengthen the decision-making and intervention capacity of ECOWAS by streamlining and strengthening the link between information analysis, option preparation and implementation.

ECOWARN appears to have made great strides towards implementing the provisions of the 1999 Protocol. At least on paper, it covers all 15 ECOWAS member states with a network of data collectors who are linked with the OMC through a sophisticated reporting system akin to that used by CEWARN. Also, as John Opoku has pointed out, "the close involvement of civil society organizations in the operationalization of the system and the strengthening of civil peacebuilding organizations to facilitate formal and informal conflict management mechanisms in the region are quite encouraging".[62] However, a number of challenges remain. For instance, the lack of adequate IT equipment to facilitate the process of data collection, processing and dissemination continues to hamper the early warning efforts even though the recent introduction of the web-based ECOWARN Reporter has helped to alleviate the situation somewhat. Despite the ongoing capacity-building initiatives of the AU, USAID and civil society actors like WANEP there is also a notable lack of analytical capacity in the OMC. These challenges notwithstanding, the establishment of the ECOWAS early warning system is a promising example of inter-state security cooperation in Western Africa. Very different in scope and concept from the CEWARN Mechanism described in the previous section, ECOWARN is nonetheless a similarly impressive case of regional collaboration and the institutionalization of effective conflict prevention structures at a supra-national level.

The Other Regional Mechanisms

Many of the other regional groupings have also begun efforts to design and implement early warning systems. While they are not (yet) as advanced as those by IGAD and ECOWAS, the mechanisms of the EAC, ECCAS, COMESA and SADC have become increasingly sophisticated over the last few years.

The East African Community comprising Kenya, Uganda, Tanzania and since 2007 also Burundi and Rwanda has developed a draft Protocol on Early Warning and Response Mechanism though it has not yet put into practice an early warning system. The protocol establishes an institutional conflict prevention mechanism which includes a Regional Centre for Early Warning and Early Warning Units situated within the member states.[63] It is envisaged that the Early Warning Centre will be situated at the EAC secretariat in Arusha and consist of a situation room linked directly with the national Early Warning Units. The early warning mechanism will have three functions, namely, (1) to promote exchange of information and collaboration among member states on early warning and response on the basis of the principles of timeliness, transparency, cooperation and the free flow of information, (2) to gather, verify, process and analyze information about conflicts in the region according to the guidelines provided in the protocol's annex, and (3) communicate all such information and analysis to decision makers of EAC policy organs. In addition, the mechanism is also to strengthen and complement other regional mechanism for conflict prevention, management and resolution in line with the provisions of Article 124 of the EAC Treaty.[64] The Protocol on Early Warning is currently in its second draft and is being presented to national stakeholders for validation and input. Thereafter, the EAC will convene a regional stakeholders' workshop including experts to review and approve it for adoption. Thus far, the EAC has decided to begin its early warning activities with monitoring livestock robbery as this is the driving factor for clashes, unrest and border conflict in the sub-region.[65]

The Economic Community of Central African States is also in the progress of establishing an early warning mechanism. Its *Mechanisme d'Alerte Rapide pour l'Afrique Centrale* (MARAC) was formally initiated at a summit conference of the United Nations' Standing Advisory Committee on Security Questions in Central Africa which took place in Yaoundé in February 1999. There the ten ECCAS member states decided to create a Council for Peace and Security in Central Africa (COPAX) as an organization for the promotion, maintenance and consolidation of peace and security in the region and signed a protocol relating to its structure and functioning.[66] In June 2002, the ECCAS Conference of Heads of State and Government adopted Standing Orders for MARAC which outline its form and purpose.[67] Article 2 of the standing orders provides for the establishment of a central structure based at the ECCAS headquarters in Libreville and decentralized national monitoring networks in each member state. The central structure is to consist of three operational units. The first is a bureau in charge of permanent monitoring and collection of information on the security situation in the region from national and international networks, the UN, the AU and other public, private, national and international organizations and institutions. The second is a bureau responsible for information analysis and evaluation, whose mission shall be to identify situations that may pose a threat to peace and security in a state or group of states in the region. The third is a bureau responsible for the Central African data base whose task shall be to store, file, keep and disseminate information by way of any appropriate media, especially MARAC's written, magnetic and numerical aids. The national networks which serve as observation and monitoring zones include both governmental and legislative organs, agencies of international organizations, NGOs, civil society as well as members of academic and research organizations. Very similar to the early warning mechanism of ECOWAS, MARAC has three primary objectives, namely, (1) to regularly monitor the political, socio-economic and security situation throughout the region, (2) to identify all sources of tensions and detect those that appear likely to degenerate into political conflicts, and (3) to alert the political leaders about potential sources of conflict and assist in implementing preventive measures decided by the region's political leaders.

Since February 2007, the European Union's Development Fund is supporting the community's efforts at detection, prevention and management of conflict within the Central African region with a € 4 million grant. The EU project envisages equipping MARAC with early warning equipment similar to that used in the other regions which will enable the Mechanism to examine, analyze and respond to crises in the region. Designed for the duration of three and a half years, the project also hopes to strengthen the relationship between MARAC and civil society actors given that this approach has worked so well for ECOWARN. While not as advanced as the latter MARAC has lately regained significant momentum following a workshop in Kinshasa in December 2007.[68]

The COMESA mandate on early warning is derived from its conflict prevention mandate rooted in Article 3(d) of its treaty. During its 10th summit held in June 2005, the COMESA Authority – the organization's ultimate decision-making body – called for the establishment of an early warning and response mechanism "with a focus on the dynamics of the conflicts in the COMESA region" that could fill the gap left by other regional early warning systems.[69] Following several rounds of discussions, it was decided that the COMESA system would begin by focusing on two particular issue areas which were not yet covered by other early warning system. The first such area is the prevalence of war economies and the competition for mineral resources which continue to fuel conflict in the region. The second area is counter-terrorism. COMESA has subsequently been designated a focal point for the African Union Center for Study and Research in Terrorism with which it has recently begun to share information on suspicious activities and trends. While COMESA's lack of funds has prevented the operationalization of the mechanism until late 2008, recent support from the EU's African Peace Facility and the GTZ has enabled the recruitment of dedicated staff as well as the development of analytical tools and IT infrastructure.[70]

The Southern African Development Community is developing a system for early warning that is much less open than those of the other RECs as it is integrated into the intelligence community and based on classified information. It was only in 2004 that SADC's Strategic Indicative Plan for the Organ (SIPO) mandated the community's Organ on Politics, Defense and Security Cooperation to establish an early warning system in order to "facilitate timeous action to prevent the outbreak or escalation of conflict".[71] The envisaged system is based on the establishment of National Early Warning Centers in each of the member states and a Regional Early Warning Centre based at the SADC Secretariat in Gaborone. Thus far, SADC has made considerable progress in operationalizing its system. By September 2004, the structural, documental, administrative and financial framework conditions had been settled. In February 2006, the community's Interstate Defense and Security Committee began to institutionalize the decisions and agreements between the member states. The central situation room in Gaborone is now in place as are the national warning cells and SADC has completed its insecurity and conflict indicators which are currently being integrated into the warning software. The most remarkable aspect of the SADC early warning system, however, is a mechanism that allows regional institutional decisions to overrule individual member states' concerns with regard to specific early warning recommendations.

Inter-African Cooperation within the CEWS Framework

The brief introduction to the Continental Early Warning System and its component regional early warning mechanisms presented above allows for a number of tentative conclusions with respect to the extent and quality of contemporary inter-African security cooperation. First, early warning cooperation at the regional level has made remarkable progress over the last two to three years. Supported by international partners such as the UN, the EU, USAID and GTZ, the continent's regional organizations have begun to institutionalize sophisticated early warning structures and improve their data collection and analysis capacities. With the notable exception of SADC, the resultant early warning systems are all based on open and transparent processes which rely on input from civil society actors to monitor the situation in the region. Through the skilled use of uncontroversial entry points, RECs like IGAD and the EAC have been able to overcome their member states' initial skepticism and have made first steps towards developing more comprehensive early warning systems. Despite a long list of remaining challenges ranging from a lack of financial and human resources to cultural sensitivities, the regions thus finally seem to have overcome the conceptual inhibitions that hampered the development of effective early warning mechanisms during the OAU-era.[72] Pressed hard by international partners and African interest groups alike, they have begun to realise the importance of conflict prevention to their economic and social development strategies and are increasingly acting accordingly.

Second, the establishment of an early warning system at the continental level has also made notable progress. Building on the meager foundations left behind by the OAU, the African Union has begun to institutionalize an elaborate conflict prevention architecture which relies on a combination of regional input and open source research to monitor peace and security throughout the continent. The CEWS situation room located in the AU's Peace and Security Department in Addis is already fully operational and produces a wide range of reports and news highlights. Several international workshops and seminars have been conducted to improve the analytical capacities of the growing numbers of staff and streamline the flow of information. Various ongoing capacity building programs such as those by the EU (worth a total of €27 million) are supporting the AU in overcoming the remaining challenges such as the lack of appropriate IT infrastructure, the design and operationalization of tailored software and the harmonization of the various regional mechanisms. Especially the latter is crucial to the effective working of the CEWS. Without a common approach to the choice and categorization of conflict indicators and agreed terms, the very basic tools for gathering and classifying information for the purposes of subsequent exchange and analysis will be flawed. Realizing this, the AU and the RECs have begun to harmonize their activities and intensify their cooperation.[73] The Memorandum of Understanding between the AU and the RECs, for example, provides for the establishment of regional liaison offices in the PSD (Article XIX), the exchange of early warning staff and lessons learnt (Article XX) and the institutionalized exchange of information (Article XVII). While the Roadmap for the Operationalization of the CEWS specifies the system's "ability to generate timely information and effective response options for AU decision-makers" as true test for its success,[74] its ability to unite the continent's various actors in a common conflict prevention effort will be no less important.

In general, it seems fair to say that the operationalization of the Continental Early Warning System and its regional component mechanisms is a promising sign of intensifying inter-African security cooperation. A particularly noteworthy development is that contrary to the OAU's often uneasy relationship with the continent's various regional organizations, the interplay between today's layers of cooperation seems almost symbiotic. Applying the principles of subsidiarity, burden-sharing and sub-contracting the AU does not seem to regard the regional organizations as competitors in a zero-sum game, but instead relies on them as essential building blocks and implementation agencies for its continental programs. The following part of this book will analyze these and other insights into contemporary inter-state security cooperation in Africa in more detail.

Notes

[1]   Report of the Secretary-General on the Prevention of Armed Conflict (UN Document A/55/985-S/2001/574, June 2001, New York).

[2]   See, for example, John Davies and Ted Robert Gurr, eds., Preventive Measures: Building Risk Assessment and Crisis Early Warning Systems (Boulder: Rowman&Littlefield Publishers, 1998), Anna Matveeva, Early Warning and Early Response: Conceptual and Empirical Dilemmas, Issue Paper No. 1 (The Hague: European Centre for Conflict Prevention, 2006), Sean O'Brien, "Anticipating the Good the Bad and the Ugly: An Early Warning Approach to Conflict and Instability Analysis," Journal for Conflict Resolution 46, no. 6 (2002), Susanne Schmeidel and Howard Adelman, eds., Early Warning and Early Response (New York: Columbia International Affairs Online, 1998), Klaas van Walraven, ed., Early Warning and Conflict Prevention: Limitations and Possibilities (The Hague: Kluwer Law International, 1998). For Africa-specific literature see Jakkie Cilliers, "Towards a Continental Early Warning System for Africa," ISS Occasional Papers, no. 102 (2005), Ulf Engel and Andreas Mehler, Closing the Gap between Early Warning and Early Action: Applying Political Science to Violent Conflicts in Africa (Leipzig: Institut für Afrikanistik, 2000), Bertrand Ramcharan, "The Continental Early Warning System of the African Union," in Conflict Prevention in Practice: Essays in Honour of James Sutterlin, ed. Bertrand Ramcharan (Leiden: Martinus Nijhoff Publishers, 2005).

[3]   There seems to be a consensus that in order to identify the causes of conflict, predict the outbreak of violence and mitigate the conflict an early warning system should contain six core mechanisms, namely, (1) data collection, (2) data analysis, (3) assessment for warning or identification of different scenarios, (4) formulation of action proposals, (5) transmission of recommendations and (6) assessment of early response. See Berghof Handbook for Conflict Transformation (Berlin: Berghof Research Center for Constructive Conflict Management, 2003). For more information see www.berghof-handbook.net

[4]   See, for example, E Azar, The Codebook of the Conflict and Peace Data Bank (University of Maryland at College Park: Center for International Development, 1982). The most extensive empirical research evaluation of early warning models has been conducted as part of the ongoing White House-initiated State Failure Project and the derivative Genocide Early Warning Center in the Department of State

[5]   A Dorn and D Bell, "Intelligence and Peacekeeping: The UN Operation in the Congo," International Peacekeeping 1, no. 2 (1995).

[6]   Howard Adelman, "Humanitarian and Conflict-Orientated Early Warning: A Historical Background Sketch," in Early Warning and Conflict Prevention: Limitations and Possibilities, ed. Klaas van Walraven (The Hague: Kluwer Law International, 1998).

[7]   Kumar Rupesinghe, "A New Generation of Conflict Prevention: Early Warning, Early Action and Human Security," in Global Conference on the Role

---

of Civil Society in the Prevention of Armed Conflict and Peace Building (New York: 2005).

[8]   FAST is an event-based political early warning mechanism that relies on monitoring information from open sources in order to enhance the ability of decision-makers to identify critical developments timeously and support the development of strategies to prevent armed conflicts or to prevent further escalation of violent conflicts. For more information see Heinz Krummenacher, Susanne Schmeidel, and Daniel Schwarz, Practical Challenges in Predicting Violent Conflict: Fast, an Example of a Comprehensive Early Warning Methodology (Bern: Schweizerische Friedensstiftung, 2001). Also see www.swisspeace.ch. For more information on the International Crisis Group's Crisis Watch see www.crisisgroup.org.

[9]   Alex Schmid, Thesaurus and Glossary of Early Warning and Conflict Prevention Terms (Leiden: Pioom Foundation, 2000). For a more detailed discussion of indicators see Alex Schmid, "Indicator Development: Issues in Forecasting Conflict Escalation," in Preventive Measures: Building Risk Assessment and Crisis Early Warning Systems, ed. John Davies and Ted Robert Gurr (Boulder: Rowman&Littlefield Publishers, 1998).

[10]   Figure adapted from A. Walter Dorn, Early Warning of Armed Conflict: An Introduction (Ottawa: Pearson Peacekeeping Center, 2002).

[11]   O'Brien, "Anticipating the Good the Bad and the Ugly: An Early Warning Approach to Conflict and Instability Analysis."

[12]   See Matveeva, Early Warning and Early Response: Conceptual and Empirical Dilemmas, 11. For more on the difficulties associated with early warning see Howard Adelman, "Difficulties in Early Warning: Networking and Conflict Management," in Early Warning and Conflict Prevention: Limitations and Possibilities, ed. Klaas van Walraven (The Hague: Kluwer Law International, 1998), 51-82, Walraven, ed., Early Warning and Conflict Prevention: Limitations and Possibilities.

[13]   OAU, Summary Record of the Seminar for the Establishment, within the OAU, of an Early Warning System on Conflict Situations in Africa, 15-18 January 1996, Addis Ababa.

[14]   Yaoundé Declaration (Africa: Preparing for the 21st Century); 32nd OAU Summit, July 1996, Yaounde- AHG/Decl.3 (XXXII), para. 25.

[15]   Africa Conflict Resolution Act: Inter-Agency Report (Washington, DC: USAID, April 1995).

[16]   Ramcharan, "The Continental Early Warning System of the African Union," 73.

[17]   John Davies, Conflict Early Warning and Early Response for Sub-Saharan Africa (University of Maryland: Center for International Development and Conflict Management, 2000).

[18]   AU, Protocol Relating to the Establishment of the Peace and Security Council, Durban, 9 July 2002, Article 12, para. 2(a) and (b).

[19]   Figure adapted from Cilliers, "Towards a Continental Early Warning System for Africa," 6.

[20]   AU, Roadmap for the Operationalization of the Continental Early Warning System (CEWS), 2006, Article 3, para. 37.

[21]   The PSC Protocol is clear in providing that the CEWS should obtain its information from a variety of sources – the CEWS is therefore envisaged as

an open source system. In this regard, the CEWS is specifically mandated to collaborate with the United Nations, its agencies, other relevant international organizations, research centers, academic institutions and NGOs. This collaboration, defined in Article 12, para 3, is meant to "facilitate the effective functioning of the Early Warning Mechanism". See AU, Roadmap for the Operationalization of the Continental Early Warning System (CEWS), 2006, Appendix A. The inherent openness and transparency of the CEWS is further evident when looking at the modalities for meetings of the PSC. Although the Protocol requires that meetings of the PSC be closed (Article 8, para. 9), the Council may decide to hold open meetings to which "civil society organizations involved and/or interested in a conflict or situation under consideration by the Peace and Security Council may be invited to participate, without the right to vote, in the discussion relating to that conflict or situation" (Article 8, para. 10). The PSC may also hold informal consultations with civil society organizations "as may be needed for the discharge of its responsibilities" (Article 8, para. 11). See Cilliers, "Towards a Continental Early Warning System for Africa," 7.

[22]   AU, Protocol Relating to the Establishment of the Peace and Security Council, 9 July 2002, Durban, Article 12, para. 5.

[23]   Ibid., para. 7.

[24]   EU MIL LO, First Impression Report on the CEWS Workshop in Addis Ababa from 25-27 April 2006, Addis Ababa, 2 May 2006.

[25]   Simone Kopfmüller, GTZ-Kooperation mit der AU: Unterstützung beim Aufbau des Kontinentalen Frühwarnsystems (Eschborn: Gesellschaft für Technische Zusammenarbeit, 2007).

[26]   Interview with Professor Ulf Engel from the Institut für Afrikanistik of the University of Leipzig who serves as one of the GTZ's three consultants for the CEWS (the others being Professor Douglas Bond from Harvard University and Dr. Joao Porto from the University of Bradford) in Cambridge, 20 January 2008. Parts of this chapter are based on the CEWS handbook.

[27]   The EMM is a fully automated media monitoring system. Together with the EU's European Joint Research Centre in Milan/Italy and the European Commission, the AU hopes to create a similar system for Africa. For the moment, the Joint Research Centre has granted the AU Conflict Management Division access to the EMM servers. The basic elements for the AU software version (Africa News Brief) have already been developed and are theoretically operational, but will have to be further adapted to AU work processes.

[28]   See AU, Roadmap for the Operationalization of the Continental Early Warning System (CEWS), 2006, Article 2, para. 22.

[29]   See, for example, Kasaija Apuuli, IGAD's Protocol on Conflict Early Warning and Response Mechanism (CEWARN): A Ray of Hope in Conflict Prevention (Utrecht: Arbeitsgruppe Internationale Politik, 2004), Douglas Bond and Patrick Meier, "CEWARN: IGAD's Conflict Early Warning and Response Mechanism," in Conflict Prevention in Practice: Essays in Honour of James Sutterlin, ed. Bertrand Ramcharan (Leiden: Martinus Nijhoff Publishers, 2005), 75-90, Ciru Mwaura and Susanne Schmeidel, eds., Early Warning and Conflict Management in the Horn of Africa (Trenton: Red Sea Press, 2001).

[30]   IGAD, Agreement Establishing the Intergovernmental Authority on Development (IGAD), 21 March 1996, Nairobi.

[31]   IGAD, Khartoum Declaration of the 8th Summit of Heads of State and Government, 23 November 2000, Khartoum, Article 3(a).

[32]   IGAD, Protocol on the Establishment of a Conflict Early Warning and Response Mechanism for the IGAD Member States, 9 January 2002, Khartoum.

[33]   Ibid., Part I, Article 1(a)-(e)

[34]   Ibid., Part II, Article 1.

[35]   Interview with Ambassador Abdelrahim Khalil, Director of the IGAD CEWARN Unit in Addis Ababa, 6 September 2007.

[36]   As CEWARN's field reporting and data analysis have revealed, the resultant violence and the death rate of conflicts in the pastoral zones is far higher than had expected. Over the three-year period 2003-2006, CEWARN has recorded over almost 2,200 conflict-related deaths in the region, of which at least 150 were women and children. Over the same period, around 138,000 livestock were lost in more than 1,500 violent incidents. In the July 2005 massacre in Turbi (Marsabit District of Kenya) an estimated 70 people including 25 school children were killed in a violent attack that was carried out by armed parties from both Ethiopia and Kenya. The Turbi massacre demonstrated how the conduct of warfare has changed and that modern raids are no longer part of traditional cultural practices. Moreover, incidents like Turbi highlight the potential regional implications of pastoralist conflicts. In this connection, conflicts in the pastoralist zones must be considered as a serious source of internal insecurity and regional instability.

[37]   CEWARN has established a structured system of quality control on daily, monthly and quarterly bases to ascertain and maintain the reliability, credibility, timeliness and quality of data and information collected from the field.

[38]   Figure adapted from IGAD-CEWARN Unit, "CEWARN Strategy, 2007-2011" (Addis Ababa, November 2006), 16

[39]   Decision adopted by the 5th CPS Meeting, May 2006, Nairobi

[40]   IGAD-CEWARN Unit, "CEWARN Strategy, 2007-2011" (Addis Ababa, November 2006), 8

[41]   IGAD-CEWARN Unit, "CEWARN Strategy, 2007-2011" (Addis Ababa, November 2006), 8. See also Apuuli, IGAD's Protocol on Conflict Early Warning and Response Mechanism (CEWARN): A Ray of Hope in Conflict Prevention.

[42]   Howard Adelman (2004) as quoted in IGAD-CEWARN Unit, "CEWARN Strategy, 2007-2011" (Addis Ababa, November 2006), 19

[43]   The currently planned expansion of the number of CEWERUs is complicated by the ongoing conflicts in Somalia and Ethiopia.

[44]   Interview with Ambassador Abdelrahim Khalil, Director of the IGAD CEWARN Unit in Addis Ababa, 6 September 2007.

[45]   Several states have supported the CEWARN effort through dedicated contributions of individuals who have taken an active role in establishing the Mechanism. However, there needs to be a commensurate shift in orientation from a project dependent upon external funds to a sustainable program financed and fully owned by member states. So far the conceptual development, establishment and operation of CEWARN has been mainly funded by two core partners: USAID (60 percent) and GTZ (30 percent), whereas IGAD member

states contributed around 10 percent of the budget in kind. This is planned to increase to 30 percent by 2011.

[46] Ciru Mwaura et al., "Building CEWARN around Entry Points," in Early Warning and Conflict Management in the Horn of Africa, ed. Ciru Mwaura and Susanne Schmeidel (Trenton: Red Sea Press, 2002), 147-167.

[47] Bond and Meier, "CEWARN: IGAD's Conflict Early Warning and Response Mechanism," 88.

[48] See Emmanuel Aning, "Towards the New Millennium: ECOWAS's Evolving Conflict Management System," African Security Review 9, no. 5 (2000).

[49] See ECOWAS, Revised Treaty of the Economic Community of West African States, 1993, Article 58(f).

[50] ECOWAS, Protocol Relating to the Mechanism for Conflict Prevention, Management, Resolution, Peacekeeping and Security, 1999. For more information on the protocol and the security mechanism see Ademola Abass, "The New Collective Security Mechanism of ECOWAS: Innovations and Problems," Journal of Conflict and Security Law 5, no. 2 (2000): 211-229, Adekeye Adebajo, "The ECOWAS Security Mechanism: Toward a Pax West Africana," in CODESRIA General Assembly Meeting (Kampala: 2002), Apuuli, IGAD's Protocol on Conflict Early Warning and Response Mechanism (CEWARN): A Ray of Hope in Conflict Prevention, Dorina Bekoe and Aida Mengistu, Operationalizing the ECOWAS Mechanism for Conflict Prevention, Management, Resolution, Peacekeeping and Security (New York: International Peace Academy, 2002).

[51] ECOWAS, Protocol Relating to the Mechanism for Conflict Prevention, Management, Resolution, Peacekeeping and Security, 1999, Chapter IV Article 23.

[52] ECOWAS, Protocol Relating to the Mechanism for Conflict Prevention, Management, Resolution, Peacekeeping and Security, 1999, Article 24.

[53] The ECOWARN Reporter is available online at http://ecowarn.org.

[54] Cilliers, "Towards a Continental Early Warning System for Africa," 11. Also see Adekeye Adebajo, "Pax West Africana? Regional Security Mechanisms," in West Africa's Security Challenges - Building Peace in a Troubled Region, ed. Adekeye Adebajo and Ismail Rashid (Boulder: Lynne Rienner, 2004), 306-307.

[55] See Institute for Security Studies, Workshop Report on Training ECOWAS on Early Warning and Conflict Prevention Systems, 28 November – 4 December 2004, Pretoria, 10-11.

[56] Figure adapted from John Opoku, "West African Conflict Early Warning and Early Response System: The Role of Civil Society Organizations," KAIPTC Paper, no. 19 (2007): 9.

[57] Adebajo, "Pax West Africana? Regional Security Mechanisms," 306.

[58] WANEP was originally set up by the African Strategic and Peace Research Group (AFSTRAG), a small Nigerian-based research and policy institute. It began as a network of 26 NGOs, but has since grown to a network of over 430 member organizations spread across 12 countries in West Africa. For more information on WANEP see www.wanep.org.

---

⁵⁹   Correspondence with John Opoku, GTZ Technical Officer, Kofi Annan International Peacekeeping Training Centre, 21 January 2008. For a detailed discussion of the role of civil society actors in the operationalization of West Africa's early warning mechanism see Opoku, "West African Conflict Early Warning and Early Response System: The Role of Civil Society Organizations." See also Ekiyor Thelma, "Civil Society's Perspective on the ECOWAS Early Warning System," (Capetown: Center for Conflict Resolution, 2006).

⁶⁰   See WANEP Press Release, ECOWAS Early Warning & Early Response (ECOWARN) System, Sensation Workshop, 27 March 2007, Accra.

⁶¹   Report of the Joint UN Inter-Agency Mission to ECOWAS on Conflict Prevention and Peacebuilding as quoted in Office of the Special Adviser on Africa, The Emerging Role of the AU and ECOWAS in Conflict Prevention and Peacebuilding, Background Paper prepared for Experts Group Meeting, December 2007, para. 46.

⁶²   Opoku, "West African Conflict Early Warning and Early Response System: The Role of Civil Society Organizations," 16.

⁶³   See Meeting the Challenge of Conflict Prevention in Africa – Towards the Operationalization of the Continental Early Warning System (AU Document PSD/EW/EXP/2(I), 17-19 December 2006, Kempton Park).

⁶⁴   EAC, Treaty Establishing the East African Community, Arusha, 10 November 1999.

⁶⁵   See EU Mil LO to the AU, First Impression Report Workshop Continental Early Warning System (CEWS), 25 – 27 April 2007, Addis Ababa.

⁶⁶   ECCAS, Protocol on the Central African Council for Peace and Security, Yaoundé, February 1999.

⁶⁷   Decision to Adopt the Standing Orders of the Central African Early Warning Mechanism (ECCAS Document 09/ECCAS/CHSG/X/02, June 2002, Malabo).

⁶⁸   Correspondence with Catherine Guicherd, Chef de Projet PAPS-CEEAC, 20 January 2008.

⁶⁹   Status of Implementation of Early Warning Systems in the Regional Economic Communities (AU Document PSD/EW/EXP/9(I), Background Paper No. 4 presented at the Meeting of Governmental Experts on Early Warning and Conflict Prevention, 17-19 December 2006, Kempton Park).

⁷⁰   Phone interview with Elisabeth Mutunga, COMESA Project Officer for Early Warning, 19 December 2008. Correspondence with Simone Kopfmüller, GTZ Project Coordinator for Peace and Security, 20 December 2008.

⁷¹   SADC, Strategic Indicative Plan for the Organ on Politics, Defense and Security Cooperation, 2004, Article 11, para. 3(b).

⁷²   For a discussion of these inhibitions see William Nhara, "Early Warning and Conflict in Africa," ISS Occasional Papers, no. 1 (1996): 2.

⁷³   See, for example, Thelma Ekiyor and Jacob Enoh-Eben, "Workshop Report on Enhancing Conflict Early Warning and Training Methodologies in Africa," (Cape Town: Centre for Conflict Resolution, 2006).

⁷⁴   AU, Roadmap for the Operationalization of the Continental Early Warning System (CEWS), 2006, Article 2, para. 25.

10
Characteristics of Security Cooperation in Africa

The previous chapters have shown the extent to which inter-African security cooperation has evolved over the last decade. They have also pointed towards a number of key characteristics of this cooperation, the most important of which are the Africanization of security, the diffusion of liberal norms, the institutionalization of cooperation, the emergence of (security) communities, the consolidation of institutional partnerships as well as the dependence on international support.

The Africanization of Security

One of the most notable developments with regard to security cooperation in Africa has been the extent to which the provision – not the ownership – of security has been internalized over the last decade. While the continent had to rely on the whims of the Security Council for much of its independent existence, the last ten to fifteen years have seen an unprecedented acceptance of responsibility for the provision of peace and security by Africa's states. Since 2003 alone, they have not only launched several independent peace support operations, concluded various mutual assistance pacts and institutionalized an elaborate peace and security architecture, but they have also begun to establish regional standby brigades, early warning systems and peacekeeping training centers. As touched upon earlier, there are five principal reasons for this Africanization of security on the continent, namely, (1) the drastic deterioration in Africa's security landscape following the end of the Cold War, (2) waning superpower interest and the international community's reluctance to get involved in the continent's proliferating conflicts, (3) the successful precedent set by the ECOWAS intervention in Liberia's civil war in August 1990, (4) the growing acceptance of and support for regionalized approaches to security by the UN and other international actors and (5) a two-fold change in the continental self-conception. Rather than going through each of these points in turn, this section will briefly elaborate on their cumulative impact.

Theorizing about the evolution of cooperation, Adler and Barnett identified a number of exogenous and endogenous factors that "propel states to look into each other's direction".[1] Among these trigger mechanisms or precipitating conditions they found "cataclysmic events that produce changes in material structures, mindsets and sensibilities" to be particularly important.[2] Bruce Cronin similarly argued that "transnational communities are most likely to form during and following periods of social upheaval, when domestic institutions are challenged, international orders are undermined and traditional structures are eroded".[3] These predictions of theory appear to be confirmed by the African experience. As argued in chapter five, the idea of closer security cooperation was muted by the constant background music of the Cold War until the end of the bipolar standoff changed many of the underlying dynamics. After more than three decades of futile attempts at establishing some sort of cooperative security arrangement on the continent, the upheavals of the immediate post-Cold War era and the simultaneous disengagement of the West made the states of Africa painfully aware of the need for cooperation and led to a twofold change in Africa's self-conception.

First, in what Uganda's President Yoweri Museveni later called a "decade of awakening",[4] Africa began to experience a new wave of cooperative Pan-Africanism which differed markedly from preceding ones.[5] Previous attempts at inter-state security cooperation had been dominated by the Westphalian notion of sovereignty so entrenched in the OAU's Charter since Africa's Heads of State had pledged non-interference in each other's internal affairs at the organization's founding conference in 1963. The new wave, however, was the result of a genuine need to cooperate in the face of an increasingly-felt impact of globalization on Africa's desolate economies, waning superpower interest and the prevalence of horrific humanitarian catastrophes on the continent. Africa's leaders realized that if they wanted to contain the spread of conflict and break the cycle of violence, poverty and underdevelopment they had to overcome the obstacles that had plagued previous attempts at security cooperation. As a result, Africa finally seemed ready to make some qualifications to the principle of the sovereign rights of nations.[6]

Second, the effect of this realization was amplified by the emergence of an idealistic undercurrent in inter-African relations. Encouraged by the end of Apartheid and the elimination of corrupt dictatorships and autocratic one-party systems, inefficient structures and unresponsive social institutions in Eastern Europe, pro-democracy movements began to flourish on the continent and with them what looked like a new generation of politically-responsible leaders.[7] Spurred by the hope for an African renaissance, these leaders quickly rediscovered the usefulness of the unifying ideology of Pan-Africanism as vehicle for their cooperative efforts. While the vision of a strong and united Africa was utopian, the promotion of a collective African identity and the resultant desire to minimize non-African interference in the affairs of the continent (by providing "African solutions to African problems") nonetheless advanced the formation of what Benedict Anderson had called an "imagined community".[8] In his book of the same name, Anderson had argued that collective self-imagination and identity formation can help community-building between states, or in other words, that communities can be constructed even in the absence of cultural similarities or economic transactions between groups through the creation and manipulation of norms, institutions, symbols and practices.[9] Naturally, not all states on the continent were equally part of this process of collective identity formation, but it seems fair to say that most states in sub-Saharan Africa (whose sense of identity had been nurtured over decades as part of their struggle against colonialism and Apartheid) came to rediscover their commonalities in the early 1990s.

The end of the Cold War thus represented a watershed in how African states interacted with each other.[10] Taken together, the growing sense of urgency arising from the developmental failures and humanitarian catastrophes of the recent past and the international community's waning interest in addressing them, the spread of democratic values as well as the rediscovery of a collective African identity paved the way for increasing cooperation and integration on the continent. Accordingly, the first half of the 1990s saw an unprecedented surge in joint endeavors such as the establishment of the African Economic Community (AEC) through the adoption of the Abuja Treaty in 1991. In the same year the African Leadership Forum also convened an all-African Conference on Security, Stability, Development and Cooperation in Kampala whose final document provided an impressive framework for collective political action.[11] Even the OAU eventually realized the need to replace its obviously inadequate ad hoc approach to conflict management with an institutionalized Mechanism for Conflict Prevention, Management and Resolution.

These promising developments on the continental level, however, could not halt the ongoing devolution of security cooperation to the regional levels. Too deep had been the regions' disappointment with the OAU's cautious approach which prevented it from establishing the mechanisms and framework necessary to tackle the security problems of the continent.[12] As argued in chapter four, regional organizations began to fill the void created by the OAU's inactivity with Operation Liberty, ECOMOG's intervention in Liberia in August 1990 when 3,500 West African soldiers deployed under Nigerian leadership to halt an armed rebellion against President Samuel Doe.[13] This intervention received widespread praise as "the first real attempt by African countries to (re)solve an African conflict" (ignoring the OAU's feeble mission in Chad) and OAU Secretary-General Salim A. Salim anticipated that the experience would make "Africans realise the potential of and need for security cooperation".[14] Salim was right in more than one way. The intervention in Liberia did not only set a remarkable precedent and provide a model for future operations, but it also increased the international community's support for the concept of "African solutions to African problems" as a feasible alternative to its own involvement.[15] It thereby reinforced the trend of Africa's regional organizations adding security initiatives to their previous (mostly economic) *raisons d'être*.[16]

As Ademola Abass has pointed out, Africa's regional organizations have justified their increasing activities in the area of peace and security on many grounds.[17] Some have argued that the provisions of Chapter VIII of the UN Charter which regulate the use of regional organizations have fallen out of step with the challenges facing states in contemporary Africa. For instance, ECOWAS argued that the speed with which conflicts explode in Africa coupled with the often innocuous nature of these conflicts does not afford African states the luxury of waiting for the Security Council authorization.[18] Others have expressed the view that the selective nature of the collective security administered by the Security Council leaves them with no other choice but to get engaged themselves as they have lost faith in the council's commitment to act on their behalf. The UN's hasty withdrawal from Somalia and the costly prevarication of the Security Council in the face of unraveling genocide in Rwanda reinforced the underlying perception that the UN was less vigorously committed to African conflicts than, for example, those in the Middle East or the Balkans. At a summit meeting of the OAU in Tunis in June 1994, Nelson Mandela used his speech to drive home his sense of bewilderment and disappointment and called on Africa to look more inwardly for solutions to its collective security problems:

> Rwanda stands out as a stern and severe rebuke to all of us for having failed to address Africa's security problems. As a result of that, a terrible slaughter of the innocent has taken place and is taking place in front of our very eyes. We know it is a matter of fact that we must have it in ourselves as Africans to change all this. We must, in action assert our will to do so.[19]

Despite many similar pleads and the institutionalization of regional conflict management mechanisms, the rest of the decade was characterized by appalling humanitarian catastrophes with the DRC being the most glaring but far from the only casualty. At the time regarded as the ultimate proof for and expression of the unwillingness of African states to cooperate with each other, these tragedies helped to galvanize the continent into action. More than anything, they clarified the need to follow up on the promises of inter-African cooperation and reinvigorated the debate on which form this cooperation should take.

It was in this atmosphere of re-engagement that Colonel Gaddafi put forth his radical reform proposals for the defunct OAU that triggered the revival of continental security cooperation. As alluded to in chapter five, this revival was accompanied by the same feeling of disappointment and distrust in the international community and its motives, capabilities and willingness to engage in African affairs that had already motivated the continent's regional organizations to get involved in matters of peace and security. While the feeling of disappointment was a direct result of the international community's disastrous track record in Africa, the feeling of distrust sprang from the recognition that Africa's infant regionalization had been accompanied by an altered outside perception of its growing significance to international politics.

In fact, it had become obvious that given the two global phenomena of terrorism and resource scarcity far more instrumentalist attention was being paid to the African continent at the turn of the millennium than at any time since its independence.[20] Given that this attention was in most cases quite noticably not concerned with the well-being of the continent and its inhabitants *per se*, but with narrow self-interests such as access to a secure and diversified energy supply and the continent's abundance of precious (and rare) metals and minerals; the prevention of mass migration as well as the denial of safe havens to terrorist organizations and other matters of national security,[21] it is not surprising that many Africans began to fear the advent of yet another scramble for their continent.[22] A conference study conducted on the desirability of military interventions in Africa by the Fund for Peace thus unsurprisingly showed that many Africans would not only prefer that intervening troops come from their own region, but also that they put more trust into the ability and willingness of regional organizations such as ECOWAS, SADC and even ECCAS to intervene on their behalf than they put in the UN.[23]

This feeling of distrust combined with the long-standing desire for continental self-emancipation to advance the Africanization of security within the framework of the new African Union. Determined to cultivate and instrumentalize the emancipative notions of *African Renaissance* (that is, the concept that African people and nations will overcome the current challenges confronting the continent and achieve cultural, political and economic renewal) and *African Century* (that is, the belief that the 21st century will bring peace, prosperity and cultural revival to Africa) and to overcome the image of the "hopeless continent",[24] the leaders of South Africa and Nigeria pushed for the AU to assume a much more proactive role with regard to peace and security than the OAU had done.[25] The elaborate form of security cooperation agreed upon in the Protocol Relating to the Establishment of the Peace and Security Council and the Protocol Relating to the Establishment of the African Standby Force and the Military Staff Committee as well as the national commitments to its implementation speak to the seriousness with which Africa's states headed President Mbeki's call "to do everything they can to rely on their own capacities to secure their continent's renaissance".[26] While there was a general awareness that African efforts would continue to remain dependent on external support for at least the foreseeable future, the creation of the AU was seen as an important step in transferring the responsibility for peace and security back from the international community to the African continent.[27] The underlying sentiment that the time had come for Africa to take charge of its own problems was well summed up by the AU's first Commissioner for Peace and Security, Ambassador Said Djinnit:

> No more, never again. Africans cannot watch the tragedies developing in the continent and say it is the UN's responsibility or somebody else's responsibility. We have moved from the concept of non-interference to non-indifference. We cannot as Africans remain indifferent to the tragedy of our people.[28]

Even though this acceptance of responsibility implies a return to the "Try Africa First" approach originally called for in the early 1960s following the UN's ill-fated intervention in Congo-Kinshasa (today's DRC), it is important to understand that neither the creation of an African security regime nor the much-maligned slogan "African solutions to African problems" should be seen as a call for African isolationism, but rather as a (legitimate) plea for African ownership and originality in matters of peace and security. As Abdou Diouf, former president of the Senegal and Secretary-General of the Francophonie put it "increased involvement of African bodies in favor of the continent should not exonerate the Security Council and the international community from the obligations of assisting an endangered Africa".[29]

As will be discussed further below, their insistence on African ownership, however, has proven a double-edged sword for the continent's leaders. While the concept offers obvious political benefits, it has also provided non-African actors with a convenient way to substitute their direct involvement in the continent's messy security affairs with a much more effective form of influence.[30] Through the selective, conditional and purpose-bound provision of financial and logistical assistance under the pretext of "enabling Africans to help themselves", states like the US, the UK and France thus continue to maintain full control over the African security agenda with the added benefit of having outsourced the actual work to the Africans. The Machiavellian character of the US support to the Ethiopian operations in Somalia, purportedly in support of AMISOM, or the French support to the African peacekeeping ventures in Western Africa speak volumes to the meager extent to which African ownership is really owned by Africa.

Nonetheless and despite recent setbacks such as the quick demise of AMIS, the lack of contributions to AMISOM and the failure to respond to the post-electoral crises in Kenya and Zimbabwe, there are no signs that the African attempts to take charge of the provision of security on the continent are about to abate. On the contrary, lacking comparable progress in other fields like economics the ongoing process of Africanizing security has evolved into the ideological centerpiece of a new African utopia, one in which, in the words of Ali Mazrui, "a Pax Africana is protected and maintained by Africa herself".[31]

The Diffusion of Liberal Norms

The Africanization of security has been accompanied by a notable change in the continent's security culture. As discussed in chapter two, security cultures are "patterns of thought and argumentation that establish pervasive and durable security preferences by formulating concepts of the role, legitimacy and efficacy of particular approaches to protecting values".[32] As such, they are the result of two interrelated processes, namely, a process of socialization and a process which Amitav Acharya has described as "norm localization".[33] While the former denotes the induction into a society's ways of behavior through the gradual institutionalization, habitualization and internalization of that society's norms,[34] the latter refers to the "contestation between emerging transnational norms and pre-existing regional normative and social orders".[35] In the case of Africa, the increasing diffusion of liberal norms and their, albeit uneven, internalization by the continent's states have led to a notable shift away from some of the central tenets of the OAU's security culture.[36]

For example, for most of the OAU's existence, its security culture was based on the norm of non-interference. As described above, this meant that its member states agreed not to interfere in each other's internal affairs thus essentially turning a blind eye to human rights abuses and political oppression.[37] For a number of reasons ranging from the increasing realization that this norm stood in sharp contrast to most of its conflict management rhetoric to growing international pressure to conform to liberal norms, the OAU eventually softened its persistence on state rights with a tentative endorsement of human rights. Described in detail in chapter five, this shift from non-interference to non-indifference was institutionalized in a number of documents such as the OAU's Declaration on the Framework for a Response to Unconstitutional Changes in Government,[38] the AU's Constitutive Act and the Solemn Declaration on a Common African Defense and Security Policy. The Constitutive Act in particular broke new ground by recognizing the right of the AU to intervene in a member state "in respect of grave circumstances, namely, war crimes, genocide and crimes against humanity (Article 4h) and "the right of member states to request intervention from the AU in order to restore peace and security" (Article 4j).

However, much more important than this rhetorical commitment is that the diffusion of liberal norms and the resultant change in security culture is beginning to manifest itself in graspable actions. Paul Williams, for example, draws attention to the AU's increasingly adamant reaction to unconstitutional changes of government.[39] Whereas the OAU had remained largely indifferent to coups and counter-coups in its member states,[40] the AU has condemned the unconstitutional changes of governments in Togo (2005), Mauritania (2005) and Guinea (2008) and subsequently suspended the countries from its activities. In the case of Togo, it even mandated ECOWAS "to take all such measures as it deems necessary to restore constitutional legality in Togo within the shortest time".[41] While the AU has not (yet) reacted in a similar fashion to fraudulent elections and other more subtle subversions of the constitutional processes in its member states, its open condemnation of *coups d'Etats* is an important step away from the OAU's infamous culture of impunity and towards the gradual internalization of liberal norms across the continent. Even though there are still enormous differences in the degree to which norms like the responsibility to protect, human rights and democratization have been internalized by Africa's states,[42] the existence of what Acharya has called a "dynamic congruence-building process" in which such transnational norms are spread is hard to ignore.[43]

The Institutionalization of Cooperation

One particularly noteworthy development that has accompanied the processes of Africanization and norm diffusion is the move from *ad hoc* initiatives to institutionalized security cooperation. While inter-state security cooperation in the early 1990s was characterized mainly by its provisionality, the last decade has seen an increasing formalization of regional and continental security arrangements and the emergence of corresponding political steering mechanisms. Given the pervasiveness of this formalization and the extent to which Africa's states have agreed upon principles, norms, procedures and programs to regulate their activities and pattern their anticipations, it is not surprising that scholars like Shannon Fields have already seen the emergence a "collaborative security regime" on the continent.[44]

There are many theories on the development of institutions and the various processes by which an informal, extra-legal, *ad hoc*, improvised system gradually fosters the achievement of cooperative outcomes and progressively enhances its own procedures to improve the prospects for these outcomes. In his book on the institutionalization of security cooperation within the European Union, Michael Smith draws attention to the circular nature of this process and the reciprocal links between institutional development and the propensity of states to cooperate.[45] According to him, "cooperation can encourage actors to build institutions and institutions themselves again foster cooperative outcomes which later influence the process of institution-building through feedback mechanisms".[46] While substantially different from the European experience in general, the process of institutionalization in Africa appears to be similar to that described by Smith in the extent to which it is based on positive experiences made during *ad hoc* instances of cooperation. As referred to repeatedly throughout this study, the relative success of the initial ECOMOG operations encouraged both the members of ECOWAS and those of other African security actors to intensify their cooperation. Learning from its interventions, ECOWAS, for example, adopted a protocol formalizing its mechanism for conflict prevention, management, resolution, peacekeeping and security in

December 1999.[47] According to Emmanuel Aning, this mechanism and its supplementary protocol on good governance and democracy "sought to consolidate and build on the experiences of ECOMOG and undertake deepening institutionalization processes to improve its capacity to resolve conflicts in the West African region".[48] The member states of other regional organizations such as SADC, IGAD and ECCAS soon followed suit and also began to create formal institutions to increase the effectiveness of their hitherto relatively unstructured cooperation in the field of peace and security.

In 2002, the process of institutionalization reached the continental layer of security cooperation when the OAU's existing peace and security framework was transformed into a "qualitatively higher form of cooperation and integration" as part of the new African Union.[49] Since then, the institutionalization processes at the regional and continental levels have evolved in a surprisingly disjoint manner and it was only with the recent adoption of the Memorandum of Understanding on security cooperation between the AU and the RECs that both processes have begun to converge. Article XVI of the MoU now specifies four ways in which both institutional layers of inter-African security cooperation are to be harmonized, namely, through (1) the continuous exchange of information, (2) regular meetings at all levels, (3) an institutional presence at each other's headquarters, and (4) joint activities and field coordination. While rational choice considerations certainly played a central role in the institutionalization of security cooperation on the continent, it is important not to underestimate the influence of additional push and pull factors such as external donor pressure, a long-standing desire for self-emancipation and the gradual changes in the continent's security culture.

The Emergence of (Security) Communities

The extent and quality of contemporary security cooperation in Africa suggests that parts of the continent have moved beyond the occasional socialization of norms and the simple institutionalization of security cooperation and have begun to evolve into security communities as defined in chapter two. Representative for all of these communities, this section will briefly elaborate on the evolutionary patterns and defining traits of two particular cases, namely, the AU (for the continental level) and SADC (for the regional level).

In order to delineate the conceptual evolution of a security community, Adler and Barnett created a three-tiered framework specifying the factors contributing to peaceful change.[50] Their first tier concerns the precipitating conditions that are necessary to induce closer cooperation. In the second tier "states and their peoples have become involved in a series of social interactions that have begun to transform the environment in which they are embedded".[51] The third tier is defined by the presence of mutual trust and collective identity formation as necessary conditions of dependable expectations of peaceful change and thus the emergence of a security community.

The African Union: A Loosely-Coupled Security Community

As Maxi Schoeman has pointed out, the precipitating conditions for the building of a continental security community in Africa "have been present all along and political leaders have been aware of them and the need for cooperation ever since the start of decolonization".[52] The previous sections have elaborated on these conditions in great detail when they discussed the progressive institutionalization of security cooperation on the continent and the replacement of the defunct OAU with a structurally more promising AU. They also touched upon the conceptual shift from regime security to human security and the incorporation of regional security structures into a continental architecture both of which are characteristic expressions of what Adler and Barnett have defined as their second tier, namely the emergence of factors conducive to the development of mutual trust and collective identity.[53] That these factors have indeed begun to alter the stringent environment in which inter-African relations have been embedded for so long is most clearly demonstrated by the unprecedented deepening of security cooperation over the last few years. Africa's previously so non-committal states have not only agreed on the establishment of the ASF and the CEWS, but they have also formulated a Common African Defense and Security Policy in February 2004 and adopted a Non-Aggression and Common Defense Pact in January 2005.[54] In addition, they have also begun to undertake joint peace operations such as AMIS.[55] The level of cooperation underlying these achievements would have been thought utopian merely a decade ago and thus reflects a remarkable growth in trust and community spirit.

It thus appears from the previous sections that the evolutionary pattern of inter-African (security) cooperation indeed corresponds to the approximate growth path of a security community as outlined by Adler and Barnett. The foundations for an African security community were therefore laid when so-called "trigger mechanisms" induced closer cooperation among the continent's states in the early 1990s (tier one). As shared meanings and understandings continued to evolve over the following decade, these foundations were strengthened and cooperation deepened (tier two). In order to verify the actual emergence of a security community in Africa (tier three) it is necessary to contrast the characteristics of today's system of cooperative security with the defining traits of such a community.

In 1961, Deutsch defined a security community as "a group that has become integrated, where integration is defined as the attainment of a sense of community, accompanied by formal or informal institutions or practices, sufficiently strong and widespread to assure peaceful change among members of the group".[56] John Baylis and Nick Rengger subsequently listed the consolidation of common values, meanings and understandings as basis of a collective identity, a shared commitment to the peaceful resolution of conflicts and the increasing institutionalization of cooperation as key indicators for the existence of a security community.[57] Adler and Barnett added that the depth of trust and the nature and degree of institutionalization within a group provide the basis for distinguishing between loosely and tightly-coupled security communities.[58]

According to Michael Taylor, one of the three key characteristic of a community is that its members share identities, values and meanings.[59] While most post-Deutschian scholars have focused on the proliferation of liberal ideas in explaining the convergence of actors' identities, values and meanings, Adler and Barnett also grant alternative (that is, non-liberal) ideas a role in community formation. In the case of Africa, the pressures of the post-Cold War environment combined with a return of Pan-Africanist ideology to promote the emergence of a shared developmentalist project and a common security culture (that is, an inter-subjective system of meanings about security problems and their required solutions). Even though there obviously remain substantial differences in political and economic values among the continent's states, the resultant increase in transnational exchanges, policy coordination and common institutions helped to reinforce a shared identity, form compatible core values and deduct collective purposes.[60] All of the latter are enshrined in the Constitutive Act of the AU (Article 4, paragraphs 1-o) and have provided the basis for the emergence of a common African position on a range of concerns (amongst them the issues of debt relief, better access to Western markets and a permanent

African seat in the UN Security Council). In order to encourage increasing conformity in regard to political, economic and corporate governance values, codes and standards, Africa's states have agreed on the establishment of an African Peer Review Mechanism (APRM) as part of NEPAD. More than half of the continent's states have already ratified their participation in this unique self-monitoring mechanism which aims to accelerate the process of inter-African cooperation and integration.[61]

However, in order to qualify as members of a security community, states need to share more than merely some core values. Most importantly, they need to display a shared commitment to the peaceful resolution of conflict and optimally have institutionalized a practical knowledge of such in some kind of rule or regulation structure that generates trust.[62] In this respect, it is essential to understand that it is not the total absence of conflicts or power struggles, but their peaceful resolution and the expression of power by means short of physical violence that characterize a security community. As in other security communities, power in the African Union should thus manifest itself in the ability to "create the underlying rules of the game, to define what constitutes acceptable play and to be able to get other actors to commit to these rules" and not in military domination.[63] Both, the treaty arrangements and the actual behavior of Africa's states seem to meet this stipulation. Articles 4(e) and 4(f) of the Constitutive Act of the AU, for example, specifically call for "the peaceful resolution of conflicts among Member States of the Union" and "the prohibition of the use of force or the threat to use force among Member States of the Union".

Maxi Schoeman has called the establishment of the African Union "the most obvious manifestation of the continent's intention to create a community".[64] Whether or not one agrees, it is difficult to deny that the organization has been (surprisingly) successful in advancing cooperation and integration in Africa since its inception in 2002. Like the Organization of Security and Cooperation in Europe (OSCE) it seems to fulfill at least six of the seven functions of a community-building institution specified by Emanuel Adler.[65] First, it promotes political consultation and bilateral and multilateral agreements among its members. Second, it sets liberal standards – applicable both within each state and throughout the community – that are used to judge democratic and human rights performance and monitors compliance with them (that the AU is much more serious about these standards than its institutional predecessor is shown by its repeated refusal to appoint Sudan's President Omar al-Bashir as chair of its Council due to the human rights accusations leveled against him). Third, by establishing a sophisticated

Continental Early Warning System it attempts to prevent violent conflict before it occurs. Fourth, it helps to develop the practices of peaceful settlement of disputes and has enshrined these in its official documents. Fifth, it builds mutual trust by promoting military cooperation and integration as, for example, through the establishment of the African Standby Force. Sixth, it supports the building of democratic institutions and the transformation to market-based economies. All this is achieved through an increasing institutionalization of cooperation that indeed reflects the ideals of a security community as earlier defined.

Given the above, it seems as if the continent currently displays all the essential characteristics of (at least) a loosely-coupled security community.[66] For in spite of the penumbra of cynicism and doubt over Africa's ability to deal with its many troubles, the last decade has seen several important developments. Driven by a fresh wave of Pan-Africanism promoting unity, solidarity and cohesion among the peoples of Africa and their states as much as by the pressures of the post-Cold War world, the parameters of inter-African relations have clearly shifted in the direction of a heightened political will to cooperate. As a result, Africa's states have made great strides in establishing a viable continental security architecture based on what Garth Le Pere has called "a different kind of Lockean social contract" in which they secure their own interests by maximizing the continent's peace and security.[67] Even more importantly, however, they have also begun to institutionalize an interpretation of social reality that differs from the past in its approach to the polarizing effects of anarchy and sovereignty and thus points to a new beginning for large parts of the continent.

SADC: Southern Africa's Regional Security Community

With regards to the regional layer of security cooperation, there has been a growing body of literature on the existence (or the non-existence) of security communities in Western and Southern Africa as well as in parts of Eastern Africa.[68] While both ECOWAS and the EAC would also make interesting case studies, the divisive history of Southern Africa makes the emergence of a security community there a particularly fascinating subject of study.[69] While it is certainly true that Southern Africa has had a violent past, it is equally true that it has for quite some time seen sustained cooperative efforts by many of its states. The history of the Frontline States (FLS) and the Southern African Development Coordinating Conference (SADCC), two of SADC's predecessors, bears testimony to these efforts. Even though the two organizations had very different *raisons d'être* – the primary purpose of the FLS was the coordination of liberation struggles and negotiations, while SADCC was set up to reduce the economic dependence of the region's states on South Africa – both were instrumental in creating and fostering a sense of community and belonging among the states of Southern Africa. Moreover, through institutionalizing regular meetings and encouraging a relatively open dialogue among the top political and military leaders of the region, the FLS and SADCC also sowed the seeds for increased interaction and further cooperation and thus helped to create the precipitating conditions of Adler and Barnett's first tier.[70]

Regional cooperation intensified substantially following the end of both the Cold War and the system of Apartheid in the early 1990s. Driven like the whole of Africa by the pressures of globalization, but also by post-Apartheid euphoria and a growing feeling of disappointment and distrust in universalism (both at the global and continental level) the states of Southern Africa increasingly looked for regional solutions to their political, economic and military problems.[71] To this end, they transformed SADCC into the more formal SADC in 1992 and formulated a Framework and Strategy for Community-Building in 1993.[72] Encouraged by the example of ECOWAS, they also deepened their security cooperation by incorporating the Front Line States' Inter-State Defense and Security Committee into the SADC structure and establishing an Organ on Politics, Defense and Security (OPDS).

However, even though the OPDS was meant to "promote political cooperation among member states" and "develop a common foreign and security policy" growing tensions over its form and functions threatened to pull the region apart.[73] As on the continental level, it was the realization of the disastrous effects of their disharmony that finally galvanized the region's states into action. As a result, they adopted the Protocol on Politics, Defense and Security Cooperation in August 2001. This Protocol not only clarified the structure of the OPDS and brought it firmly under SADC control, but also provided for many elements that Adler and Barnett consider symptomatic of their second and third tiers. For example, it called for the establishment of a collective security capability and the conclusion of a Mutual Defense Pact.[74] Given that both have since been realized – the states of SADC signed a Mutual Defense Pact in August 2003 and the region's standby brigade has been declared operational in 2007 – Naison Ngoma's argument that Southern Africa has developed into a true security community does not seem far fetched. This becomes even more obvious when briefly comparing the communality of values, the commitment to a peaceful resolution of conflict and the institutionalization of cooperation in today's Southern Africa with the defining traits of such a community.

With the end of Apartheid, the states of Southern Africa "lost" their central focal point for communality on both sides of the racial divide (one side being united in favoring racism, the other being united in opposing it). However, far from subsequently tumbling into an identity crisis, the region's states quickly found a new unifying purpose in jointly confronting transnational problems such as the spread of HIV/AIDS, the adverse impacts of economic globalization and the prevalence of conflict. This purpose was embedded in a growing feeling that the region's "common cultural and social affinities, common historical experiences, common problems and aspirations" implied the existence of a foundation for common actions and thus a clear indication of a shared future.[75] First manifested in the move from a "coordination conference" to a "community" during the transformation of SADCC into SADC, this rediscovered communality has become increasingly entrenched over the last decade. The formulation of a Common Agenda for SADC as well as the adoption of more than 20 SADC protocols, reaching from the Protocol on Principles and Guidelines Governing Democratic Elections to the aforementioned Protocol on Politics, Defense and Security Cooperation bear witness to this process of assimilation and point towards the existence of a shared developmentalist ideology, the convergence of core norms and values as well as the development of a collective identity in the region.[76]

As members of the AU, the states of Southern Africa have expressed a steadfast commitment to the peaceful resolution of conflict at the continental level. In addition, they have repeatedly reaffirmed this commitment at the regional level. As early as 1992, the Treaty and Declaration establishing SADC clearly spelt out the "peaceful settlement of disputes" as one of the community's five basic principles (Article 4e). Subsequent documents such as the Protocol on Politics, Defense and Security Cooperation, the Strategic Indicative Plan for the Organ on Politics, Defense and Security Cooperation as well as the Mutual Defense Pact have continued to stress the importance of avoiding the threat or use of violence as means of resolving conflicts.

Very much like the AU or the OSCE, SADC displays Adler's characteristics of a community-building institution. It not only furthers cooperation and contributes to the development of mutual trust and a collective identity among its member states, but also provides the framework for a system of collective security and even military integration.[77] While there are some, such as Paul-Henri Bischoff, who believe that SADC had already crossed the threshold towards attaining the status of a security community when it established its Organ on Politics, Defense and Security in 1996, its more recent institutional achievements seem an even clearer indicator for the emergence of such a community in Southern Africa.[78] Especially the increasing institutionalization of military cooperation, reaching from regular joint exercises and the development of a common SADC peace operations doctrine to the sharing of intelligence, reveals the seriousness with which the region's states are attempting to overcome the suspicions of the past and assure a lasting non-conflictual relationship among each other.[79] Combined with the ongoing institutionalization of cooperation in many other areas such as, for example, infrastructure development, agriculture and education, this seriousness underlines the region's increasing self-conception as a (security) community.

Even though there obviously remain substantial problems such as Robert Mugabe's authoritarian grip on Zimbabwe (and the region's regrettable acquiescence thereof) or the proliferation of "competing regionalisms", Southern Africa thus seems to have developed into a security community as defined by Adler and Barnett.[80] As at the continental level, distinct trigger mechanisms like the end of the Cold War encouraged closer cooperation at the regional level and helped to reinforce a shared identity, form compatible core values and deduct collective purposes. However, unlike the continent at large, the Southern African region not only seems to conform to the definition of a loosely-coupled security community (exhibiting, for example, a self-identification as community, multilateral decision-making and compatible core values), but also displays traits of its tightly-coupled variant such as a system of collective security and a steadily rising level of military integration.

There are several possible explanations for the tighter integration of the regional layer such as the significantly lower number of actors involved (14 as compared to 53), their greater homogeneity or the higher level of outside (that is, non-African) support. Another explanation may be found in Buzan and Waever's Regional Security Complex Theory (RSCT). The central idea in RSCT is that, since most threats or security problems travel more easily over short distances than over long ones, security interdependence is normally patterned into regionally based clusters, so-called security complexes.[81] According to Buzan and Waever, Southern Africa is such a complex and its higher level of security interdependence could explain why it has integrated faster and further than the continent at large.[82] However, both layers of security cooperation continue to evolve and the last two years have seen several remarkable developments in this respect.

At the continental level, the AU's 9th Ordinary Summit held in Accra in July 2007 recommended the establishment of a Union Government as transitory institutional arrangement on the way towards total political unification of the continent.[83] In a surprising return to Kwame Nkrumah's dream of a United States of Africa, this decision alludes to the rediscovered attractiveness of Pan-Africanist ideology in the face of the diverse problems and challenges facing the continent.[84] The proposed Union Government would consist of a more focused Assembly and an Executive Council backed by an effective Permanent Representatives Committee and result-orientated specialized technical committees. In addition, its commission would have executive authority on matters totally or partially delegated by Union members.[85] Following his recent election as AU Chairperson, Libya's leader Muammar Gaddafi promised a swift implementation of the Union Government plans.[86]

At the regional level, the decision of ECOWAS at its 32nd Summit in Abuja in June 2007 to replace its Executive Secretariat with a more powerful Commission and to embrace a ten-pillar vision of integration to fast-track the creation of a border-less West Africa is an equally noteworthy development. The institutional transformation of ECOWAS is particularly pioneering as it is accompanied by the adoption of a new legal regime which emphasizes supra-nationality and de-emphasizes the importance of national ratification processes in order to overcome some of the inhibitions that have characterized West African integration thus far. In the enthusiastic words of Gboyega Akinsanmi:

> From what transpired at the summit, it is more glaring now than any time in the history of the region that its leaders are now ready to jettison the factors that have remained as a clog in the wheel of a borderless West Africa. This represents a major milestone in the history of the region. The summit was a major development meant to sever the Gordian knots of barriers and impediments to the process of integration.[87]

The Consolidation of Organizational Partnerships

Africa's emerging peace and security architecture is built upon an increasingly strong basis of institutional partnerships between African actors as well as between African and non-African actors. The partnerships between African actors include those between different regional organizations, those between such regional organizations and the AU, and those between all these organizations and civil society actors such as WANEP.[88] The partnerships between African and non-African actors comprise those of the aforementioned African actors with the UN, the EU and other international entities like NATO and SHIRBRIG. The last few years have seen an unprecedented deepening of all these partnerships and this section will briefly discuss two essential aspects of this phenomenon, namely, the institutional interplay that is developing between the various organizational layers of inter-state security cooperation in Africa and the role of international partnerships in its consolidation. In the process, it will clarify a number of concepts such as multiple identities, organized complementarity, poly-centric governance and multi-level security communities all of which help to illustrate the atypical form of inter-state security cooperation that has emerged on the continent.[89]

The Interplay between Africa's Institutional Layers

The first facts to note when discussing the partnerships developing between Africa's various peace and security institutions are that the continent's states belong to both, the continental <u>and</u> the regional layer of cooperation, and that the majority of states belongs to more than one regional organization. In fact, of the 53 AU member states, 26 are members of two such regional organizations and 19 are members of three. Two countries (the DRC and Swaziland) even belong to four. Only six countries maintain membership in just one regional community.[90] In one of his earlier essays on security communities, Emmanuel Adler acknowledges the possibility of states being members of more than one community-region as a result either of their "liminal" status or of concentric circles of identity.[91] The latter concept is based on Barry Buzan's argument that, contrary to the nineteenth-century view of exclusive nationalisms, people are quite capable of holding several identities in parallel and that therefore there is no contradiction in, for example, being English, British, European and Western all at the same time.[92] Naturally, however, such concentric circles of identity presuppose the existence of a shared cognitive space, that is, an agreement among the members of all "layers" on certain core constitutive norms. The absence of such an agreement, most clearly demonstrated by the refusal of ECOWAS to identify with the OAU norm on non-interference and its subsequent intervention in Liberia, must be seen as one of the reasons for the withering of the continental organization in the early 1990s and the resultant devolution of interstate cooperation to the regional level. Accordingly, the (re)emergence and gradual consolidation of a shared cognitive space over the last couple of years was a major facilitator in the reconciliation between the two layers and thus the parallel development of continental and regional security communities in Africa. Combined with the particular attractions of each layer of cooperation – the greater cohesiveness of the regional level seems to allow for better cooperation in areas such as security and conflict management, while the continental level offers greater economies of scale, international bargaining power and synergies in the fight against region-transcending problems such as the spread of HIV/AIDS – the existence of concentric circles of identity thus helps to explain the simultaneous involvement of African states in more than one layer of inter-state security cooperation.

Contrary to the OAU's often uneasy relationship with the continent's various regional organizations, the interplay between today's layers of cooperation seems almost symbiotic. Applying the principles of subsidiarity, burden-sharing and sub-contracting the AU does not regard the regional organizations as competitors in a zero-sum game, but instead relies on them as essential building blocks and implementation agencies for its continental programs.[93] This multi-layered approach to inter-African security cooperation is best described as a system of de-centralized collective security or, in the words of Edmond Keller, "regional security-management complexes nested within the context of an aspiring continental security complex". It is characterized by its firm reliance on existing regional security initiatives and their incorporation into continental policy.[94] The regional mechanisms for conflict prevention, management and resolution act as executive organs and first line of response, while the AU's Peace and Security Council and its ancillary structures such as the AU Peace Support Operations Division serve as authoritative clearinghouse and overarching framework for all initiatives.[95] Illustrated by the heavily regionalized character of central AU projects like the ASF (based on five regionally administered standby brigades) or the CEWS (based on five regional early warning mechanisms), this "division of labor" allows both layers of inter-African security cooperation to profit from each other's comparative advantages without sacrificing their individual concerns. The AU, for example, gains from the regions' experience in international security cooperation and – in the case of Western, Eastern and Southern Africa – their established security structures and mechanisms. The regions, on the other hand, profit from the increased credibility and donor attention inherent in a continent-wide project. Given this positive relationship, the fear that regionalism would be inimical to universalism expressed by functionalists like David Mitrany seems, at least for the time being, relatively unfounded in the case of inter-African security cooperation.[96]

Besides offering tangible benefits to each layer of cooperation, the decentralized nature of the emerging system also seems to have overcome a crucial shortcoming of previous attempts at continental cooperation. While the latter were often characterized by outright rivalry between the layers, today's steadfast incorporation of regional initiatives as pillars and implementation agencies ensures that the regions feel direct ownership in the process of establishing a continental security architecture.[97] With the regions maintaining a significant stake and central role in the decision-making structure, the new system not only reduces the risk of competition between the layers, but also helps to overcome the skepticism of states previously opposed to centralizing the responsibility for peace. Organized complementarity between the continental and the regional layers of collective security is thus more than simply a pragmatic way in which the gap between the continent's capabilities and its conflicts can be bridged. It is the conceptual centerpiece of Africa's emerging security architecture and the theoretical foundation for the idea of multi-level security communities.

Even though there have been repeated attempts to liken Africa's emerging institutional order to a "peace pyramid", so far no conceptual epithet has been able to accurately explain the nature of the relationship that has developed between the different layers of security cooperation in Africa.[98] While there certainly is a hierarchical/pyramidal element in the relationship between the continent and its regions (after all, the AU retains the primary responsibility for promoting peace and security in Africa), this element is not necessarily dominant. Instead, the Protocol Regarding the Establishment of the PSC states that the modalities of the partnership between the layers shall be determined by the comparative advantage of each and the prevailing circumstances (Article 16b). Not surprisingly then, security cooperation between the layers has taken many forms. Sometimes the regions act on behalf of the AU (as in Liberia in 2003), other times they act in concert with it (as currently in Darfur and Somalia). The relationship between the two layers thus often appears unordered.

The concept of multi-layered security communities is an attempt to explain this seemingly unsystematic interplay between Africa's layers of security cooperation and provide a theoretical framework for its discussion. Built around the aforementioned notions of multiple identities and organized complementarity the concept shares many of the characteristics of Karl Deutsch's original security community theory (and its adaptation by Emmanuel Adler and Michael Barnett). However, it differs in its approach to states' underlying motives for participation in such communities. For contrary to that of a pluralistic security community in the classical Deutschian sense – which Ole Waever once described as "simply a non-war community" – the *raison d'être* for the aforementioned African security communities does not seem to lie in the avoidance of inter-state war (after all, African countries have hardly fought each other since independence).[99] Instead, certain push and pull factors have led the states of Africa to reach out for the benefits of security cooperation.

Because they have done so on several levels of territorial aggregation (regional and continental) even the more complex theory adaptation of Adler and Barnett (which does allow for cooperative gains as *raison d'être* of security communities) cannot account for all aspects of the resultant security system. Hoping to fill the theoretical void, the concept of multi-layered security communities combines the strengths of constructivist thinking on security cooperation inherent in the security community terminology with the descriptive power of public administration concepts such as multi-level governance (MLG) and poly-centric governance (PCG).

Equally seldomly applied to the African continent as the idea of security communities itself (they are most often associated with the European Union or the process of political devolution in Great Britain), both terms help to conceptualize the non-hierarchical multi-level security community system with multiple, often overlapping jurisdictions that has developed in Africa. MLG is often described as an arrangement for making binding decisions that engages a multiplicity of politically independent but otherwise interdependent actors at different levels of territorial aggregation in more-or-less continuous interactions and that does not assign exclusive policy competence or assert a stable hierarchy of political authority to any of these levels.[100] PCG on the other hand includes the functional dimension along with the territorial one and can be defined as an arrangement for making binding decisions over a multiplicity of actors that delegates authority over functional tasks to a set of dispersed and relatively autonomous agencies that are not controlled – *de jure* or *de facto* – by a single collective institution.

Built around these two concepts, the notion of a multi-layered security community thus describes the continent's emerging security architecture as a poly-centric collective security system in which the regional layers function as relatively autonomous implementation agencies of the continental layer within a framework of organized complementarity. The two layers thereby interact with each other in two ways: first, across different levels of cooperation (vertical dimension) and second, with other relevant actors within the same level (horizontal dimension). In that respect, multi-layered security communities have to be clearly distinguished from overlapping security communities such as NATO and the EU which exclusively interact in the horizontal dimension (see Figure 10.1).

Figure 10.1: Multi-Layered and Overlapping Security Communities[101]

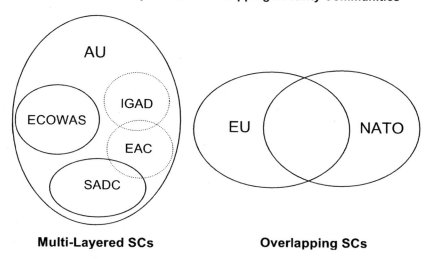

Multi-Layered SCs   **Overlapping SCs**

Despite the obvious functionality and success of this relationship between the AU and regional and sub-regional conflict management actors, the AU has learned from the mistakes of its institutional predecessor and recognized the dangers that can arise from an unchecked proliferation of organizations and initiatives.[102] Consequently, the AU's decision to limit its official collaboration to seven RECs (ECOWAS, SADC, IGAD, AMU, ECCAS, COMESA and EAC) and to dedicate its 2006 summit in Banjul mainly to the rationalization of RECs must be seen in light of the continental organization's desire to lessen the likelihood of competing rather than complementary security efforts.[103] This desire for rationalization, harmonization and integration is enshrined in every major AU document, be it the Constitutive Act, the Protocol on the Establishment of the PSC or the Memorandum of Understanding between the African Union and the RECs signed in January 2008. The appointment of an AU delegate to interface with the RECs, the establishment of an AU liaison office at the headquarters of ECOWAS in Abuja, the creation of REC liaison offices in Addis Ababa as well as the institutionalization of regular meetings and exchange of notes between the AU and the RECs are only some of the steps that have been taken to ensure the various organizations' effective partnership.[104]

The Deepening of International Partnerships

The refinement of inter-African partnerships is only one of the reasons for the institutional consolidation of the African Peace and Security Architecture. Another is the deepening of partnerships with international actors like the UN or the EU. This process has many fathers among them Africa's return into the geo-strategic limelight, the changing notion of security, the prevalence of violent conflict and humanitarian catastrophes on the continent, the promising transformation of the feeble OAU into a more inclusive and action-orientated AU and its suitability as attractive focal point for international attention, the strategic overstretch of the UN as well as the attempt of the EU to assume a greater foreign policy and development role.

The partnership between Africa's institutional actors and the United Nations has evolved substantially over the years. As alluded to repeatedly throughout this book, the end of the Cold War precipitated the increased involvement of Africa's regional organizations in the maintenance of peace and security. This development, launched by the ECOWAS intervention in Liberia in 1990, has been hailed by the UN as opening a new era in which "regional arrangements or agencies can render great service if their activities are undertaken in a manner consistent with the Purposes and Principles of the Charter, and if their relationship with the UN is governed by Chapter VIII".[105] Following a series of ups and downs,[106] the experiences of the last five years and especially those of the operations in Burundi (2003), Liberia (2003) and Darfur (2004) have indeed revealed a functioning division of labor between Africa's security institutions and the UN that appears to play into the strengths and compensate for the weaknesses of both types of organizations.[107] Under this layered approach to conflict management, the initial response to a crisis comes from African actors either in the form of interventions mandated and executed by a regional organization (as happened in Liberia) or continental operations under the leadership of the AU (as happened in Burundi and Darfur). Once the situation is stabilized, the UN takes over.

This division of labor allows all organizations to employ their respective comparative advantages. While the African organizations are able to deploy faster than the UN (mainly because of lower minimum standards in medical evacuation and operational readiness) and are able to adopt a more robust approach to peace enforcement, only the UN has the capability and resources to pull together the various components needed to form a complex integrated peace building response that can address the long-term post-conflict reconciliation and reconstruction needs of most conflict zones. Organized complimentarity between the UN and Africa's organizations in the field of collective security can thus be seen as a logical, necessary and pragmatic way in which the gap between the resources available to the UN and the increasing numbers of conflicts can be bridged, without sacrificing the pivotal importance of the Security Council as the custodian of international peace or infringing on African ownership concerns.[108] It was with this complementarity in mind that Hédi Annabi, the Assistant Secretary-General for Peacekeeping Operations, used a speech before the Security Council Session to emphasize that

> ... close ties between the UN and Africa's organizations are crucial, not just for the success of African regional endeavors, but for the UN and international security. The more complex the challenges of our globalized world grow, the more crucial partnership between our respective organizations has become for the pursuit of a security that is truly collective, effective and equitable for all men and women.[109]

With the transformation of AMIS into the first UN-AU hybrid mission, the partnership between Africa's institutional actors and the UN has deepened once more. Pursuant to UN Security Council Resolution 1769 and Article 17 of the AU's PSC Protocol which states that "where necessary recourse will be made to the UN to provide financial, logistical and military support to the AU's activities in the promotion and maintenance of peace, security and stability in Africa", the 26,000 strong UNAMID began to replace the much weaker AMIS on 31 December 2007.[110] While the UN is now responsible for the overall political control of the mission, the operational command remains with the AU which has transformed its Darfur Integrated Task Force (DITF) into a joint AU-UN planning and management cell. Given that a hybrid mission is much more complex with respect to command, control and coordination than the simple "re-hatting" of forces practiced in the past, it is not surprising that the institutional cooperation between the AU PSOD and the UN DPKO has intensified substantially over the last year.[111] In addition to this operational partnership, Africa's institutional actors and the UN have also expanded their cooperation on capacity-building and long-term development issues and have held the first of a series of joint workshops to formulate a ten-year cooperation strategy in November 2007.

The partnership between Africa's institutional actors and the European Union is of a different kind.[112] Ever since it adopted its Africa Strategy *The EU and Africa: Towards a Strategic Partnership* in December 2005, the EU has focused on material and financial support to the AU and the RECs rather than direct participation in African peacekeeping initiatives. The EU-AU Joint Strategy adopted at the 2nd AU-EU Joint Summit in Lisbon in December 2007 further consolidated this passive role. While the strategy aims to "take the Africa-EU relationship to a new, strategic level with a strengthened political partnership and enhanced cooperation at all levels", it is unlikely that the EU will become as deeply involved with joint operational issues as the UN. Its recent military missions in Africa such as EUFOR Congo (2006) and EUFOR Chad (ongoing) have generally been planned and executed with only "minimal involvement of African organizations" and its operational support to the AU's missions in Darfur and Somalia has been limited to the provision of civilian police and occasional air lifts.[113]

However, this is not to say that the EU is not deeply involved with Africa's emerging peace and security architecture. On the contrary, the EU is not only the largest financial contributor to many of the continent's initiatives, but it also highly active in liaising with African actors like the AU's Conflict Management Division. Its Military Liaison Officer in Addis Ababa, Colonel Reinhard Linz, for example, has been deeply engaged with the establishment of the DITF, the formulation and translation of key ASF documents including the ASF Doctrine and the Standard Operating Procedures as well as the restructuring and expansion of the PSOD.[114] The EU has also provided a legal advisor for AMIS and has been instrumental in the establishment of the AMISOM Strategic Planning and Management Unit in Addis Ababa and the Force HQ in Mogadishu. In order to increase partnership coherence on its side, the EU has recently established its own permanent delegation to the AU.

The Dependence on International Support

One of the most notable characteristic of contemporary inter-African security cooperation is the crucial importance of external financial and material support. Both case studies have demonstrated the extent to which non-African actors have become involved with the establishment of the African Peace and Security Architecture and they leave no doubt about Africa's dependence on this support and the risks associated with it. In fact, as much as 90 percent of the costs of establishing the APSA have been shouldered by international actors for reasons ranging from virtually pure altruism to unveiled self-interest.[115]

Given that most of its current peacekeeping operations are taking place in African theatres, it is hardly surprising that the UN wants to strengthen African capacities to deal with the continent's many perils.[116] As described in the previous section, the UN increasingly sees African actors as valuable partners in a worthwhile enterprise for which the UN alone has neither the necessary capacity nor the political support. As the mandates of UN peace operations continue to increase in complexity, becoming more comprehensive, including holding elections, protecting civilians and building government institutions, there is a notable gap between the demand for UN services and the current possible supply.[117] It is this fact which makes Africa's emerging security architecture and its potential to provide an initial muscle to peace operations so essential to the future of the UN and has led Secretary-General Kofi Annan to rally behind them.

> Within the context of the United Nations primary responsibility for matters of international peace and security, providing support for regional and sub-regional initiatives in Africa is both necessary and desirable. Such support is necessary, because the United Nations lacks the capacity, resources and expertise to address all problems that may arise in Africa. It is desirable because wherever possible the international community should strive to complement rather than supplant African efforts to resolve Africa's problems.[118]

As a result of the reports of the Brahimi Commission (2000) and the High-Level Panel on Threats, Challenges and Change (2004), the AU has increasingly emerged as the focal point for UN capacity building support. Since late 2006, the UN maintains a permanent liaison team to the AU HQ in order to coordinate its support activities, assist with operational planning and management and strengthen headquarters capabilities.[119]

According to a 2007 study on donor involvement in the continent's emerging peace and security architecture, "the G8 represents the AU's most important international partner [after the UN] as it provides a point of departure for many national initiatives".[120] The G8's involvement in capacity building in Africa began at the Genoa Summit in 2001. It has since grown steadily and culminated in the 2007 Heiligendamm Summit which declared Africa's development one of the group's top priorities (the others being climate change and economic growth). To this purpose, the G8 leaders pledged to increase their capacity building support in line with the 1992 Paris Declaration, their own Africa Action Plan (AAP) agreed to in Kananaskis in 2002 and the so-called Joint Plan adopted in 2003. A fundamental aim of the latter was to "mobilize technical and financial assistance so that, by 2010, African partners are able to engage more effectively to prevent and resolve violent conflict on the continent, and undertake peace support operations in accordance with the United Nations Charter".[121] Realizing that implementation of the ambitious Joint Plan was lacking, one problem being that the G8 has no bureaucracy or other machinery through which to implement its policies and thus has to rely on coherent actions of its member states, the G8 begun to narrow its focus on particular areas of the African peace and security architecture.[122] These areas include the ASF, and specifically its civilian and police components, as well as capacity building for conflict prevention and stabilization, reconstruction, reconciliation and development in post-conflict situations.[123]

Just like the G8, the European Union has become increasingly involved in the African continent over the last couple of years and it is now widely regarded as "one of the most important supporters of the AU peace and security agenda, in terms of the volume and the predictability of funds".[124] Beginning in earnest with its Africa strategy of 2005 which, in the words of Stephan Klingebiel and his associates, "treated Africa as one for the first time", the EU has steadily increased its support for the continent's peace and security activities and initiatives.[125] Based on the implementation policies outlined in its Concept for Strengthening African Capabilities for the Prevention, Management and Resolution of Conflicts as well as various action plans, the EU has focused on long-term capacity building, including military and civilian crisis management support for the ASF. To this effect, it has earmarked €35 million out of its €250 million African Peace Facility (APF) for capacity-building purposes and has begun to fund personnel recruitment, staff costs, equipment, rent of office space and duty travel, a series of ASF workshops, the creation of liaison offices of RECs with the AU as well as the development of early warning capacities. The EU has recently replenished the APF with €300 million for the period 2008-2010 and has dedicated a large part of this money for capacity building efforts. Furthermore, it has Europeanized the successful French RECAMP initiative which will serve as framework for the validation exercises of the ASF.

In addition to their engagement through the multilateral channels of institutions like the UN, the G8 and the EU, several states have launched their own national efforts to support Africa's emerging capabilities. The German GTZ, for example, has emerged as the principal supporter of the operationalization of CEWS. It has organized and paid for several workshops, contracted three external experts as early warning consultants for the AU, supported the development of an authoritative CEWS Handbook and installed the necessary IT-components throughout the continent. Besides its work on the CEWS, the GTZ has also provided temporary office space for the AU's PSOD and facilitated the formulation of the MoU between the AU and the RECs. During her widely-publicized speech at the AU in October 2007, Chancellor Angela Merkel promised further German support initiatives. The Foreign Ministry has since, amongst other things, provided €20 million for the construction of the new PSOD building on the AU compound.

The United States, for many reasons ranging from the Global War on Terrorism and resource interests in Western Africa to the wish to counteract China's rising influence on the continent, is an even more active capacity builder than Germany.[126] Besides its long-existent programs like ACOTA and the Enhanced International Peacekeeping Capabilities Assistance, the US has established a separate embassy to the AU and announced the creation of a new African Command (AFRICOM) which aims to "provide a comprehensive and multi-dimensional approach to capacity building".[127] Officially inaugurated in October 2008 at its provisional headquarters in Germany, AFRICOM is supposed to streamline the multitude of US initiatives by offering a focal point through which to channel all support to the continent. Thus far, US assistance still comes from a variety of independent and often mal-coordinated offices including at least three in the State Department, several in the Department of Defense, and more from EUCOM and other overseas commands.[128]

Contrary to the US which still lacks "a single overall plan and a single point of coordination for assisting the range of African conflict resolution and peacekeeping activities", the United Kingdom pooled the peacekeeping capacity-building programs of its three pertinent departments – the Foreign and Commonwealth Office, the Department for International Development and the Ministry of Defense – into what is known as the Africa Conflict Prevention Pool (ACPP) as early as 2001. In 2008, the ACPP was merged with the Global Conflict Prevention Pool in order to further increase its effectiveness. With a yearly budget of about €100 million (GBP 60 million), the ACPP "is a tool for joint analysis, financing and coordination utilizing in-country DFID offices, Defense Attaches and Diplomatic Missions as well as four regional conflict advisors".[129] Based on a Pan-African strategy and several regional work plans, the ACPP supports a variety of African peace and security initiatives ranging from community safety programs in Sierra Leone, security sector reforms in Nigeria and the implementation of the Nuba Mountain Cease Fire Agreement in Sudan to conceptual support to the AU's Conflict Management Centre and the development of policy documents for the ASF.

More so than the UK, France has found it difficult to relinquish its traditional role in Africa and give up its bilateral programs with former colonies in exchange for more multilateral approaches to capacity building.[130] Since 1997, the bulk of France's support to the continent's emerging peace and security architecture has been channeled through RECAMP which aims to strengthen Africa's capacities for peacekeeping through training, the provision of equipment and the organization of multinational exercises.[131] Under RECAMP, France has set up four training centers in Mali, Côte d'Ivoire, Gabon and Ghana and has conducted five exercise cycles involving more than 20 African countries and several international observers. Following the partial Europeanization of RECAMP in 2007,[132] France will continue to provide equipment and training to selected African countries while the EU will, at least on paper, take over the organization of the exercise cycle. The importance France attaches to Africa's emerging security architecture is also aptly demonstrated by the fact that its liaison officer at the AU HQ in Addis Ababa is a Brigadier-General (as opposed to all other countries and institutions who generally send a Colonel).[133]

Other noteworthy national initiatives include China's provision of $100 million for an urgently-needed expansion of the AU Headquarters in Addis Ababa in 2007,[134] Italy's extensive support for AMISOM and the various development programs of Canada and the Scandinavian countries.[135] Both NATO and SHIRBRIG have also provided substantial levels of support to African institutions, the former mostly in form of strategic transport for AMIS/UNAMID and AMISOM and the latter through the training of regional standby brigades.[136]

It is beyond doubt that without all these external support initiatives, hardly any of the aforementioned developments in inter-African security cooperation would have been possible. The case studies on the ASF and the CEWS, moreover, have clearly shown that any further progress will continue to depend on external assistance for (at least) the foreseeable future. While critics often use this fact to point to the potential for neo-colonial blackmailing or the notable incongruence between the popular rhetoric of "African Ownership" and the continent's material and financial dependence on external resources, the changing nature of this dependence is rarely noted. It is, however, a central aspect of and telling indicator for the continent's progress in the institutionalization of security cooperation. Two things in particular have changed, namely, the nature of the assistance and its recipient(s).

Writing on the dependence of African security initiatives on outside support in 1997, Roy May and Gerry Cleaver called on the continent's states "to get themselves organized so as to make better use of the external assistance offered and gradually reduce their dependence thereon".[137] Little more than ten years later, this is exactly what African states have done. Their emerging peace and security architecture epitomizes a much needed common objective which helps to channel the multiplicity of resources, initiatives and ambitions devoted to African peace and security efforts into one direction, or as Cedric de Coning put it in 2004:

> The development of the African security architecture is a significant achievement because it provides Africa with a common policy framework for capacity building. This means that the various capacity building initiatives underway, and any new programs, can be directed to support this common objective, regardless of whether such initiatives are taking place at the regional, sub-regional or national level.[138]

One direct result of the emergence of an attractive focal point for external assistance is that most of the support now goes to the regional and continental bodies rather than to the states. Another is that external actors whose motivations range from a genuine desire to help to strategic calculations about burden-sharing increasingly seek to further African self-sufficiency through long-term capacity-building. Both changes are important and their significance to inter-African security cooperation should not be underestimated. It should, however, also be noted that Africa's return into the geo-strategic limelight and the corresponding changes in donors' motivations which will be discussed in the next chapter may eventually reverse the progress made thus far.

Notes

¹   Emanuel Adler and Michael Barnett, "A Framework for the Study of Security Communities," in *Security Communities*, ed. Emanuel Adler and Michael Barnett (Cambridge: Cambridge University Press, 1998).

²   Ibid., 51.

³   Bruce Cronin, *Community under Anarchy: Transnational Identity and the Evolution of Cooperation* (New York: Columbia University Press, 1999), 36.

⁴   Yoweri Museveni, *Address to the South African Parliament*, Cape Town, 27 May 1997.

⁵   For an excellent introduction to Pan-Africanism see P. Olisanwuche Esedebe, *Pan-Africanism: The Idea and Movement, 1776-1991*, 2nd ed. (Washington, D.C.: Howard University, 1994). For the idea of waves of Pan-Africanism see Christopher Landsberg, "The Fifth Wave of Pan-Africanism," in *West Africa's Security Challenges: Building Peace in a Troubled Region*, ed. Adekeye Adebajo and Ismail Rashid (Boulder: Lynne Rienner, 2004).

⁶   Landsberg, "The Fifth Wave of Pan-Africanism," 117.

⁷   Olusegun Obasanjo, "A Balance Sheet of the African Region and the Cold War," in *Africa in the New International Order: Rethinking State Sovereignty and Regional Security*, ed. Edmond Keller and Donald Rothchild (Boulder: Lynne Rienner, 1996), 18.

⁸   Benedict Anderson, *Imagined Communities* (London: Verso, 1992).

⁹   See A Cohen, *The Symbolic Construction of Community* (New York: Tavistock Publishers, 1985), Alexander Wendt, "Collective Identity Formation and the International State," *American Political Science Review* 88 (1994).

¹⁰   See Edmond Keller and Donald Rothchild, eds., *Africa in the New International Order: Rethinking State Sovereignty and Regional Security* (Boulder: Lynne Rienner, 1996).

¹¹   See Francis Deng and William Zartman, *A Strategic Vision for Africa: The Kampala Movement* (Washington DC: Brookings Institution Press, 2002).

¹²   See O. Obodozie, *Security Concerns: Nigeria's Peacekeeping Efforts in Liberia and Sierra Leone, 1990-1999* (PhD Thesis, University of South Africa, 2004), 61.

¹³   See Katharina Coleman, *International Organizations and Peace Enforcement: The Politics of International Legitimacy* (Cambridge: Cambridge University Press, 2007), 73-115.

¹⁴   N Echezons and E Duru, "Conflict Prevention, Management and Resolution: Establishing a Regional Force for Africa," *European Journal of Scientific Research* 8, no. 3 (2005): 39.

¹⁵   See Comfort Ero, *ECOMOG: A Model for Africa?*, Monograph Series No. 46 (Pretoria: Institute for Security Studies, 2000), Margaret Vogt, ed., *The Liberian Crisis and ECOMOG: A Bold Attempt at Regional Peacekeeping* (Lagos: Gabumo Press, 1992).

[16] See Terry Mays, "African Solutions to African Problems: The Changing Face of African-Mandated Peace Operations," *Journal of Conflict Studies* (2003).

[17] Ademola Abass, *Regional Organizations and the Development of Collective Security - Beyond Chapter VIII of the UN Charter* (Oxford: Hart Publishing, 2004).

[18] Ibid., xxii.

[19] Nelson Mandela as quoted in African Rights, *Rwanda: Death, Despair and Defiance*, Revised Edition, August 1995, 1138.

[20] Stephan Klingebiel, *How Much Weight for Military Capabilities? Africa's New Peace and Security Architecture and the Role of External Actors* (Bonn: Deutsches Institut für Entwicklungspolitik, 2005).

[21] Ibid. The latter have featured especially prominently in the US considerations to re-engage in Africa's destiny. In the words of US Representative Edward Royce: "With the development of terrorist sanctuaries in Africa we have an increasing stake in the continent's peace and its stability". Edward Royce, Opening Statement, *Hearing on Peacekeeping in Africa: Challenges and Opportunities* (House of Representatives, Subcommittee on Africa, Committee on International Relations, 8 October 2004), 1.

[22] The first scramble for Africa occurred during the colonization, the second was a natural by-product of the independence movements during the 1950s and early 60s and the third is associated with the various attempts of the Cold War superpowers to carve out spheres of influence for themselves.

[23] Fund for Peace, *African Perspectives on Military Intervention*, Conference Summary of the Regional Reponses to Internal War Program (Washington DC: Fund for Peace, 2004), 2 and 13; also Jason Ladnier, *Neighbors on Alert - Regional Views on Humanitarian Intervention*, Summary Report of the Regional Responses to Internal War Program (Washington DC: Fund for Peace, 2003), 3 as well as interview with Jason Ladnier and Patricia Taft (both Fund for Peace) in Washington DC, 22 November 2005.

[24] Cover title of *The Economist*, 13 May 2000.

[25] For a discussion of the role of South Africa and Nigeria in the creation of the AU see Thomas Tieku, "Explaining the Clash of Interests of Major Actors in the Creation of the African Union," *African Affairs* 103, no. 411 (2004): 228-49.

[26] Thabo Mbeki as quoted in Theo Neethling, "Realizing the African Standby Force as a Pan-African Deal: Progress, Prospects and Challenges," *Journal of Military and Strategic Studies* 8, no. 1 (2005): 10-11.

[27] Interview with Ambassador Said Djinnit, 1 June 2007, Addis Ababa.

[28] Ambassador Said Djinnit, AU Commissioner for Peace and Security, 28 June 2004, Addis Ababa, as quoted in Kristiana Powell, *The African Union's Emerging Peace and Security Regime - Opportunities and Challenges for Delivering on the Responsibility to Protect*, Monograph Series No. 119 (Pretoria: Institute for Security Studies, 2005), 1.

[29] Closing Address at the 8th Institut des Hautes Etudes de Défense Nationale (IHEDN) Forum on the African Continent, Paris, 9 June 2007.

[30] For a more detailed discussion on the idea of African ownership and its limits see Benedikt Franke and Romain Esmenjaud, "Who Owns African

---

Ownership? The Africanization of Security and Its Limits," *South African Journal of International Affairs* 14, no. 2 (2008): 137-58.

[31]   Ali Mazrui, *Towards a Pax Africana: A Study in Ideology and Ambition* (Chicago: Chicago University Press, 1967), 216.

[32]   Paul Williams bases his definition on the work of Alastair Johnston, *Cultural Realism: Strategic Culture and Grand Strategy in Chinese History* (Princeton: Princeton University Press, 1995).

[33]   Amitav Acharya, "How Ideas Spread: Whose Norms Matter? Norm Localization and Institutional Change in Asian Regionalism," *International Organization* 58, no. 2 (2004).

[34]   For a good discussion of the process of socialization see Thomas Risse, Stephen Ropp, and Kathryn Sikkink, "The Socialization of International Human Rights Norms into Domestic Practices," in *The Power of Human Rights*, ed. Thomas Risse (Cambridge: Cambridge University Press, 1999).

[35]   Acharya, "How Ideas Spread: Whose Norms Matter? Norm Localization and Institutional Change in Asian Regionalism," 241.

[36]   For a good discussion of regional security cultures in Africa see, for example, Thomas Jaye, "The Security Culture of ECOWAS: Origins, Development and the Challenges of Child Trafficking," *Journal of Contemporary African Studies* 26, no. 2 (2008): 151-68, Jürgen Haacke and Paul Williams, "Security Culture and Transnational Challenges: ECOWAS in Comparative Perspective," *Journal of Contemporary African Studies* 26, no. 2 (2008): 213-22.

[37]   For more evidence on this see Rachel Murray, *Human Rights in Africa* (Cambridge: Cambridge University Press, 2004).

[38]   See *Declaration on the Framework for an OAU Response to Unconstitutional Changes in Government* (OAU Document AHG/Decl.5 (XXXVI), 10-12 July 2000).

[39]   For more information on this shift see Paul Williams, "From Non-Intervention to Non-Indifference: The Origins and Development of the African Union's Security Culture," *African Affairs* 106, no. 423 (2007): 253-79.

[40]   See Patrick McGowan, "African Military Coups d'Etats, 1956-2001," *Journal of Modern African Studies* 41, no. 3 (2003).

[41]   AU Document PSC/PR/Comm. (XXV), AU PSC, 25th Meeting, Addis Ababa, 25 February 2005.

[42]   See Paul Williams, "The responsibility to protect, norm localization and African international society," Paper presented at the International Studies Association annual convention, 16 February 2009, New York.

[43]   Acharya, "How Ideas Spread: Whose Norms Matter? Norm Localization and Institutional Change in Asian Regionalism," 250.

[44]   Shannon Field, ed., *Peace in Africa: Towards a Collaborative Security Regime* (Johannesburg: Institute for Global Dialogue, 2004).

[45]   See Michael Smith, *Europe's Foreign and Security Policy: The Institutionalization of Cooperation* (Cambridge: Cambridge University Press, 2004), 17-36.

[46]   Ibid., 17.

[47]   Emmanuel Aning, "From Eco-Pessimism to Eco-Optimism: ECOMOG and the West African Integration Process," *African Journal of Political Science* 4, no. 1 (1999): 25-39.

[48] ———, "Investing in Peace and Security in Africa: The Case of ECOWAS," in *Security and Development: Investing in Peace and Prosperity*, ed. Robert Picciotto and Rachel Weaving (London: Routledge, 2006), 156. See also Emmanuel Aning, "The Transformation of ECOWAS: Towards an Emerging Security Regime," *African Journal of Politics* 10, no. 1 (2007).

[49] Quoted in Joram Biswaro, *Perspectives on Africa's Integration and Cooperation from OAU to AU: Old Wine in New Bottles?* (Dar es Salaam: Tanzania Publishing House, 2005), 73.

[50] Adler and Barnett, "A Framework for the Study of Security Communities," 37-48. Naison Ngoma rightly argues that even though the evolution of security communities in regions is a product of their histories and thus not confined to the growth path model suggested by Adler and Barnett, the latter's characterization of the development of security communities remains the most comprehensive manner in which such developments can the studied in the African region. See Naison Ngoma, *Prospects for a Security Community in Southern Africa: An Analysis of Regional Security in the Southern African Development Community* (Pretoria: Institute for Security Studies, 2005), 52.

[51] Adler and Barnett, "A Framework for the Study of Security Communities," 39.

[52] M. Schoeman, "Imagining a Community: The African Union as an Emerging Security Community," *Strategic Review for Southern Africa* 24, no. 1 (2002): 9-10.

[53] Adler and Barnett, "A Framework for the Study of Security Communities," 39.

[54] For an excellent collection of key documents on peace and security in Africa see Monica Juma, ed., *Compendium of Key Documents Relating to Peace and Security in Africa* (Pretoria: University of Pretoria Law Press, 2006). For more information on the CADSP see Omar Touray, "The Common African Defense and Security Policy," *African Affairs* 104, no. 417 (2005).

[55] For information on AMIB see Festus Agoagye, "The African Mission in Burundi: Lessons Learned from the First African Union Peacekeeping Operation," *Conflict Trends*, no. 2 (2004): 9-15. For information on AMIS see Seth Appiah-Mensah, "The African Mission in Sudan: Darfur Dilemmas," *African Security Review* 15, no. 1 (2006).

[56] Karl W. Deutsch, "Security Communities," in *International Politics and Foreign Policy*, ed. James Rosenau (New York: Free Press, 1961), 98.

[57] John Baylis and Nick Rengger, eds., *Dilemmas of World Politics: International Issues in a Changing World* (Oxford: Clarendon Press, 1992), 54-55.

[58] Adler and Barnett, "A Framework for the Study of Security Communities," 30.

[59] Michael Taylor, *Community, Anarchy and Liberty* (New York: Cambridge University Press, 1982), 25.

[60] For Deutsch a consensus on main values is sufficient to create a pluralistic security community and differences in political and economic values do not need to undermine such a community. Karl W. Deutsch, *Political Community and the North Atlantic Area - International Organization in the Light of Historical Experience* (Princeton: Princeton University Press, 1957), 123-25.

[61]   For more information on the APRM see Ravi Kanbur, "The African Peer Review Mechanism (APRM): An Assessment of Concept and Design," *SAGA Working Paper*, no. 161 (2004).

[62]   Emanuel Adler, "Imagined (Security) Communities: Cognitive Regions in International Relations," *Millennium: Journal of International Studies* 26, no. 2 (1997): 258-59.

[63]   Michael Williams, "Hobbes and International Relations: A Reconsideration," *International Organization* 50 (1996): 213-47. See also Adler, "Imagined (Security) Communities: Cognitive Regions in International Relations," 261.

[64]   See Schoeman, "Imagining a Community: The African Union as an Emerging Security Community," 16.

[65]   See Adler, "Imagined (Security) Communities: Cognitive Regions in International Relations," 270. See also Emanuel Adler, "Seeds of Peaceful Change: The OSCE's Security Community-Building Model," in *Security Communities*, ed. Emanuel Adler and Michael Barnett (Cambridge: Cambridge University Press, 1998).

[66]   With respect to the type of security community, the deep divisions that continue to permeate Africa certainly confine it to the loosely-coupled category for the moment, even though some of its characteristics point to a level of development congruent with what Adler and Barnett described as tightly-coupled security community (for example, its system of collective security). According to Adler and Barnett it is perfectly possible that elements of an ascendant or even mature security community might already be present in an earlier (nascent phase). See also Schoeman, "Imagining a Community: The African Union as an Emerging Security Community," 8. In the case of Africa, the replacement of the norm of non-intervention with the norm of mutual accountability is another such characteristic that would generally be associated with more a developed form of a security community. See Michael Barnett and Emanuel Adler, "Studying Security Communities in Theory, Comparison and History," in Security Communities, ed. Emanuel Adler and Michael Barnett (Cambridge: Cambridge University Press, 1998), 432.

[67]   Garth le Pere in Field, ed., *Peace in Africa: Towards a Collaborative Security Regime*, 17.

[68]   For Western Africa see Alhaji Bah, "West Africa: From a Security Complex to a Security Community," *African Security Review* 14, no. 2 (2005). For Southern Africa see the works of Naison Ngoma.

[69]   In view of the region's long history of violent conflict and deep divisions, it is hardly surprising that there are many skeptics such as Jan Isaksen and Elling Tjonneland or Laurie Nathan. See Jan Isaksen and Elling Tjonneland, "Assessing the Restructuring of SADC: Positions, Policies and Progress," (Oslo: Norwegian Agency for Development Cooperation, 2001), Laurie Nathan, "SADC's Uncommon Approach to Common Security, 1992-2003," Journal of Southern African Studies 32, no. 3 (2006).

[70]   For a more detailed discussion on the FLS see W. Breytenbach, "Conflict in Sub-Saharan Africa: From Frontline State to Collective Security," in *The Arusha Paper 2* (1995), Gilbert Khadiagala, *Allies in Adversity: The Frontline States in Southern African Security, 1975-1993* (Athens: Ohio University Press, 1994), Robert Jaster, "A Regional Security Role for Africa's

Front Line States: Experience and Prospects," in *Adelphi Paper No. 180* (London: International Institute for Strategic Studies, 1983). For more information on SADCC see, for example, Samir Amin, Derrick Chitala, and Ibbo Mandaza, eds., *SADCC: Prospects for Disengagement and Development in Southern Africa* (Tokyo: United Nations University Press, 1987), Fadzai Gwaradzimba, "SADCC and the Future of Southern African Regionalism," *Issue: A Journal of Opinion* 21, no. 1/2 (1993).

[71]   On the global level, the perception that international interest in the continent was receding and that as a result the Security Council became less vigorously committed to African conflicts caused many African states to look more inwardly for solutions to their collective security problems. On the continental level, the failure of the OAU to provide a true continental framework for such solutions was one of the reasons for the growth in regionalisms. Consequently, the devolution was a historically and politically logical process resulting from the OAU's cautious approach which prevented it from establishing the mechanisms and framework necessary to tackle the security problems of the continent. Regional initiatives such ECOWAS or SADC eventually filled the void that had been created by the OAU's inability.

[72]   For a more detailed analysis of events between 1992 and 1995, see Maxi van Aardt, "Doing Battle with Security: The Emergence of a Southern African Approach " *South African Journal of International Affairs* 3, no. 2 (1996), L Gumbi and Jakkie Cilliers, "South Africa, SADC and a Regional Security Regime," *AI Bulletin* 34, no. 4 (1994), Greg Mills, "South Africa and Africa: Regional Integration and Security Cooperation," *African Security Review* 4, no. 2 (1995).

[73]   For more information on the OPDS and its difficulties see, for example, W. Breytenbach, "Failure of Security Cooperation in SADC: The Suspension of the Organ for Politics, Defense and Security " *South African Journal of International Affairs* 7, no. 1 (2000).

[74]   Ngoma, *Prospects for a Security Community in Southern Africa: An Analysis of Regional Security in the Southern African Development Community*, 223-24.

[75]   SADC, Towards a Southern African Development Community, August 1992, Windhoek.

[76]   For an opposing view on Southern Africa's communality see, for example, Laurie Nathan, "The Absence of Common Values and Failure of Common Security in Africa, 1992-2003," *LSE Crisis States Program Working Paper*, no. 50 (2004), Mwesiga Baregu, "Economic and Military Security," in *From Cape to Congo: Southern Africa's Evolving Security Challenges*, ed. Mwesiga Baregu and Christopher Landsberg (Boulder: Lynne Rienner, 2003), 29.

[77]   See Benedikt Franke, "Military Integration in Southern Africa: SADC's Standby Brigade," in *South African Yearbook of International Affairs 2006* (Cape Town: South African Institute of International Affairs, 2007).

[78]   Paul-Henri Bischoff, "SADC as a Foreign Policy Actor: The Challenges of Cooperation in Southern Africa," in *Africa Institute of South Africa 40th Anniversary Conference* (Pretoria: 2001), 1.

[79]   See Naison Ngoma, "SADC: Towards a Security Community?," *African Security Review* 12, no. 3 (2003), Naison Ngoma, "SADC's Mutual

Defense Pact: A Final Move to a Security Community?," *The Round Table* 93, no. 375 (2004).

[80]   Competing regionalisms are defined as the occurrences of competition between intergovernmental institutions with overlapping memberships and quasi-identical *raisons d'être* but different underlying motives and/or conceptions of cooperation and regional integration. For more information on the concept of competing regionalisms see Benedikt Franke, "Competing Regionalisms in Africa and the Continent's Emerging Security Architecture," *African Studies Quarterly* 10, no. 1 (2007).

[81]   Barry Buzan and Ole Waever, *Regions and Powers - the Structure of International Security* (Cambridge: Cambridge University Press, 2003), 4. See also David Francis, *Uniting Africa - Building Regional Peace and Security Systems* (Aldershot: Ashgate, 2006), 102-07.

[82]   Buzan and Waever argue that transnationality of insecurity, the existence of a regional hegemon (that is, South Africa) as well as the tendency of Southern African states to confine their security interactions to their immediate neighborhood (for reasons as varied as a lack of resources or the aforementioned disillusionment with continental cooperation) led to the emergence of such a complex in Southern Africa. Buzan and Waever, *Regions and Powers - the Structure of International Security*, 233-38.

[83]   For a more detailed discussion of this summit and the idea of the United States of Africa see Benedikt Franke, "Die Vereinigten Staaten Von Afrika," *Kulturaustausch: Zeitschrift für internationale Perspektiven* 58, no. 1 (2008).

[84]   Kwame Nkrumah, *Africa Must Unite* (New York: F.A. Praeger, 1963).

[85]   See *Assembly Decision on the Report of the 9th Extraordinary Session of the Executive Council on the Proposal for the Union Government* (AU Document AU/DEC.156 (VII), January 2007, Addis Ababa). See also, *Assembly Decision on the "Study on an African Union Government: Towards the United States of Africa"* (AU Document AU/DEC. 123 (VII), July 2006, Banjul) and *Africa and the Challenges of the Changing World Order: Desirability of a Union Government*, Conclusions and Recommendations of the Conference on the Desirability of a Union Government, November 2005, Abuja.

[86]   See Muammar Gaddafi, *Inaugural Speech on the Occasion of the Election of the AU Chairperson*, 7 February 2009, Addis Ababa.

[87]   Gboyega Akinsanmi, "Borderless West Africa Primary Goal of ECOWAS," *This Day*, 24 June 2007.

[88]   For a good treatment of the issues surrounding civil society partnerships see Chris Landsberg and Shaun McKay, *Engaging the New Pan-Africanism: Strategies for Civil Society* (Johannesburg: ActionAid International, 2005).

[89]   For an interesting discussion of the evolution of inter-organization security cooperation in international peace operations see Kristin Haugevik, *New Partners, New Possibilities: The Evolution of Inter-Organizational Security Cooperation in International Peace Operations* (Oslo: Norsk Utenrikspolitisk Institutt (NUPI), 2007).

[90]   UNECA, *Assessing Regional Integration in Africa*, 2004, Addis Ababa, 39-40.

[91] Adler, "Imagined (Security) Communities: Cognitive Regions in International Relations," 256.

[92] Barry Buzan, "From International System to International Society: Structural Realism and Regime Theory Meet the English School," *International Organization* 47, no. 3 (1992): 339.

[93] Article 16 of the PSC Protocol and the CADSP stress that the regional mechanisms will form the "building blocks" of the AU's peace and security architecture; See also Articles 3c, j and k of the AU Constitutive Act and Article 3p of the 2003 Amendment to the Constitutive Act. For more information on the principles of subsidiarity, burden-sharing and sub-contracting see Abass, *Regional Organizations and the Development of Collective Security - Beyond Chapter VIII of the UN Charter*, 154, Malcolm Chalmers, *Sharing Security - the Political Economy of Burdensharing* (Basingstoke: Macmillan 2000).

[94] Edmond Keller, "Rethinking African Regional Security," in *Regional Orders: Building Security in a New World*, ed. David Lake and Patrick Morgan (University Park: Pennsylvania State University Press, 1997), 298.

[95] See Protocol Regarding the Establishment of the Peace and Security Council, Article 16. See also Decisions of the Lusaka Summit 2001, Decision 1, Article 8b (iii).

[96] See David Mitrany, *A Working Peace System: An Argument for the Functional Development of International Organizations* (Oxford: Oxford University Press, 1943).

[97] See Benedikt Franke, "In Defense of Regional Peace Operations in Africa," *Journal of Humanitarian Assistance*, no. 185 (2006).

[98] For more information on the notion of a peace pyramid see Mark Malan, "The OAU and African Sub-Regional Organizations - a Closer Look at the Peace Pyramid," (Pretoria: Institute for Security Studies, 1999).

[99] Ole Waever, "Insecurity, Security and Asecurity in the West European Non-War Community," in *Security Communities*, ed. Emanuel Adler and Michael Barnett (Cambridge: Cambridge University Press, 1998), 69. Using the standard definition of the Correlates of War Project, there have only been three events in post-colonial African history qualifying as inter-state wars, namely, the so-called Ogaden War between Somalia and Ethiopia (1977-78), the war between Uganda and Tanzania (1978) and the border war between Ethiopia and Eritrea (1998-2000). See Douglas Lemke, *Regions of War and Peace* (Cambridge: Cambridge University Press, 2002), 161-94.

[100] For a detailed discussion of the MLG concept see the works of Liesbet Hooghe and Gary Marks. For a good summary see Ian Bache and Matthew Flinders, eds., *Multi-Level Governance* (Oxford: Oxford University Press, 2004).

[101] Note that there can be overlapping security communities within multi-layered ones. For example, several members of the Intergovernmental Authority on Development (IGAD) are also members of the East African Community (EAC).

[102] For an in-depth discussion of these dangers see Franke, "Competing Regionalisms in Africa and the Continent's Emerging Security Architecture."

[103] See AU, *Final Report on the 7th African Union Summit*, 25 June – 2 July 2006, Banjul.

[104]   At the time of writing, five RECs (ECOWAS, EAC, COMESA, IGAD and ECCAS) had established liaison offices near the AU compound in Addis Ababa. The others were to follow soon.

[105]   See *An Agenda for Peace, Preventive Diplomacy, Peacemaking and Peacekeeping*, Report of the Secretary-General (UN Document A/47/277-S/24111, 17 June 1992, New York).

[106]   See Jane Boulden, *Dealing with Conflict in Africa: The United Nations and Regional Organizations* (Basingstoke: Palgrave Macmillan, 2003).

[107]   See Adebayo Adedeji and Christopher Landsberg, "Back to the Future: UN Peacekeeping in Africa," in *Managing Armed Conflict in the 21st Century*, ed. Adebayo Adedeji and C Sriram (London: Frank Cass, 2001). Also see Thomas Weiss, ed., *Beyond UN Subcontracting: Task-Sharing with Regional Security Arrangements and Service-Providing NGOs* (Basingstoke: Macmillan Press, 1998).

[108]   Ademola Abass has argued that even though Africa's regional organizations have joined up with the UN in a number of ways, they do not necessarily subscribe to the unquestionable authority of the Security Council. In an interview with Abass, AU Ambassador Sam Ibok stated that "the AU is not an arm of the United Nations. We accept the UN's global authority but we will not wait for the UN to authorize an action that we intend to take. We are in a tacit agreement with the United Nations on this and there is an agreement to that effect". See Abass, *Regional Organizations and the Development of Collective Security - Beyond Chapter VIII of the UN Charter*, 166. Also see Ademola Abass, "The Security Council and the Challenges of Collective Security in the Twenty-First Century: What Role for African Regional Organizations?," in *Global Governance and the Quest for Justice - International and Regional Organizations*, ed. Douglas Lewis (Oxford: Hart, 2006).

[109]   Hédi Annabi, UN Assistant Secretary-General for Peacekeeping Operations, *Spoken Remarks to the UN Security Council*, 28 March 2007, New York.

[110]   For an excellent treatment of UNAMID see Sarah Kreps, "The United Nations-African Union Mission in Darfur: Implications and Prospects for Success," *African Security Review* 16, no. 4 (2007).

[111]   For critical views of the cooperation between the UN and African actors see Timothy Othieno and Nhamo Samasuwo, "A Critical Analysis of Africa's Experiments with Hybrid Missions and Security Collaboration," *African Security Review* 16, no. 3 (2007): 25-40. See also David Francis et al., *Dangers of Co-Deployment - UN Cooperative Peacekeeping in Africa* (Aldershot: Ashgate, 2005).

[112]   For a detailed discussion of the emerging EU-Africa partnerships see Mark Malan, "The European Union and the African Union as Strategic Partners in Peace Operations: Not Grasping the Planning and Management Nettle," *KAIPTC Paper*, no. 13 (2006), Mary Farrell, "A Triumph of Realism over Idealism? Cooperation between the European Union and Africa," *Journal of European Integration* 27, no. 3 (2005).

[113]   Interview with Maj.-Gen. Karl-Heinz Viereck, Commander of EUFOR RD Congo, 25 April 2007, London.

[114]   Interview with Col. Reinhard Linz, EU MIL LO, 30 January 2008, Addis Ababa.

[115] For an introduction to the role of external support see Stephan Klingebiel, "Regional Security in Africa and the Role of External Support," *European Journal of Development Research* 17, no. 3 (2005): 437-48.

[116] The current UN missions in Africa are UNMIS (Sudan), UNAMID (Darfur), ONUB (Burundi), UNOCI (Côte d'Ivoire), UNML (Liberia), MONUC (Democratic Republic of the Congo), UNMEE (Ethiopia and Eritrea), UNIOSIL (Sierra Leone) and MINURSO (Western Sahara).

[117] Eric Berman and Katie Sams, *Peacekeeping in Africa: Capabilities and Culpabilities* (Geneva: United Nations Institute for Disarmament Research, 2000), 379-80.

[118] UN, *The Causes of Conflict and the Promotion of Durable Peace and Sustainable Development in Africa*, Report of the Secretary-General, 16 April 1998, New York.

[119] Report of the High-Level Panel on Threats, Challenges and Change, *A more secure world: Our shared responsibility* (New York: United Nations, 2004), para. 272c.

[120] Lindsay Scorgie, "Building African Peacekeeping Capacity: Donors and the African Union's Emerging Peace and Security Architecture," *KAIPTC Paper*, no. 16 (2007): 13.

[121] Implementation Report by Africa Representatives to Leaders on the G8 Africa Action Plan, para. 12.

[122] Alex Ramsbotham, Alhaji Bah, and Fanny Calder, *The Implementation of the Joint Africa/G8 Plan to Enhance African Capabilities to Undertake Peace Support Operations: Survey of Current G8 and African Activities and Potential Areas for Further Collaboration* (London: Chatham House, 2005).

[123] G8 Summit Declaration, Growth and Responsibility in Africa, 8 June 2007, Articles 39-45.

[124] S Klingebiel et al., *Donor Contributions to Strengthening the African Peace and Security Architecture* (Final Report of the DIE Country Working Group: Institute for Security Studies, 2006), 59.

[125] Ibid. For more information on EU-Africa relations see Gilbert Khadiagala, "Euro-African Relations in the Age of Maturity," in *Africa in World Politics: Reforming Political Order*, ed. John Harbeson and Donald Rothchild (Boulder: Westview Press, 2009), 305-22.

[126] For a more detailed description of US capacity building in Africa see Benedikt Franke, "Enabling a Continent to Help Itself: US Military Capacity Building and Africa's Emerging Security Architecture," *Strategic Insights* VI, no. 1 (2007).

[127] For a taste of the growing literature on AFRICOM see Otto Sieber, "Africa Command: Forecast for the Future," *Strategic Insights* VI, no. 1 (2007).

[128] One-Day Conference on AFRICOM, Royal United Services Institute (RUSI), 18 February 2008, London.

[129] DFID, *The Africa Conflict Prevention Pool: An Information Document: A Joint UK Government Approach to Preventing and Reducing Conflict in Sub-Sahara Africa*, DFID, Ministry of Defense and Foreign and Commonwealth Office, 2004, London. Interview with Simon Bond, Pan-Africa Policy Unit, Africa Directorate, Foreign and Commonwealth Office, 9 August 2006, London. See also DFID, *Africa Conflict Prevention Program Annual Report 2007/8*, London, October 2008. According to this plan, the UK spent

GBP 2.38 million on Pan-African conflict prevention initiatives, GBP 24 million on West African initiatives, GBP 7 million on Southern African initiatives, GPB 19 million on Central African initiatives and GBP 7.5 million on initiatives in the Horn of Africa in 2007/8

[130] Scorgie, "Building African Peacekeeping Capacity: Donors and the African Union's Emerging Peace and Security Architecture," 18. For more information on France's occasional relapse into colonial policies see Franke, "Competing Regionalisms in Africa and the Continent's Emerging Security Architecture."

[131] For more information on RECAMP see Niagalé Bagayoko, *The EU and the Member States: The African Capabilities Building Programs* (Paris: Centre d'Analyse Stratégique, 2007), Oliver de Cevins, "Pour Que RECAMP Ne Rime Plus Avec Décampe," *Défense Nationale* 59, no. 3 (2003): 80-90.

[132] See Sébastien Bergeon, "Vers Une Européanisation De La Politique De Sécurité Et De Défense De La France En Afrique?," *Défense Nationale* 63, no. 1 (2007): 58-60.

[133] Interview with Brig.-Gen. Francois Bigand, French MIL LO to the AU, 14 May 2007, Addis Ababa

[134] For more information on China's growing involvement in Africa see, for example, Ian Taylor, "China's Oil Diplomacy," *International Affairs* 82, no. 5 (2006): 937-59, Ian Taylor, *China and Africa: Engagement and Compromise* (New York: Routledge, 2006), Peter Brookes and Ji Hye Shin, "China's Influence in Africa: Implications for the United States," *Heritage Foundation Backgrounder*, no. 1916 (2006), Denis Tull, "China's Engagement in Africa: Scope, Significance and Consequences," in *Africa in World Politics: Reforming Political Order*, ed. John Harbeson and Donald Rothchild (Boulder: Westview, 2009), 323-44.

[135] See Scorgie, "Building African Peacekeeping Capacity: Donors and the African Union's Emerging Peace and Security Architecture," 18-21.

[136] SHIRBRIG has signed a MoU with EASBRIG regarding cooperation in this respect. Written correspondence with LTC Ugo Bani, Public Information Officer, SHIRBRIG, 3 February 2008. Note that the future of SHIRBRIG is currently uncertain.

[137] R May and G Cleaver, "African Peacekeeping: Still Dependent," *International Peacekeeping* 4, no. 3 (1997): 18.

[138] Cedric de Coning, *Towards a Common Southern African Peacekeeping System, Electronic Briefing Paper No. 16* (Pretoria: Center for International Political Studies, 2004), 4.

11
Challenges to Security Cooperation in Africa

Despite the undeniable progress made over the last few years and the extraordinarily high level of international support, many challenges and obstacles to effective inter-African security cooperation remain. In fact, there are so many that their discussion could (and one day probably will) easily fill several books. This section briefly summarizes some of the most pressing challenges beyond the obvious ones like the scarcity of financial and military resources which have already been covered in great detail elsewhere.[1] These fall into four broadly related categories, namely, (1) challenges associated with the current state of and trends in regional integration, (2) challenges associated with the nature and quality of the international support measures for inter-African security cooperation, (3) challenges associated with the nature of the African support for inter-African security cooperation and (4) challenges associated with the lack of institutional capacity. The challenges associated with the current state of and trends in regional integration include the continuing proliferation of regional groupings, the extensive overlap of memberships within them as well as the competitions between them, the consequences of asymmetrical regionalization and the temptations of formalistic regionalism. The challenges associated with the nature of international support include the hidden agendas, inappropriate interference and overly selective commitment of international donors as well as the resultant inexpedience of many international support measures. The challenges associated with the nature of African support generally relate to the ulterior motives of African states, the fact that the burden of establishing the elaborate security architecture described throughout this book still rest on merely a few shoulders as well as the unfinished nature of Africa's process of self-emancipation. The last category of challenges arises from the serious lack of institutional capacity that still limits the effectiveness of most African organizations. Overcoming these challenges will be the key to a successful African security regime and a huge step towards ending the continent's history of conflict and instability.

The Excessive Number of Regional Organizations

Despite the AU's aforementioned rationalization efforts, the African continent is still overcrowded with organizations and initiatives which share the same purpose but operate independently of each other. Encouraged by the post-Cold War policy preferences of Western powers – most notably the US, Britain and, to some extent, France – for "African solutions to African problems", a multiplicity of these players has also established peace and security structures.[2] The absence of clear lines of communications or a hierarchical structure amongst the latter not only complicates the increasing willingness of sub-regional, regional and continental organizations to take a more proactive role in protecting human security, but also breeds the danger of confusion, duplication of effort and a dissipation of energies and resources. Consequently, it is essential that the AU continues to strengthen its role as authoritative clearinghouse for all cooperative initiatives and clarifies its relations with these initiatives in order to avoid the impression that the various layers of cooperation of inter-African security cooperation are competing for foreign support, political influence and institutional pre-eminence in promoting peace and stability on the continent. For if such perceptions of inter-organizational competition were to arise it might not only undermine all initiatives, but could also lead to a division of Africa's institutional landscape into rivalrous regional blocs as seen in the 1960s.[3]

There are currently at least 42 organizations and institutions on the continent that would need to be integrated into the AU's structure. This task is compounded by the fact that despite the similarities there exist distinct differences in institutional structures, financial patrons as well as ideologies and strategies between these organizations and the AU from which only the former benefit.[4] Fearing a substantial reduction in independence and direct support, these organizations have proven difficult to integrate into the continental framework. While events like the merger of the Accord on Non-Aggression and Defense (ANAD) with ECOWAS raise the hopes for a lasting harmonization of Africa's many confusing and duplicating mechanisms, there thus remains much need for further rationalization and integration of the continent's plethora of peace and security initiatives.

Overlapping Memberships

The institutional chaos is further complicated by the fact that many African states simultaneously belong to more than one intergovernmental body that aspires to a role in security maintenance and conflict management (see Figure 11.1). While this problem of overlapping memberships is, of course, not unique to Africa, its extent and effects may prove particularly detrimental to the continent's infant security architecture.[5] As mentioned before, of the 53 AU member countries, 26 are members of two regional organizations, and 19 are members of three. Two countries (DRC and Swaziland) even belong to four. Only six countries maintain membership in just one regional community.[6] Even though the AU has limited its official collaboration to seven RECs with whom it has signed a Memorandum of Understanding on security cooperation in January 2008, there are at least 14 institutional arrangements within Africa which have established some sort of peace and security mechanism. In West Africa, ECOWAS cohabits with the *Union Économique et Monétaire Ouest-Africaine* (UEMOA), the Manu-River Union (MRU) and the Community of Sahel and Saharan States (CENSAD). In Central Africa, ECCAS overlaps with the *Communauté Économique et Monétaire d'Afrique Centrale* (CEMAC) and the Economic Community of Great Lakes Countries (CEPGL). In Southern Africa, SADC, the South African Customs Union (SACU) and the Indian Ocean Commission (IOC) share their integration spaces with COMESA which, in turn, extends over the whole of Eastern Africa, some states of Northern Africa and Central Africa.[7] This overlap among Africa's organizations not only leads to wasteful duplications of effort and counterproductive competition among countries and institutions, but also tends to dissipate collective efforts towards the common goal of the African Union and muddy the goals of integration. It also adds to the burdens of member states as a country belonging to two or more organizations not only faces multiple financial obligations, but must cope with different meetings, policy decisions, instruments, procedures and schedules.[8]

Given these negative aspects, the AU must strengthen its efforts to disentangle Africa's confusing web of institutional overlaps.[9] However, this may not prove easy as countries often benefit politically from multiple memberships which are seen to justify the extra expenses by increasing a country's regional influence and donor attractiveness. Nonetheless, the AU should, at the very least, clarify the many procedural questions arising from the resultant overlaps. For example, there needs to be a better understanding of priorities and procedures when troops, pre-identified for use by both a sub-regional and regional body, are simultaneously needed in two places at once. Without a well-defined understanding of which organization or crisis area has primacy in these situations, problems with force projection and force generation will continue to be a major hurdle.[10]

Figure 11.1: Membership(s) in Africa's Main Integration Arrangements

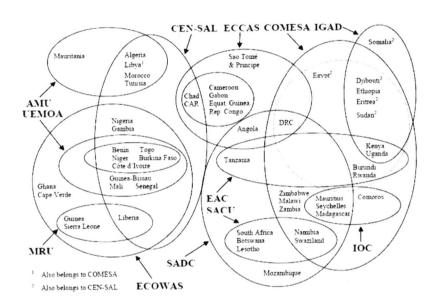

Regionalism as Formalism

While the challenges to continental cooperation arising from Africa's institutional chaos and overlap are relatively straightforward, the difficulties arising from regionalism as formalism and asymmetrical regionalization are less well known though equally serious. The former denotes the problem that Africa seems to have slithered back into a situation whereby the progress of development and integration is measured by the increasing elaborateness of bureaucratic structures and the number of institutions created and protocols passed without necessarily paying any particular attention to the political will or capacity that exist to make sure that these institutions function or that the protocols get implemented.[11] This dichotomy between appearance and capacity and the notable tendency to concentrate on policy formulation rather than implementation has already cost the lives of many a cooperative venture in Africa and will continue to do so until the AU's ongoing rationalization efforts and the concomitant separation of the continent's organizations into viable partners and mere Potemkin villages finally bears fruit.[12]

Asymmetrical Regionalization

Asymmetrical regionalization refers to the uneven development of regional and sub-regional organizations and initiatives due to their differing colonial heritages, political and security agendas, incompatible visions, differing development of member states and widely varying levels of outside support. While there is hardly anyone to blame for these differences, they inevitably hamper the AU's integrationist efforts and undermine the consensus required to pursue a collective security mandate and execute effective responses to conflict through regional and continental initiatives. The resultant tensions are potentially further aggravated by donor-driven capacity-building initiatives which are not always well coordinated and tend to favor some regions and states over others as well as the existence of regional hegemons or hegemonic pretenders.

The Nature of International Support

While the notion of "helping Africans to help themselves" remains the backbone of the West's pro-Africanization rhetoric, the rationale for it has changed with Africa's recent return to the geo-strategic limelight. Instead of the mere burden-shifting of the immediate post-Cold War period, contemporary support activities are once again driven by strategic considerations as a growing number of states are competing for political influence and access to raw materials on the continent. While in theory it should not matter for what reason a political entity supports the process of Africanizing peace and security on the continent as long as it does so, the selective and self-centered nature of this renewed international engagement has already begun to undermine the very foundations of inter-state cooperation in Africa.

First, it has led to a creeping Westernization of African security efforts. Through their increasing involvement in the continent's security affairs and the selective application of their financial muscle, external actors like the US and France but also the UN and the EU have essentially shaped the discussion about the meaning of "African security" in their own image. As a result, a notable dichotomy has developed between how Africans think about the concept of "African security" and how non-Africans think about it.[13] While for many African leaders regime survival continues to play the central role, non-African decision-makers generally focus on the increasingly popular and easier-to-sell notions of "new threats" and "human security" which they have superimposed on the African debate.[14] By focusing their badly-needed support on initiatives which they themselves see in accordance with this distorted debate like the creation of an AU Counter-Terrorism Center, Western actors – China and other non-Western actors have been very careful not to attach conditions to their financial and material support – have essentially abused Africa's dependence on foreign aid in order to shape the emerging security structures to their liking. Even though this coercive institutional isomorphism – that is, the forced assimilation of organizational structures – may have positive side-effects with respect to the bureaucratic efficiency, political sustainability and international compatibility of the resultant African structures, it naturally leads to the question as to how Western the Africanization of Africa's security can become before it looses the crucial support of the Africans themselves.[15]

Second, the commitment of many states, particularly of France and the US, to the notion of "African solutions to African problems" is far from steadfast. In fact, the experience of the last five years clearly shows that Western actors generally only resort to the "African solution" if the problem at hand fulfills one or more of the following criteria: (1) they do not have any immediate interest in it; (2) they do have an immediate interest but do not want to engage directly or alone; (3) it requires a long-term and sustained approach they are unwilling to commit to.[16] France's Janus-faced security policy in Western Africa (once called its *chasse gardée*), America's decision to encourage and actively support Ethiopia's invasion of Somalia and its establishment of a separate combatant command for Africa are all unmistakable signs that the West continues to see the Africanization of African security merely as one policy option of many. Without in any way wishing to diminish the enormous contribution international actors have made to the African missions in Burundi, Darfur, Somalia and the Comoros, the disadvantages of the resultant selectiveness and *ad hoc* nature of most international support measures are hard to miss. For one, it is once again

Western and not African actors that decide on when, where and how the "African solution" is applied because without significant financial and military means of their own African states (and organizations) have no choice but to bow to the strategic, operational and tactical demands of their "benefactors". Cedric de Coning foresaw this negative dependence and its likely consequences for the continent's freedom of action even before the AU was inaugurated.

> Its reliance on foreign funding means that donors could influence which missions the AU can undertake based on their national interests. Donors can determine the duration of a mission, and can influence a mission's mandate by placing terms and conditions on continued funding, or by withdrawing funding if they no longer agree with the scope of the mission.[17]

What he did not foresee, however, was to what extent the West would really make use of its financial muscle to define, shape and control the process of Africanization. Happy to hide behind their support for the principle of "African solutions for African problems" whenever they need to justify their inaction in geo-strategically unimportant places like Darfur or Somalia states like France and the US are quick to ignore this principle when they see vital interests at stake.[18] Over the years this has led to a macabre division of labor between Africans and non-Africans in which the latter have practically outsourced the handling of conflicts they are not themselves willing to engage in to the former under the flimsy banner of Africanization, or as Adekeye Adebajo has put it:

> The battle cry of "African solutions to African problems", coined during the Cold War to rid the continent of foreign meddlers, has cynically been appropriated in the current era. It has been hijacked to promote an apartheid system of peacekeeping in which Africans are expected to spill most of the blood, while the West pays some of the bills in a macabre aristocracy of death.[19]

Given the West's thinly-veiled desire for peacekeeping by proxy, sub-contracting and outsourcing, it is not surprising that its support programs are increasingly seen as yet another instrument of external domination. Rather than "enabling Africans to help themselves", it seems to many that they are merely aimed at "enabling Africans to help the West". If this perceived gap between the West's postulated commitment to the principle of African ownership and the actual level of African control continues to widen, it may eventually erode African support for the emerging structures and thereby undermine the progress made thus far.

The Quality of International Support

A related problem is the actual quality and suitability of the international capacity-building programs. The most serious structural deficiencies cited in the burgeoning literature on international support initiatives are (1) their undue emphasis on peacekeeping training at the expense of the provision of badly-needed military equipment and machinery, (2) their greater responsiveness to immediate crises than to long-term measures and (3) the lack of harmonization and coordination between the multitude of donor initiatives.

Given that their capacity-building commitments also have to appeal to their domestic electorates and international partners, it is not surprising that many donor states (and their institutions) prefer the easy-to-sell provision of peacekeeping training to the supply of deadly military hardware like guns, armored personnel carriers and combat helicopters. Even though the success of robust peace operations like UNAMID and AMISOM depends on the latter, little has changed in the ten years since Eric Berman and Katie Sams argued the following:

> Supplying the type and amount of military equipment that might enable African peacekeepers to respond effectively to crises on their continent is neither financially nor politically feasible; providing low-level peacekeeping training and instruction is. Western initiatives respond principally to domestic political concerns — not African limitations.[20]

Another crucial shortcoming of today's capacity-building programs is that despite their often impressive-looking budgets – the EU's African Peace Facility, for example, has just been replenished with €300 million and the US has committed over US$ 660 million to its Global Peace Operations Initiative – actual funding is rather sporadic and seemingly more responsive to immediate crises than longer-term projects like the ASF or the CEWS. While the readiness of donors to sacrifice the latter for urgently-needed crisis relief is politically understandable, it has nonetheless severely hampered the sustainable development of Africa's security capabilities.

Lastly, the insufficient coordination of donor activities means that the overall impact of international capacity-building support remains far below potential. Even though the G8 Africa Action Plan has identified the unnecessary duplication of efforts and the divisive impact of uncoordinated measures as significant obstacles to capacity-building in Africa and has subsequently called for a better harmonization of bilateral support initiatives, the coordination between the various programs is still weak. Widely differing agendas and political rivalries among the donors have inhibited efforts to overcome this problem which thus continues to undermine the development of strategic approaches and multiplies transaction costs for the AU and other recipients in Africa. Interestingly, insufficient coordination of support activities is not a problem confined to the international level. Even within donor states the various development and security agencies often fail to coordinate their efforts for reasons ranging from inter-agency rivalries and personal turf battles to asymmetric information and constitutional restraints. US assistance, for example, still comes from a variety of independent and often mal-coordinated offices including at least three in the Department of State, several in the Department of Defense, and more from EUCOM and other overseas commands.[21]

The Lack of Commitment by the Majority of Africa's States

Quite naturally, African leaders have been among the most fervent advocates of total and immediate Africanization of Africa's security affairs. Alpha Oumar Konaré, the first chairperson of the AU Commission, for example, used a special meeting of the UN Security Council in September 2007 to remind the world that "the primary responsibility for ensuring peace in Africa belongs to Africans themselves and they must shoulder that responsibility".[22]   This noble rhetoric, however, contrasts starkly with the grim reality on the continent. Instead of the "traditional African values of burden-sharing and mutual assistance" evoked in their Solemn Declaration on a Common African Defense and Security Policy, most of Africa's 53 states have displayed a remarkable lack of political and financial commitment to and interest in the continent's security affairs. As a result, the enormous burden of attempting to Africanize these affairs rests on merely a few shoulders – most notably those of Nigeria, Rwanda, Uganda and South Africa where troop contributions to African-led missions are concerned and Ethiopia, Libya and Kenya where financial support to the emerging security structures is concerned.[23] Consequently, the AU finds it ever more difficult to man, equip and sustain its growing array of security initiatives. Its faltering mission in Somalia, for example, remains woefully understaffed – almost two years after its launch it still consists of nothing but a handful of Ugandan troops – and it is also still more than two thirds short of its promised troop contribution to the UN's hybrid force in Darfur.

While the reluctance of many states to contribute more than words to the process of Africanization has to be seen in the context of their often disastrous economic situation (after all, 38 out of the world's 50 least developed countries are in Africa), the lack of broad support beyond the occasional common declaration undermines the very idea of Africanization. Most crucially, it erodes the illusion of Africanization as a Pan-African project. Instead it feeds suspicions that those states that do promote the process and actively contribute to it do so for purely self-serving rather than universally beneficial reasons. Especially Nigeria, Kenya, Libya and Ethiopia have regularly been accused of abusing the AU's emerging security architecture as vehicle for their hegemonic ambitions. This in turn deters many smaller states from increasing their commitments to the AU-led process and instead leads them to concentrate their support on their respective sub-regional and/or regional organizations where they expect greater and more direct returns on their investments (that is, more control over the use of their contributions). Despite the Memorandum of Understanding between the AU and the seven regional organizations it officially recognizes as pillars of its security architecture, this continues to prevent a unitary African approach. Instead, it advances the fragmentation of the process of Africanization into several broadly-related but not fully compatible sub-processes that had begun with the devolution of security initiatives in the early 1990s. While nothing in the underlying idea of "African solutions to African problems" actually requires the Africanization of security to be a centralized process, its fragmentation is undoubtedly fraught with certain disadvantages (even though it may help to keep the smaller states committed). First, it leads to an unnecessary duplication of efforts and structures. Second, it dilutes the potential impact of the international support measures.[24] Lastly, it also raises the question of how the continent's current plethora of intergovernmental organizations and institutions are going to evade the self-destructive rivalries which have characterized Africa's institutional landscape for so long and which have prevented effective sub-regional and regional cooperation ever since the beginning of decolonization?

The Nature of African Support

Just as in the case of the international actors, the specific reasons for which African states support the emerging system of inter-African cooperation should not be too important as long as they do not have any adverse effects on the realization of the system itself. Some of these reasons and the states' resultant behavior, however, severely restrict the quality and sustainability of the ongoing cooperation in security affairs. For example, the tendency of some states to openly declare themselves part of the Africanization process seems to be motivated more by a desire for Western arms and training which they can use for internal security measures than by the willingness to be part of a continental conflict management effort, or as Paul Omach once argued: "States participating [in international capacity building programs] do so with the primary motive of strengthening their military forces to deal with internal conflicts rather than the need to participate in regional peacekeeping."[25] The last few years have seen states like Nigeria, Senegal and Uganda using military hardware and training obtained under the pretext of Africanization to crush their domestic opposition and rebel movements.[26] Another motivation that has already begun to undermine the credibility of African efforts is their use as excuse for and justification of African inaction. Examples that immediately come to mind include the continent's unfortunate insistence on an "African solution" for the crisis in Zimbabwe and the AU's mishandling of Kenya's electoral impasse in 2008.

The Unfinished Nature of Africa's Self-Emancipation

The unfinished nature of Africa's self-emancipation is another factor that limits the sustainability of the ongoing process of Africanization and quality of the resultant inter-African cooperation. Especially the deep-running divisions and rivalries that continue to exist between many African states (for example, between Anglophones and Francophones) as well as their susceptibility to outside interference and manipulation must foster serious doubts about the continent's ability to promote the Africanization of security beyond its current level. As long as Africa's states continue to think and act in artificially-created categories and maintain closer links with their colonial or neo-colonial masters than with each other, further progress is unlikely. Unfortunately, the geo-strategically motivated reengagement of the international community in the continent's affairs has already begun to reverse the process of African self-emancipation that seemed so promising not even a decade ago.

The AU's Lack of Institutional Capacity

As argued earlier in this study, the functionality of Africa's emerging peace and security architecture is heavily dependent on an efficient and credible African Union as an embodiment of a renewed Pan-Africanism and a catalyst for continental integration. However, as an organization with a huge and diverse membership representing a poor and conflict-ridden continent the AU faces a number of challenges to its unifying efforts such as managing the impending "implementation crisis" from within or fulfilling the world's high expectations despite its meager funding and enormous capacity constraints. The legacy of the OAU is one of repeated implementation crises, in which the high-reaching goals of the organization's initiatives regularly failed to attain sufficient commitment from the continent's leaders and the international community. Many fear that a similar fate may await the AU's current security initiatives, a concern based significantly on recent events such as the operational shortcomings and financial bankruptcy of AMIS, the recurrence of conflict in Somalia, the organization's lenient attitude towards Mugabe's Zimbabwe as well its failure to react to both the electoral crisis in Kenya as well as the civil war in the DRC's eastern provinces, all of which were widely seen as signs of the AU's dysfunction. With these failures adding up to the trenchant memories of past misdeeds and antagonistic interactions, it is hardly surprising that the level of trust African countries currently put in the AU occasionally appears insufficient for building a durable and truly collaborative security architecture.

The effect of this lack of trust is compounded by the AU's inability to restore confidence in its leadership role through financial means. Despite the fact that a large proportion of the AU's budget is spent on peace and security initiatives (more than $70 million out of a total of $139 million in 2008) member states appear to feel very little direct impact. Instead, there is a growing feeling among regional lead states that the meager benefits of membership do not justify an increasing submission to the AU's authority in the delicate field of security. While the calls for the AU to finally earn the right to be the senior authoritative structure on the continent are thus growing louder, the AU is simply lacking the resources to fulfill this demand. Despite substantial outside support through the aforementioned international initiatives, the AU is suffering from an enormous resource and capacity constraint which has impacted and will continue to impact on the extent to which the organization is able to commit meaningfully to continental security through both the support of regional and sub-regional efforts as well as its own initiatives. Identified as *"the* major problem of the AU" by Alex Ramsbotham and Alhaji Bah in 2005 and reconfirmed by an external audit in 2007, the lack of institutional human resource capacity continues to cripple the organization's institutional effectiveness.[27] For instance, the AU's PSC has a huge mandate but still has no sufficiently-staffed secretariat to support its work. Its Peace Support Operations Division tries to run several operations and simultaneously coordinate the establishment of the ASF and the CEWS while being as much as 55 percent short of the personnel strength agreed upon at the 2003 Maputo Summit. Operational pressures such as those to respond to the crises in Darfur and Somalia further exacerbate already weak headquarters capacity for strategic, long-term planning and development. Naturally, such shortcomings cause many difficulties for international capacity building efforts. For example, the AU's resultant inability to determine clearly the specifics of what support it wants and how that support should be delivered weakens its capacity to secure coherent donor assistance for identified priorities and the lack of financial audit and administrative staff dealing with peace funds reduces its absorption capacity for aid.

Summary

These are just some of the thorny issues and Herculean tasks that Africa will have to face on its way to achieving effective and sustainable inter-state security cooperation. There are countless other difficulties such as the inherent weakness of many African states, the still insufficient involvement of civil society and the prevalence of divisive conflict and rivalry on virtually every corner of the continent. Even though notable progress has been made with respect to the Africanization of security, the diffusion of norms, the institutionalization of cooperation and the consolidation of partnerships, without further commitment by its member states and the international community the AU's peace and security architecture risks the same tragic fate as the organization's erstwhile flagship operation in Darfur.

Notes

[1]   For a taste of the literature on the scarcity of financial and military resources and its impact on inter-African security cooperation see Theo Neethling, "Realizing the African Standby Force as a Pan-African Deal: Progress, Prospects and Challenges," *Journal of Military and Strategic Studies* 8, no. 1 (2005).

[2]   Mats Berdal, "Peacekeeping in Africa, 1990-1996: The Role of the United States, France and Britain," in *Peacekeeping in Africa*, ed. Oliver Furley and Roy May (Aldershot: Ashgate, 1998), 50.

[3]   Meant is the rivalry between the Casablanca and Monrovia blocs of states described in chapter three.

[4]   For example, Francis Cupri argued in the US Army War College Quarterly (Parameters) that the United States should support sub-regional organizations such as ECOWAS rather than the AU as they offer "a greater return on US investment". See Francis V. Crupi, "Why the United States Should Robustly Support Pan-African Organizations," Parameters, no. 4 (2005): 106-123.

[5]   Europe also has a highly complex regional security architecture that includes the UN, the EU and its various institutions, the 55-member Organization for Security and Co-operation in Europe (OSCE), the 26-member NATO and the 28-member West European Union (WEU). Contrary to Africa, these arrangements can draw on the support of wealthy industrialized states which adds to the viability of such arrangements, even though it may not relieve the confusion.

[6]   United Nations Economic Commission for Africa, *Assessing Regional Integration in Africa* (UNECA, Addis Ababa, 2004), 39-40.

[7]   African Union Commission/Economic Commission for Africa, *Report on Meeting of Experts on the Rationalization of the Regional Economic Communities* (AU Document EX.CC/220(VIII), 2005, Addis Ababa) 3.

[8]   United Nations Economic Commission for Africa, *Assessing Regional Integration in Africa* (UNECA, Addis Ababa, 2004), 41. Burundi has recently suspended its membership in ECCAS in order to limit its integration obligation to fewer regional organizations. This could be seen as a sign of a beginning rationalization of multiple memberships had Burundi not almost simultaneously joined the EAC in order to be part of Eastern Africa's integrationist efforts.

[9]   For ongoing efforts to rationalize these overlaps see African Union, Report of the Consultative Meeting on the Rationalization of the Regional Economic Communities (RECs) for Eastern and Southern Africa, 2006, Addis Ababa, 5-6.

[10]   Patricia Taft and Jason Ladnier, *Realizing "Never Again" - Regional Capacities to Protect Civilians in Violent Conflicts* (Washington DC: Fund for Peace, 2006), 6.

[11]   For a good but somewhat out of date discussion on this issue see, for example, Senzo Ngubane and Hussein Solomon, *Projects Gone Too Far: Sub-*

Regional Security Efforts in Africa (Pretoria: Centre for International Political Studies, 2001), 6.

[12] Jeffrey Herbst, "Crafting Regional Cooperation in Africa," in *Crafting Cooperation: Regional International Institutions in Comparative Perspective*, ed. Amitav Acharya and Alastair Johnston (Cambridge: Cambridge University Press, 2007), 129.

[13] David Chuter, *Into Africa, Always Something New: Telling Africans what their Security Problems Are*, Conference Presentation, Royal United Services Institute Conference on AFRICOM, 18 February 2008.

[14] This is the result of a study presented by Major Shannon Beebe at the Royal United Services Conference on AFRICOM, 18 February 2008, London. For a detailed discussion see Caroline Thomas and Peter Wilkin, eds., *Globalization, Human Security and the African Experience* (Boulder: Lynne Rienner, 1999).

[15] For more information on the notion of coercive institutional isomorphism see Paul DiMaggio and Walter Powell, "The Iron Cage Revisited: Institutional Isomorphism and Collective Rationality in Organizational Fields," *American Sociological Review* 48 (1983): 147-160.

[16] For an informative discussion of the argument that "the growing reliance on regional organizations is a result of an unwillingness to commit rather than because the idea has intrinsic merit" see Jane Boulden, *Dealing with Conflict in Africa: The United Nations and Regional Organizations* (Basingstoke: Palgrave Macmillan, 2003), 30.

[17] Cedric de Coning, "Peacekeeping in Africa: The Next Decade," *Conflict Trends*, no. 3 (2002): 53.

[18] There are a couple of good examples. For instance, many African leaders were taken by surprise by the UK's intervention in Sierra Leone in 2002 and the second EU operation in the Democratic Republic of Congo (Operation Artemis, April-November 2006) was launched despite the protests of many African countries.

[19] Adekeye Adebajo, "Tread Warily through the Politics of Peacekeeping," *Sunday Times*, 29 April 2007.

[20] Eric Berman and Katie Sams, *Constructive Disengagement: Western Efforts to Develop African Peacekeeping, Monograph Series No. 33* (Pretoria: Institute for Security Studies, 1998).

[21] See Benedikt Franke, "Enabling a Continent to Help Itself: US Military Capacity Building and Africa's Emerging Security Architecture," *Strategic Insights* VI, no. 1 (2007).

[22] Special Meeting of the UN Security Council on Africa, September 2007.

[23] For more information on African troop contributions to ongoing peace operations see *Annual Review of Global Peace Operations 2007*. New York: Center on International Cooperation

[24] Cedric de Coning has rightly argued that the AU's emerging peace and security architecture "epitomizes a much needed common objective which helps to channel the multiplicity of resources, initiatives and ambitions devoted to African peace and security efforts into one direction". See Cedric de Coning, *Towards a Common Southern African Peacekeeping System, Electronic Briefing Paper No. 16* (Pretoria: Center for International Political Studies, 2004), 4.

25   Paul Omach, "The African Crisis Response Initiative: Domestic Politics and Convergence of National Interests," *African Affairs* 99 (2000): 73.

26   Nigeria has used material and training originally provided for its ECOWAS activities to fight the rebels in the Niger Delta. Uganda has used troops trained and equipped through Western capacity-building programs in its counter-insurgency campaign against the Lord's Resistance Army while Senegal has done likewise in its operations in the Casamance region.

27   Alex Ramsbotham, Alhaji Bah, and Fanny Calder, "Enhancing African Peace and Security Capacity: A Useful Role for the UK and the G8?," *International Affairs* 81, no. 2 (2005): 334.

12
Conclusion

Over 2000 years ago, the Roman statesman Pliny the Elder marvelled *"Ex Africa semper aliquid novi"* (always something new from Africa). While it is unlikely that Pliny made this comment with regard to inter-African security cooperation, it fits the subject of this book very well. For the empirical findings discussed above show that the conceptual debate about inter-state security cooperation would be incomplete without a critical understanding of the developments in Africa. The insights gained from the detailed analysis of the AU's emerging security architecture reconfirm the suspicion uttered in chapter two that mono-causal theories of cooperation like realism and neo-liberal institutionalism are inadequate to explain fully the evolution and contemporary pattern of inter-state security cooperation on the continent. The findings instead suggest that there are a number of additional issue areas which a more appropriate theory has to take into account if it is to make sense of inter-African cooperation. First, the central role of socialized identities and ideational factors in motivating African states to cooperate with each other clearly demonstrates that inter-subjective factors cannot be ignored when studying security relations on the continent. Second, the role of institutions in fostering these relations must not be underestimated. Third, an appreciation of the various logics of regionalism is essential to understand the observed extent and quality of contemporary inter-African security cooperation.

Before concluding the book with a summary of its main arguments, this chapter will briefly elaborate on the theoretical implications of these three insights. It thereby argues that none of them is to be taken to mean that the material forces of realist theory have lost their importance to the study of international cooperation. Instead, the African experience merely shows that the attention to the concern for power and sovereignty that undoubtedly continues to permeate international relations must be complemented by an understanding of the occasions where these concerns are balanced against competing objectives or even muted altogether. Without such an understanding it is simply impossible to comprehend the recent proliferation of cooperative ventures on the African continent, particularly in the field of peace and security.

The Role of Inter-Subjectivity

Undoubtedly the most important insight to emerge from this study is the prominence of inter-subjective factors in the reasons motivating African states to intensify their security cooperation. The previous chapters have shown that it is virtually impossible to understand the dynamics of this cooperation without reference to constructivist concepts such as collective identity formation, norm diffusion, social learning and community-building. Even though it is hard to measure their impact empirically, these factors have unquestionably advanced inter-African security cooperation through the fostering of shared meanings and the generation of collective interests.

A telling example is the role played by Pan-Africanism and related concepts like the African Renaissance or the African Century. Pan-Africanism has a long history as unifying factor in inter-African relations. As mentioned before, it was first utilized as a political instrument and ideology in the struggle for decolonization in the late 1950s and early 1960s. During this period, political leaders like Kwame Nkrumah used it to mobilize the continent and its goal of African unity was regarded as "the locomotive to solve the myriad of problems faced by the newly independent states".[1] The resultant Pan-African euphoria, however, was only short-lived. Once independence was achieved, the meaning and objectives of Pan-Africanism were generally domesticated and national integration and development took precedence over the concern for inter-African cooperation. It was not until the end of the Cold War that Pan-Africanism began to resurface as a political force when, in the words of David Francis, the diverse and pressing problems of the era again forced on African leaders the "imperative for unity".[2] Spurred by a growing sense of urgency and hope for an African renaissance, these leaders quickly rediscovered the usefulness of the unifying ideology of Pan-Africanism as vehicle for their cooperative efforts. While it is difficult to gauge the impact of the resultant wave of cooperative Pan-Africanism, the promotion of a collective African identity and the resultant desire to minimize non-African interference in the affairs of the continent certainly advanced the formation of what Benedict Anderson has called an "imagined community".

Very much in contrast to traditional theories of regional cooperation and integration, this imagined community in many ways preceded rather than resulted from political, strategic and functional interactions and interdependence. Karl Deutsch is representative of those scholars who hold that a community is the final product, or terminal condition, of a process of integration which is driven by the need to cope with the conflict-causing effects of increased transactions. According to him, the growing volume and range of transactions – political, economic or cultural – increases the opportunities for possible conflict among the actors, forcing them to devise institutions and practices for peaceful adjustment and change.[3] But in the case of Africa, regional cooperation was undertaken in the absence of high levels of functional interdependence or interaction. The African Union and many of its regional sub-groupings evolved despite low levels of economic transactions and the existence of substantial political and situational differences among their members. Central to this process was a set of Pan-African norms, among which continental solidarity and an increasing desire to minimize reliance on the "goodwill" of the international community were the most salient.

In 1995, Ali Mazrui suggested that the emerging wave of Pan-Africanism was based on the dual rationales of "poetry and imperialism".[4] He argued that the collective historical experiences of colonial suppression and memories of marginalization and socio-cultural and racial affinities shared by most African states made them particularly receptive for concepts like Thabo Mbeki's African Renaissance which suggested that the future would bring peace, prosperity and cultural revival to Africa if only its states were finally prepared to cooperate in light of the otherwise insurmountable challenges ahead. The resultant collective solidarity – a sense of oneness akin to the feeling of "we-ness" described by Deutsch – became a powerful mobilizing and unifying force which contributed substantially to the revival of continental security cooperation. Naturally, not all states of the continent were equally part of this process of community-building and some, like Libya, even manipulated it for their own purposes, but in general it seems fair to say that most states in sub-Saharan Africa came to rediscover the benefits of a communal approach to problem-solving in the 1990s and increasingly formulated their objectives in the light of Pan-African norms and understandings.

Hence, while the process-based integrationist models of liberal theory may provide a key rationale for the evolution of cooperation in Europe, they miss important aspects of the African experience because they ignore the powerful motivational impact of inter-subjective factors such as collective identities and shared values. This is, however, not to say that the conceptual pathway suggested by the liberal school in which increasing interaction provides the basis necessary for the development of mutual trust and thus sustainable cooperation is not applicable to Africa. Inter-African security cooperation certainly did not appear out of thin air.

Instead, the book showed that the states of the continent were able to take a number of shortcuts on the liberals' conceptual pathway, because the basis for the development of trust had long been established by their shared histories of subjugation and marginalization, unmarred for the most part by historic enmities (naturally, there are exceptions like Ethiopia and Eritrea). The resultant sense of what Anderson had called a "deep, horizontal comradeship" and the shared desire for emancipation nurtured over decades of external domination thus provided at least part of the basis for cooperation normally fostered through long interactive processes.[5]

Process nonetheless remains essential. As illustrated by Monica Juma with reference to the experiences in the IGAD and EAC regions, "sustainable security is process-based, as opposed to being a quick fix, deliverable product".[6] Devoting attention to process is of the utmost importance, because it forms the building blocks of trust, a critical prerequisite for all cooperative ventures. In the context of regionalized conflicts, process acquires even greater significance because of the psycho-political dynamics involved. As observed by Michelle Parlevliet, "to overcome negative feelings and perceptions so that structural issues can be addressed, protagonists have to develop trust in the process and in those who guide it".[7] Thus, whether security is sought in a conflict-ridden environment (IGAD), or as a conflict prevention strategy (EAC), it is a process that is based on consensus-building, trust and networking between various sectors of society at the local, national and international level.

The Importance of Institutions

Another important insight to emerge from this study is the pivotal role played by institutions in the development and maintenance of inter-African cooperation. This role is interesting not so much because it differs from that predicted by conventional theories like neo-liberal institutionalism, but because it expands on it. In addition to the commonly cited functions of institutions (that is, they encourage communication, disseminate information, reduce transaction costs and synthesize state interests), the African experience has shown them to contribute in at least three other crucial ways to inter-state security cooperation on the continent. First, they help to socialize their member states according to group norms. Second, they shape the processes of goal selection and the strategies adopted to achieve these goals. Third, they provide the vital link between the different layers of inter-state security cooperation and reduce the number of actors in a complex setting to a manageable level.

Contrary to the traditional rational choice theories of cooperation that assume actors' preferences and interests to be fixed, social constructivism allows for the possibility that interests, and even the identities on which these interests are based, are conditioned by institutional or social structures. Bruce Cronin, for example, has argued that while transnational identities play a crucial role in determining the type of security arrangement states enter into, causality can also work the other way.[8] According to him, transnational identities are often institutionalized within international associations that help to socialize their members according to group norms.[9] To the degree that the association is taken as a positive reference group, the participants take on the roles associated with them. The exclusive nature of these associations thereby helps to highlight the self-other distinction that forms the basis of an identity and strengthens the transnational identities the institutions embody. Thus, Cronin would predict that states become more "African" by participating in the African Union and more "West African" by participating in ECOWAS. According to Michael Smith, such an identity development does not even require a "transfer" of loyalty to the institution, but only a redefinition or expansion of national identity to include also the collectivity symbolized by it.[10]

While there is a substantial body of literature on the European dimension of this phenomenon, Africa's institutional landscape has not yet attracted any attention in this respect.[11] This study suggests that there is indeed evidence that increasing participation in institutional projects has conditioned how African states have defined their goals and how they have behaved in order to achieve those goals. Take, for example, the case of the new legal regime of ECOWAS described in chapter ten. Its emphasis on supra-nationality at the expense of national ratification processes clearly shows that the states of West Africa have at least partly reconstituted their behavior and interests in terms of regional norms rather than national ones and there are many indications that this reconstitution is the result of their positively perceived membership in ECOWAS. The same holds true for the continental level. The ongoing discussion about a Union Government as a stepping stone towards a political unification of the continent, however utopian it may be, illustrates how far African states have come since the establishment of the AU in 2002. Even though it is difficult to ascertain to what extent the internalization of collective norms that can be observed throughout Africa's institutional landscape is the result of what has once been referred to as the "Helsinki Effect", it is unquestionable that there is a conditioning momentum within many of Africa's institutions that is not captured by traditional theories of cooperation.[12]

Another noteworthy characteristic of the AU and its institutional pillars is the extent to which their bureaucratic components shape the processes of goal selection and the strategies adopted to achieve these goals in a way that fosters further cooperation. Contrary to most national bureaucracies in Africa, the multi-national bureaucracies of organizations like SADC, ECOWAS and the AU are staffed by well-trained professionals whose generally positive disposition towards greater functional cooperation is a factor whose role in the factual intensification of inter-African cooperation should not be underestimated. Again, there is much research on this issue of bureaucratic "self-actualization" with respect to international organizations like the EU or the UN, but hardly any relating to the African continent and its institutions even though the principal-agent problem underlying this phenomenon appears to be much more pronounced there for two reasons.[13] First, the capacity of national structures to control and influence decisions at the level of international organizations is significantly more limited in Africa than in, for example, Europe. Second, in contrast to institutions in the developed world, there is substantial outside pressure on African institutions to stimulate and structure political discourse and facilitate cognitive convergence in a way that leads to greater and more sustainable cooperation among their member states. Coupled with the bureaucracies' generally positive attitude towards functional cooperation (which in itself may be the result of the aforementioned conditioning momentum as well as a certain degree of institutional isomorphism[14]), these factors may mean that the member states of African institutions like the AU or SADC have potentially less limiting control over the cooperative initiatives of these institutions than is commonly assumed.

The third insight with respect to the role of institutions is the extent to which inter-state cooperation can thrive within a group of well-coordinated institutions, so-called policy networks, with a clear governance structure.[15] The analyses of the ASF and the CEWS have shown that the level of security cooperation in all five regions of the continent has increased significantly as a result of the clearinghouse activities of the AU and the particular design of the emerging security architecture. The latter's poly-centric and multi-level structure in which the regional layers function as relatively autonomous implementation agencies of the continental layer within a framework of organized complementarity is particularly well-suited to overcome the inhibitions to cooperation usually associated with large numbers of actors.[16] The reliance on the regions as intermediate level of interaction not only significantly reduces the number of actors the AU PSOD has to deal with (from 53 states to 5 regions) and thus eases the identification and realization of common interests, but it also allows all states to continue to feel ownership in inter-African security cooperation and thereby reduces the risk of failure.

The Logics of Regionalism

The book has also shown the importance of regionalism for theorizing inter-state security cooperation. As briefly alluded to in the introduction, the concepts of regionalism and regionalization have long been an important part of the academic discourse on inter-state cooperation, but it has only been with Björn Hettne's so-called new regionalisms that the apparent resurgence of regional cooperation throughout the world has found adequate theoretical coverage.[17] Arguing that the present round of regionalization is qualitatively different from that observed in the 1950s and 1960s, Hettne called for a reappraisal of the traditional approaches to the logic of regionalism. An unquestionable advantage of the resultant new regionalisms concept is its multidimensionality and compatibility with constructivist reasoning as both characteristics are essential to understand the continuous growth in popularity of regional actions among Africa's states.

Over fifty years ago, Louis Wirth observed that "regionalism is not one thing, but many things".[18] This seems to be particularly true for Africa. Even a cursory glance at the continent's regional organizations suggests that a single logic of regionalism is not sufficient to explain the multitude of cooperation and integration arrangements that have sprung up over the last decade. While the idea that one theory (or set of theories) may provide appropriate understandings of them all has long been criticized, this has not stopped scholars from producing universal models of integration or reapplying theories based on highly specific contexts such as the European. This study, however, has found that, at least as far as the regionalization of inter-state security cooperation is concerned, there are substantial differences between the logics of regionalism across the continent and the various layers of cooperation. In the EAC, for example, inter-subjective factors such as the existence of a common East African identity including a common language (Swahili) certainly played a much larger role in the intensification of inter-state security relations than they did in IGAD or ECCAS. There other logics of regionalism such as the need to counteract the increasing regionalization of domestic instability and civil wars or external donor pressure provided the main rationales for and paths to increasing security cooperation. Also, while the institutionalization of security cooperation in some regions broadly resembles the European experience in the extent to which they were preceded by increasing functional integration in other fields (mostly economics) and several *ad hoc* initiatives, other regions have intensified their security relations without high levels of economic and political interaction to build upon. A crucial characteristic all paths to regional cooperation appear to share, however, is the central role of hegemonic ambitions.[19]   Nigeria's instrumentalization of ECOWAS, Kenya's rivalry with Ethiopia over primacy in the Horn of Africa and IGAD as well as the competition between South Africa and Zimbabwe over the control of SADC have all, for better or worse, shaped the evolution of the respective regional organizations. On the continental level, the importance of hegemons or hegemonic pretenders seems less pronounced. Africa's large states have not always seen their goals realized nor have they always taken the lead on every major policy or institutional innovation. Instead, the smaller states have often played more important roles in the development of Africa's collaborative security regime in terms of its policies and procedural development than most theories of regionalization would expect.[20]

This last point sheds light on another important finding. There appears to be a significant difference between the motivations for security cooperation at the regional and the continental levels. Naturally, this is at least partly due to the particular attractions of each layer of cooperation, but there is also evidence that the inter-subjective aspect of security cooperation is generally less pronounced at the regional level because hard power considerations often remain the dominating rationale. At the continental level, however, inter-subjective factors seem to be less overshadowed by such considerations. Whether this is because states feel that they have less to lose or more to gain from ideologically charged cooperation at this level is an issue that will have to be clarified in further research.

All the above shows that the regionalization of security cooperation has taken many paths in Africa and that no single logic of regionalism can provide a coherent explanation for all of them. Instead, the variety of motivations for and contemporary patterns of regionalization efforts in the field of peace and security necessitates a certain theoretical flexibility, once referred to as the "diversity approach" by Ademola

Abass.[21] While one particular case may be best explained by Barry Buzan's regional security complex theory, Arie Kacowicz's concept of zones of peace may be better suited to explain others.[22] The challenge is to avoid the temptation to succumb to the many commonalities of the various regionalisms which have been covered in this study and, as a result, to believe in a single logic of regionalization.

While the lack of a unifying theory is certainly disappointing from an academic perspective, it fits well into the multi-dimensional framework of Hettne's new regionalisms. Its constructivist ontologies serve well to fuse distinct theoretical approaches, not only because they often provide some of their explanatory power,[23] but also because they are able to incorporate insights such as the notion of issue-linkage of more traditional analyses of regional integration like those by Ernst Haas and Philippe Schmitter without falling prey to their materialistic focus.[24] Contrary to rationalist approaches which attempt to explain regional processes and international cooperation purely with the help of strategic interests and relative gains and losses, a constructivist approach to regional cooperation thus allows for "a theoretically rich and promising way of conceptualizing the interaction between material incentives, inter-subjective structures and the identity and interests of the actors".[25] The findings of this study have shown that only such an open, non-deterministic approach can hope to provide an appropriate theoretical framework for the study of inter-state security cooperation in Africa.

Bringing the Traditional Theories Back in

Despite the fact that most of the above findings appear to challenge the very substance of traditional theories like realism and neo-liberal institutionalism, this study does not argue that these theoretical approaches have become totally irrelevant to the analysis of inter-state cooperation. Far from it, the study has actually highlighted the continuing relevance of material and rationalist explanations for cooperation, but not without drawing attention to the previously neglected inter-subjective component of African security relations. For this reason, its purpose should not be seen so much as an attempt to refute a positivist approach to cooperation, but rather as an effort to expand on it.

There is substantial evidence that realist theory in particular continues to hold many insights for assessing inter-African relations, particularly with respect to the self-interested rationales for cooperation.

For contrary to the new regionalists' insistence that the effects of globalization are inevitably eroding the Westphalian nation state,[26] the African experience has shown that the end of the era of nationalism is not remotely in sight. Instead, a key to understanding the rise of regional cooperation in Africa, as Jeffrey Herbst has pointed out, is to "discard the assumption that there is an inevitable conflict between sovereignty (or, more precisely, the prerogatives of individual leaders) and regional cooperation".[27] Herbst attributes the African style of socialization and regional institution-building to a shared predicament of the rulers in securing regime legitimacy and a common aversion to external interference in their domestic affairs. According to him, the behavior of Libya's Muammar al-Gaddafi, Sudan's Omar al-Bashir and Zimbabwe's Robert Mugabe shows the extent to which African leaders promote regional or continental cooperation with the aim of enhancing their own domestic standing and cementing their state's regional power status.[28] Herbst concluded that African leaders are only enthusiastic about those types of cooperation that help to secure national power structures and ask for little in return and that this is proven by the fact that the type of cooperation statistically most likely to fail does not adhere to these characteristics.[29]

Even if one rejects Herbst's personality-driven characterization of Africa's political landscape, it is hard to miss the extent to which narrow state interests continue to shape the design of cooperation arrangements on the continent, especially at the regional level. However, rather than presenting a potent challenge to the constructivist approach advocated throughout this study, this "rational design of international institutions" once again helps to show the heuristic beauty of Alexander Wendt's concept of multiple realizability.[30] As argued in chapter two, this concept is based on the argument that there are (at least) three reasons why actors observe cultural norms, namely, (1) because they are forced to, (2) because it is in their self-interest, and (3) because they perceive the norms as legitimate.[31] Rather than accepting these three rationales as expressions of three different (and mutually exclusive) theoretical approaches to the impact of norms on international relations, namely, neo-realist, neo-liberal and idealist theories respectively, Wendt takes them to reflect different degrees to which norms have been internalized by the actors.

Applied to the African context, this means that instead of holding deep structure responsible for the "realist" behavior observed across the continent, his version of constructivism points to the endurance of interactive practices that reproduce and sustain such behavior. Coupled with the idea that the same effect can be reached through different causes, this constructivist explanation holds the key for "bringing traditional theories back in" because it allows for different logics of, and paths to, security cooperation. A Kantian culture like that embodied by Africa's emerging Peace and Security Architecture (APSA) which is characterized by a high degree of cooperation does therefore not necessarily have to be associated with cultural internalization of the third degree but can also be a product of purely self-interested compliance resulting from the threat of punishment (first degree) or the simple benefits of cooperation (second degree).[32] This means that the constructivist framework can account for both extremes of motivational factors, the "egoistic" motivation for cooperation identified by Herbst as well as the ideological motivation so typical of the security community argument.

Figure 12.1: The Multiple Realization of Inter-African Security Cooperation[33]

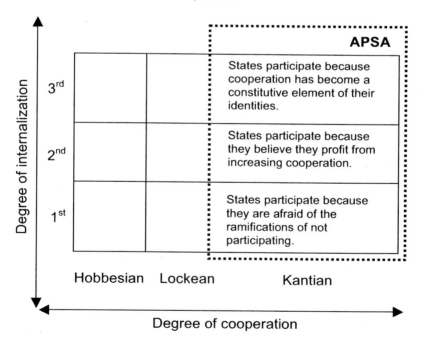

Figure 12.1 uses Wendt's stylized representation of the three cultures of anarchy to illustrate the multiple realizability of inter-African security cooperation within the framework of APSA. It shows that there are (at

least) three paths to participation in the continental security architecture, beginning with participation on the basis of fear of the ramifications of refusal like regional ostracism or a reduction in international assistance. Given that no African leader wants to be seen as opposing the Pan-African project, this might be a widespread rationale. The second path to inter-state cooperation is probably the most common among the states of Africa. They participate in APSA because of its benefits such as international recognition and military support. Gaddafi's Libya is a clear case in point. The last path is the one described in detail in the section on security communities and, certainly, the rarest at the present time. Here states participate in the collective security effort because it has become a constitutive element of their identities and interests. Naturally, all three paths may overlap and rationales may differ for different layers of cooperation, but the underlying idea remains relatively straightforward. African states cooperate with each other for very different reasons and even though the concern for power and sovereignty enshrined in the traditional theories continues to permeate most of them, constructivist approaches have the added benefit of also being able to account for those instances where this concern is balanced against competing objectives or muted altogether.

Summary

The end of the immediate post-Cold War era and the dissatisfaction with prevailing approaches to international relations have opened new spaces for theorizing about world politics. This book took a fresh look at inter-state security cooperation in Africa. Its main theoretical conclusions are that the developments on the continent provide a powerful understanding of the motivations for, and evolutionary patterns of inter-state security cooperation and that a constructivist approach offers a useful theoretical lens through which to examine and explore these motivations and evolutionary patterns as well as their institutional manifestations.

More specifically, the study has found that inter-subjective factors such as collective identities – ranging from a simple sense of belonging based on common historical experiences and shared developmentalist ideologies to a determination for political unification according to Pan-African ideals – have played a central role in the way African states have come to interact with each other over the last decade. This importance of the inter-subjective in inter-African security relations is one of the reasons why constructivist thinking so substantially enriches the analysis of inter-state cooperation on the continent. While traditional theories of cooperation like realism and neo-liberal institutionalism severely downplay the social and ideational aspects of trans-national security relationships, constructivism bases much of its explanatory power on ideas, norms and sociological processes such as collective identity formation, social learning and community building. As argued in the previous section, this emphasis on the inter-subjective, however, does not mean that constructivism cannot also account for the obvious validity of key aspects of the traditional theories in the context of Africa's emerging peace and security architecture. On the contrary, Alexander Wendt has shown that constructivist ideas about the importance of ideational structures and the mutually constitutive relationship between actors and structures can sit comfortably with the prevalence of "realist" behavior in some parts of the continent. Rather than holding deep structure responsible for the radically self-interested and competitive conceptions of inter-state relations observed across Africa, constructivism simply points to the endurance of interactive practices that reproduce and sustain those conceptions.

The study has also drawn attention to the importance of the African experience for theorizing inter-state security cooperation. It has attempted to show that the continent's theoretical marginalization has impoverished the academic debate on international cooperation by limiting it to the experiences of the developed world. The unfortunate assumption by many scholars that Africa has little to contribute to theory-building has not only glossed over the conceptually rich patterns of inter-state relations on the continent, but is has also left large parts of IR theory untested in a variety of important circumstances. As a result, theories like realism and neo-liberal institutionalism that allegedly expound a universal message fail to capture essential African realities and misinterpret both the motivations of African states for security cooperation as well as the evolutionary patterns of such cooperation.

While this elision of African realities is a long-standing problem – as early as 1974 Basil Davidson warned that the stereotypical and largely Eurocentric presentation of Africa failed to capture the essence and theoretical relevance of Africa's socio-political unity in diversity – it has never been so inexcusable.[34] The analysis of the African Standby Force and the Continental Early Warning System has shown the astonishing extent and quality of contemporary inter-state security cooperation in Africa. Coupled with the historical retrospect in chapters three, four and five, it clearly illustrates the continent's enormous political progress and institutional advancements over the last decade.

Remarkable in itself, this positive development is the more noteworthy against the backdrop of the economic marginalization and underdevelopment of the states involved and the prevalence of violent conflict throughout the continent. Given its pioneering character, an understanding of the dynamics underlying the growing interaction of Africa's states in the field of peace and security is therefore bound to yield important insights for a theoretical reappraisal of inter-state security cooperation in the developing world in general. It has been the central ambition of this book to lay the conceptual foundation for such a reappraisal.

Besides this conceptual ambition, the book also sought to foster the emergence of a less cynical view of inter-African security cooperation. Although the tensions and rivalries that have characterized Africa's institutional landscape thus far have cast a penumbra of doubt over the ability of the continent to establish a viable peace and security architecture, it is hard to ignore the enormous progress made over the last few years. It is certainly true that violent conflicts continue to rage in wide parts of the continent like the Democratic Republic of the Congo, the Sudan, the Central African Republic, Chad and Somalia and that the African attempts to jointly overcome these conflicts have not always yielded convincing results, but the trend towards ever closer and more effective security relationships is nonetheless clear.

For several decades, political differences among the independent states, the unfinished nature of the continent's liberation and profound external (non-African) interference prevented any meaningful cooperation in the field of peace and security. It was only with the end of the Cold War, the concomitant proliferation of conflicts throughout the continent and the sudden marginalization in world affairs, that the states of Africa were finally galvanized into action in the early 1990s. Since then, much has been achieved. Regional organizations like SADC, ECOWAS and ECCAS have forged ahead with institutionalizing elaborate mechanisms for conflict prevention, management and resolution while the AU has slowly consolidated its strategic leadership role. Administrative, financial, institutional and operational structures have been established to serve as benchmarks and guidelines for future missions and several international initiatives have begun to remedy the significant military deficiencies of African countries and their organizations.

The African interventions in Burundi, Liberia, Darfur, Somalia and the Comoros testify to the dedicated efforts to provide "African solutions to African problems". Yet, it is certainly true that many challenges remain. For a start, the institutional carcasses and Potemkin villages that litter Africa's history of interstate cooperation show that the continent has always been better at policy formulation than implementation and that elaborate bureaucratic structures alone do not necessarily guarantee an improvement in the extent and quality of inter-state cooperation. The omnipresent resource constraints and political idiosyncrasies as well as the problems inherent in the continent's asymmetrical regionalizations and remaining conflict systems such as the Manu River Union (Liberia, Sierra Leone, Guinea, Côte d'Ivoire), the Great Lakes (DRC, Rwanda, Burundi and Uganda), the Sahel (Sudan, Chad, Central African Republic) and the Horn (Somalia, Eritrea, Ethiopia, Somaliland, Puntland) are further obstacles on the path ahead. Consequently, even though the Deutschian terminology of security communities suits the conditions in some parts of Africa well, since there has indeed been a gradual development towards improved security relations, this should not be interpreted to mean that there is something inevitable about this process. There is no guarantee that security relations in wide parts of Africa will continue to improve. In fact, current events in Darfur and Somalia unfortunately suggest quite the opposite.

Acknowledging these difficulties on the road ahead, this study has nonetheless taken the view that the undeniable progress made thus far merits an in-depth assessment of the emerging patterns of cooperation. Naturally, given the breadth of the subject, any attempt to distil theoretical lessons from the African experience inevitably runs the risk of oversimplifying what is a long and complex story. Its findings must thus not be taken as conclusive, but merely as an indication for future research agendas. At the very least, they should generate further debate and discussion on inter-African security cooperation and thus help to address the notable imbalance in the academic literature on inter-state cooperation that originally motivated this study.

Among the many issues worth exploring are the influence of specific security cultures on states' propensity to cooperate and the extent to which the African experience corresponds to or differs from other instances of complex inter-state security cooperation in the developing world such as, for example, that of ASEAN. One aspect that has surfaced so consistently throughout this study that it certainly deserves its own in-depth assessment and theoretical discussion is the role of individual leaders in advancing or inhibiting inter-state security cooperation as well as the nature of the domestic forces that encourage them to do so. The particular character of Africa's political systems where the widespread weakness of state institutions contrasts starkly with the dominant role of the political elites means that the Head of

State usually wields such remarkable decision-making power that those invested in the leaders of strong presidential democracies like France or the United States pale in comparison. Without the moderating influence of a strong national parliament, leaders like Gaddafi, Mugabe, Olusegun Obasanjo and Meles Zenawi have thus been able to push through many of the difficult reforms of Africa's institutional landscape which have been covered in this book, hoping to profit from them. It is thus paradoxically the weakness of the African state which has advanced inter-state security cooperation in Africa. Given the extent to which the future of such cooperation depends on individuals and the associated risks for the continent's cooperative ventures ranging from the sudden withdrawal of support to being degraded to mere instruments of personal ambitions, more research needs to be done on the influence of personal power politics on inter-African security cooperation.

An even more important academic imperative, however, is to reunite conceptually what this book has deliberately sought to disentangle for the sake of clarity, namely inter-state cooperation in the field of peace and security and cooperation in all other fields. While it was necessary to keep both kinds of cooperation separate in order to ensure the intellectual purity of the study's central arguments, they naturally interact closely and often even have mutually constitutive effects. These effects are already clearly visible on the continent where it is hard to miss that the Africanization of security has a very real and valuable emancipative impact on African politics in general. A unifying common defense and security policy agenda, increased political institution-building and the establishment of an administrative base for cooperative ventures in other fields such as economics are only a few of the positive spill-over effects of the ongoing intensification of inter-state security cooperation in Africa. In this respect, the increasing momentum in inter-African security cooperation observed throughout this study may well prove to be the onset of a real African renaissance.

Notes

[1]   David Francis, *Uniting Africa - Building Regional Peace and Security Systems* (Aldershot: Ashgate, 2006), 11. Also see Immanuel Wallerstein, *Africa: The Politics of Unity: An Analysis of a Contemporary Social Movement* (London: Pall Mall Press, 1968).

[2]   Francis, *Uniting Africa - Building Regional Peace and Security Systems*, 25.

[3]   Karl W. Deutsch, "Security Communities," in International Politics and Foreign Policy, ed. James Rosenau (New York: Free Press, 1961), 99.

[4]   Ali Mazrui, "Pan-Africanism: From Poetry to Power," *Issue: A Journal of Opinion* 23, no. 1 (1995): 35-8.

[5]   Benedict Anderson, *Imagined Communities* (London: Verso, 1992), 7.

[6]   See Monica Juma, "The Intergovernmental Authority on Development and the East African Community," in *From Cape to Congo: Southern Africa's Evolving Security Challenges*, ed. Mwesiga Baregu and Christopher Landsberg (Boulder: Lynne Rienner, 2003), 245-6.

[7]   Michelle Parlevliet, "The Role of Civil Society in Preventing Deadly Conflicts in Africa," in *Fifth Meeting of the Independent International Commission on Kosovo* (University of the Witwatersrand: South African Institute for International Affairs, 2000), 15.

[8]   Bruce Cronin, *Community under Anarchy: Transnational Identity and the Evolution of Cooperation* (New York: Columbia University Press, 1999), 36-7.

[9]   See also Alastair Johnston, "Treating International Institutions as Social Environments," *International Studies Quarterly* 45, no. 4 (2001).

[10]   Michael Smith, *Europe's Foreign and Security Policy: The Institutionalization of Cooperation* (Cambridge: Cambridge University Press, 2004), 30.

[11]   See, for example, Thomas Risse, "European Institutions and Identity Change: What Have We Learned?," in *Identities in Europe and the Institutions of the European Union*, ed. Marilynn Brewer, Richard Herrmann, and Thomas Risse (Lanham: Rowman & Littlefield, 2004).

[12]   The Helsinki Effect refers to the potential of human rights norms to affect domestic political change. The effect takes its name from the Helsinki Final Act of 1975 which is said to have contributed to the downfall of communism by providing protest movements with a common platform. See Daniel Thomas, *The Helsinki Effect: International Norms, Human Rights and the Demise of Communism* (New Haven: Princeton University Press, 2001).

[13]   For a detailed discussion of the Principal-Agent Problem and its role in international institutions see, for example, Darren Hawkins et al., eds., *Delegation and Agency in International Organisations* (Cambridge: Cambridge University Press, 2006).

[14]   For more information on the concept of institutional isomorphism see Paul DiMaggio and Walter Powell, "The Iron Cage Revisited: Institutional

Isomorphism and Collective Rationality in Organizational Fields," *American Sociological Review* 48 (1983): 147-60.

[15] For more information on the role of policy networks see Tanja Börzel, "What's So Special About Policy Networks?," *European Integration Online Papers* 1, no. 16 (1997).

[16] For a discussion of these inhibitions see Kenneth Oye, "Explaining Cooperation under Anarchy: Hypotheses and Strategies," *World Politics* 38, no. 1 (1985): 19-20.

[17] See, for example, Björn Hettne and Fredrik Söderbaum, "Theorising the Rise of Regioness," in *New Regionalisms in the Global Political Economy*, ed. S Breslin, et al. (London: Routledge, 2002). See also Björn Hettne, "The New Regionalism Revisited," in *Theories of New Regionalism: A Palgrave Reader*, ed. F Söderbaum and T Shaw (Basingstoke: Palgrave, 2003), 22-42.

[18] Louis Wirth as quoted in Rupert Vance, "The Regional Concept as Tool for Social Research," in *Regionalism in America*, ed. Merrill Jensen (Madison: University of Wisconsin Press, 1951), 392.

[19] See Hari Singh, "Hegemons and the Construction of Regions," in *The State and Identity Construction in International Relations*, ed. Sarah Vandersluis (Basingstoke: Macmillan, 2000), Thomas Pedersen, "Cooperative Hegemony: Power, Ideas and Institutions in Regional Integration," *Review of International Studies* 28, no. 4 (2002).

[20] See Thomas Christensen and Jack Snyder, "Chain Gangs and Passed Bucks: Predicting Alliance Patterns in Multipolarity," *International Organization* 44, no. 2 (1990): 137-68.

[21] Ademola Abass, *Regional Organizations and the Development of Collective Security - Beyond Chapter VIII of the UN Charter* (Oxford: Hart Publishing, 2004), 19-20.

[22] See Barry Buzan, *People, States and Fear*, 2nd ed. (Boulder: Lynne Rienner, 1991), Barry Buzan and Ole Waever, *Regions and Powers - the Structure of International Security* (Cambridge: Cambridge University Press, 2003), Arie Kacowicz, *Zones of Peace in the Third World: South America and West Africa in Comparative Perspective* (Albany: State University of New York Press, 1998). For a treatment of the security complex theory with specific reference to Africa see Francis, *Uniting Africa - Building Regional Peace and Security Systems*, 102-7.

[23] Hettne and Söderbaum, "Theorising the Rise of Regioness," 45.

[24] Philippe Schmitter, "A Revised Theory of Regional Integration," *International Organization* 24, no. 4 (1970), Ernst Haas, "Why Collaborate? Issue-Linkage and International Regimes," *World Politics* 32, no. 3 (1980).

[25] Andrew Hurrell, "Regionalism in Theoretical Perspective," in *Regionalism in World Politics: Regional Organisations and International Order*, ed. L Fawcett and A Hurrell (Oxford: Oxford University Press, 1995).

[26] See, for example, Bjorn Hettne, Andreas Inotai, and Osvaldo Sunkel, eds., *Globalism and the New Regionalism* (Basingstoke: MacMillan, 1999).

[27] Jeffrey Herbst, "Crafting Regional Cooperation in Africa," in *Crafting Cooperation: Regional International Institutions in Comparative Perspective*, ed. Amitav Acharya and Alastair Johnston (Cambridge: Cambridge University Press, 2007), 129.

[28]   For a brief discussion of the role of Gaddafi in the creation of the AU and his personal motivations see Francis, *Uniting Africa - Building Regional Peace and Security Systems*, 25.

[29]   Herbst, "Crafting Regional Cooperation in Africa," 129-30.

[30]   Barbara Koremenos, Charles Lipson, and Duncan Snidal, "The Rational Design of International Institutions," *International Organization* 55, no. 4 (2001): 762.

[31]   Alexander Wendt, *Social Theory of International Politics* (Cambridge: Cambridge University Press, 1999), 250.

[32]   On multiple realisability see Benjamin Most and Harvey Starr, "International Relations Theory, Foreign Policy, Substitutability And "Nice" Laws," *World Politics* 36, no. 3 (1984): 383-406.

[33]   Figure adapted from Wendt, *Social Theory of International Politics*, 254.

[34]   Basil Davidson, *Africa in History* (London: Paladin, 1974), 70. See also Francis, *Uniting Africa - Building Regional Peace and Security Systems*, 241.

Acronyms

A

AAFC	Allied Armed Forces of the Community
AAP	[G8] Africa Action Plan
ACDS	African Chiefs of Defense Staff
ACHPR	African Commission on Human and Peoples' Rights
ACOTA	African Contingency Operations Training&Assistance
ACPP	[UK] African Conflict Prevention Pool
ACRF	[US] African Crisis Response Force
ACRI	[US] African Crisis Response Initiative
ADO	African Defense Organization
AEC	African Economic Community
AfDB	African Development Bank
AFSTRAG	African Strategic and Peace Research Group
AHC	African High Command
AMIB	African Union Mission in Burundi
AMIS	African Union Mission in Sudan
AMISEC	Mission for the Support of Elections in the Comoros
AMISOM	African Mission in Somalia
AMOD	African Ministers of Defense
AMU	Arab Maghreb Union
ANC	African National Congress
APRM	African Peer Review Mechanism
APSA	African Peace and Security Architecture
ASAS	Association of Southern African States
ASEAN	Association of South-East Asian Nations
ASF	African Standby Force
AU	African Union

B

BG	[EU] Battlegroup
BMATT	British Military Advisory and Training Team
BMVg	Bundesministerium für Verteidigung
BPST	British Peace Support Team

C

C^2	Command and Control
C^3I	Command, Control, Communications and Intelligence
CADSP	Common African Defense and Security Policy
CEAO	Communauté de l'Afrique de l'Ouest
CEN-SAD	Community of Sahel-Saharan States
CEWARN	Conflict Early Warning and Response Mechanism
CEWERU	Conflict Early Warning and Early Response Unit
CEWS	Continental Early Warning System

CFSP	[EU] Common Foreign and Security Policy
CIMIC	Civil Military Cooperation/Coordination
CIVPOL	Civilian Police
CJTF-HOA	Combined Joint Task Force – Horn of Africa
CMC	[OAU] Conflict Management Center
CMD	[AU] Conflict Management Division
COMESA	Common Market for Eastern / Southern African States
COPAX	Le Conseil de Paix et de Sécurité de l'Afrique Centrale
CPF	[ECOWAS] Conflict Prevention Framework
CPMR	Conflict Prevention, Management and Resolution
CPX	Command Post Exercise
CSBM	Confidence and Security Building Measures
CSCE	Conference on Security and Cooperation in Europe
CSS	Critical Security Studies

D

DDR	Disarmament, Demobilization and Re-Integration
DHA	[UN] Department of Humanitarian Affairs
DITF	[AU] Darfur Integrated Task Force
DPA	[UN] Department for Political Affairs
DPA	Darfur Peace Agreement
DPKO	[UN] Department of Peace Keeping Operations
DRC	Democratic Republic of Congo
DSC	Defense and Security Commission

E

EAC	East African Community
EASBRIG	Eastern African Standby Brigade
EASBRICOM	[EASBRIG] Coordination Mechanism
ECCAS	Economic Community of Central African States
ECOSOC	[UN] Economic and Social Council
ECOSOCC	[AU] Economic, Social and Cultural Council
ECOMIL	ECOWAS Mission in Liberia
ECOMOG	ECOWAS Monitoring Group
ECOWAS	Economic Community of West African States
EDSC	[EASBRIG] Development Support Committee
EMM	European Media Monitoring System
ESDP	European Security and Defense Policy
ESF	ECOWAS Standby Force
EU	European Union
EUMC	[EU] Military Committee
EUMS	[EU] Military Staff
EWS	Early Warning System

F

FAST	Frühanalyse von Spannungen und Tatsachenermittlung
FCO	Foreign and Commonwealth Office
FEWER	Forum on Early Warning and Early Response

FEWS	Famine Early Warning System
FfP	Fund for Peace
FLS	Front Line States
FNL	Forces Nationales de Libération
FOMAC	Force Multinationale d'Afrique Centrale
FY	Fiscal Year

G

GPOI	Global Peace Operations Initiative
GTZ	Gesellschaft für Technische Zusammenarbeit

I

ICISS	Int. Commission on Intervention & State Sovereignty
IGAD	Inter-Governmental Authority on Development
IGADD	Inter-Gov. Authority on Drought and Development
IGASOM	[IGAD] Mission to Somalia
IGO	Inter-Governmental Organization
IISS	International Institute for Strategic Studies
IPI	International Peace Institute
IR	International Relations
ISCDS	Inter- State Committee for Defense and Security
ISDSC	Inter-State Defense and Security Committee
ISS	Institute for Security Studies

J

JEM	[Sudanese] Justice and Equality Movement

K

KAIPTC	Kofi Annan Int. Peacekeeping Training Centre

M

MAES	[AU] Mission d'assistance électorale et sécuritaire
MARAC	Mécanisme d'Alerte Rapide de l'Afrique Centrale
MDP	Mutual Defense Pact
MISAB	Mission de Surveillance des Accords de Bangui
MLG	Multi-Level Governance
MLO	Military Liaison Officer
MONUC	Mission de l'ONU en RD Congo
MOOTW	Military Operations Other Than War
MoU	Memorandum of Understanding
MPMC	[ECOWAS] Mission Planning and Management Cell
MRU	Mano River Union
MS	Member State(s)
MSC	[AU] Military Staff Committee
MSC	[ECOWAS] Mediation and Security Council

N

NARC	Northern African Regional Capability

NATO	North Atlantic Treaty Organization
NEPAD	New Partnership for African Development
NGO	Non-Governmental Organization
NMOG	[OAU] Neutral Military Observer Group
NRF	[NATO] Response Force
NRI	National Research Institute

O

OAS	Organization of American States
OAU	Organization of African Unity
OCCLA	Coordinating Committee for the Liberation of Africa
OLMEE	[OAU] Liaison Mission in Ethiopia and Eritrea
OMC	Observation and Monitoring Center
OMIB	[OAU] Mission in Burundi
OMIC	[OAU] Mission in Comoros
OMZ	Observation and Monitoring Zone
ONUB	Opération des Nations Unies au Burundi
OPDS	[SADC] Organ on Politics, Defense and Security
OPDSC	Organ on Politics, Defense and Security Cooperation
OSCE	Organization for Security and Co-operation in Europe

P

PCG	Poly-Centric Governance
PDF	[Sudanese] Popular Defense Forces
PfP	[NATO] Partnership for Peace
PSC	[AU] Peace and Security Council
PSD	[AU] Peace and Security Directorate
PSO	Peace Support Operation
PSOD	[AU] Peace Support Operations Department
PSTC	Peace Support Training Centre

R

RDC	Rapid Deployment Capability
RDL	[UNSAS] Rapid Deployment Level
REC	Regional Economic Community
RISDP	Regional Indicative Strategic Development Plan
ROE	Rules of Engagement
RPTC	Regional Peacekeeping Training Centre
RSC	Regional Security Complex
RSCT	Regional Security Complex Theory
RSF	Regional Standby Force

S

SADC	Southern African Development Community
SADCC	SA Development Coordination Conference
SADF	South African Defense Force
SAPSD	South African Protection Support Detachment
SCARF	Strategic Conflict Analysis and Response Framework

SDS	Strategic Deployment Stock
SG	[UN] Secretary General
SHIRBRIG	[UN] Standby Forces High Readiness Brigade
SIPO	[SADC] Strategic Indicative Plan for the Organ
SIRPI	Stockholm International Peace Research Institute
SLM/A	Sudan Liberation Movement/Army
SMC	[ECOWAS] Standing Mediation Committee
SMPU	[AMISOM] Support Management and Planning Unit
SRSG	[UN] Special Representative of the Secretary General

T

TCC	Troop Contributing Country
TCEW	[IGAD] Technical Committee on Early Warning
TFG	Transitional Federal Government

U

UIC	Union of Islamic Courts
UN	United Nations
UNAMID	[UN] African Mission in Darfur
UNAVEM	[UN] Angola Verification Mission
UNDP	[UN] Development Program
UNECA	[UN] Economic Commission for Africa
UNEP	[UN] Environmental Program
UNHCR	[UN] High Commissioner for Refugees
UNMIS	[UN] Mission in Sudan
UNSAS	[UN] Standby Arrangement System
UNSC	[UN] Security Council
USAID	[US] Agency for International Development

W

WANEP	West African Network for Peacebuilding
WEU	Western European Union
WARN	West African Early Warning and Response Network

Bibliography

Aardt, Maxi van. "Doing Battle with Security: The Emergence of a Southern African Approach, "*South African Journal of International Affairs* 3, no. 2 (1996).

————. "The Emerging Security Framework in Southern Africa: Regime or Community?" *Strategic Review for Southern Africa* 19, no. 1 (1997): 1-30.

Abass, Ademola. "The Implementation of ECOWAS New Protocol and Security Council Resolution 1270 in Sierra Leone: New Development in Regional Intervention." *University of Miami International and Comparative Law Review* 10, no. 1 (2002).

————. "The New Collective Security Mechanism of ECOWAS: Innovations and Problems." *Journal of Conflict and Security Law* 5, no. 2 (2000): 211-29.

————. Regional Organizations and the Development of Collective Security - Beyond Chapter VIII of the UN Charter. Oxford: Hart Publishing, 2004.

————. "The Security Council and the Challenges of Collective Security in the Twenty-First Century: What Role for African Regional Organizations?" In Global Governance and the Quest for Justice - International and Regional Organizations, edited by Douglas Lewis, 91-112. Oxford: Hart, 2006.

Abass, Ademola, and M. Baderin. "Towards Effective Collective Security and Human Rights Protection in Africa: An Assessment of the Constitutive Act of the New African Union." *Netherlands International Law Review* 49, no. 1 (2002).

Aboagye, Festus. "The ECOWAS Security Regime and Its Utility for Africa." In Peace in Africa - Towards a Collaborative Security Regime, edited by Shannon Field, 163-92. Johannesburg: Institute for Global Dialogue, 2004.

Acharya, Amitav. "The Association of Southeast Asian Nations: Security Community or Defence Community?" *Pacific Affairs* 64, no. 2 (1991): 159-78.

————. "Beyond Anarchy: Third World Instability and International Order after the Cold War." In International Relations Theory and the Third World, edited by Stephanie Neuman, 159-212. New York: St. Martin's Press, 1998.

————. "Collective Identity and Conflict Management in Southeast Asia." In Security Communities, edited by Emanuel Adler and Michael Barnett, 198-227. Cambridge: Cambridge University Press, 1998.

————. Constructing a Security Community in Southeast Asia: ASEAN and the Problem of Regional Order. London: Routledge, 2001.

————. "How Ideas Spread: Whose Norms Matter? Norm Localization and Institutional Change in Asian Regionalism." *International Organization* 58, no. 2 (2004).

————. "The Periphery as the Core: The Third World and Security Studies." York University Centre for International and Strategic Studies Occasional Paper, no. 28 (1995).

————. "Regional Military-Security Cooperation in the Third World: A Conceptual Analysis of the Relevance and Limitations of ASEAN." *Journal of Peace Research* 29, no. 1 (1992): 7-21.

Acharya, Amitav, and Barry Buzan. "Why Is There No Non-Western International Relations Theory? An Introduction." *International Relations of the Asia-Pacific* 7, no. 3 (2007): 287-312.

Acharya, Amitav, and Alastair Johnston. "Comparing Regional Institutions." In Crafting Cooperation: Regional Institutions in Comparative Perspective, edited by Amitav Acharya and Alastair Johnston, 1-31. Cambridge: Cambridge University Press, 2007.

Adebajo, Adekeye. Building Peace in West Africa: Liberia, Sierra Leone, and Guinea-Bissau. Boulder: Lynne Rienner, 2002.

————. Liberia's Civil War: Nigeria, ECOMOG and Regional Security in West Africa. Boulder: Lynne Rienner, 2002.

————. "Pax West Africana? Regional Security Mechanisms." In West Africa's Security Challenges - Building Peace in a Troubled Region, edited by Adekeye Adebajo and Ismail Rashid, 291-318. Boulder: Lynne Rienner, 2004.

————. "The Peacekeeping Travails of the AU and the Regional Economic Communities." In The African Union and Its Institutions, edited by John Akokpari, Angela Ndinga-Muvumba and Tim Murithi, 131-61. Auckland Park: Fanele, 2008.

Adebajo, Adekeye, and Christoph Landsberg. "The Heirs of Nkrumah: Africa's New Interventionists." *Pugwash Occasional Papers* 2, no. 1 (2000).

————. "South Africa and Nigeria as Regional Hegemons." In From Cape to Congo - Southern Africa's Evolving Security Challenges, edited by Mwesiga Baregu and Christoph Landsberg. Boulder: Lynne Rienner, 2003.

Adebajo, Adekeye, and Michael O'Hanlon. "Africa: Toward a Rapid Reaction Force." *SAIS Review* 17, no. 2 (1997): 153-64.

Adebajo, Adekeye, and Ismail Rashid, eds. West Africa's Security Challenges: Building Peace in a Troubled Region. Boulder: Lynne Rienner Publishers, 2004.

Adedeji, Adebayo. Comprehending and Mastering African Conflicts. London: Zed Book, 1999.

————. "ECOWAS: A Retrospective Journey." In West Africa's Security Challenges - Building Peace in a Troubled Region, edited by Adekeye Adebajo and Ismail Rashid, 21-50. Boulder: Lynne Rienner, 2004.

Adejumobi, S. "Conflict and Peacebuilding in West Africa: The Role of Civil Society and the African Union." *Conflict, Security and Development* 4, no. 1 (2004): 59-77.

Adeleke, Ademola. "The Politics and Diplomacy of Peacekeeping in West Africa: The ECOMOG Operation in Liberia." *Journal of Modern African Studies* 33, no. 4 (1995): 569-93.

Adelman, Howard. "Difficulties in Early Warning: Networking and Conflict Management." In Early Warning and Conflict Prevention: Limitations and Possibilities, edited by Klaas van Walraven, 51-82. The Hague: Kluwer Law International, 1998.

————. "Humanitarian and Conflict-Orientated Early Warning: A Historical Background Sketch." In Early Warning and Conflict Prevention:

Limitations and Possibilities, edited by Klaas van Walraven, 45-50. The Hague: Kluwer Law International, 1998.

———. "Theoretical Approaches to Developing an Early Warning Model." *The Journal of Ethno-Development* 4, no. 1 (1994): 124-31.

Adi, Hakim, and Marika Sherwood. The 1945 Manchester Pan-African Congress Revisited. Edited by George Padmore. London: New Beacon Books, 1995.

Adler, Emanuel. "Cognitive Evolution: A Dynamic Approach for the Study of International Relations and Their Progress." In Progress in Post-War International Relations, edited by Emanuel Adler and Beverly Crawford, 43-88. New York: Columbia University Press, 1991.

———. Communitarian International Relations: The Epistemic Foundations of International Relations. New York: Routledge, 2005.

———. "Condition(s) of Peace." *Review of International Studies* 24 (1998): 165-92.

———. "Imagined (Security) Communities: Cognitive Regions in International Relations." *Millennium: Journal of International Studies* 26, no. 2 (1997): 249-77.

———. "Seeds of Peaceful Change: The OSCE's Security Community-Building Model." In Security Communities, edited by Emanuel Adler and Michael Barnett, 119-60. Cambridge: Cambridge University Press, 1998.

———. "Seizing the Middle Ground: Constructivism in International Relations." *European Journal of International Relations* 3, no. 3 (1997).

Adler, Emanuel, and Michael Barnett. "A Framework for the Study of Security Communities." In Security Communities, edited by Emanuel Adler and Michael Barnett, 29-68. Cambridge: Cambridge University Press, 1998.

———. "Governing Anarchy: A Research Agenda for the Study of Security Communities." *Ethics and International Affairs* 10 (1996): 63-98.

———. "Pluralistic Security Communities: Past, Present, Future." Working Paper Series on Regional Security, no. 1 (1994).

———. Security Communities. Cambridge: Cambridge University Press, 1998.

———. "Security Communities in Theoretical Perspective." In Security Communities, edited by Emanuel Adler and Michael Barnett, 3-28. Cambridge: Cambridge University Press, 1998.

Adler, Emanuel, and Beverly Crawford, eds. Progress in Post-War International Relations. New York: Columbia University Press, 1991.

Agbi, S. The OAU and African Diplomacy, 1963-1979. Ibadan: Impact Publishers, 1986.

Agoagye, Festus. "The African Mission in Burundi: Lessons Learned from the First African Union Peacekeeping Operation." *Conflict Trends*, no. 2 (2004): 9-15.

Agyeman, Opoku. Nkrumah's Ghana and East Africa: Pan-Africanism and African Interstate Relations. London: Fairleigh Dickinson University Press, 1992.

Ahluwalia, Pal. "The African Renaissance: Reinventing African Identity." In Africa Beyond 2000: Essays on Africa's Political and Economic Development in the Twenty-First Century, edited by S. Saxena. Delhi: Kalinga Publications, 2001.

Ajala, Adekunle. Pan-Africanism: Evolution, Progress and Prospects. London: André Deutsch, 1973.

Akinrinade, Sola, and Amadu Sesay. Africa in the Post-Cold War International System. London: Washington, 1998.

Akokpari, John, Angela Ndinga-Muvumba, and Tim Murithi, eds. The African Union and its Institutions. Auckland Park: Fanele, 2008.

Alagappa, Muthiah. "Regional Arrangements, the UN, and International Security: A Framework for Analysis." In Beyond UN Subcontracting - Task-Sharing with Regional Security Arrangements and Service-Providing NGOs, edited by Thomas Weiss, 3-29. Basingstoke: Macmillan, 1998.

———. "Regionalism and Conflict Management: A Framework for Analysis." *Review of International Studies* 21, no. 4 (1995): 359-87.

Alden, Chris. "From Neglect to 'Virtual Engagement': The United States and Its New Paradigm for Africa." *African Affairs* 99, no. 396 (2000): 355-71.

Aluko, O. Ghana and Nigeria 1957-70. A Study in Inter-African Discord. London: Rex Collings, 1976.

Amate, C. O. C. Inside the OAU: Pan-Africanism in Practice. New York: St. Martin's Press, 1986.

Amponsem-Boateng, Richard. "Prospects of the Economic Community of West African States Standby Force." US Army Command and General Staff College, 2006.

Anderlini, Sanam, and David Nyheim. "Preventing Future Wars: State of the Art Conflict Early Warning Systems." *Conflict Trends* 2, no. 1 (1999): 20-3.

Anderson, Benedict. Imagined Communities. London: Verso, 1992.

Andrain, Charles F. "The Pan-African Movement: The Search for Organization and Community." *Phylon* 23, no. 1 (1962): 5-17.

Andrew, K, and Victoria Holt. United Nations - African Union Coordination on Peace and Security. Washington DC: Henry L. Stimson Centre, 2007.

Aning, Emmanuel. "African Commitments to Conflict Prevention and Peacemaking: A Review of Eight NEPAD Countries." African Human Security Initiative, 2004.

———. "African Crisis Response Initiative and the New African Security (Dis-)Order." *African Journal of Political Science* 6, no. 1 (2001): 43-67.

———. "From Eco-Pessimism to Eco-Optimism: ECOMOG and the West African Integration Process." *African Journal of Political Science* 4, no. 1 (1999): 21-39.

———. "Towards the New Millennium: ECOWAS's Evolving Conflict Management System." *African Security Review* 9, no. 5 (2000).

———. "The Transformation of ECOWAS: Towards an Emerging Security Regime." *African Journal of Politics* 10, no. 1 (2007).

Appiah-Mensah, Seth. "The African Mission in Sudan: Darfur Dilemmas." *African Security Review* 15, no. 1 (2006): 2-19.

Apuuli, Kasaija. IGAD's Protocol on Conflict Early Warning and Response Mechanism (CEWARN): A Ray of Hope in Conflict Prevention. Utrecht: Arbeitsgruppe Internationale Politik, 2004.

Arnold, Guy. Africa: A Modern History London: Atlantic Books, 2005.

Art, Robert, and Robert Jervis. International Politics. 2nd ed. Boston: Little & Brown, 1986.

Asante, S. "Pan-Africanism and Regional Integration." In General History of Africa - Africa since 1935, edited by Ali Mazrui. California: Heinemann, 1993.

————. The Political Economy of Regionalism in Africa: A Decade of the Economic Community of West African States (ECOWAS). New York: Praeger, 1986.

————. Regionalism and Africa's Development : Expectations, Reality, and Challenges. New York: St. Martin's Press, 1997.

Austin, Dennis. "Pax Africana?" In Military Power and Politics in Black Africa, edited by Simon Baynham, 166-76. London: Croom Helm, 1986.

Axelrod, Robert. The Complexity of Cooperation: Agent-Based Models of Competition and Collaboration. Princeton: Princeton University Press, 1997.

————. "Conflict of Interest: An Axiomatic Approach." *Journal of Conflict Resolution* 11 (1967): 87-99.

————. The Evolution of Cooperation. New York: Basic Books, 1984.

————. "An Evolutionary Approach to Norms." *American Political Science Review* 80, no. 4 (1986): 1095-111.

Axelrod, Robert, and Robert O. Keohane. "Achieving Cooperation under Anarchy: Strategies and Institutions." *World Politics* 38, no. 1 (1985): 226-54.

Ayoob, Mohammed. "From Regional System to Regional Society: Key Variables in the Construction of Regional Order." *Australian Journal of International Affairs* 53, no. 3 (1999): 247-60.

————. "Inequality and Theorising in International Relations: The Case for Subaltern Realism." *International Studies Review* 4, no. 3 (2002): 27-48.

————. "Security in the Third World: The Worm About to Turn?" *International Affairs* 60, no. 1 (1984): 41-51.

————. "Squaring the Circle: Collective Security in a System of States." In Collective Security in a Changing World, edited by Thomas Weiss, 45-62. Boulder: Lynne Rienner, 1993.

————. "Subaltern Realism: International Relations Theory Meets the Third World." In International Relations Theory and the Third World, edited by Stephanie Neuman. New York: St. Martin's Press, 1998.

————. The Third World Security Predicament: State Making, Regional Conflict and the International System Boulder: Lynne Rienner, 1995.

Bach, Daniel. Regionalization in Africa: Integration & Disintegration. Oxford: Bloomington, 1999.

Bache, Ian, and Mathew Flinders, eds. Multi-Level Governance. Oxford: Oxford University Press, 2004.

Bah, Alhaji. "West Africa: From a Security Complex to a Security Community." *African Security Review* 14, no. 2 (2005).

Baker, Bruce. "Twilight of Impunity for Africa's Presidential Criminals." *Third World Quarterly* 25, no. 8 (2004).

Baker, Regina. "Cooperation, Collusion and Coercion: The Third World and International Relations Theory." Paper presented at the annual meeting of the Midwest Political Science Association in Chicago, 2006.

Bakwesegha, Chris. "The Emerging Role of Sub-Regional Organisations." *Conflict Trends*, no. 4 (2003): 15-19.

————. "The Role of the Organization of African Unity in Conflict Prevention, Management and Resolution in the Context of the Political Evolution of Africa." *African Journal on Conflict Prevention, Management and Resolution* 1, no. 1 (1997).

Baldwin, David. "The Concept of Security."*Review of International Studies* 23, no. 1 (1997): 5-26.

Baregu, Mwesiga, and Christopher Landsberg, eds. From Cape to Congo: Southern Africa's Evolving Security Challenges. Boulder: Lynne Rienner, 2003.

Barnett, Michael. "Radical Chic? Subaltern Realism: A Rejoinder." *International Studies Review* 4, no. 3 (2002): 49-62.

Barnett, Michael, and Emanuel Adler. "Studying Security Communities in Theory, Comparison and History." In Security Communities, edited by Emanuel Adler and Michael Barnett, 413-41. Cambridge: Cambridge University Press, 1998.

Barnett, Michael, and Martha Finnemore. "The Politics, Power and Pathologies of International Organizations." *International Organization* 53, no. 4 (1999): 699-732.

Baylis, John, and Nick Rengger, eds. Dilemmas of World Politics: International Issues in a Changing World. Oxford: Clarendon Press, 1992.

Beaton, Leonard. The Struggle for Peace. London: Praeger, 1967.

Bekoe, Dorina, and Aida Mengistu. Operationalizing the ECOWAS Mechanism for Conflict Prevention, Management, Resolution, Peacekeeping and Security. New York: International Peace Academy, 2002.

Bellamy, Alex. Security Communities and Their Neighbours: Regional Fortresses or Global Integrators. New York: Palgrave Macmillan, 2004.

Bellamy, Alex, and Paul Williams. Understanding Peacekeeping. 2nd ed. Oxford: Polity, 2009.

Bergeon, Sébastien. "Vers une Européanisation de la Politique de Sécurité et de Défense de la France en Afrique?" *Défense Nationale* 63, no. 1 (2007): 58-60.

Berkowitz, Peter. Virtue and the Making of Modern Liberalism. Princeton: Princeton University Press, 2000.

Berman, Eric. French, UK and US Policies to Support Peacekeeping in Africa: Current Status and Future Prospects, Paper No. 622. Oslo: Norwegian Institute of International Affairs, 2002.

———. "The Security Council's Increasing Reliance on Burden-Sharing: Collaboration or Abrogation." *International Peacekeeping* 4, no. 1 (1998).

Berman, Eric, and Katie Sams. Constructive Disengagement: Western Efforts to Develop African Peacekeeping, Monograph Series No. 33. Pretoria: Institute for Security Studies, 1998.

———. Peacekeeping in Africa: Capabilities and Culpabilities. Geneva: United Nations Institute for Disarmament Research, 2000.

Bially-Mattern, Janice. "Power in Realist-Constructivist Research." *International Studies Review* 6, no. 2 (2004): 343-46.

———. "The Power Politics of Identity." *European Journal of International Relations* 7, no. 3 (2001): 349-97.

Biermann, Werner, ed. African Crisis Response Initiative: The New US Africa Policy. Piscataway: Transaction Publishers, 1999.

Bischoff, Paul-Henri. "SADC as a Foreign Policy Actor: The Challenges of Cooperation in Southern Africa." In Africa Institute of South Africa 40th Anniversary Conference. Pretoria, 2001.

Biswaro, Joram. Perspectives on Africa's Integration and Cooperation from OAU to AU: Old Wine in New Bottles? Dar es Salaam: Tanzania Publishing House, 2005.

Blumer, Herbert. Symbolic Interactionism: Perspective and Method. Englewood Cliffs: Prentice Hall, 1969.

Bøås, Morten. "Nigeria and West Africa: From a Regional Security Complex to a Regional Security Community?" In Ethnicity Kills? The Politics of Peace, War and Ethnicity in Sub-Saharan Africa, edited by Einar Braathen, Morten Bøås and Gjermund Saether. Basingstoke: Palgrave, 2000.

———. Regions and Regionalization: A Heretic's View. Uppsala: Nordiska Afrikainstitutet, 2001.

Bogland, Karin, Robert Egnell, and Maria Lagerström. The African Union - a Study Focusing on Conflict Management. Stockholm: Swedish Defense Research Agency, 2008.

Bond, Douglas, and Patrick Meier. "CEWARN: IGAD's Conflict Early Warning and Response Mechanism." In Conflict Prevention in Practice: Essays in Honour of James Sutterlin, edited by Bertrand Ramcharan, 75-90. Leiden: Martinus Nijhoff Publishers, 2005.

Boon, Catherine. Political Topographies of the African State: Territorial Authority and Institutional Choice. Cambridge: Cambridge University Press, 2003.

Booth, Ken. "Security and Emancipation." Review of International Studies 17 (1991).

———. "A Security Regime in Southern Africa: Theoretical Considerations." Centre for Southern African Studies Working Paper Series, no. 30 (1994).

———. Theory of World Security. Cambridge: Cambridge University Press, 2007.

Booth, Ken, and Peter Vale. "Critical Security Studies and Regional Insecurity: The Case of Southern Africa." In Critical Security Studies: Concepts and Cases, edited by Keith Krause and Michael Williams. London: UCL Press, 1997.

———. "Security in Southern Africa: After Apartheid, Beyond Realism." International Affairs 71, no. 2 (1995): 285-304.

Börzel, Tanja. "What's so Special About Policy Networks?" European Integration Online Papers 1, no. 16 (1997).

Boshoff, Henri, and Dara Francis. "The AU Mission in Burundi: Technical and Operational Dimensions." African Security Review 12, no. 3 (2003): 41-44.

Boulden, Jane. Dealing with Conflict in Africa: The United Nations and Regional Organizations. Basingstoke: Palgrave Macmillan, 2003.

Brecher, Michael. "International Studies in the Twentieth Century and Beyond: Flawed Dichotomies." International Studies Quarterly 43, no. 2 (1999): 213-64.

Breytenbach, W. "Failure of Security Cooperation in SADC: The Suspension of the Organ for Politics, Defense and Security " South African Journal of International Affairs 7, no. 1 (2000).

Broderick, Francis. W.E.B. Dubois: Negro Leader in a Time of Crisis. Stanford: Stanford University Press, 1959.

Brooks, Stephen. "Dueling Realisms." International Organization 51, no. 3 (1997): 445-78.

Browne, Dallas. "Libya and the African Union." In History Behind the Headlines, edited by Megan O'Meara. New York: Gale Cengage, 2003.

Bull, Hedley. The Anarchical Society: A Study of Order in World Politics. London: Macmillan, 1977.

Buzan, Barry. "The Concept of National Security for Developing Countries." In Workshop on "Leadership and Security in Southeast Asia". Institute of Southeast Asian Studies, Singapore, 1987.

———. "A Framework for Regional Security Analysis." In South Asian Insecurity and the Great Powers, edited by Barry Buzan and Gowher Rizvi, 3-33. London: Croom Helm, 1986.

———. "From International System to International Society: Structural Realism and Regime Theory Meet the English School." International Organization 47, no. 3 (1992): 327-52.

———. From International to World Society? English School Theory and the Social Structure of Globalisation. Cambridge: Cambridge University Press, 2004.

———. People, States and Fear. 2nd ed. Boulder: Lynne Rienner, 1991.

———. "Third World Regional Security in Historic and Structural Perspective." In The Insecurity Dilemma: National Security of Third World States, edited by Brian Job. Boulder: Lynne Rienner, 1992.

Buzan, Barry, Charles Jones, and Richard Little. The Logic of Anarchy: Neo-Realism to Structural Realism. New York: Columbia University Press, 1993.

Buzan, Barry, and Ole Waever. Regions and Powers - the Structure of International Security. Cambridge: Cambridge University Press, 2003.

Callaghy, Thomas, Ronald Kassimir, and Robert Latham, eds. Intervention and Transnationalism in Africa. Cambridge: Cambridge University Press, 2001.

Carr, E.H. The Twenty Year Crisis, 1919-1939: An Introduction to the Study of International Relations. New York: St. Martin's, 1946.

Cevins, Oliver de. "Pour que RECAMP ne Rime plus avec Décampe." Défense Nationale 59, no. 3 (2003): 80-90.

Chabal, Patrick, and Jean-Pascal Daloz. Africa Works: Disorder as Political Instrument. Oxford: James Currey, 1999.

Chalmers, Malcolm. Sharing Security - the Political Economy of Burdensharing. Basingstoke: Macmillan 2000.

Checkel, Jeffrey. "The Constructivist Turn in International Relations Theory." World Politics 50, no. 2 (1998).

Chemarin, Elodie. "Les enjeux des programmes francais et américans de renforcement des capacités africaines de maintien de la paix," (Geneva: Graduate Institute of International and Development Studies, 2007).

Chimelu, C. Integration and Politics among African States. Uppsala: Scandinavian Institute of African Studies, 1977.

Christensen, Thomas, and Jack Snyder. "Chain Gangs and Passed Bucks: Predicting Alliance Patterns in Multipolarity." International Organization 44, no. 2 (1990): 137-68.

Cilliers, Jakkie. "From Acronyms to Action: The Seminal Assembly of the African Union." African Security Review 11, no. 1 (2002).

———. "From Durban to Maputo: A Review of the 2003 Summit of the African Union." ISS Occasional Papers, no. 76 (2003).

————. "The SADC Organ for Defense, Politics and Security." ISS Occasional Papers, no. 10 (1996).

————. "Towards a Continental Early Warning System for Africa." ISS Occasional Papers, no. 102 (2005).

Cilliers, Jakkie, and Mark Malan. Progress with the African Standby Force, ISS Papers No. 98. Pretoria: Institute for Security Studies, 2005.

Cilliers, Jackie, and Kathryn Sturman. "Challenges Facing the AU's Peace and Security Council." *African Security Review* 13, no. 1 (2004): 97-104.

Clapham, Christopher. Africa and the International System: The Politics of State Survival. Cambridge: Cambridge University Press, 1996.

————. "Degrees of Statehood." *Review of International Studies* 24, no. 2 (1998).

Clark, John, ed. The African Stakes of the Congo War. Basingstoke: Palgrave Macmillan, 2004.

————. "Foreign Policy Making in Central Africa: The Imperative of Regime Security in a New Context." In African Foreign Policies: Power and Process, edited by Gilbert Khadiagala and Terrence Lyons, 67-86. Boulder: Lynne Rienner, 2001.

————. "Realism, Neo-Realism and Africa's International Relations in the Post-Cold War Era." In Africa's Challenge to International Relations Theory, edited by Kevin Dunn and Timothy Shaw, 85-102. Basingstoke: Palgrave, 2001.

Clayton, Tony. "African Military Capabilities in Insurrection, Intervention and Peace Support Operations." In African Interventionist States, edited by Oliver Furley and Roy May, 51-68. Aldershot: Ashgate, 2001.

Cleaver, G, and R May. "Peacekeeping: The African Dimension." *Review of African Political Economy* 22 (1995).

Clough, Michael. "The United States and Africa: The Policy of Cynical Disengagement." *Current History* 91 (1992): 193-98.

Cohen, A. The Symbolic Construction of Community. New York: Tavistock Publishers, 1985.

Coleman, Katharina. International Organizations and Peace Enforcement: The Politics of International Legitimacy. Cambridge: Cambridge University Press, 2007.

Collins, Alan. "Forming a Security Community: Lessons from ASEAN." *International Relations of the Asia-Pacific* 7, no. 2 (2007): 203-25.

Coning, Cedric de. "The Civilian Dimensions of the African Standby System." *Conflict Trends*, no. 4 (2005): 10-16.

————. "Peace Operations in Africa: The Next Decade." Norwegian Institute of International Affairs Working Paper, no. 721 (2007).

————. "Peacekeeping in Africa: The Next Decade." *Conflict Trends*, no. 3 (2002): 46-55.

————. "Refining the African Standby Force Concept." *Conflict Trends*, no. 2 (2004).

————. "The Role of the OAU in Conflict Management in Africa." ISS Monograph, no. 10 (1997).

Coning, Cedric de, and Hussein Solomon. "Enhancing the OAU Mechanism for Conflict Prevention, Management and Resolution." *Politeia* 8, no. 4 (1999): 22-33.

Copeland, Dale. "The Constructivist Challenge to Structural Realism." In Constructivism and International Relations, edited by Stefano Guzzini and Anne Leander, 1-20. London: Routledge, 2006.

Cox, Robert. The New Realism: Perspectives on Multilateralism and World Order. London: Macmillan, 1997.

Cox, Richard. Pan-Africanism in Practice: An East African Study, PAFMESCA 1958-1964. London: Oxford University Press, 1964.

Crawford, Beverly, and Emanuel Adler, eds. Progress in Post-War International Relations. New York: Columbia University Press, 1991.

Cronin, Bruce. Community under Anarchy: Transnational Identity and the Evolution of Cooperation. New York: Columbia University Press, 1999.

———. Institutions for the Common Good: International Protection Regimes in International Society. Cambridge: Cambridge University Press, 2003.

Crupi, Francis V. "Why the United States Should Robustly Support Pan-African Organizations." *Parameters,* no. 4 (2005): 106-23.

Daley, Patricia. "The Burundi Peace Negotiations: An African Experience of Peacemaking " *Review of African Political Economy* 34, no. 112 (2007): 333-52.

David, Steven. "Explaining Third World Alignment." *World Politics* 43, no. 2 (1991): 233-56.

———. "Why the Third World Matters." *International Security* 14, no. 1 (1989): 50-85.

Davidson, Basil. Africa in History. London: Paladin, 1974.

———. The Black Man's Burden: Africa and the Curse of the Nation State. Oxford: James Currey, 1992.

Davies, John, and Ted Robert Gurr, eds. Preventive Measures: Building Risk Assessment and Crisis Early Warning Systems. Boulder: Rowman & Littlefield Publishers, 1998.

Deng, Francis. Mediating the Sudanese Conflict: A Challenge for IGADD, CSIS Africa Notes No. 169. Washington DC: Centre for Strategic and International Studies, 1995.

Deng, Francis, and William Zartman. A Strategic Vision for Africa: The Kampala Movement. Washington DC: Brookings Institution Press, 2002.

Desh, Michael. "Why Realists Disagree About the Third World (and Why They Shouldn't)." In Realism: Restatements and Renewal, edited by Benjamin Frankel. London: Frank Cass, 1996.

Deutsch, Karl W. The Analysis of International Relations. Englewood Cliffs: Prentice Hall, 1988.

———. Political Community and the North Atlantic Area - International Organization in the Light of Historical Experience. Princeton: Princeton University Press, 1957.

———. "Security Communities." In International Politics and Foreign Policy, edited by James Rosenau. New York: Free Press, 1961.

Dewitt, David. "Common, Comprehensive and Cooperative Security." *The Pacific Review* 7, no. 1 (1994): 1-15.

DiMaggio, Paul, and Walter Powell. "The Iron Cage Revisited: Institutional Isomorphism and Collective Rationality in Organizational Fields." *American Sociological Review* 48 (1983): 147-60.

Donnelly, Jack. Realism and International Relations. Cambridge: Cambridge University Press, 2000.

Doom, Ruddy. "From Information to Political Action: Some Political Prerequisites." In Early Warning and Conflict Prevention: Limitations and Possibilities, edited by Klaas van Walraven. The Hague: Kluwer Law International, 1998.

Doornbos, Martin. "The African State in Academic Debate: Retrospect and Prospect." *Journal of Modern African Studies* 28, no. 2 (1990).

Dorn, Walter. "Regional Peacekeeping Is Not the Way." *Peacekeeping and International Relations* 27, no. 2 (1998).

Downs, George. "Beyond the Debate on Collective Security." In Collective Security Beyond the Cold War edited by George Downs, 1-16. Michigan: University of Michigan Press, 1994.

Downs, G. Collective Security Beyond the Cold War. Michigan: University of Michigan Press, 1994.

Duffield, Ian. "Pan-Africanism since 1940." In The Cambridge History of Africa, edited by Michael Crowder. Cambridge: Cambridge University Press, 1984.

Dunn, Kevin. "Africa and International Relations Theory." In Africa's Challenge to International Relations Theory, edited by Kevin Dunn and Timothy Shaw. Basingstoke: Palgrave, 2001.

———. "Madlib #32: The (Blank) African State: Rethinking the Sovereign State in International Relations Theory." In Africa's Challenge to International Relation's Theory, edited by Kevin Dunn and Timothy Shaw. Basingstoke: Palgrave, 2001.

———. "Tales from the Dark Side: Africa's Challenge to International Relations Theory." *Journal of Third World Studies* 17, no. 1 (2000).

Dunn, Kevin, and Timothy Shaw, eds. Africa's Challenge to International Relations Theory. Basingstoke: Palgrave, 2001.

Dunne, Tim. Inventing International Society: A History of the English School. London: Macmillan, 1998.

———. "The New Agenda." In International Society and Its Critics, edited by Alex Bellamy. Oxford: Oxford University Press, 2004.

Durkheim, Emile. The Division of Labour in Society. New York: Free Press, 1984.

———. Ethics and the Sociology of Morals. Buffalo: Prometheus Books, 1993.

East, Maurice A., and Phillip M. Gregg. "Factors Influencing Cooperation and Conflict in the International System." *International Studies Quarterly* 11, no. 3 (1967): 244-69.

Eberwein, Wolf-Dieter. "The Future of International Warfare: Toward a Global Security Community " *International Political Science Review* 16, no. 4 (1995): 341-60.

Echezons, N, and E Duru. "Conflict Prevention, Management and Resolution: Establishing a Regional Force for Africa." *European Journal of Scientific Research* 8, no. 3 (2005).

Elbe, Stephan. "Strategic Implications of HIV/AIDS." *Adelphi Papers*, no. 357 (2003).

Emerson, Rupert. "Pan-Africanism." *International Organization* 16, no. 2 (1962).

Engel, Ulf, and Andreas Mehler. Closing the Gap between Early Warning and Early Action: Applying Political Science to Violent Conflicts in Africa. Leipzig: Institut für Afrikanistik, 2000.

Ero, Comfort. ECOMOG: A Model for Africa?, Monograph Series No. 46. Pretoria: Institute for Security Studies, 2000.

Esedebe, P. Olisanwuche. Pan-Africanism: The Idea and Movement, 1776-1991. 2nd ed. Washington, D.C.: Howard University, 1994.

Esty, Daniel, et al. "The State Failure Project: Early Warning Research for US Foreign Policy Planning." In Preventive Measures: Building Risk Assessment and Crisis Early Warning Systems, edited by John Davies and Ted Robert Gurr, 27-38. Boulder: Rowman & Littlefield Publishers, 1998.

Evera, Stephen van. Causes of War: Power and the Roots of Conflict. Ithaca: Cornell University Press, 1999.

———. Guide to Methods for Students of Political Science. Ithaca: Cornell University Press, 1997.

———. "Why Europe Matters. Why the Third World Doesn't." *Journal of Strategic Studies* 13, no. 2 (1990): 1-51.

Falk, Richard, and Saul Mendlovitz, eds. Regional Politics and World Order. San Francisco: W.H. Freeman and Company, 1973.

Farer, Tom. "The Role of Regional Collective Security Arrangements." In Collective Security in a Changing World, edited by Thomas Weiss, 153-84. Boulder: Lynne Rienner, 1993.

Farrell, Mary. "A Triumph of Realism over Idealism? Cooperation between the European Union and Africa." *Journal of European Integration* 27, no. 3 (2005): 263-83.

Fasehun, O. "Nigeria and the Issue of an African High Command: Towards a Regional and/or Continental Defense System." *Afrika Spektrum* 80, no. 3 (1980).

Fawcett, Louise. "Exploring Regional Domains: A Comparative History of Regionalism." *International Affairs* 80, no. 3 (2004).

Fawcett, Louise, and Andrew Hurrell, eds. Regionalism in World Politics: Regional Organization and International Order. Oxford: Oxford University Press, 1995.

Fayemi, Kayode. Deepening the Culture of Constitutionalism: Regional Institutions and Constitutional Development in Africa. Ikeja: Centre for Democracy and Development, 2003.

———. "Framework for Cooperative Security in a Region in Transition." *Conflict Trends* 4 (2002): 48-53.

Field, Shannon, ed. Peace in Africa: Towards a Collaborative Security Regime. Johannesburg: Institute for Global Dialogue, 2004.

Finnemore, Martha. National Interests in International Society. Ithaca: Cornell University Press, 1996.

Fisher, L., and Naison Ngoma. "The SADC Organ: Challenges in the New Millennium." ISS Occasional Papers, no. 114 (2005).

Fitzke, Susan. "The Treaty for East-African Cooperation: Can East-Africa Successfully Revive One of Africa's Most Infamous Economic Groupings?" *Minnesota Journal of Global Trade* 8 (1999): 127-59.

Flint, Julie, and Alex de Waal. Darfur: A New History of a Long War London: Zed, 2008.

Foucault, Michel. Power/Knowledge. New York: Pantheon, 1980.

———. "The Subject and Power." *Critical Inquiry* 22 (1982): 381-404.

Francis, David, ed. Peace & Conflict in Africa. London: Zed Books, 2008.

————. Uniting Africa - Building Regional Peace and Security Systems. Aldershot: Ashgate, 2006.

Francis, David, Mohammed Faal, John Kabia, and Alex Ramsbotham. Dangers of Co-Deployment - UN Cooperative Peacekeeping in Africa Aldershot: Ashgate, 2005.

Franke, Benedikt. "Africa's Evolving Security Architecture and the Concept of Multi-Layered Security Communities." *Cooperation and Conflict* 43, no. 3 (2008): 313-340.

————. "Competing Regionalisms in Africa and the Continent's Emerging Security Architecture." *African Studies Quarterly* 10, no. 1 (2007).

————. "Enabling a Continent to Help Itself: US Military Capacity Building and Africa's Emerging Security Architecture." *Strategic Insights* VI, no. 1 (2007).

————. "In Defense of Regional Peace Operations in Africa." *Journal of Humanitarian Assistance*, no. 185 (2006).

————. "Military Integration in Southern Africa: SADC's Standby Brigade." In South African Yearbook of International Affairs 2006. Cape Town: South African Institute of International Affairs, 2007.

————. "A Pan-African Army: The Evolution of an Idea and Its Eventual Realization in the African Standby Force." *African Security Review* 15, no. 4 (2006): 2-16.

————. "The Politics of Defence in Africa." In Politics of Defence: International and Comparative Perspectives, edited by Isaiah Wilson and James Forest. London: Routledge, 2008.

Franke, Benedikt, and Romain Esmenjaud. "Who Owns African Ownership? The Africanization of Security and its Limits." South African Journal of International Affairs 14, no. 2 (2008): 137-158.

Frankel, Benjamin, ed. Realism: Restatements and Renewal. London: Frank Cass, 1996.

————, ed. Roots of Realism. London: Frank Cass, 1996.

Furley, Oliver, and May Roy. Ending Africa's Wars: Progressing to Peace. Aldershot: Ashgate, 2006.

Gallie, Walter Bruce, "Essentially Contested Concepts," Proceedings of the Aristotelian Society 56 (1956): 167-98.

Galtung, Johan. "Violence, Peace and Peace Research." *Journal of Peace Research* 6, no. 6 (1969).

Garofano, John. "Power, Institutions, and the ASEAN Regional Forum: A Security Community for Asia?" *Asian Survey* 42, no. 3 (2002): 502-21.

Geiss, Imanuel. The Pan-African Movement. London: Methuen & Co, 1968.

————. "Pan-Africanism." *Journal of Contemporary History* 4, no. 1 (1969): 187-200.

George, Alexander, and Andrew Bennett. Case Studies and Theory Development in the Social Sciences. Cambridge: MIT Press, 2004.

Giddens, Anthony. The Constitution of Society: Outline of the Theory of Structuration. Cambridge: Polity Press, 1984.

Gilpin, Robert. The Political Economy of International Relations. Princeton: Princeton University Press, 1987.

Glaser, Charles L. "Realists as Optimists: Cooperation as Self-Help." *International Security* 19, no. 3 (1994): 50-90.

Goldgeier, James, and Michael McFaul. "A Tale of Two Worlds: Core and Periphery in the Post-Cold War Era." *International Organization* 46, no. 2 (1992): 467-92.

Goldstein, Judith, and Robert Keohane, eds. Ideas and Foreign Policy: Beliefs, Institutions and Political Change. Ithaca: Cornell University Press, 1993.

Gomes, Solomon. "The OAU, State Sovereignty and Regional Security." In Africa in the New International Order: Rethinking State Sovereignty and Regional Security, edited by Edmond Keller and Donald Rothchild, 37-51. Boulder: Lynne Rienner, 1996.

Gourevitch, Peter. "The Second Image Reversed: The International Source of Domestic Politics." International Organization 32, no. 4 (1978): 881-912.

Grant, Andrew, and Fredrik Söderbaum, eds. The New Regionalism in Africa. Aldershot: Ashgate, 2003.

Grieco, Joseph. "Anarchy and the Limits of Cooperation: A Realist Critique of the Newest Liberal Institutionalism." International Organization 42 (1988): 485-507.

———. "Understanding the Problem of International Cooperation: The Limits of Neo-Liberal Institutionalism and the Future of Realist Theory." In Neo-Realism and Neo-Liberalism: The Contemporary Debate, edited by David Baldwin, 301-38. New York: Columbia, 1993.

Grieco, Joseph, Robert Powell, and Duncan Snidal. "The Relative-Gains Problem for International Cooperation." *The American Political Science Review* 87, no. 3 (1993): 729-43.

Griffith, Cyril. The African Dream: Martin R. Delany and the Emergence of Pan-African Thought. London: Pennsylvania State University Press, 1975.

Groom, A.J.R., and Paul Taylor, eds. Functionalism. London: Hodder Arnold, 1975.

Gross-Stein, Janice. "Detection and Defection: Security Regimes and the Management of International Conflict." *International Journal* 40 (1985).

Grunberg, Isabelle. "Exploring The "Myth" Of Hegemonic Stability." *International Organization* 44, no. 4 (1990): 431-77.

Gurr, T. "Early Warning Systems: From Surveillance to Assessment to Action." In Preventive Diplomacy, edited by M Cahill. New York, 1996.

Gurr, T, and B Harff. "Conceptual Research and Policy Issues in Early Warning: An Overview." *The Journal of Ethno-Development* 4, no. 1 (1994): 3-14.

Guzzini, Stefano, and Anna Leander, eds. Constructivism and International Relations: Alexander Wendt and his Critics. London: Routledge, 2006.

Haacke, Jürgen. ASEAN's Diplomatic and Security Culture: Origins, Development and Prospects. London: Routledge, 2003.

Haacke, Jürgen, and Paul Williams. "Security Culture and Transnational Challenges: ECOWAS in Comparative Perspective." *Journal of Contemporary African Studies* 26, no. 2 (2008): 213-22.

———. "Thinking About Regional Security Cultures in Africa and Asia." In ISA Annual Convention. Chicago, 2007.

Haas, Ernst. Beyond the Nation State. Stanford: Stanford University Press, 1964.

———. "The Challenge of Regionalism." *International Organization* 12 (1958): 440-59.

————. "Collective Conflict Management: Evidence for a New World Order " In Collective Security in a Changing World, edited by Thomas Weiss, 63-120. Boulder: Lynne Rienner, 1993.

————. "The Study of Regional Integration: Reflections on the Joy and Anguish of Pre-theorizing." In Regional Politics and World Order, edited by Richard Falk and Saul Mendlovitz, 103-32. San Francisco: W.H. Freeman and Company, 1973.

————. "Why Collaborate? Issue-Linkage and International Regimes." *World Politics* 32, no. 3 (1980): 357-405.

Haftel, Yoram. "Designing for Peace: Regional Integration Arrangements, Institutional Variation and Militarised Inter-State Disputes." *International Organization* 61 (2007): 217-37.

Haftendorn, Helga. "The Security Puzzle: Theory-Building and Discipline-Building in International Security." *International Studies Quarterly* 35 (1991): 3-17.

Haftendorn, Helga, Robert Keohane, and Celeste Wallander, eds. Imperfect Unions: Security Institutions over Time and Space. Oxford: Oxford University Press, 1999.

Haggar, Ali. "The Origins and Organization of the Janjawiid in Darfur." In War in Darfur and the Search for Peace, edited by Alex de Waal, 113-39. Cambridge: Global Equity Initiative, Harvard University, 2007.

Halperin, Sandra. "International Relations Theory and the Hegemony of Western Conceptions of Modernity." In Decolonizing International Relations, edited by Branwen Jones. London: Rowman & Littlefield, 2006.

Hammerstad, Anne. "Domestic Threats, Regional Solutions? The Challenge of Security Integration in Southern Africa." *Review of International Studies* 31, no. 1 (2005): 69-87.

Handel, Michael. Weak States in the International System. London: Frank Cass, 1981.

Handy, Russell. "The Africa Contingency Operations Training and Assistance: Developing Training Partnerships for the Future of Africa " *Air & Space Power Journal*, no. 3 (2003): 57-64.

Hansen, Roger. "Regional Integration: Reflections on a Decade of Theoretical Efforts." *World Politics* 21, no. 1 (1969): 242-71.

Harbeson, John, ed. The Military in African Politics. New York: Praeger, 1987.

Harbeson, John, and Donald Rothchild, eds. Africa in World Politics: Reforming Political Order. Boulder: Westview Press, 2008.

Harsch, Ernest. "Africa Builds its own Peace Forces." *Africa Recovery* 17, no. 3 (2003).

Harvey, David. A Brief History of Neo-Liberalism. Oxford: Oxford University Press, 2005.

Haslam, Jonathan. No Virtue like Necessity: Realist Thought in International Relations since Machiavelli. New Haven: Yale University Press, 2002.

Haugevik, Kristin. New Partners, New Possibilities: The Evolution of Inter-Organizational Security Cooperation in International Peace Operations. Oslo: Norsk Utenrikspolitisk Institutt (NUPI), 2007.

Hawkins, Darren, David Lake, Daniel Nielson, and Michael Tierney, eds. Delegation and Agency in International Organisations. Cambridge: Cambridge University Press, 2006.

Heimsoeth, H. "Die Auflösung der Ostafrikanischen Gemeinschaft." *Verfassung und Recht in Übersee* 13 (1980): 55-59.

Heitman, Helmoed-Römer. "Comoros Operation: The Positives and Negatives" *Jane's Defense Weekly* 45, no. 15 (2008).

Henk, Dan, and Steven Metz. The United States and the Transformation of African Security: The African Crisis Response Initiative and Beyond: Strategic Studies Institute, US Army War College, 1997.

Henk, Dan, and Martin Rupiya. "Funding Defense: Challenges of Buying Military Capability in Sub-Saharan Africa." Carlisle: US Army Strategic Studies Institute, 2001.

Hentz, James. South Africa and the Logic of Regional Cooperation. Bloomington: Indiana University Press, 2005.

Hentz, James, and Bøås Morten. New and Critical Security and Regionalism: Beyond the Nation State. Aldershot: Ashgate, 2003.

Herbst, Jeffrey. "Crafting Regional Cooperation in Africa." In Crafting Cooperation: Regional International Institutions in Comparative Perspective, edited by Amitav Acharya and Alastair Johnston, 129-44. Cambridge: Cambridge University Press, 2007.

Hertz, John. "Idealist Internationalism and the Security Dilemma." *World Politics* 2, no. 1 (1950): 157-80.

———. Political Realism and Political Idealism. Chicago: University of Chicago Press, 1951.

Hettne, Björn. "The New Regionalism Revisited." In Theories of New Regionalism: A Palgrave Reader, edited by F Söderbaum and T Shaw, 22-42. Basingstoke: Palgrave, 2003.

Hettne, Björn, and András Sunkel Osvaldo Inotai. The New Regionalism and the Future of Security and Development, New York: St. Martin's Press, 2000.

Hettne, Björn, and Fredrik Söderbaum. "The New Regionalism." *Politeia* (Special Issue) 17, no. 3 (1998).

———. "Theorizing the Rise of Regioness." In New Regionalisms in the Global Political Economy, edited by S Breslin, C Hughes, N Phillips and B Rosamond. London: Routledge, 2002.

Hill, Christopher. "The Capability-Expectations Gap or Conceptualizing Europe's International Role." *Journal of Common Market Studies* 31, no. 3 (1993): 305-28.

Hill, Robert, ed. The Marcus Garvey and Universal Negro Improvement Papers I-IX. Manchester: Manchester University Press, 1983.

Holsti, Ole. Unity and Disintegration in International Alliances: Comparative Studies. London: Wiley, 1976.

Holt, Victoria. African Capacity Building for Peace Operations: UN Collaboration with the African Union and ECOWAS. Washington DC: Henry L. Stimson Center, 2005.

Hooghe, Liesbet, and Gary Marks. "Unravelling the Central State, but how? Types of Multi-Level Governance." *American Political Science Review* 97, no. 2 (2003): 233-43.

Hooker, J. Black Revolutionary: George Padmore's Path from Communism to Pan-Africanism. London: Pall Mall Press, 1967.

Hopf, Ted. "The Promise of Constructivism in International Relations Theory." *International Security* 23, no. 1 (1998).

Hough, M. "Collective Security and its Variants: A Conceptual Analysis with Specific Reference to SADC and ECOWAS." *Strategic Review for Southern Africa* 20, no. 2 (1998): 23-43.

Howe, Herbert M. Ambiguous Order: Military Forces in African States. Boulder: Lynne Rienner Publishers, 2001.

Huban, Mark. The Skull beneath the Skin: Africa after the Cold War. Boulder: Westview Press, 2003.

Hull, Cecilia, and Emma Svensson. African Union Mission in Somalia (AMISOM): Exemplifying African Union Peacekeeping Challenges. Stockholm: Swedish Defense Research Agency, 2008.

Hume, Cameron. Ending Mozambique's War: The Role of Mediation and Good Offices. Washington DC: United States Institute of Peace Press, 1994.

Hunter-Gault, Charlayne. New News out of Africa: Uncovering the African Renaissance. New York: Oxford University Press, 2006.

Hurd, Ian. "Legitimacy and Authority in International Politics." *International Organization* 53 (1999): 379-408.

Hurrell, Andrew. "Regionalism in Theoretical Perspective." In Regionalism in World Politics: Regional Organisations and International Order, edited by L Fawcett and A Hurrell. Oxford: Oxford University Press, 1995.

Hyden, Goran. African Politics in Comparative Perspective. Cambridge: Cambridge University Press, 2006.

Ijomah, B. "The African Military Interventions: A Prelude to Military High Command." *Journal of African Activist Association* 5, no. 5 (1974): 51-63.

Imobighe, Thomas. "An African High Command: The Search for a Feasible Strategy of Continental Defense." *African Affairs* 79, no. 315 (1980): 241-54.

―――. "The Analysis of Political Issues Raised by OAU Peacekeeping in Chad." In Peacekeeping as a Security Strategy in Africa: Chad and Liberia as Case Studies, edited by Margaret Vogt and S. Aminu, 241-59. Enugu: Fourth Dimension Publishing, 1996.

Isaksen, Jan, and Elling Tjonneland. "Assessing the Restructuring of SADC: Positions, Policies and Progress." Oslo: Norwegian Agency for Development Cooperation, 2001.

Jackson, Patrick, and Daniel Nexon. "Constructivist Realism or Realist-Constructivism?" *International Studies Review* 6, no. 2 (2004): 337-41.

Jackson, Richard. "Violent Internal Conflict and the African State: Towards a Framework of Analysis." *Journal of Contemporary African Studies* 20, no. 1 (2002): 29-52.

Jackson, Robert, and Carl Rosberg. "Why Africa's Weak States Persist: The Empirical and the Juridical in Statehood." *World Politics* 35, no. 1 (1982).

Jackson, Stephen. The United Nations Operation in Burundi (ONUB) - Political and Strategic Lessons Learned. New York: UN Peacekeeping Best Practices Unit, 2006.

Jaye, Thomas. Issues of Sovereignty, Strategy, and Security in the Economic Community of West African States (ECOWAS) Intervention in the Liberian Civil War: Edwin Mellen Press, 2003.

―――. "The Security Culture of ECOWAS: Origins, Development and the Challenges of Child Trafficking." *Journal of Contemporary African Studies* 26, no. 2 (2008): 151-68.

Jervis, Robert. "Cooperation under the Security Dilemma." *World Politics* 30, no. 2 (1978).

―――. Perception and Misperception in International Politics. Princeton: Princeton University Press, 1976.

―――. "Realism, Neo-Liberalism and Cooperation: Understanding the Debate." *International Security* 24, no. 1 (1999): 42-63.

―――. "Security Regimes." *International Organization* 36, no. 2 (1982).

Job, Brian. "The Insecurity Dilemma." In The Insecurity Dilemma: National Security of Third World States, edited by Brian Job. Boulder: Lynne Rienner, 1992.

Johnson, Douglas. The Root Causes of Sudan's Civil Wars. London: James Currey, 2003.

Johnston, Alastair. "Treating International Institutions as Social Environments." *International Studies Quarterly* 45, no. 4 (2001): 487-515.

Jones, Branwen, ed. Decolonizing International Relations. London: Rowman & Littlefield 2006.

Jordan, Robert. International Organizations: A Comparative Approach to the Management of Cooperation. 4th ed. Westport: Praeger, 2001.

Juma, Monica, ed. Compendium of Key Documents Relating to Peace and Security in Africa. Pretoria: University of Pretoria Law Press, 2006.

―――. "IGAD and the East African Community." In From Cape to Congo: Southern Africa's Evolving Security Challenges, edited by Mwesiga Baregu and Christopher Landsberg, 225-54. Boulder: Lynne Rienner, 2003.

Kacowicz, Arie. "Explaining Zones of Peace: Democracies as Satisfied Powers?" *Journal of Peace Research* 32, no. 3 (1995): 265-76.

―――. "Negative International Peace and Domestic Conflicts, West Africa 1957-96." *Journal of Modern African Studies* 35 (1997): 367-85.

―――. "Pluralistic Security Communities and 'Negative Peace' in the Third World." Working Paper Series on Regional Security no. 2 (1994).

―――. Zones of Peace in the Third World: South America and West Africa in Comparative Perspective. Albany: State University of New York Press, 1998.

Kagwanja, P. "Power and Peace: South African and the Refurbishing of Africa's Multilateral Capacity for Peacemaking." *Journal of Contemporary African Studies* 24, no. 2 (2006).

Kalu, Kelechi. "Post-Cold War Realism, Liberal Internationalism and the Third World." *African and Asian Studies* 36, no. 2 (2001): 225-36.

Kamala, Diodorus. "The Achievements and Challenges of the New East-African Community Cooperation." University of Hull Research Memoranda, no. 58 (2006).

Kanbur, Ravi. "The African Peer Review Mechanism (APRM): An Assessment of Concept and Design." SAGA Working Paper, no. 161 (2004).

Kanderege, Théodore. "Towards a Sub-Regional Force in the Great Lakes Region." *African Geopolitics*, no. 23 (2006): 125-48.

Kappeler, D. "Causes Et Conséquences de la Désintegration de la Communauté Est-Africaine." *Politique Étrangère* 43 (1978): 319-30.

Katzenstein, Peter, ed. The Culture of National Security: Norms and Identity in World Politics. New York: Columbia University Press, 1996.

Keller, Edmond. "African Conflict Management and the New World Order." Institute on Global Conflict and Cooperation Policy Paper, no. 13 (1995).

————. "Rethinking African Regional Security." In Regional Orders: Building Security in a New World, edited by David Lake and Patrick Morgan, 296-317. University Park: Pennsylvania State University Press, 1997.

Keller, Edmond, and Donald Rothchild, eds. Africa in the New International Order: Rethinking State Sovereignty and Regional Security. Boulder: Lynne Rienner, 1996.

Keohane, Robert. After Hegemony: Cooperation and Discord in the World Political Economy. Princeton: Princeton University Press, 1984.

————. "The Demand for International Regimes." *International Organization* 36 (1982).

————. "International Institutions: Two Approaches." *International Studies Quarterly* 32 (1988): 379-96.

————. "Neo-liberal Institutionalism: Perspective on World Politics." In International Institutions and State Power: Essays in International Relations Theory, edited by Robert Keohane, 1-20. Boulder: Lynne Rienner, 1989.

————. Power and Governance in a Partially Globalized World. London: Routledge, 2002.

Keohane, Robert, and Joseph Nye. "International Interdependence and Integration." In Handbook of Political Science, edited by F Greenstein and N Polsby. Reading: Addison-Wesley, 1975.

————. Power and Interdependence: World Politics in Transition. Boston: Little & Brown, 1977.

Khadiagala, Gilbert, ed. African Foreign Policies: Power and Process. Boulder: Lynne Rienner Publishers, 2001.

————. Allies in Adversity: The Frontline States in Southern African Security, 1975-1993. Athens: Ohio University Press, 1994.

————. "Burundi." In Dealing with Conflict in Africa: The United Nations and Regional Organizations, edited by Jane Boulden, 215-51. Basingstoke: Palgrave Macmillan, 2003.

————. "Euro-African Relations in the Age of Maturity." In Africa in World Politics: Reforming Political Order, edited by John Harbeson and Donald Rothchild, 305-22. Boulder: Westview Press, 2009.

————. "Foreign Policy Decision-Making in Southern Africa's Fading Frontline." In African Foreign Policies: Power and Process, edited by Gilbert Khadiagala and Terrence Lyons, 131-58. Boulder: Lynne Rienner, 2001.

————. "Mediating Civil Conflicts in Eastern Africa." *Politeia* 24, no. 3 (2005): 295-314.

————. "Prospects for a Division of Labor: African Regional Organizations in Conflict Prevention." In Early Warning and Conflict Prevention: Limitations and Possibilities, edited by Klaas van Walraven. The Hague: Kluwer Law International, 1998.

Khadiagala, Gilbert, and Terrence Lyons. "Foreign Policy Making in Africa: An Introduction." In African Foreign Policies: Power and Process, edited by Gilbert Khadiagala and Terrence Lyons, 1-14. Boulder: Lynne Rienner, 2001.

Khobe, Mitikishe. "The Evolution and Conduct of ECOMOG Operations in West Africa." In Boundaries of Peace Support Operations: The African Dimension, edited by Mark Malan. Pretoria: Institute for Security Studies, 2000.

Khosa, Meshack M. Muthien Yvonne G. Regionalism in the New South Africa: The Making of Modern Africa. Aldershot: Brookfield, 1998.

Kibasomba, Roger. "Financing a Credible Standby Force via the AU's Peace Fund " In Peace in Africa - Towards a Collaborative Security Regime, edited by Shannon Field, 225-50. Johannesburg: Institute for Global Dialogue, 2004.

Kioko, Ben. "The Right of Intervention under the African Union's Constitutive Act." *International Review of the Red Cross* 85, no. 852 (2003).

Klingebiel, Stephan. "Africa's New Peace and Security Architecture - Converging the Roles of External Actors and African Interests." *African Security Review* 14, no. 2 (2005): 35-44.

———. "Regional Security in Africa and the Role of External Support." *European Journal of Development Research* 17, no. 3 (2005): 437-48.

Kloman, Erasmus. "African Unification Movements." *International Organization* 16, no. 2 (1962): 387-404.

Klotz, Audie. Norms in International Relations: The Struggle against Apartheid. Ithaca: Cornell University Press, 1995.

Kolodziej, Edward. Security and International Relations. Cambridge: Cambridge University Press, 2005.

Koremenos, Barbara, Charles Lipson, and Duncan Snidal. "The Rational Design of International Institutions." *International Organization* 55, no. 4 (2001).

Kornegay, Francis. "The Geopolitics of Redress: Reconfiguring Africa's Diplomacy." *Global Insight* 13 (2001).

Krasner, Stephen. International Regimes. Ithaca: Cornell University Press, 1983.

———. "Sovereignty and its Discontents." 1996.

Kratochwil, Friedrich. "Constructing a New Orthodoxy? Wendt's Social Theory of International Politics and the Constructivist Challenge." *Millennium: Journal of International Studies* 29, no. 1 (2000): 73-101.

Krause, Keith. "Theorizing Security, State Formation and The "Third World" In the Post-Cold War World." *Review of International Studies*, no. 24 (1998): 125-36.

Kreps, Sarah. "The United Nations-African Union Mission in Darfur: Implications and Prospects for Success." *African Security Review* 16, no. 4 (2007): 67-79.

Krummenacher, Heinz, Susanne Schmeidel, and Daniel Schwarz. Practical Challenges in Predicting Violent Conflict: FAST, an Example of a Comprehensive Early Warning Methodology. Bern: Schweizerische Friedensstiftung, 2001.

Kühne, Winrich. Africa and the End of the Cold War. Ebenhausen: Stiftung Wissenschaft und Politik, 1990.

———. Afrika Auf dem Wege zu eigenen Kapazitäten für Konfliktprävention und Peacekeeping? Geschichte, Organisation und Perspektiven des OAU Mechanismus von 1993. Ebenhausen: Stiftung Wissenschaft und Politik, 1998.

Laakso, Liisa. "Beyond the Notion of a Security Community: What Role for the African Regional Organisations in Peace and Security." *The Round Table* 94, no. 381 (2005): 489-502.

————. Regional Integration for Conflict Prevention and Peace Building in Africa: Europe, SADC and ECOWAS. Helsinki: University of Helsinki, 2002.

Ladnier, Jason. Neighbours on Alert: Regional Views on Humanitarian Intervention, Summary Report of the Regional Responses to Internal War Program. Washington DC: Fund for Peace, 2003.

Lakatos, Imre. "Falsification and the Methodology of Scientific Research Programmes." In Criticism and the Growth of Knowledge, edited by Imre Lakatos and Alan Musgrave. Cambridge: Cambridge University Press, 1970.

————. The Methodology of Scientific Research Programmes: Philosophical Papers. Cambridge: Cambridge University Press, 1978.

Lake, David. "Regional Security Complexes: A Systems Approach." In Regional Orders: Building Security in a New World, edited by David Lake and Patrick Morgan, 45-67. University Park: Pennsylvania State University Press, 1997.

Lake, David, and Patrick Morgan. "Building Security in the New World of Regional Orders." In Regional Orders: Building Security in a New World, edited by David Lake and Patrick Morgan, 343-54. University Park: Pennsylvania State University Press, 1997.

————. "The New Regionalism in Security Affairs." In Regional Orders: Building Security in a New World, edited by David Lake and Patrick Morgan, 3-19. University Park: Pennsylvania State University Press, 1997.

Landsberg, Christopher. "The Fifth Wave of Pan-Africanism." In West Africa's Security Challenges: Building Peace in a Troubled Region, edited by Adekeye Adebajo and Ismail Rashid. Boulder: Lynne Rienner, 2004.

Landsberg, Chris, and Shaun McKay. Engaging the New Pan-Africanism: Strategies for Civil Society. Johannesburg: ActionAid International, 2005.

Laremont, Ricardo, ed. Borders, Nationalism and the African State. Boulder: Lynne Rienner, 2005.

————. The Causes of War and the Consequences of Peacekeeping in Africa: Heinemann, 2002.

Lefever, Ernst. "The Military Assistance Training Program." *Annals of the American Academy of Political and Social Science* 424 (1976): 85-95.

Legro, Joseph. "Which Norms Matter? Revisiting the Failure of Internationalism." *International Organization* 51, no. 1 (1997).

Legro, Jeffrey W., and Andrew Moravcsik. "Is Anybody Still a Realist?" *International Security* 24, no. 2 (1999): 5-55.

Legum, Colin. Pan-Africanism: A Short Political Guide. New York: F.A. Praeger, 1965.

Lemarchand, Rene. Burundi: Ethnic Conflict and Genocide. Cambridge: Cambridge University Press, 1996.

Lemke, Douglas. "African Lessons for International Relations Research." *World Politics* 56, no. 1 (2003): 114-38.

————. Regions of War and Peace. Cambridge: Cambridge University Press, 2002.

Levitt, Jeremy. "The African Crisis Response Initiative: A General Survey." *Africa Insights* 28, no. 3 (1998).

————. "The Peace and Security Council of the African Union: The Known Unknowns." *Transnational Law & Contemporary Problems* 13, no. 1 (2003): 109-38.

Lewis, Rupert, and Patrick Bryan, eds. Garvey: His Work and Impact Trenton: Africa World Press, 1991.

Liebenberg, Ian. "The African Renaissance: Myth, Vital Lie or Mobilizing Tool?" *African Security Review* 7, no. 3 (1998).

Lijphart, A. "Karl W. Deutsch and the New Paradigm in International Relations." In From Development to Global Community: Essays in Honour of Karl W. Deutsch, edited by R Merritt and B Russett. London: George Allen and Unwin, 1981.

Likoti, Fako. "The 1998 Military Intervention in Lesotho: SADC Peace Mission or Resource War?" *International Peacekeeping* 14, no. 2 (2007): 251-63.

Linklater, Andrew, and Hidemi Suganami. The English School of International Relations: A Contemporary Reassessment. Cambridge: Cambridge University Press, 2006.

Little, Richard. The Balance of Power in International Relations: Metaphors, Myths and Models. Cambridge: Cambridge University Press, 2007.

Luck, Edward. UN Security Council: Practice and Promise. London: Routledge, 2006.

Lund, Michael, and Enrique Roig. "An Emerging Security Community." In Searching for Peace in Africa: An Overview of Conflict Prevention and Management Activities, edited by Monique Mekenkamp, Paul van Tongeren and Hans van de Veen, 391-95. Utrecht: European Platform for Conflict Prevention and Transformation, 1999.

Lyman, Princeton. "The War on Terrorism in Africa." In Africa in World Politics: Reforming Political Order, edited by John Harbeson and Donald Rothchild, 276-304. Boulder: Westview Press, 2009.

Lynch, Hollis. Edward Wilmot Blyden: Pan-Negro Patriot, 1832-1912. Oxford: Oxford University Press, 1970.

MacFarlane, Fiona, and Mark Malan. "Crisis and Response in the Central African Republic: A New Trend in African Peacekeeping?" *African Security Review* 7, no. 2 (1998).

MacLean, Sandra. "Challenging Westphalia: Issues of Sovereignty and Identity in Southern Africa." In Africa's Challenge to International Relations Theory, edited by Kevin Dunn and Timothy Shaw, 146-62. Basingstoke: Palgrave, 2001.

Magubane, Bernard. "The African Renaissance in Historical Perspective." In African Renaissance, edited by M Makgoba. Cape Town: Mafube & Tafelberg, 1999.

Makinda, Sam, and Wafula Okumu. The African Union: Challenges of Globalization, Security and Governance. London: Routledge, 2008.

Malan, Mark. Boundaries of Peace Support Operations: The African Dimension, ISS Monograph Series No 44. Pretoria: Institute for Security Studies, 2000.

————. "The European Union and the African Union as Strategic Partners in Peace Operations: Not Grasping the Planning and Management Nettle." KAIPTC Paper, no. 13 (2006).

————. "Keeping the Peace in Africa: A Renaissance Role for South Africa?" *Indicator SA* 15, no. 2 (1998).

————. "New Tools in the Box? Towards a Standby Force for Africa." In Peace in Africa - Towards a Collaborative Security Regime, edited by Shannon Field, 193-224. Johannesburg: Institute for Global Dialogue, 2004.

————. "The OAU and African Sub-Regional Organizations - a Closer Look at the Peace Pyramid." Pretoria: Institute for Security Studies, 1999.

————. "Regional Power Politics under Cover of SADC - Running Amok with a Mythical Organ." ISS Occasional Papers, no. 35 (1998).

Malaquias, Assis. "Reformulating International Relations Theory: African Insights and Challenges." In Africa's Challenge to International Relations Theory, edited by Kevin Dunn and Timothy Shaw, 11-29. Basingstoke: Palgrave, 2001.

Maloka, Eddy. "The South African "African Renaissance" Debate: A Critique." *Polis* 8 (2001).

Maluwa, Tiyanjana. "The Constitutive Act of the African Union and Institution-Building in Postcolonial Africa." *Leiden Journal of International Law*, no. 16 (2003): 157-70.

March, James, and Johan Ohlsen. Rediscovering Institutions: The Organisational Basis of Politics. New York: Free Press, 1989.

Marks, Gary, and Liesbet Hooghe. "Contrasting Visions of Multi-Level Governance." In Multi-Level Governance, edited by Ian Bache and Mathew Flinders, 15-30. Oxford: Oxford University Press, 2004.

Martin, Guy. Africa in World Politics: A Pan-African Perspective. Asmara: Africa World Press, 2002.

Martin, Tony. "International Aspects of the Garvey Movement." *Jamaica Journal* 20, no. 3 (1987): 32-36.

Mathiasen, Flemming. "The African Union and Conflict Management." US Army War College, 2006.

Mathurin, Owen. Henry Sylvester Williams and the Origins of the Pan-African Movement, 1869-1911. Westport: Greenwood Press, 1976.

Matveeva, Anna. Early Warning and Early Response: Conceptual and Empirical Dilemmas, Issue Paper No. 1. The Hague: European Centre for Conflict Prevention, 2006.

May, R, and G Cleaver. "African Peacekeeping: Still Dependent." *International Peacekeeping* 4, no. 3 (1997).

Mayall, James. "National Identity and the Revival of Regionalism." In Regionalism in World Politics: Regional Organisation and International Order, edited by Louise Fawcett and Andrew Hurrell. Oxford: Oxford University Press, 1995.

Mays, Terry. "African Solutions to African Problems: The Changing Face of African-Mandated Peace Operations." *Journal of Conflict Studies* (2003).

————. Africa's First Peacekeeping Operation: The OAU in Chad, 1981-1982. New York: Praeger, 2002.

Mazrui, Ali. Africa's International Relations: The Diplomacy of Dependency and Change. London: Heinemann, 1977.

————. "Pan-Africanism: From Poetry to Power." *Issue: A Journal of Opinion* 23, no. 1 (1995): 35-38.

————. Towards a Pax Africana: A Study in Ideology and Ambition. Chicago: Chicago University Press, 1967.

Mazzeo, Domenico, ed. African Regional Organizations. Cambridge: Cambridge University Press, 1984.

McGowan, Patrick. "African Military Coups d'Etats, 1956-2001." *Journal of Modern African Studies* 41, no. 3 (2003): 339-70.

McGowan, Patrick, and T. Johnson. "Sixty Coups in Thirty Years - Further Evidence Regarding African Military Coups." *Journal of Modern African Studies* 24, no. 3 (1984).

McGowan, Patrick, and Dale Smith. "Economic Dependency in Black Africa: An Analysis of Competing Theories." *International Organization* 32, no. 1 (1978): 179-235.

McKay, Vernon. Africa in World Politics. New York: Harper & Row, 1963.

Mearsheimer, John. "The False Promise of International Institutions." *International Security* 19, no. 3 (1994): 5-49.

————. The Tragedy of Great Power Politics. New York: Norton, 2001.

Meinken, Arno. Militärische Kapazitäten und Fähigkeiten Afrikanischer Staaten - Ursachen und Wirkungen Militärischer Ineffektivität in Sub-Sahara Afrika, SWP Studie No. 4. Berlin: Stiftung Wissenschaft und Politik, 2005.

Meyers, David. "Intra-regional Conflict Management by the Organization of African Unity." *International Organization* 28, no. 3 (1974).

Michaels, Marguerite. "Retreat from Africa." *Foreign Affairs* 72, no. 1 (1993): 93-98.

Mills, Greg. "South Africa and Africa: Regional Integration and Security Cooperation." *African Security Review* 4, no. 2 (1995).

Mills, Greg, Garth Shelton, and Lyal White. "Comparative Security Arrangements in the Americas, Asia and the Gulf." In Peace in Africa - Towards a Collaborative Security Regime, edited by Shannon Field, 81-118. Johannesburg: Institute for Global Dialogue, 2004.

Milner, Helen. "The Assumption of Anarchy in International Relations Theory: A Critique." In Neo-realism and Neo-liberalism: The Contemporary Debate, edited by David Baldwin. New York: Columbia University Press, 1993.

Misztal, Barbara. Trust in Modern Societies. Cambridge: Polity Press, 1996.

Mitchell, Timothy. "The Limits of the State: Beyond Statist Approaches and Their Critics." *American Political Science Review* 85, no. 1 (1991).

Mitrany, David. A Working Peace System: An Argument for the Functional Development of International Organizations. Oxford: Oxford University Press, 1943.

Mohamedou, Mohammed-Mahmoud. "The Arab Maghreb Union of North Africa: The Challenge of Regional Integration and Mediterranean Cooperation." The Ralph Bunche Institute of the United Nations Occasional Paper Series, no. 26 (1997).

Møller, Björn. "Security Cooperation in Southern Africa: Lessons from the European Experience (NATO, EU, OSCE)." *Peace Research Abstracts* 39, no 1 (2002): 3-152.

Möller, Frank. "Capitalizing on Difference: A Security Community or/as a Western Project?" *Security Dialogue* 44, no. 4 (2003): 472-507.

Morgan, Patrick. "Regional Security Complexes and Regional Orders." In Regional Orders: Building Security in a New World, edited by David Lake and Patrick Morgan, 20-44. University Park: Pennsylvania State University Press, 1997.

Morgenthau, Hans. Politics among Nations: The Struggle for Power and Peace. 6th ed. New York: McGraw-Hill, 1985.

Motumi, Tsepe. "Logistical and Capacity Considerations Surrounding a Standby Force." In Peace in Africa - Towards a Collaborative Security Regime, edited by Shannon Field, 251-64. Johannesburg: Institute for Global Dialogue, 2004.

Mpangala, Gaudens, and Bismarck Mwansasu, eds. Beyond Conflict in Burundi. Dar es Salaam: Mwalimu Nyerere Foundation, 2004.

Mtimkulu, Bereng. "Opinion: The African Union and Peace Support Operations." *Conflict Trends*, no. 4 (2005): 34-36.

Muchie, Mammo. "Pan-Africanism: An Idea whose Time Has Come." *Politikon: South African Journal of Political Studies* 27, no. 2 (2000): 297-306.

Mugomba, Agrippah. "Regional Organizations and African Underdevelopment: The Collapse of the East African Community." *The Journal of Modern African Studies* 16, no. 2 (1978): 261-72.

Murithi, Timothy. The African Union: Pan-Africanism, Peacebuilding and Development. Aldershot: Ashgate, 2005.

Murithi, Tim. "The African Union's Evolving Role in Peace Operations: The African Union Mission in Burundi, the African Union Mission in Sudan and the African Union Mission in Somalia." *African Security Review* 17, no. 1 (2008): 70-82.

Murray, Rachel. Human Rights in Africa. Cambridge: Cambridge University Press, 2004.

Muyangwa, M., and M. Vogt. "An Assessment of the OAU Mechanism for Conflict Prevention, Management and Resolution, 1993-2000." New York: International Peace Academy, 2000.

Mwanasali, M. "From the Organization of African Unity to the African Union." In From Cape to Congo: Southern Africa's Evolving Security Challenges, edited by Mwesiga Baregu and Christopher Landsberg. Boulder: Lynne Rienner, 2002.

Mwanasali, Musifiky. "Politics and Security in Central Africa." *African Journal of Political Science* 4, no. 2 (1999): 89-105.

Mwaura, Ciru, Peter Nyaba, Peter Otim, and Seyoum Gebreselassie. "Building CEWARN around Entry Points." In Early Warning and Conflict Management in the Horn of Africa, edited by Ciru Mwaura and Susanne Schmeidel. Trenton: Red Sea Press, 2002.

Mwaura, Ciru, and Susanne Schmeidel, eds. Early Warning and Conflict Management in the Horn of Africa. Trenton: Red Sea Press, 2001.

Nabudere, D. "African Unity in Historical Perspective." In A United States of Africa?, edited by E Maloka. Pretoria: Africa Institute, 2001.

Naldi, Gino. "Peacekeeping Attempts by the Organization of African Unity." *The International and Comparative Law Quarterly* 34, no. 3 (1985): 593-601.

Nantambu, Kwame. "Pan-Africanism Versus Pan-African Nationalism." *Journal of Black Studies* 28, no. 5 (1998): 561-74.

Nathan, Laurie. "The Absence of Common Values and Failure of Common Security in Africa, 1992-2003." *LSE Crisis States Program Working Paper*, no. 50 (2004).

————. "Domestic Instability and Security Communities." *European Journal of International Relations* 12, no. 2 (2006): 275-99.

————. "The Making and Unmaking of the Darfur Peace Process." In War in Darfur and the Search for Peace, edited by Alex de Waal, 245-66. Cambridge: Global Equity Initiative, Harvard University, 2007.

————. "Mediation and the AU's Panel of the Wise." In Peace in Africa - Towards a Collaborative Security Regime, edited by Shannon Field, 63-80. Johannesburg: Institute for Global Dialogue, 2004.

————. "SADC's Uncommon Approach to Common Security, 1992-2003." *Journal of Southern African Studies* 32, no. 3 (2006): 605-22.

————. "Security Communities and the Problem of Domestic Instability." *Crisis States Research Centre Working Paper Series*, no. 55 (2004).

Ndongui, Bellarmin. "Central Africa: Collective Security and Regional Integration." *African Geopolitics*, no. 23 (2006): 103-24.

Neethling, Theo. "International Peacekeeping Trends: The Significance of African Contributions to African Peacekeeping Requirements." *Politikon: South African Journal of Political Studies* 31, no. 1 (2004).

————. "Military Intervention in Lesotho: Perspectives on Operation Boleas and Beyond." *The Online Journal of Peace and Conflict Resolution* 2, no. 2 (1999).

————. "Pursuing a Functional Security Community in Southern Africa: Is It Possible after All?" *Strategic Review for Southern Africa* 25, no. 1 (2003).

————. "Pursuing an Effective African Peacekeeping Capability: What Could Be Learned from Burundi and Darfur?" *Strategic Review for Southern Africa* 29, no. 2 (2007): 50-73.

————. "Realizing the African Standby Force as a Pan-African Deal: Progress, Prospects and Challenges." *Journal of Military and Strategic Studies* 8, no. 1 (2005): 1-25.

Neuman, Stephanie, ed. International Relations Theory and the Third World. New York: St. Martin's Press, 1998.

————. "International Relations Theory and the Third World: An Oxymoron?" In International Relations Theory and the Third World, edited by Stephanie Neuman, 1-30. New York: St. Martin's Press, 1998.

Newmann, Edward. "Human Security and Constructivism." *International Studies Perspectives* 2, no. 3 (2002): 239-51.

Ngoma, Naison. "An Analysis of a Security Community in the Southern African Region." University of the Western Cape, 2004.

————. "Hawks, Doves or Penguins? A Critical Review of the SADC Military Intervention in the DRC." ISS Occasional Papers, no. 88 (2004).

————. Prospects for a Security Community in Southern Africa: An Analysis of Regional Security in the Southern African Development Community. Pretoria: Institute for Security Studies, 2005.

————. "SADC: Towards a Security Community?" *African Security Review* 12, no. 3 (2003): 17-28.

————. "SADC's Mutual Defense Pact: A Final Move to a Security Community?" *The Round Table* 93, no. 375 (2004): 411-23.

Nieuwkerk, Anthoni van. "The Role of the AU and NEPAD in Africa's New Security Regime." In Peace in Africa - Towards a Collaborative Security Regime, edited by Shannon Field, 41-62. Johannesburg: Institute for Global Dialogue, 2004.

Nkiwane, Tandeka. "The End of History? African Challenges to Liberalism in International Relations." In Africa's Challenge to International Relations

Theory, edited by Kevin Dunn and Timothy Shaw, 103-11. Basingstoke: Palgrave, 2001.

Nkrumah, Kwame. Africa Must Unite. New York: F.A. Praeger, 1963.

————. Neo-Colonialism: The Last Stage of Imperialism. London: Thomas Nelson & Sons, 1965.

Nweke, Aforka. "The Organization of African Unity and Intra-African Functionalism." *Annals of the American Academy of Political and Social Science* 489 (1987): 133-47.

Nye, Joseph. "Comparative Regional Integration: Concept and Measurement." *International Organization* 22 (1968).

————, ed. International Regionalism. Boston: Little & Brown, 1968.

————. "Neorealism and Neoliberalism." *World Politics* 40, no. 2 (1988).

Nye, Joseph S. Pan-Africanism and East African Integration. Cambridge: Harvard University Press, 1965.

Nzaou, Elton. Vers la Création d'une Armée Panafricaine: La Force Africaine de Paix. Paris: L'Harmattan, 2004.

O'Brien, Sean. "Anticipating the Good the Bad and the Ugly: An Early Warning Approach to Conflict and Instability Analysis." *Journal for Conflict Resolution* 46, no. 6 (2002): 791-811.

Okafor, Obiora. "The African System on Human and Peoples' Rights, Quasi-Constructivism, and the Possibility of Peacebuilding within African States." *International Journal of Human Rights* 8, no. 4 (2004): 413-50 (38 pages).

Olonisakin, Funmi. "African 'Homemade' Peacekeeping Initiatives." *Armed Forces and Society* 23, no. 3 (1997).

————. "Changing Perspectives on Human Rights in Africa." In Africa in the Post-Cold War International System, edited by Sola Akinrinade and Amadu Sesay. London: Pinter, 1998.

————. Reinventing Peacekeeping in Africa: Conceptual and Legal Issues in ECOMOG Operations, 2000.

Olson, Mancur. The Logic of Collective Action: Public Goods and the Theory of Groups. Cambridge: Harvard University Press, 1965.

Olympio, Sylvanus. "Reflections on Togolese and African Problems." In Africa Speaks, edited by James Duffy and Robert Manners. Princeton: D. Van Nostrand, 1961.

Omach, Paul. "The African Crisis Response Initiative: Domestic Politics and Convergence of National Interests." *African Affairs* 99 (2000): 73-95.

O'Neill, William, and Violet Cassis. Protecting Two Million Internally Displaced: The Successes and Shortcomings of the African Union in Darfur. Washington DC: Brookings Institution Press, 2005.

Onuf, Nicholas. World of Our Making: Rules and Rule in Social Theory and International Relations. Columbia: University of South Carolina Press, 1989.

Opoku, John. "West African Conflict Early Warning and Early Response System: The Role of Civil Society Organizations." KAIPTC Paper, no. 19 (2007).

Ordeshook, Peter. Game Theory and Political Theory: An Introduction. New York: Cambridge University Press, 1986.

Orth, R. "African Operational Experiences in Peacekeeping." *Small Wars and Insurgencies* 7, no. 3 (1996).

Oshisanya, Samuel. The Ultimate End of Pan-Africanism. Lagos: S.A. Oshisanya, 1983.

Ould-Abdullah, Ahmedou. Burundi on the Brink, 1993-1995: A UN Special Envoy Reflects on Preventive Diplomacy. Washington, DC: US Institute of Peace, 2000.

Oye, Kenneth. "The Conditions for Cooperation in World Politics." In International Politics: Enduring Concepts and Contemporary Issues, edited by Robert Art and Robert Jervis. New York: Harper Collins, 1996.

———. "Explaining Cooperation under Anarchy: Hypotheses and Strategies." *World Politics* 38, no. 1 (1985): 1-24.

Oyebade, Adebayo. "The End of the Cold War in Africa: Implications for Conflict Management and Resolution." In Africa after the Cold War: The Changing Perspectives on Security, edited by Adebayo Oyebade and Abiodun Alao. Trenton: Africa World Press, 1998.

Packer, C., and D. Rukare. "The New African Union and its Constitutive Act." *American Journal of International Law* 96, no. 365 (2002).

Pedersen, Thomas. "Cooperative Hegemony: Power, Ideas and Institutions in Regional Integration." *Review of International Studies* 28, no. 4 (2002).

Persaud, Randolph. "Re-Envisioning Sovereignty: Marcus Garvey and the Making of a Transnational Identity." In Africa's Challenge to International Relations Theory, edited by Kevin Dunn and Timothy Shaw, 112-28. Basingstoke: Palgrave, 2001.

Powell, Kristiana. The African Union's Emerging Peace and Security Regime - Opportunities and Challenges for Delivering on the Responsibility to Protect, Monograph Series No. 119. Pretoria: Institute for Security Studies, 2005.

Powell, Kristiana, and Thomas Tieku. "Africa: Towards Durable Peace - the African Union's New Security Agenda: Is Africa Closer to a Pax Pan-Africana?" *International Journal* 60, no. 4 (2005): 937-53.

Powell, Robert. "Absolute and Relative Gains in International Relations Theory." *American Political Science Review* 85 (1991): 1303-20.

Prunier, Gerard. Darfur: The Ambiguous Genocide. Revised and updated edition ed. London: Hurst, 2007.

Ramcharan, Bertrand. "The Continental Early Warning System of the African Union." In Conflict Prevention in Practice: Essays in Honour of James Sutterlin, edited by Bertrand Ramcharan, 71-4. Leiden: Martinus Nijhoff Publishers, 2005.

Ramsbotham, Alex, Alhaji Bah, and Fanny Calder. "Enhancing African Peace and Security Capacity: A Useful Role for the UK and the G8?" *International Affairs* 81, no. 2 (2005).

———. The Implementation of the Joint Africa/G8 Plan to Enhance African Capabilities to Undertake Peace Support Operations: Survey of Current G8 and African Activities and Potential Areas for Further Collaboration. London: Chatham House, 2005.

Reno, William. "External Relations of Weak States and Stateless Regions in Africa." In African Foreign Policies: Power and Process, edited by Gilbert Khadiagala and Terrence Lyons, 185-206. Boulder: Lynne Rienner, 2001.

Renou, Xavier. "A New French Policy for Africa." *Journal of Contemporary African Studies* 20, no. 1 (2002).

Risse, Thomas. "European Institutions and Identity Change: What Have We Learned?" In Identities in Europe and the Institutions of the European Union, edited by Marilynn Brewer, Richard Herrmann and Thomas Risse. Lanham: Rowman & Littlefield, 2004.

Risse, Thomas, Stephen Ropp, and Kathryn Sikkink, eds. The Power of Human Rights: International Norms and Domestic Change. Cambridge: Cambridge University Press, 1999.

———. "The Socialization of International Human Rights Norms into Domestic Practices." In The Power of Human Rights, edited by Thomas Risse. Cambridge: Cambridge University Press, 1999.

Rotberg, Robert. "African Responses to African Crises: Creating a Military Response." In Peacekeeping and Peace Enforcement in Africa: Methods of Conflict Prevention, edited by Robert Rotberg, 98-110. Washington DC: Brookings Institution Press, 2000.

———, ed. Peacekeeping and Peace Enforcement in Africa: Methods of Conflict Prevention. Washington DC: Brookings Institution Press, 2000.

Rothchild, Donald. Managing Ethnic Conflict in Africa - Pressures and Incentives for Cooperation. Washington DC: Brookings Institution Press, 1997.

Rouvez, Alain. Disconsolate Empires: French, British and Belgian Military Involvement in Post-Colonial Sub-Saharan Africa. Lanham: University Press of America, 1994.

Rudwick, Elliot. W.E.B. Dubois: A Study in Minority Group Leadership Philadelphia: University of Pennsylvania Press, 1960.

Ruggie, John. Constructing the World Polity: Essays on International Institutionalisation. New York: Routledge, 1998.

———. "What Makes the World Hang Together? Neo-Utilitarianism and the Social Constructivist Challenge." *International Organization* 52 (1998): 855-85.

Russell, Alec. Big Men, Little People: The Leaders Who Defined Africa. New York: New York University Press, 1999.

Russett, Bruce. "International Regions and the International System." In Regional Politics and World Order, edited by Richard Falk and Saul Mendlovitz. San Francisco: W.H. Freeman, 1973.

———. "A Neo-Kantian Perspective: Democracy, Interdependence and International Organisations in Building Security Communities." In Security Communities, edited by Emanuel Adler and Michael Barnett, 368-94. Cambridge: Cambridge University Press, 1998.

Russett, Bruce, J Oneal, and D Davis. "The Third Leg of the Kantian Tripod for Peace: Organizations and Militarised Disputes 1950-1985." *International Organization* 52, no. 3 (1998).

Rwantabagu, Hermenegilde. "Explaining Intra-State Conflict in Africa: The Case of Burundi." *International Journal on World Peace* 18, no. 2 (2001): 41-54.

Sage, Andre Le, ed. African Counterterrorism Cooperation: Assessing Regional and Subregional Initiatives. Dulles: Potomac Books, 2007.

———. "Terrorism Threats and Vulnerabilities in Africa." In African Counterterrorism Cooperation: Assessing Regional and Subregional Initiatives, edited by Andre Le Sage, 1-38. Dulles: Potomac Books, 2007.

Samatar, Ahmed. The African State: Reconsiderations. London: Delay, 2002.

Santho, Sehoai. "Lesotho: Lessons and Challenges of the SADC Intervention, 1998." In Sustainable Security in Africa, edited by Diane Philander. Pretoria: Institute for Security Studies, 2000.

Saurin, Julian. "International Relations as the Imperial Illusion: The Need to Decolonize IR" In Decolonizing International Relations, edited by Branwen Jones. London: Rowman & Littlefield, 2006.

Schleicher, Hans-Georg. "Regionale Sicherheitskooperation im südlichen Afrika: SADC and OPDSC." University of Leipzig Papers on Africa, no. 78 (2006).

Schmeidel, Susanne, and Howard Adelman, eds. Early Warning and Early Response. New York: Columbia International Affairs Online, 1998.

Schmid, Alex. "Indicator Development: Issues in Forecasting Conflict Escalation." In Preventive Measures: Building Risk Assessment and Crisis Early Warning Systems, edited by John Davies and Ted Robert Gurr. Boulder: Rowman & Littlefield Publishers, 1998.

———. Thesaurus and Glossary of Early Warning and Conflict Prevention Terms. Leiden: Pioom Foundation, 2000.

Schoeman, M. "Imagining a Community: The African Union as an Emerging Security Community." *Strategic Review for Southern Africa* 24, no. 1 (2002).

Scorgie, Lindsay. "Building African Peacekeeping Capacity: Donors and the African Union's Emerging Peace and Security Architecture." *KAIPTC Paper*, no. 16 (2007).

Sebenius, James. "Challenging Conventional Explanations of International Cooperation: Negotiation Analysis and the Case of Epistemic Communities." *International Organization* 46 (1992): 323-66.

Segell, Glen. "The United Nations African Union Mission in Darfur." *Strategic Insights* VII, no. 1 (2008).

Selassie, Haile. "Towards African Unity." *Journal of Modern African Studies* 1, no. 3 (1963).

Serafino, Nina. "The Global Peace Operations Initiative: Background and Issues for Congress." Washington DC: Congressional Research Service, 2006.

Sesay, Ahmadu. "Collective Security or Collective Disaster? Regional Peace-Keeping in West Africa." *Security Dialogue* 26, no. 2 (1995).

———. "The Limits of Peacekeeping by a Regional Organization: The OAU Peacekeeping Force in Chad." *Conflict Quarterly* 11, no. 1 (1991): 7-26.

Shannon, V. "Norms Are What States Make of Them: The Political Psychology of Norm Violation." *International Studies Quarterly* 44, no. 2 (2000): 355-74.

Shaw, Timothy. "African Foreign Policy in the New Millenium: From Coming Anarchies to Security Communities? From New Regionalisms to New Realisms?" In Africa's Challenge to International Relations Theory, edited by Timothy Shaw and Kevin Dunn, 204-19. Basingstoke: Palgrave, 2001.

———. "New Regionalisms in Africa in the New Millennium: Comparative Perspectives on Renaissance, Realisms and/or Regressions." In New Regionalism in the Global Political Economy, edited by Shaun Breslin, Christopher Hughes, Nicola Phillips and Ben Rosamond, 177-89. London: Routledge, 2002.

Shaw, Timothy, Sandra Maclean, and Katie Orr. "Peace-Building and African Organisations: Towards Subcontracting or a New and Sustainable Division of Labor?" In Early Warning and Conflict Prevention: Limitations and Possibilities, edited by Klaas van Walraven. The Hague: Kluwer Law International, 1998.

Shepperson, George. "Pan-Africanism And "Pan-Africanism": Some Historical Notes." *Phylon* 23, no. 4 (1962): 346-58.

Shircliffe, James. "Tip of the African Spear: Forging an Expeditionary Capability for a Troubled Continent." *The Royal United Services Institute Journal* 152, no. 4 (2007): 58-62.

Sidaway, James. Imagined Regional Communities: Integration and Sovereignty in the Global South. London: Routledge, 2002.

Sieber, Otto. "Africa Command: Forecast for the Future." *Strategic Insights* VI, no. 1 (2007).

Singh, Hari. "Hegemons and the Construction of Regions." In The State and Identity Construction in International Relations, edited by Sarah Vandersluis. Basingstoke: Macmillan, 2000.

Smaldone, Joseph. "African Military Spending: Defense versus Development?" *African Security Review* 15, no. 4 (2006): 17-32.

Smith, Michael. Europe's Foreign and Security Policy: The Institutionalization of Cooperation. Cambridge: Cambridge University Press, 2004.

Smith, Steve. "Wendt's World." *Review of International Studies* 26 (2000): 151-63.

Snidal, Duncan. "The Game Theory of International Politics." *World Politics* 38 (1985): 25-57.

———. "International Cooperation among Relative Gains Maximizers." *International Studies Quarterly* 35, no. 4 (1991): 387-402.

———. "The Limits of Hegemonic Stability Theory." *International Organization* 39, no. 4 (1985): 579-614.

———. "Relative Gains and the Pattern of International Cooperation." *The American Political Science Review* 85, no. 3 (1991): 701-26.

Snyder, Glenn. "Alliance Theory: A Neorealist First Cut." In The Evolution of Theory in International Relations: Essays in Honor of William T.R. Fox, edited by Robert Rothstein, 83-103. Columbia: University of South Carolina Press, 1991.

Solomon, Hussein, and Jakkie Cilliers. "Southern Africa and the Quest for Collective Security." *Security Dialogue* 28, no. 2 (1997): 191-207.

Solomon, Hussein, and Gerrie Swart. "Defending African Unity: Can the Peace and Security Council of the African Union Succeed?" *Conflict Trends*, no. 1 (2004): 10-15.

Souaré, Issaka. Africa in the United Nations System, 1945-2005. London: Adonis & Abbey, 2006.

Southall, Roger, and Kristina Bentley. An African Peace Process: Mandela, South Africa and Burundi. London: Human Science Research Council, 2005.

Starr, Harvey. "Democracy and War: Choice, Learning and Security Communities." *Journal of Peace Research* 29, no. 2 (1992): 207-13.

Stein, Arthur. "Coordination and Collaboration: Regimes in an Anarchic World." In Neo-Realism and Neo-Liberalism: The Contemporary Debate, edited by David Baldwin. New York: Columbia University Press, 1993.

———. Why Nations Cooperate: Circumstance and Choice in International Relations. Ithaca: Cornell University Press, 1990.

Stein, Arthur, and Steven Lobell. "Geostructuralism and International Politics: The End of the Cold War and the Regionalization of International Security." In Regional Orders: Building Security in a New World, edited by David Lake and Patrick Morgan, 101-24. University Park: Pennsylvania State University Press, 1997.

Sturman, Kathryn. "The Rise of Libya as a Regional Player." *African Security Review* 12, no. 2 (2003).

Sutherland, Bill, and Matt Meyer. Guns and Gandhi in Africa: Pan-African Insights on Non-Violence, Armed Struggle and Liberation in Africa. Trenton: Africa World Press, 2000.

Svensson, Emma. The African Mission in Burundi: Lessons Learned from the African Union's First Peace Operation. Stockholm: Swedish Defense Research Agency, 2008.

———. The African Union's Operations in the Comoros. Stockholm: Swedish Defense Research Agency, 2008.

Taft, Patricia, and Jason Ladnier. Realizing "Never Again" - Regional Capacities to Protect Civilians in Violent Conflicts. Washington DC: Fund for Peace, 2006.

Taylor, Ian. China and Africa: Engagement and Compromise. New York: Routledge, 2006.

Taylor, Ian, and Paul Williams, eds. Africa in International Politics: External Involvement on the Continent. London: Routledge, 2003.

———. "Political Culture, State Elites and Regional Security in West Africa." *Journal of Contemporary African Studies* 26, no. 2 (2008): 137-49.

Taylor, P. International Organization in the Modern World. London: Pinter, 1993.

Thelma, Ekiyor. "Civil Society's Perspective on the ECOWAS Early Warning System." Capetown: Center for Conflict Resolution, 2006.

Thomas, Caroline, and Peter Wilkin, eds. Globalization, Human Security and the African Experience. Boulder: Lynne Rienner, 1999.

Thomas, Daniel. The Helsinki Effect: International Norms, Human Rights and the Demise of Communism. New Haven: Princeton University Press, 2001.

Thomas, Scott. "Africa and the End of the Cold War: An Overview of Impacts." In Africa in the Post-Cold War International System, edited by Sola Akinrinade and Amadu Sesay, 3-27. London: Pinter, 1998.

Thompson, Vincent. Africa and Unity: The Evolution of Pan-Africanism. London: Longmans, 1969.

Thompson, William. "The Regional Subsystem: A Conceptual Explication and a Propositional Inventory." *International Studies Quarterly* 17, no. 1 (1973).

Tickner, A. "Seeing IR Differently: Notes from the Third World." *Millennium: Journal of International Studies* 32, no. 2 (2003): 295-324.

Tieku, Thomas. "African Union Promotion of Human Security in Africa." *African Security Review* 16, no. 2 (2007): 26-37.

———. "Explaining the Clash of Interests of Major Actors in the Creation of the African Union." *African Affairs* 103, no. 411 (2004): 249-67.

Tilly, Charles. "International Communities, Secure or Otherwise." In Security Communities, edited by Emanuel Adler and Michael Barnett. Cambridge: Cambridge University Press, 1998.

Tirole, Jean. "Hierarchies and Bureaucracies: On the Role of Collusion in Organizations." *Journal of Law, Economics & Organisation* 2, no. 2 (1986): 181-214.

Toga, Dawit. "The African Union Mediation and the Abuja Peace Talks." In War in Darfur and the Search for Peace, edited by Alex de Waal, 214-44. Cambridge: Global Equity Initiative, Harvard University, 2007.

Touray, Omar. "The Common African Defense and Security Policy." *African Affairs* 104, no. 417 (2005): 635-56.

Tuck, Richard, ed. Hobbes: Leviathan. Cambridge: Cambridge University Press, 1991.

Turner, John. Continent Ablaze: The Insurgency Wars in Africa - 1960 to the Present. London: Arms and Armour Press, 1998.

Vale, Peter. "New Ways to Remember: Community in Southern Africa." *International Relations* 18, no. 1 (2004): 73-89.

———. Security and Politics in South Africa: The Regional Dimension. Boulder: Lynne Rienner, 2003.

Vale, Peter, and Sipho Maseko. "South Africa and the African Renaissance." *International Affairs* 74, no. 2 (1998).

Väyrynen, Raimo. "Stable Peace through Security Communities? Steps Towards Theory-Building." In Stable Peace among Nations, edited by Arie Kacowicz, Ole Elgstrom and Magnus Jerneck, 156-93. Lanham: Rowman & Littlefield, 2000.

Vogt, Andreas. "Towards a Comprehensive Self-Sufficient African Peace Operation Capacity: Fact or Fiction?" *Conflict Trends*, no. 4 (2005): 24-29.

Vogt, Margaret, ed. The Liberian Crisis and ECOMOG: A Bold Attempt at Regional Peacekeeping. Lagos: Gabumo Press, 1992.

Vogt, Margaret, and S. Aminu, eds. Peacekeeping as a Security Strategy in Africa: Chad and Liberia as Case Studies. Vol. 1. Enugu: Fourth Dimension Publishing, 1996.

Waal, Alex de, ed. War in Darfur and the Search for Peace. Cambridge: Global Equity Initiative, Harvard University, 2007.

Waever, Ole. "Insecurity, Security and Asecurity in the West European Non-War Community." In Security Communities, edited by Emanuel Adler and Michael Barnett. Cambridge: Cambridge University Press, 1998.

———. "Power, Principles and Perspectivism: Understanding Peaceful Change in Post-Cold War Europe." In Peaceful Changes in World Politics, edited by Heikki Patomki, 208-82. Tampare: Tampare Peace Research Institute, 1995.

Wagenen, Richard van. "The Concept of Community and the Future of the United Nations." *International Organization* 19, no. 3 (1965): 812-27.

———. Research in the International Organisation Field: Some Notes on a Possible Focus. Princeton: Center for Research on World Political Institutions, 1952.

Wallander, Celeste, and Robert Keohane. "Risk, Threat and Security Institutions." In Imperfect Unions: Security Institutions over Time and Space, edited by Helga Haftendorn, Robert Keohane and Celeste Wallander. Oxford: Oxford University Press, 1999.

Wallerstein, Immanuel. Africa: The Politics of Unity: An Analysis of a Contemporary Social Movement. London: Pall Mall Press, 1968.

————. "The Early Years of the OAU: The Search for Organizational Pre-eminence." *International Organization* 20, no. 4 (1966): 774-87.

Walraven, Klaas van. Dreams of Power - the Role of the Organisation of African Unity in the Politics of Africa 1963-1993. Aldershot: Ashgate, 1999.

————, ed. Early Warning and Conflict Prevention: Limitations and Possibilities. The Hague: Kluwer Law International, 1998.

————. The Pretence of Peacekeeping: ECOMOG, West Africa and Liberia, 1990-1998. The Hague: Netherlands Institute of International Relations, 1999.

Walt, Stephen. "The Enduring Relevance of the Realist Tradition." In Political Science: State of the Discipline, edited by Ira Katznelson and Helen Milner. New York: Norton, 2002.

————. "International Relations: One World, Many Theories." *Foreign Policy* 110 (1998).

————. The Origins of Alliances. Ithaca: Cornell University Press, 1987.

Waltz, Kenneth. Man, the State and War: A Theoretical Analysis. New York: Columbia University Press, 1959.

————. "Reflections on Theory of International Politics: A Response to My Critics." In Neorealism and its Critics, edited by Robert Keohane. New York: Columbia University Press, 1986.

————. Theory of International Politics. New York: Random House, 1979.

————. "Theory of International Relations." In The Handbook of Political Science, edited by Fred Greenstein and Nelson Polsby. Reading: Addison-Wesley, 1975.

Weber, Katja. Hierarchy Amidst Anarchy: Transaction Costs and Institutional Choice. Albany: State University of New York Press, 2000.

Weiss, Thomas, ed. Beyond UN Subcontracting: Task-Sharing with Regional Security Arrangements and Service-Providing NGOs. Basingstoke: Macmillan Press, 1998.

————, ed. Collective Security in a Changing World. Boulder: Lynne Rienner, 1993.

Weiss, Thomas, and Meryl Kessler, eds. Third World Security in the Post Cold War Era. Boulder: Lynne Rienner, 1991.

Welch, Claude Emerson. Dream of Unity: Pan Africanism and Political Unification in West Africa. Ithaca: Cornell University Press, 1966.

Wendt, Alexander. "Anarchy Is What States Make of It: The Social Construction of Power Politics." *International Organization* 46, no. 2 (1992).

————. "Collective Identity Formation and the International State." *American Political Science Review* 88 (1994): 384-96.

————. "Constructing International Politics." *International Security* 20, no. 1 (1995).

————. Social Theory of International Politics. Cambridge: Cambridge University Press, 1999.

Williams, Michael. "The Discipline of the Democratic Peace: Kant, Liberalism and the Social Construction of Security Communities." *European Journal of International Relations* 7, no. 4 (2001): 525-53.

————. "The Institutions of Security: Elements of a Theory of Security Organizations." *Cooperation and Conflict* 32, no. 3 (1997).

Williams, Michael, and Iver Neumann. "From Alliance to Security Community: NATO, Russia and the Power of Identity." *Millennium: Journal of International Studies* 29, no. 2 (2000): 357-87.

Williams, Paul. "From Non-Intervention to Non-Indifference: The Origins and Development of the African Union's Security Culture." *African Affairs* 106, no. 423 (2007): 253-79.

———. "Keeping the Peace in Africa: Why "African" Solutions Are Not Enough " *Ethics and International Affairs* 22, no. 3 (2008): 309-29.

———. "Military Responses to Mass Killing: The African Union Mission in Darfur." *International Peacekeeping* 13, no. 2 (2006): 168-83.

———. "The Peace and Security Council of the African Union: Evaluating an Embryonic International Institution." In ISA Annual Convention. San Francisco, 2008.

———, ed. Security Studies: An Introduction. London: Routledge, 2008.

———. "Thinking About Security in Africa." *International Affairs* 83, no. 6 (2007): 1021-38.

Wolfers, Arnold. Discord and Collaboration: Essays on International Politics. Baltimore: Johns Hopkins University Press, 1962.

Wolfers, Michael. Politics in the Organization of African Unity. London: Methuen & Co, 1976.

Woronoff, Jon. "The Case for an African Defense Organization." *Africa Report* 16, no. 6 (1971): 23-25.

———. Organizing African Unity. Metuchen: Scarecrow Press, 1970.

Wright, Stephen. African Foreign Policies. Boulder: Westview Press, 1999.

Yoon, M. Y. "Internal Conflicts and Cross-Border Military Interventions in Sub-Saharan Africa in the Post-Cold War Era." *Journal of Political & Military Sociology* 33, no. 2 (2005): 277-93.

Zan, Banagoun. "African Armies and Sustainable Development." *African Geopolitics*, no. 23 (2006): 75-102.

Zartman, I. William. "Africa as a Subordinate State System in International Relations." In Regional Politics and World Order, edited by Richard Falk and Saul Mendlovitz, 384-98. San Francisco: W.H. Freeman & Co, 1973.

———. "African Regional Security and Changing Patterns of Relations." In Africa in the New International Order: Rethinking State Sovereignty and Regional Security, edited by Edmond Keller and Donald Rothchild, 52-70. Boulder: Lynne Rienner, 1996.

———. "Decision-Making among African Governments in Inter-African Affairs." *Journal of Development Studies* 2, no. 2 (1966).

Zartman, William, and Katharina Vogeli. "Prevention Gained and Prevention Lost: Collapse, Competition and Coup in Congo." In Opportunities Missed, Opportunities Seized: Preventive Diplomacy in the Post-Cold War World, edited by Bruce Jentleson, 265-92. Lanham: Rowman & Littlefield, 2000.

Zehfuss, Maja. "Constructivism and Identity: A Dangerous Liaison." *European Journal of International Relations* 7, no. 3 (2001): 315-48.

———. Constructivism in International Relations: The Politics of Reality. Cambridge: Cambridge University Press, 2002.

Zimmerman, William. "Hierarchical Regional Systems and the Politics of System Boundaries." *International Organization* 26, no. 1 (1972): 18-36.

Zorgbibe, Charles. "The Right of Interference and Africa." *African Geopolitics*, no. 23 (2006): 169-20.

Index

About the Book

In the midst of the atrocities reported in the Democratic Republic of Congo, the seemingly constant strife in the Horn of Africa, and the ongoing violence in Darfur, how do we make sense of the simultaneous increase in interstate security cooperation in Africa? To what extent, and why, does this cooperation differ from previous initiatives? In what direction is it heading? Benedikt Franke assesses the peace and security architecture that is taking shape under the nominal leadership of the African Union, analyzing the emerging structures and trends and also rethinking prevailing notions and theoretical assumptions about interstate security relations.

Benedikt Franke is visiting research fellow at the University of Oxford.